The Myth of the Missing Black Father

The Myth of the Missing Black Father

EDITED BY Roberta L. Coles and Charles Green

Columbia University Press   New York

Columbia University Press
Publishers Since 1893
New York   Chichester, West Sussex
Copyright © 2010 Columbia University Press
All rights reserved

Library of Congress Cataloging-in-Publication Data

The myth of the missing black father / edited by Roberta L. Coles and Charles Green.
p. cm.
Includes bibliographical references and index.
ISBN 978-0-231-14352-3 (cloth : alk. paper)—ISBN 978-0-231-14353-0
(pbk. : alk. paper)—ISBN 978-0-231-52086-7 (e-book)
1. African American fathers. 2. Absentee fathers. 3. African American families. I. Coles,
Roberta L. II. Green, Charles (Charles St. Clair) III. Title.
HQ756.M98 2010
306.874'208996073—dc22
2009019270

♾

Columbia University Press books are printed on permanent and durable acid-free
paper.
This book is printed on paper with recycled content.
Printed in the United States of America

C 10 9 8 7 6 5 4 3 2 1
P 10 9 8 7 6 5 4 3 2 1

This book is dedicated to all committed black fathers and their children living in the United States and around the globe.

Contents

Acknowledgments

Most books, beginning with research and continuing through the writing stage, require at least a couple years of preparation before they appear in print. Edited volumes, particularly those for which chapters have been specifically prepared by the contributors, can be that much more challenging. Thus, in the process of coordinating and organizing this book project the need for outside resources and special assistance was ever more demanding. While the benefits of the computer and information age were extremely helpful in communicating with contributors who were spread across several states, there was still the need for other support in the form of funding for research-related costs, such as research assistants, travel, and supplies, to mention a few. For this, we are indebted to our academic institutions—Marquette University and Hunter College of the City University of New York—for approving small research grants: specifically, from Marquette University, the Regular Research Grant and the Summer Faculty Fellowship, and from Hunter College, the Professional Staff Congress—CUNY Award Program.

In addition to funding sources, there are number of colleagues as well as sociology students and personal contacts whom we would like to thank for their support in the areas of technical consultation, referral of subjects for the interviews, and their unearthing of journal articles, newspaper clippings, Web sites, and other relevant research information on the topic of black fatherhood that we might otherwise have overlooked. Our gratitude goes out to Ted Anderson, Marie Lesly Auguste, Dawn Bonnett, Erica Chito-Childs, Claire Green, Marguerite Holm, Tammy Jones, Naomi Kroeger, Dominic Lewis, Tina Mangum, Felicia Martin, Janina McCormack, James Mitchell, Joong-Hwan Oh, Sandy Ramer, Ruth Sidel, Naseive Smith, Janice Staral, the George Sanders Fathers Resource Center, Mieko Manuel-Timmons, and Basil Wilson.

Our gratitude is extended to the anonymous reviewers for their favorable support, to editors at Columbia University Press—Lauren Dockett, Avni Majithia, and Michael Haskell—for their help at all stages in preparing the manuscript, and to the contributors to this volume, who persisted through multiple revisions. And, finally, we are indebted to the many father-respondents for telling stories that bring insight into fathering.

The Myth of the Missing Black Father

Introduction

The black male. A demographic. A sociological construct. A media caricature. A crime statistic. Aside from rage or lust, he is seldom seen as an emotionally embodied person. Rarely a father. Indeed, if one judged by popular and academic coverage, one might think the term "black fatherhood" an oxymoron. In their parenting role, African American men are viewed as verbs but not nouns; that is, it is frequently assumed that Black men *father* children but seldom *are* fathers. Instead, as the law professor Dorothy Roberts (1998) suggests in her article "The Absent Black Father," black men have become the symbol of *fatherlessness*. Consequently, they are rarely depicted as deeply embedded within and essential to their families of procreation. This stereotype is so pervasive that when black men are seen parenting, as Mark Anthony Neal (2005) has personally observed in his memoir, they are virtually offered a Nobel Prize.

But this stereotype did not arise from thin air. As shown in table 0.1, in 2000, only 16 percent of African American households were married couples with children, the lowest of all racial groups in America. On the other hand, 19 percent of Black households were female-headed with children, the highest of all racial groups. From the perspective of children's living arrangements, shown in table 0.2, over 50 percent of African American children lived in mother-only households in 2004, again the highest of all racial groups. Although African American teens experienced the largest decline in births of all racial groups in the 1990s,

Table 0.1

Family and Non-Family Households Total and by Race, 2000

	Number of households	Percentage of all households that were family							Percentage of households that were nonfamily		
		Family total	Married-couple households total	Married couples with children under 18	Female-headed households total	Female-headed households with children under 18	Male-headed households total	Male-headed households with children under 18	Total	Live alone	2 or more
U.S. population		68.1	51.7	23.5	12.2	7.2	4.2	2.1	31.9	25.8	6.1
Non-Hispanic white	79,093,136	67	54	23	9	5	3.4	1.7	34.5	28.3	6.2
Hispanic	9,222,402	80	54	36	18	12	8	4	20.0	13.9	6.1
Black	11,862,087	68	31	16	31	19	6	3	32.2	27.1	5.1
Asian	3,101,668	74	61	34	9	4	5	1	26.0	19	7
Pacific Islander	94,361	77	55	33	16	9	7	4	23.0	15	8
American Indian and Alaskan native	665,047	72	44	24	21	13	7	4	29.0	22	7

Source: U.S. Department of Commerce (2000), Quick Table-P10, Matrices PCT8, PCT17, PCT18, PCT26, PCT27, and PCT28.

Table 0.2
Living Arrangements of Black Children, 2004

Living arrangements	Black children
Two parents	37.6%
Married	33.9
Unmarried	3.7
Mother-only	50.4
Father-only	3.3
Neither parent	8.8

Source: Kreider (2008).

still in 2000, 68 percent of all births to African American women were nonmarital, suggesting the pattern of single-mother parenting may be sustained for some time into the future (Martin et al. 2003). This statistic could easily lead observers to assume that the fathers are absent.

While it would be remiss to argue that there are not many absent black fathers, absence is only one slice of the fatherhood pie and a smaller slice than is normally thought. The problem with "absence," as is fairly well established now, is that it's an ill defined pejorative concept usually denoting nonresidence with the child, and it is sometimes *assumed* in cases where there is no legal marriage to the mother. More importantly, absence connotes invisibility and noninvolvement, which further investigation has proven to be exaggerated (as will be discussed below). Furthermore, statistics on children's living arrangements (table 0.2) also indicate that nearly 41 percent of black children live with their fathers, either in a married or cohabiting couple household or with a single dad.

These African American family-structure trends are reflections of large-scale societal trends—historical, economic, and demographic—that have affected all American families over the past centuries. Transformations of the American society from an agricultural to an industrial economy and, more recently, from an industrial to a service economy entailed adjustments in the timing of marriage, family structure, and the dynamics of family life. The transition from an industrial to a service economy has been accompanied by a movement of jobs out of cities; a decline in real wages for men; increased labor-force participation for women; a decline in fertility; postponement of marriage; and increases in divorce, nonmarital births, and single-parent and nonfamily households.

These historical transformations of American society also led to changes in the expected and idealized roles of family members. According to Lamb (1986), during the agricultural era, fathers were expected to be the "moral teachers"; during industrialization, breadwinners and sex-role models; and during the service economy, nurturers. It is doubtful that these idealized roles were as discrete as implied. In fact, LaRossa's (1997) history of the first half of the 1900s reveals that public calls for nurturing, involved fathers existed before the modern era. It is likely that many men had trouble fulfilling these idealized roles despite the legal buttress of patriarchy, but it was surely difficult for African American men to fulfill these roles in the context of slavery, segregation, and, even today, more modern forms of discrimination. A comparison of the socioeconomic status of black and white fathers illustrates some of the disadvantages black fathers must surmount to fulfill fathering expectations. According to Hernandez and Brandon (2002), in 1999 only 33.4 percent of black fathers had attained at least a college education, compared to 68.5 percent of white fathers. In 1998, 25.5 percent of black fathers were un- or underemployed, while 17.4 percent of white fathers fell into that category. Nearly 23 percent of black fathers' income was half of the poverty threshold, while 15 percent of white fathers had incomes that low.

The historical transformations were experienced across racial groups but not to the same extent. The family forms of all racial groups in America have become more diverse, or at least recognition of the diversity of family structure has increased, but the proportions of family types vary across racial groups (as indicated in table 0.1). Because African American employment was more highly concentrated in blue-collar jobs, recent economic restructuring had harsher implications for black communities and families (Nelson 2004). The higher and more concentrated poverty levels and greater income and wealth inequality—both among African Americans and between African Americans and whites—expose African American men, directly and indirectly, to continued lower life expectancy, higher mortality, and, hence, a skewed gender ratio that leaves black women outnumbering black men by the age of eighteen.

All of these societal and family-level trends affect black men's propensity to parent and their styles of parenting in ways we have yet to fully articulate. For instance, Americans in general have responded to these trends by postponing marriage by two to four years over the last few decades, but that trend is quite pronounced among African Americans, to the point that it is estimated that whereas 93 percent of whites born from 1960 through 1964 will eventually marry, only 64 percent of blacks born in the same period ever will (Goldstein and Kenney 2001). Consequently, in 1970 married-couple families accounted for about 68 percent of all black families, but in 2000, after several decades of deindustrialization, only 46 percent were married couples. The downstream effect of marriage decline is that the majority of black children no longer live in married-couple homes.

Certainly, the skewed gender ratio mentioned earlier contributes to this declining marriage trend, but the role of other factors is under debate. Wilson (1987) and others have suggested that black men's underemployment, along with black women's higher educational attainment in relation to black men (and smaller wage gap than between white men and women, according to Roberts 1994) may decrease both men's and women's desire to marry and may hinder some black men's efforts to be involved fathers (Marsiglio and Cohan 2000). However, other research (Lerman 1989; Ellwood and Crane 1990) has found that even college-educated and employed black men have exhibited declines in marriage, and yet additional research points to attitudinal factors (South 1993; Tucker and Mitchell-Kernan 1995; Crissey 2005), with black men desiring marriage less than white and Latino men.

Other parenting trends may also be affected by black men's unique status. Their higher mortality rate and lower life expectancy may affect the timeline of parenting, increasing pressure to reproduce earlier. If married or cohabiting, black women's higher employment rate may increase the amount of time black men spend with their children (Fagan 1998). Higher poverty and collective values also pull extended family members into the mix, diffusing parenting responsibilities, which may lead to more protective or more neglectful styles of parenting.

Because of these society-wide and race-specific changes in family formation and gender roles, academia and popular culture have exhibited an increasing fascination with the diversifying definitions of masculinity and the roles men play in families, particularly as fathers. Research and publications on fatherhood have increased exponentially, and courses on fatherhood are popping up in the nation's colleges and universities. However, most of the research has been based on samples of respondents who are all racially white. And when men of color have been included in small numbers, the researchers do not address race as a variable; hence their conclusions are stated generically.

In conjunction with this increased amount of research and, in fact, frequently fueling the research, has been a proliferation of public and private programs and grants aimed at creating "responsible fatherhood." While many of the programs have been successful in educating men on how to be qualitatively better fathers, many have aimed primarily either at encouraging fathers to marry the mothers of their children or at securing child support. Marriage and child support are important aspects of family commitment, but marriage is no guarantee of attentive fathering, and garnished child support alone, particularly if it goes to the state and not to the mother and child, is hardly better parenting. Within this policy focus, African American men are most frequently attended to under the rubric of "fragile families" (Hobson 2002; Gavanas 2004; Mincy, Garfinkel, and Nepomnyaschy 2005). Although this classification may be intended to bring attention to structural supports that many families lack, once again it promulgates the idea that black men cannot be strong fathers.

Given the increased focus on fatherhood in scholarly and popular venues, what do we really know about black men and parenting? We know more than we used to but less than we should. Scanning recent anthologies on fatherhood still reveals that despite the interest in broadening the scope of fatherhood, African American fathers, when discussed at all, continue to be addressed predominantly under categories frequently associated with parenting from afar, as nonresident, nonmarital fathers; see Lamb (1997, 2004), Daniels (1998), Dowd (2000), Tamis-LeMonda and Cabrera (2002). Even books specifically on black fathers concentrate almost exclusively on nonresident fathers (Barras 2000; Hamer 2001; Clayton, Blankenhorn, and Mincy 2003).

So let's start there, with what we know about nonresident or so-called absent fathers. Studies on this ilk of fathers indicate that generally a large portion of nonresident fathers are literally absent from their children's lives or, if in contact, their involvement decreases substantially over time. A number of memoirs by black men and women, sons and daughters of literally absent fathers, attest to the painful experience that this can be for the offspring—both sons and daughter—of these physically or emotionally missing fathers. For instance, writing in his 1999 book *Becoming Dad: Black Men and the Journey to Fatherhood*, award-winning journalist Leonard Pitts wrote of his own father and others:

He was one thing many other fathers were not: He was there. Present and accounted for every day. Emotionally absent, mind you. But there, at least, in body. I know so many men, so many black men, who cannot say the same. So many men for whom the absence of father is a wound that never scabbed over.

(12)

Similarly, journalist Michael Datcher (2001:3) wrote in his memoir, *Raising Fences: A Black man's love story,* that in his east-side Long Beach, California, apartment building of thirty families, he never saw a father visit, let alone live in, a household. Because of that, he says, "I've been obsessed with being a husband and father since I was seven years old. Quiet as it's kept, many young black men have the same obsession. Picket-fence dreams. . . . But usually we strike a cool pose. Hide Huxtable-family dreams in the corner: Can't let someone catch us hoping that hard."

Whereas we usually think of sons as being naturally more affected by the absence of a father, daughters, too, hurt, as journalist Jonetta Rose Barras's self-revealing book *Whatever Happened to Daddy's Little Girl? The Impact of Fatherlessness on Black Women* illustrates. Speaking from her own experience and those of women she interviewed, Barras said (2000:5) that she wrote the book because

> I wanted other women to know that someone understood. I know fatherlessness. I know the emptiness it creates, the years searching for something to help fill the void, looking for a substitute to make me whole. I know the insecurity; the endless battles with doubts that are re-created with each new relationship—battles that are never won; the pain that resurfaces after each departure of a man in my life. I wanted women to understand the distinct patterns of sadness, insecurity, confusion, and unresolved pain that connects those of us who experience father loss either through death, divorce, or abandonment.

Although these anguished experiences are too common, they remain only one part, though often the more visible part, of the larger fatherhood picture. An increasing number of quantitative and qualitative studies find that of men who become fathers through nonmarital births, black men are least likely (when compared to white and Hispanic fathers) to marry or cohabit with the mother (Mott 1994; Lerman and Sorensen 2000). But they were found to have the highest rates (estimates range from 20 percent to over 50 percent) of visitation or provision of some caretaking or in-kind support (more than formal child support). For instance, Carlson and McLanahan's (2002) figures indicated that only 37 percent of black nonmarital fathers were cohabiting with the child (compared to 66 percent of white fathers and 59 percent of Hispanic), but of those who weren't cohabiting, 44 percent of unmarried black fathers were visiting the child, compared to only 17 percent of white and 26 percent of Hispanic fathers. These studies also suggested that black nonresident fathers tend to maintain their level of involvement over time longer than do white and Hispanic nonresident fathers (Danziger and Radin 1990; Taylor et al. 1990; Seltzer 1991; Stier and Tienda 1993; Wattenberg 1993; Coley and Chase-Lansdale 1999).

Sometimes social, fictive, or "other" fathers step in for or supplement nonresident biological fathers. Little research has been conducted on social fathers, but it is known they come in a wide variety: relatives, such as grandfathers and uncles; friends, romantic partners and new husbands of the mother, cohabiting or not; and community figures, such as teachers, coaches, or community-center staff. Although virtually impossible to capture clearly in census data, it is known that a high proportion of black men act as social fathers of one sort or another, yet few studies exist on this group of dads. Lora Bex Lempert's 1999 study of black grandmothers as primary parents found that many families rely on grandfathers, other male extended family members, or community members to fill the father's shoes, but unfortunately her study did not explore the experience of these men.

Jarrett, Roy, and Burton's (2002:234) review of qualitative studies of black fathers managed to capture the perspectives of a few low-income social fathers. One sixteen-year-old talked about his fatherlike relationship with the young daughter of a friend.

> Tiffany (a pseudonym) is not my baby, but she needs a father. To be with her, I work in the day care center at school during my lunch hour. I feed her, change her diapers, and play with her. I buy her clothes when I can because I don't make much money. I keep her sometimes. Her mother and her family appreciate what I do and Tiffany loves me too. Every time she sees me she reaches for me and smiles.

Fagan's (1998) study of low-income biological and stepfathers in two-parent homes found that the two types of fathers of black children were equally involved (contrary to findings from other studies on stepfathers generally). Similarly, McLanahan and Sandefur (1994) found that, compared to those who live in single-parent homes, black male teens who lived with stepfathers were significantly less likely to drop out of school and black teen females were significantly less likely to become teen mothers. The authors speculated that the income, supervision, and role models that stepfathers provide may help compensate for communities with few resources and social control. Although they are often pictured as childless men, these social fathers may also be some other child's biological father, sometimes a nonresident father himself. Consequently, it is not easy and is certainly misleading to discuss fathers as if they come in discreet, nonoverlapping categories of biological or social.

A smaller amount of research has been conducted on black fathers in two-parent families, which are more likely to also be middle-class families. Allen (1981), looking at wives' reports, found black wives reported a higher level of father involvement in childrearing than did white wives. McAdoo (1988) and Bowman (1993) also concluded that black fathers are more involved than white fathers in childrearing. However, Roopnarine and Ahmeduzzaman (1993), and Hossain and Roopnarine (1994) find no or insignificant racial differences in the level and quality of married fathers' involvement. Across races, fathers in married-couple families were about equally involved with their children, which in all cases was less than mothers.

In terms of parenting style, studies of black two-parent families have found that African American parenting styles tend to be more authoritarian, with an emphasis on obedience and control or monitoring, than those of white parents. This style difference is frequently explained by lower income and neighborhood rather than by race itself (Garcia-Coll 1990; Hofferth 2003). Bright and Williams (1996) conducted a small qualitative study of seven low- to middle-income black fathers in two-parent families in an urban area. They found these fathers worked collaboratively with their wives to nurture their children and that chief among their concerns were rearing children with high self-esteem, protecting their family members in unsafe environments, securing quality education, and having a close relationship with their children. Marsiglio (1991) also found black fathers to talk more and have positive engagement with their older children.

Finally, and ironically, most *absent* in the literature on black fatherhood have been those fathers who are most *present*: black, single full-time fathers. About 6 percent of black households are male-headed, with no spouse present; about half of those contain children under eighteen years old (see table 0.1). These men also may be biological or adoptive fathers, but little is known about them. Aside from the contributors to this volume (Coles 2001a, 2001b, 2001c, 2003, 2009; Green, this volume; Osgood and Schroeder, this volume), Hamer and Marchiorio (2002) are the only ones who have researched this group of fathers. Brett Brown's (2000) study of single fathers included black men, but his findings and conclusions did not disarticulate the data by race.

In sum, research on black fathers has been limited in quantity and has narrowly focused on nonmarital, nonresident fathers and only secondarily on dads in married-couple households. This oversight is not merely intentional, for black men are only about 6 percent of the U.S. population and obviously a smaller percent are fathers. They are not easy to access, particularly by an academy that remains predominantly white. We hope to use this volume to fill in some of the gaps and to broaden the scope of what people see when they look at black men as parents. We want to adjust the public's visual lens from a zoom to a wide angle to view black fathers in a realistic landscape, to illustrate that they are quite varied in their living arrangements, marital status, and styles of parenting.

In this volume, we do not intend to decide which set of dads is better (whether by race or by type of father within races). We are not interested in the good dad–bad dad typology. We make the assumption that good fathering is best for children, but we also assume good fathering can take many forms and styles. We want to explore how black men perceive and decipher their various parenting experiences and give them voice in the pages of this anthology. We want to consider policies, tried or suggested, that impede or facilitate parenting on the part of black men. We seek to provide a forum in which black fathers in their full range of parenting take center stage. We feel that the timing of this book is opportune, with the recent election of the first black president of the United States. Many African Americans are optimistic that President Barack Obama, who experienced the absence of his own father and is expressly committed to furthering involved fatherhood, will be able to significantly weaken the existing stereotype of the black father, both through his own public example and through facilitative policy.

The Organization of the Book

The Myth of the Missing Black Father is an interdisciplinary volume with contributors from sociology but also from the disciplines of social work, family studies, and psychology. It comprises sixteen chapters—all of which were specifically prepared for this volume—organized into six parts. Consistent with one of the main objectives of the volume—to showcase the diversity of African American fatherhood in contrast to the often unidimensional portrayal of black fathers as largely absent single fathers—these sections explore key categories of black fathers in contemporary society and some of the challenges they encounter. They also explore children's perceptions of their fathers alongside certain legal and social policies that contradict the objective of responsible fathering.

Three chapters are included in part 1, "Married Fathers," that draw attention to the persistence of this basic familial typology in the Black community. Loren Marks, Katrina Hopkins-Williams, Cassandra Chaney, Olena Nestruk, and Diane Sasser's interviews with married fathers underscore this point. A quantitative study by Ron Bulanda examines the intersection of poverty and the parenting styles of married African American moms and dads, while Erica Chito-Childs and Heather Dalmage examine the sensitive matter of black fathers in interracial unions who have undertaken the gargantuan task of socializing their biracial children as African Americans.

Part 2 focuses on the emerging family type, "Single Resident Fathers." Until now, single custodial fathers have been underrepresented in the literature in part because of demographics but also the larger society's reluctance to fully embrace this family type. Roberta Coles's lead essay uses a qualitative study to provide an overview of this emerging family type. With the perplexing debate about gendered nurturing as a backdrop, Charles Green's qualitative study compares single mothers' and fathers' views of one another as parents. This section ends with a quantitative study by Aurea Osgood and Ryan Schroeder, who compare black and white single custodial fathers' use of public assistance benefits.

Another expanding typology of fatherhood is captured in part 3, "Social Fathering." While this category is not new to the black community, it has nonetheless taken on increased importance in the past few decades. Mark King's quantitative examination of the movement of various father figures in and out of low-income families further clarifies the conceptual aspects of social fathering. Aaron Smith's essay considers the special but overlooked role that grandfathers play as social fathers. The final essay in this section, by Bethany L. Letiecq, navigates us through fathering in violent inner-city neighborhoods, with a critical eye on the differences between biological fathers and social fathers.

Part 4, "Young Fathers," derails the stereotype of young fathers as irresponsible. Kevin Roy and Colleen Vesely's qualitative analysis of thirty-five young, low-income African American fathers shows the receptiveness of these young men to supporting their children and illustrates that father involvement is shaped by the support and expectations of kin systems. Further reason for optimism concerning young fathers is advanced in Jacqueline Smith's essay on Division I college athletes who are also fathers and who are determined to dismiss the myth by demonstrating their ability to balance fatherhood, athletics, and academics.

Whereas most of the studies in this volume examine the problem of fatherhood through the lens of fathers, part 5 offers a snapshot of fathers as they are perceived through children's eyes. Eunice Matthews-Armstead's essay reports on her extensive interviews with adult black women whose fathers were absent for most if not all of their lives and how they have narratively reconstructed those fathers as adults. Suzanne Lamorey creatively addresses the matter of father absence and portrayals of father figures in children's literature and analyzes how fathers affect meaning making for children.

The final section in this volume, "Policies Affecting Black Fathers" addresses the all too often negative effects of social policies and certain legal institutions on fathering, particularly among black fathers. The first chapter, coauthored by Amy Smoyer, Kim Blankenship, and Tracy Macintosh, examines the plight of black fathers who seek to fulfill their responsibilities as parents but are trapped by their legal status as parolees or probationers and the bureaucratic rules that govern their lives. The final two chapters, by Cheryl Mills and David Pate, respond to the radical welfare policy changes that began in 1996 during the Clinton administration, which introduced new welfare and child-support-payment legislation that in some cases has weakened rather than strengthened the involvement of fathers in their children's lives. Mills concentrates on the history and background of the problem, while Pate focuses on the hotly debated "marriage promotion" plan.

A Word About Methods

Since the primary objective of *The Myth of the Missing Black Father* is to broaden our understanding of Black fathers, who for too long have remained in the background and invisible to the public eye, we wanted the essays in this volume to contribute to changing that image by placing fathers' voices in narrative form. Thus, the majority of the studies are based chiefly on qualitative research procedures, though a few rely heavily on quantitative methodology. Qualitative methods aim for depth of information concerning subjects' inner feelings and viewpoints but are not without limitations. A key limitation is the tendency for these studies to rely upon small samples, making it difficult to generalize findings across wider populations.

Despite this, we hope that the studies in this anthology will cumulatively provide the reader with rich information on how black fathers feel about their circumstances, choices, regrets, and aspirations as related to their own and their children's futures. These studies should inspire us to increase our efforts to attract more resources to expand our samples, extend the research, and strengthen our findings.

References

Allen, W. 1981. "Mom, Dads, and Boys: Race and Sex Differences in the Socialization of Male Children." In *Black Men*, ed. L. Gary, 99–114. Beverly Hills, Calif.: Sage.

Barras, J. R. 2000. *Whatever Happened to Daddy's Little Girl? The Impact Of Fatherlessness On Black Women*. New York: Ballantine.

Bowman, P. 1993. "The Impact of Economic Marginality on African-American Husbands and Fathers." In *Family Ethnicity*, ed. H. McAdoo, 120–137. Newbury Park, Calif.: Sage.

Bright, J. A., and C. Williams. 1996. "Child-rearing and Education in Urban Environments: Black Fathers' Perspectives." *Urban Education* 31 (3): 245–60.

Brown, B. V. 2000. "The Single-Father Family: Demographic, Economic, and Public Transfer Use Characteristics." *Marriage and Family Review* 29:203–23.

Carlson, M. J. and S. S. McLanahan. 2002. "Fragile Families, Father Involvement, and Public Policy" In *Handbook of Father Involvement: Multidisciplinary Perspectives*, ed. Catherine Tamis-LeMonda and Natasha Cabrera, 461–88. Mahwah, N.J.: Lawrence Erlbaum.

Clayton, O., D. Blankenhorn, and R. B. Mincy, eds. 2003. *Black Fathers in Contemporary American Society*. New York: Russell Sage Foundation.

Coles, R. L. 2001a. "African American Single Full-time Fathers." *Journal of African American Men* 6 (2): 63–82.

Coles, R. L. 2001b. "Black Single Fathers: Choosing to Parent Full-Time." *Journal of Contemporary Ethnography* 31 (4): 411–39.

Coles, R. L. 2001c. "The Parenting Roles and Goals of Single Black Full-time Fathers." *Western Journal of Black Studies* 25 (2): 101–16.

Coles, R. L. 2003. "Black Single Custodial Fathers: Factors Influencing the Decision to Parent." *Families in Society* 84 (2): 247–58.

Coles, R. L. 2009. *The Best Kept Secret: Single Black Fathers.* Lanham, Md.: Rowman and Littlefield.

Coley, R. L., and P. L. Chase-Lansdale. 1999. "Stability and Change in Paternal Involvement Among Urban African American Fathers." *Journal of Family Psychology* 13 (3): 1–20.

Crissey, S. R. 2005. "Race/Ethnic Differences in the Marital Expectations of Adolescents: The Role of Romantic Relationships." *Journal of Marriage and Family* 67:697–709.

Daniels, C. R., ed. 1998. *Lost Fathers: The Politics of Fatherlessness.* London: Macmillan.

Danziger, S. and N. Radin. 1990. "Absent Does Not Equal Uninvolved: Predictors of Fathering in Teen Mother Families." *Journal of Marriage and the Family* 52 (3): 636–42.

Datcher, M. 2001. *Raising Fences: A Black Man's Love Story.* New York: Riverhead Books.

Dowd, N. E. 2000. *Redefining Fatherhood.* New York: New York University Press.

Ellwood, D. T., and J. Crane. 1990. "Family Change Among Black Americans: What Do We Know?" *The Journal of Economic Perspectives* 4 (4): 65–84.

Fagan, J. 1998. "Correlates of Low-Income African American and Puerto Rican Fathers' Involvement with Their Children." *Journal of Black Psychology* 24 (3): 351–67.

Garcia-Coll, C. 1990. "Developmental Outcome of Minority Infants: A Process-Oriented Look Into our Beginnings. *Child Development* 61:270–89.

Gavanas, A. 2004. *Fatherhood Politics in the United States: Masculinity, Sexuality, Race, and Marriage.* Chicago: University of Illinois Press.

Goldstein, J. R. and C. T. Kenney. 2001. "Marriage Delayed or Marriage Forgone? New Cohort Forecasts of First Marriage for U.S. Women," *American Sociological Review* 66 (4): 506–19.

Hamer, J. 2001. *What It Means to Be Daddy.* New York: Columbia University Press.

Hamer, J., and K. Marchiorio. 2002. "Becoming Custodial Dads: Exploring Parenting Among Low-Income and Working-Class African American Fathers." *Journal of Marriage and Family* 64:116–29.

Hernandez, D. J., and P. D. Brandon. 2002. "Who Are the Fathers of Today?" In *Handbook of Father Involvement,* ed. C. S. Tamis-LeMonda and N. Cabrera, 33–62. Mahwah, N.J.: Lawrence Erlbaum.

Hobson, B. 2002. *Making Men Into Fathers.* Cambridge: Cambridge University Press.

Hofferth, S. 2003. "Race/Ethnic Differences in Father Involvement in Two-Parent Families: Culture, Context, or Economy?" *Journal of Family Issues* 24 (2): 185–216.

Hossain, Z., and Roopnarine, J. 1994. "African-American Fathers' Involvement with Infants: Relationship to Their Functioning Style, Support, Education, and Income." *Infant Behavior and Development* 17:175–84.

Jarrett, R. L., K. M. Roy, and L. M. Burton. 2002. "Fathers in the 'Hood': Insights from Qualitative Research on Low-Income African American Men." In *Handbook of Father Involvement: Multidisciplinary Perspectives*, ed. C. Tamis-LeMonda and N. Cabrera, 221–48. New York: Lawrence Erlbaum.

Kreider, R. M. 2008. *Living Arrangements of Children: 2004*. U.S. Department of Commerce, U.S. Census Bureau.

Lamb, M. E. 1986. "The Changing Role of Fathers." In *The Father's Role: Applied Perspectives*, ed. M. E. Lamb, 3–27. New York: Wiley.

Lamb, M. E., ed. 1997. *The Role of the Father in Child Development*. 3rd ed. New York: Wiley.

Lamb, M. E., ed. 2004. *The Role of the Father in child Development*. 4th ed. Hoboken, N.J.: Wiley.

LaRossa, R. 1997. *The Modernization of Fatherhood: A Social and Political History*. Chicago: University of Chicago Press.

Lempert, L. B. 1999. "Other Fathers: An Alternative Perspective on African American Community Caring." In *The Black Family: Essays and Studies*, ed. R. Staples, 189–201. Belmont, Calif.: Wadsworth.

Lerman, R. I. 1989. "Employment Opportunities of Young Men and Family Formation." *American Economic Review* (May): 62–66.

Lerman, R. and E. Sorensen. 2000. "Father Involvement with Their Nonmarital Children: Patterns, Determinants, and Effects on Their Earnings." *Marriage and Family Review* 29 (2/3): 137–58.

Marsiglio, W. 1991. "Paternal Engagement Activities with Minor Children." *Journal of Marriage and the Family* 53:973–86.

Marsiglio, W., and M. Cohan. 2000. "Contextualizing Father Involvement and Paternal Influence: Sociological and Qualitative Themes." In *Fatherhood: Research, Interventions, and Policies*, ed. H. E. Peters, G. W. Peterson, S. K. Steinmetz, and R. D. Day, 75–95. New York: Haworth.

Martin, J. A., B. E. Hamilton, P. D. Sutton, S. J. Ventura, F. Menacker, and M. L. Munson. 2003. "Births: Final Data for 2002." *National Vital Statistics Reports* 52 (10). Washington, D.C.: Government Printing Office.

McAdoo, J. L. 1988. "The Roles of Black Fathers in the Socialization of Black Children." In *Black Families*, ed. H. P. McAdoo, 257–69. Newbury Park, Calif.: Sage.

McLanahan, S., and G. Sandefur. 1994. *Growing Up with a Single Parent: What Hurts, What Helps*. Cambridge, Mass.: Harvard University Press.

Mincy, R., I. Garfinkel, and L. Nepomnyaschy. 2005. "In-Hospital Paternity Establishment and Father Involvement in Fragile Families." *Journal of Marriage and Family* 67:611–26.

Mott, E. L. 1994. "Sons, Daughters, and Fathers' Absence: Differentials in Father-Leaving Probabilities and in Home Environments." *Journal of Family Issues* 5:97–128.

Neal, M. A. 2005. *The New Black Man*. New York: Routledge.

Nelson, T. J. 2004. "Low-Income Fathers." *Annual Review of Sociology* 30:427–51.

Pitts, L., Jr. 1999. *Becoming Dad: Black Men and the Journey to Fatherhood*. Atlanta: Longstreet.

Roberts, D. 1998. "The Absent Black Father." In *Lost Fathers: The Politics of Fatherlessness in America*, 144–61. New York: St. Martin's Press.

Roberts, S. 1994. "Black Women Graduates Outpace Male Counterparts." *New York Times*. October 31.

Roopnarine, J. L., and M. Ahmeduzzaman. 1993. "Puerto Rican Fathers' Involvement with Their Preschool-Age Children." *Hispanic Journal of Behavioral Sciences* 15 (1): 96–107.

Seltzer, J. A. 1991. "Relationships Between Fathers and Children Who Live Apart: The Father's Role After Separation." *Journal of Marriage and the Family* 53:79–101.

South, S. J. 1993. "Racial and Ethnic Differences in the Desire to Marry." *Journal of Marriage and Family* 55 (2): 357–70.

Stier, H. and M. Tienda. 1993. "Are Men Marginal to the Family? Insights from Chicago's Inner City." In *Men, Work, and Family*, ed. J. C. Hood, 23–44. Newbury Park, Calif.: Sage.

Tamis-LeMonda, C. S., and N. Cabrera. 2002. "Cross-disciplinary Challenges to the Study of Father Involvement." In *Handbook of Father Involvement: Multidisciplinary Perspectives*, ed. C. S. Tamis-LeMonda and N. Cabrera, 599–620. New York: Lawrence Erlbaum.

Taylor, R., L. Chatters, M. B. Tucker, and E. Lewis. 1990. "Developments in Research on Black Families: A Decade Review." *Journal of Marriage and the Family* 52:993–1014.

Tucker, M. B., and Mitchell-Kernan, C. 1995. "Trends in African American Family Formation: A Theoretical and Statistical Overview." In *The Decline in Marriage Among African American: Causes, Consequences, and Policy Implications*, ed. M. B. Tucker and C. Mitchell-Kernan, 3–26. New York: Russell Sage Foundation.

U.S. Department of Commerce, U.S. Census Bureau. 2000. *Households and Families: 2000*. Electronic version. Available from Census 2000 Summary File 2 (SF-2) QT-P10 at http://factfinder.census.gov.

Wattenberg, E. 1993. "Paternity Actions and Young Fathers." In *Young Unwed Fathers: Changing Roles and Emerging Policies*, ed. R. Lerman and T. Ooms, 213–34. Philadelphia: Temple University Press.

Wilson, W. J. 1987. *The Truly Disadvantaged: The Inner City, the Underclass, and Public Policy*. Chicago: University of Chicago Press.

PART ONE

Married Fathers

CHAPTER ONE

"My Kids and Wife Have Been My Life"

Married African American Fathers Staying the Course

LOREN MARKS, KATRINA HOPKINS-WILLIAMS, CASSANDRA CHANEY,
OLENA NESTERUK, AND DIANE SASSER

On the opening page of a recent edited volume titled *Black Fathers in Contemporary American Society*, Blankenhorn and Clayton (2003:1) ask, "Is any demographic fact more disturbing, more demanding of our collective attention, than the fact that the great majority of African American children do not live with their fathers?" However, they hasten to add some good news as well. The same page reads, conversely: "Is any demographic fact more hopeful, or more demanding of our collective encouragement, than the fact the proportion of African American children living with both of their biological, married parents, although still quite low, has risen significantly since 1995?" (1).

Dupree and Primus (2001) have noted that between 1995 and 2000 the proportion of black children living in two-parent, married-couple homes *increased* from 34.8 to 38.9 percent. While this increased figure is far lower than it was before 1980, when the majority of black families were still marriage based (McAdoo 2007), it is high enough to illustrate that many African American fathers and mothers and their children are sharing a marriage-based home life. Unfortunately, "little research exists on positive marital adjustment, happiness, and satisfaction among African Americans" (Lassiter 1998:35). Instead, researchers have chosen to focus almost exclusively on single mothers in poverty, leading to a great imbalance in research on black families

(Bobo 2003), an imbalance that has resulted in scholars virtually ig-noring responsible, generative black fathers (Allen and Connor 1997), and *married* black fathers in particular (Connor and White 2006). It is this condition in the literature to which Livingston and McAdoo (2007) refer, when they state, "To gain a more accurate view of the Black community, researchers will have to gain a more comprehensive sample of Black families, for only then will they be in a position to understand the unique roles that Black fathers play in nurturing and socializing their children" (233). This chapter is our effort to provide "a more comprehensive sample" by presenting some stories about a type of African American men that is rarely heard from—married fathers.

Black families and the fathers in these families face many struc-tural and systemic challenges (e.g., economic, demographic, historical-legal; Coles 2006) as well as varying levels of racism, oppression, and powerlessness (Green 2001). These are topics that require volume-length attention, and here we will only be able to briefly overview three contextualizing issues involving black men, fatherhood, and marriage: trends in African American marriage and fatherhood, barri-ers to black marriage and marriage-based fatherhood, and the impor-tance of father-child involvement.

Trends in African American Marriage and Fatherhood

In 1925, six out of every seven black households included a husband or father (Franklin 2007). In fact, "until the 1960s, a remarkable 75% of Black families included both husband and wife" (Franklin 2007:6). Sociologist Steven Nock (2003) has shown that in 1977, 69 percent of black men aged forty to forty-four in the United States were mar-ried and living with their wives. By 1987, the figure had dropped to 56 percent. Measures in 1997 revealed another 13-point drop to 43 per-cent (Mincy and Pouncy 2003; Nock 2003). Although marital rates de-clined for all races during those two decades, the downward trajectory for black marriage was especially sharp. However, in the 2000 Census (three years later), the percentage of black men living with their wives *increased* 2 points to 45 percent. In this regard, we are at an interest-ing point in history, when a sharp and steady decline has abated. It is time to examine some reasons for the recent increase, as well as an opportunity to ask, "Why did a sharp marital decline occur?" It is to the latter question that we turn to next.

Barriers to Black Marriage and Marriage-Based Fatherhood

There are several factors that have contributed to the eighty-year decline in black married fathers. These include an imbalanced gender ratio, lack of mate availability, criminality, and many other issues (for recent reviews, see Chapman 2007; Staples 2007). Here, we will briefly address two central barriers for black men: employment and education.

Employment

After years of examining African American fathers and families, William Julius Wilson (1996) concluded that "crime, family dissolution, welfare, and low levels of social organization are fundamentally a consequence of the disappearance of work" (cf. Sudarkasa 2007:180).[1] To paint a more specific picture, "45% of Black men in Chicago aged 20 to 24 [were] out of work and out of school" and "all but out of hope" (Herbert 2003). Other urban centers or "cores" have similar or even higher unemployment rates (45–55 percent) among young black men (Kunjufu 2004). In connection with the unemployment situation among Black men, the late John McAdoo (1993) stated: "The ability to provide for self and family affects a man's self-perception with regard to various family roles. [However], from an ecological perspective . . . an African American man's ability to fulfill his provider role depends on community systems over which he has little control" (30).

Christiansen and Palkovitz (2001) have pointed out that the "provider role" (referred to by McAdoo) is not just something American men *do*, it is a significant portion of their identity, of who they *are* as men. Men, black or white, have difficulty trying to assume the responsibilities of husband and father unless they are meeting the societal and instrumental requirements associated with being a "provider." This is underscored by the finding that for young, inner-city, black men in the eighteen to thirty-one age bracket, employment increases the likelihood that a young man will marry the mother of his child by *eightfold* (Testa and Krogh, 1995).

Education

The lack of employment and employability leads to a discussion of education because the industrial jobs that provided the economic foundation for the black working class in the first half of the twentieth century have dissipated (Green 1997, 2001). As African American leaders have argued in the past, education seems to be a critical key for opening the doors of opportunity—not just financial or employment opportunity but marital opportunity as well. Unfortunately, the American ideal of quality public education for all has not been realized. In many areas of the United States—most notably in inner cities and in the South—there are significant, even staggering differences between educational opportunities between black and white children and youth. Following the *Brown v. Board of Education* ruling, there was a white flight for private schools (which are often subsidized at some level by public funds [see Edelman 2007]). A significant portion of white children attend private schools that are prohibitively costly for most minorities, promoting de facto segregation (Marks et al. 2006). An extreme example is offered by Edelman (2007), who reports, "In Lee County School District in South Carolina, White students are almost 900 times more likely to attend private schools than Black students" (320). Indeed, in contexts where

> large portions of the middle- and upper-class voting contingency [a]re paying private school tuition for their child(ren), [the relatively wealthy] have little incentive to support public education tax bases. Predictably, public education is grossly underfunded as a result, and the likelihood of a child from a lower (and disproportionately Black) income bracket receiving a high quality education that will allow [a good] standard of living for their rising African American generation is remote.
>
> (Marks et al. 2006:211)

While relatively poor educational opportunities have harmed African American women, their male counterparts have fared even worse. Nearly twice as many black women are enrolled in higher education as black men—and about 40 percent of the black male population is functionally illiterate (Chapman 2007).

Education and employment are formidable barriers that stand between many (and possibly *most*) black men and marriage-based fatherhood. However, in spite of these and other barriers, many black fathers *are* highly committed to their marriage, wife, and children. Where are their stories in the social-science literature? Would it not be valuable to listen to and learn from black fathers who have enduring marriages and strong relationships with their children, children whom they raised in their own homes? While we are not the first to ask these questions, we are among the first to search out and tell the stories (cf. Connor and White 2006).

The Importance of Father-Child Involvement

Since 1980, more than seventy studies on the connection between father involvement and child well-being have been conducted. Of those, more than 80 percent indicate a significant positive relationship (Amato and Rivera 1999; Livingston and McAdoo 2007; see also Peters et al. 2000). Specifically, black children tend to have fewer behavior problems and higher academic achievement as father involvement increases (Coley 1998; Livingston and McAdoo 2007). While much is known regarding how fathers (and marriage) influence children, relatively little is known about how children influence married fathers. Married fathers tend to work more after their children are born and tend to see a dip in marital satisfaction but an increase in marital stability (Cowan and Cowan 2000; Palkovitz 2002). Some ethnographic work addressing single black fathers exists (Coles 2002, 2003, 2006), but research examining children's effects on black married fathers is scant.

A Brief Description of Our Participants

Consistent with our desire to conduct a meaningful and relevant study, we focused on married couples where the partners had been raised (and still resided) in inner-city areas (including Boston, Cleveland, Milwaukee, New Orleans, and Portland, Ore.). Approximately one-half of African Americans reside in inner-city neighborhoods "typified by poverty, poor schools, unemployment, periodic street violence, and generally high levels of stress" (Lassiter 1998:37). These are contexts where marriages are less likely to form and where divorce is more likely when marriage does occur (Tucker 2000; Clayton, Mincy, and

Blankenhorn 2003). By extension, married fathers are rare in American inner cities. However, twenty-four of our thirty interviewed couples (80 percent) resided in inner-city neighborhoods (four couples were rural, two were suburban). In terms of education, every one of the sixty people in our sample completed high school or earned a GED, and a majority had attended at least some college. Further, wives typically had as much education as their husbands or more than them, a characteristic that is a predictor of marital *instability* among whites (Veroff, Douvan, and Hatchett 1995). In terms of employment, every one of the thirty couples had had dual incomes for most of their married life, and the average combined household income was about $58,000. Except in one case of severe injury and a few cases of retirement, all wives and husbands were currently employed. Most of the husbands' jobs were industrial "blue-collar" jobs with decent pay—jobs that are disappearing rapidly from urban America (Green 2001).

The couples in our study had been married for an average of about twenty-six years, with an average age of fifty-five years for the fathers and fifty-three years for the mothers. For four of the fathers (and three of the mothers), their present long-term marriage was a remarriage. Most couples had married in their mid- to late twenties. The couples had an average of slightly less than three children, and in all but a couple of cases the children had been born after marriage. A final note on our couples is that in order to be interviewed, both the wife and husband had to report (on an independently mailed and confidential survey) that their marriage was a "happy" one. In short, these couples' marriages were not only stable or enduring, they were also happy.

Procedures

After the participants gave informed consent, each father and mother completed detailed demographic forms. The fathers and mothers were then asked twenty open-ended questions that addressed various aspects of parenting, marriage, and family life. Interviews were conducted in the participants' homes and typically lasted about two hours, although some interviews went considerably longer. The thirty transcribed couple interviews comprised roughly 1,000 double-spaced pages. Themes relating to a variety of subject areas were coded, but this chapter will focus on four central themes relating specifically to the interface between fathering and marriage for the black men we interviewed.

Narrative Themes

In this section, four key themes from our qualitative data analysis will be presented: *leaving the "bachelor mindset" behind; helping family, friends, and community; the influence of children on their fathers;* and *depth of relationship and commitment with wife.* We have previously discussed some key barriers that stand between many black men and marriage. The first two themes that will be presented address challenges the black men we interviewed reported facing *after* marriage.

Leaving the "Bachelor Mindset" Behind

The first theme addresses the fundamental issue of moving from "me" to "we" in a marriage. Many men struggle with commitment—in terms of making a marriage proposal. However, a marriage commitment does not guarantee a shift from a self-centered to couple-centered life. That is, it was a significant struggle for many of the men we interviewed, by their own reports, to move past what they referred to as "the bachelor mindset" early on in their marriages. Terrence reflected:[2]

> [I remember asking myself (about marriage)], "Can I really do this?" [And] asking God, "Really, can I do this?" 'Cause [my wife] will tell you, I still had *the bachelor mindset.* She was chasing me down in the street. Telling me when to come home. I mean, we went back and forth with that for five or six years. I mean, my thing was: "I'm a bachelor." I couldn't get [out of] that mindset that . . . I'm independent. [I'd ask her], "What are you calling me for? Why do I got to come home? Why do I have to be there with you? Why do we have to eat together? I'm over here [with my boys]. I'm okay. I'm fine. I'll be home when I get ready." I couldn't connect [the marriage vows with the actions]. [Well], I'm [fully] married now.

LaRon gave additional insight into this same struggle by discussing his transition from "opening up with buddies" to sharing with his wife. He explained:

> You have to change, you have to be willing to give up everything that you used to think about relationships, and sacrifice your buddies. The buddy mentality [has been] with you all your life. To give up that type

of thinking is tough, [but you must do it] for your spouse. . . . [You have the challenge of] convincing yourself that your spouse can be as good as [a] friend [to you] as your buddies were. . . . [I] always had a problem with that. This new person, a female at that, you have to be able to share openly—just as you would with your buddies. *Share.* That is the hardest thing! Opening up . . . opening up is not a natural thing for men with women. [With] their buddies, they talk all day long about anything, everything. We tend to save things in reserve, exclusively with our buddies. . . . [But now it is supposed to be your wife that] you share everything [with]; your thoughts, your ambitions, the things you hate. You [used to] tell your buddies everything . . . and well, that's how you have to be with your spouse. Not that I have mastered that, I have not. But I think that [is] what you need [to do].

LaRon's wife, Vanessa, agreed that she married a work-in-progress, but reported with some pride that "[over time, I have seen a lot of] maturity [and] spiritual growth [in him]. [Early on], he was extremely impulsive and selfish; very singularly absorbed. [He] just couldn't even see anything beyond what he wanted for himself. . . . That has changed." Another father similarly discussed his "turning point":

I think there were moments [early in our marriage] that I was playing that role of a kid and she was [like my] Mama, 'cause I didn't want to grow up. But now I know I [had] to grow up. That [was] a real turning point for me. I can't tell you exactly when that "Aha" moment came for me. It gradually came and continues.

We (Marks et al. 2008:181) have reported that a pattern emerges among many of these couples we have interviewed: namely,

(a) boy meets girl; (b) boy loves girl but has difficulty leaving "the single life" behind; (c) the man [faces] a choice point. In some cases, the husband changed and the marriage became unified, but in other cases, the husband did not change and/or unity was not achieved and the marriage ended. . . . [The couples whose marriages endured tended to share] a unified marital and family *vision.*

Chapman (2007) issues a call for understanding and reconciliation between the genders and implicitly touches on several issues that are reflected in our data. We similarly offer a strategy for men in overcoming the prevalent and relationally unhealthy "bachelor mindset" and penchant for "hangin' with the boys." This strategy is not offered by ivory tower scholars, but by Frank, a long-term husband and father who had to negotiate the single-to-married transition in his own life. He stated:

> One thing I've found that's good [is a] support group of men who are in like terms, [like] faith. You can't hang around with your boy[s] running the street[s]. You need men who are mature [enough to] see beyond that . . . maybe they made mistakes in the past [but they are strong now]. You need a group of *men* . . . you need that backing. I think that's vital. Other men give you strength, other men [do that]. All your life you grew up with guys hanging out and you know that numbers make strength. So faith [and] male bonding [bring strength].

The difference Frank notes between "hangin' around with your boys running the streets" and "bonding with a good support group of men" is far more than semantic. Perhaps a central difference is that *men* are not resentful of time and energy that other fathers invest in their children and wives, while "boys" are likely to be jealous. "Men" assume a supporting role in encouraging other men to build primary bonds with family. Often, as Frank mentions, such men also promote a commitment to faith and God (cf. Connor 2006; Marks and Dollahite 2007). In fact, references to God and faith by fathers (and mothers) were so prevalent in our study that we have written other papers focused solely on these sacred influences, including the influence of the black church as "church family" (Marks et al. 2005; Marks and Chaney 2006).

Helping Family, Friends, and Community

The first theme addressed the challenge of overcoming the "bachelor mindset" that is common in the early years of marriage. However, for the fathers we interviewed, this challenge tended to pass as their maturity and marital commitment increased. Our second theme is another postmarriage challenge that faces virtually all black fathers at some level: the dilemma of how much help to provide to family and friends. Unlike overcoming the "bachelor mindset," this second challenge will likely be present for the rest of one's life.

To better understand the foundation of this challenge, it is necessary to understand the sense of collectivism that prevails in African
American families and communities. Family scholars have discussed
"her" and "his" marriages over the past three decades, but in a very
real sense, African American marriages "belong" to the community.
One father named Clarence captured this idea as follows:

> [One of the most] important things [in marriage] . . . is recognizing
> that there is a need to stay together for the sake of the community
> and for the sake of the family. [Your marriage is not just for you, it's]
> for the family, [for] the community, and its wholeness. [W]e have a
> responsibility to our children, we have a responsibility to our commu-
> nity to remain together. . . . We have to be an example to our children.
> We have to show them there are parents out there who don't give up.
> When we go to the activities of our children . . . we see single parents,
> we don't know all the reasons behind it. But I feel good when me and
> my wife walk in there [together as a strong black married couple]. It
> just kind of brings a sense of wholeness for me when we can come in
> together. [W]e can represent as a couple, as a *married* couple, to our
> children [and community].

This strong community tie can be costly. Of our thirty families,
twenty-four were residing in inner-city areas. Four more families lived
in poor, rural areas, while only two were in suburbs. In brief, although
most of the families were of middle to low-middle socioeconomic status, they were relatively well-off compared with most of their single
and divorced family and friends because of the additional resources
of a marital household (i.e., two wage earners, two sets of skills, and
two adult parents in the home, etc.). We have elsewhere referred to
these couples as *the wealthy poor* (Marks et al. 2006). Dual-earner
black couples in committed marriages, like our sample, tend to have a
large network of close family and kin relationships, and many in that
network have lower income levels and no spouse to lean on in trying times. As a result, married, *wealthy poor* couples often become
a primary source of assistance—the first doors to literally and figuratively receive *knocks of need* (Marks et al. 2006). One father in our
sample, Jason, grew weary of the problems, strains, and demands of his
native, inner-city neighborhood and moved to a suburban community.
He explained:

We've been geographically away from our community for nearly twenty-five years. We've been accused at times of being different or being kind of isolated. We do this intentionally, isolate ourselves from [some of my old boys]. [Some of them say], "[You] must think [you] are better than [we] are." . . . [I]t isn't that; we just want better for ourselves and we want to put our children in a different environment and raise them in a different environment. Some of the stuff [in the inner city], granted, we *don't* want to be a part of. There's no health and there's no strength in [many aspects of that environment], [especially] as a married couple. To be truthful, part of the reason we are here today is because we didn't hang out with some of [our crowd who went down the wrong path] back in the '80s and '90s, to be very honest. . . . We have [seized] these opportunities, [while our crowd chose differently]. . . . I don't want the fellowship [with that crowd], I don't need it. That sounds kind of harsh but I don't need that fellowship anymore.

There are many potentially destructive aspects of inner-city "environment" and "fellowship" to which Jason refers. Participants addressed black-on-black violence, gang culture, and "the street life," on the one hand, but also illustrated compassionate Afro-centric collectivism, on the other. The blend is a troubling one for Jackson, a respected "old head" in his community, who was passionate in his call for more of the latter:

[What] we [all] need to do is be more supportive of each other. [W]e need to go back to the basics, go back to where we depend on ourselves more as a family. [We need to] go back to the values [of] teaching [our children] what is right and wrong. [We need] to encourage [our children] to grow [and to be more careful with spending]. It doesn't take a lot to live, you don't need a whole bunch of things to live; that's unnecessary. We *need* to have more unity, more time together, Sunday dinner has dissolved. We need to encourage [others], your house should be open. Those are the basics I'm talking about. Those are the things that will get you through anytime—*depending on each other, be[ing] there for each other [as family and community]*.

Another married father, Bryant, recalled that during his childhood, the "community" Jackson refers to was "there" to step in and help him when his own family failed. He explained:

[Although my father wasn't around, my neighborhood] was like a village for me. [There were] others [I] was connected to that gave me more of the internal stuff at a young age that I needed. I didn't get that from the nuclear family because there was too much dysfunction and turmoil within that bubble for me to get what I needed— but I found [men] throughout [my community]. [And through those] relationship[s], I found people that gave me what I needed at crucial times in my life.

Many of the men we have interviewed are committed fathers in spite of poor experiences with their own fathers. It is likely that the social fathers Bryant referred to were a critical factor in what he has made of himself; indeed, no one needs social fathers more than the fatherless boy (cf. Connor and White 2006). However, it is important to note that although social fathers (e.g., coaches, teachers, church leaders, Boy Scout leaders, etc.; cf. Coley 2001) do not *need* to be married fathers themselves, it *is* married fathers that usually fill the voluntary positions that provide the richest opportunities for social fatherhood (Nock 1998; Marks and Palkovitz 2004).

Many men in the black community find meaning in giving their time and energy to the rising generation in creative ways (Allen and Connor 1997). However, married fathers are often asked to give other resources as well. For example, Coles (2006) has pointed out that informal adoptions outnumber formal, legal adoptions about ten to one in the African American community, consistent with African tradition of taking care of extended family (Stewart 2004). We similarly found that almost all of the families in our study had provided room and board for at least one person from outside of their nuclear families at some point in time. Indeed, some of the married couples had housed *temporary children* for years with little or no compensation (cf. Marks et al. 2006). In short, these fathers and their families had "open homes" (a phrase Jackson used in his interview). Sheila and Rashaad, a rural couple in our sample, had been married for several years but had been unable to have children. Sheila was asked by a pregnant cousin who had been struggling with substance abuse if Sheila would take her to the hospital. Following the delivery, Sheila's cousin asked Sheila and Rashaad to take the baby home with them, a request they honored. The "temporary" child never left. Sheila and Rashaad ultimately raised the baby, as well as two other children from an extended family member who was abusing drugs and was an unsatisfactory parent. This pattern was familiar to other parents in our sample as well. Following this relatively sudden shift from no children to three, Sheila explained:

> Sometimes I just don't want to be a Mommy, I mean I made this decision, it wasn't something that God forced on me, but I didn't have nine months to deal with, "Oh, it's coming." I mean I got two kids in one year [and one more after that] and we were married for ten years without kids, just me and [Rashaad], doing whatever we wanted to do.

Sheila and Rashaad, like many other wealthy poor couples, offered an initial safe haven that became a long-term home for children of extended family or kin who were not prepared or willing to be responsible parents (Marks et al. 2006).

While the fathers and families in our study gave time and shelter, that was not all they gave. To frame their financial sacrifices, we will turn briefly to previous research from Mincy and Pouncy (2003), who indicate that "Black married couples earn 80% as much as White married couples but have only 27% as much net worth" (57). Low homeownership rates and different levels of access to financial information account for some of the disparity in net worth among black and white married couples, but some of the difference is likely traceable to the large amount of financial/temporal resources that black married couples pour back into their communities through informal channels (McAdoo 2007). Indeed, giving heavily to meet knocks of need in the community is

> an aspect of African American culture that can make it difficult for a married Black couple to "get ahead" (i.e., pre-pay loans, invest significant portions of income, save a nest egg, or plan for retirement) because the possibility of financial emergencies rests not only with immediate family but in their extended family and kin networks as well, thus transforming the "possibility" of financial emergency into a "probability." . . . [T]he good news is that no one goes hungry . . . the bad news is that no one gets ahead. What those outside this culture often fail to see is that while one may educationally and financially "pull *themselves* up by the bootstraps," it is difficult [probably impossible] for a single marriage to "pull up" an entire extended family.
>
> (Marks et al. 2006:217)

As mentioned earlier, the challenge of helping family, friends, and the community (in terms of time, energy, shelter, and money) was referenced by many fathers in our study of all ages. Indeed, it is a challenge and an opportunity, a curse and a blessing that seems to be lifelong (cf. Stack 1974; Comer 1988). Perhaps no one framed this constant challenge as optimistically or faithfully as Steven, one whose house had been home to many and whose wife shared his view of giving back all they could to their inner-city community. He stated:

> I look at it [this way]: God has given me a gift to do what He would want me to do, so I can't say that I sacrifice anything [through my heavy involvement in our community]. That's the same way that I look at my wife. I think that her time [and effort], [the way] that she's able to touch many people outside my family . . . [that] is a call from God. . . . If we have a relationship together [and] we both do know God, then it's my responsibility to hold up her end at home if she's out doing God's work [in our community]. So I don't look at it as a sacrifice. I think [she has] a gift that a lot of people out there are looking for, and that she has it [and] that she's able to give. I feel that it's my job to understand what God is having her to do, and to be able to cover [for] her [here at home], and vice versa, her covering me, if there's things that I need to do [for our community]. I think this allows us to work together, understanding that God is in charge of everything that we have to do in a household.

Unfortunately, the lives and stories of responsible, family- and community-focused Black fathers like Steven "are [too often] ignored and their contributions minimized" (Connor and White 2006:14).

The Influence of Children on Their Fathers

An abundance of research addresses the effect that the presence and positive involvement of a father tends to have on a child (Popenoe 1996; Peters et al. 2000). Far less is known about how children impact fathers (Palkovitz 2002; Palkovitz et al. 2003). Cowan and Cowan's (2000) book-length study, *When Partners Become Parents*, documents some of the marital influences surrounding birth and the transition to parenthood. Later influences of children on their parents' marriages are not well documented. However, one of the most prevalent influences of children reported by the fathers was their (younger and older) children's influence on the fathers' marital relationships. As we will see in this section, the fathers explain that "kids bless you and they stress you," but they do more than that—they can truly change you.

MARITAL CHANGES—"KIDS BLESS YOU AND THEY STRESS YOU." The influence of children on marriage was pervasive, but the effects and expressions varied. Frank, for example, discussed how trying to raise children together with his wife made constant communication a necessity. He explained:

> [Without our kids, our marriage] wouldn't have been as rich. I don't think it would have been as rich or as lively because a lot of the things that we discuss involve the kids. Whether it was something we agreed on or something we disagreed on, [at least my wife and I were communicating]. [We were constantly talking and saying], "[W]e want this . . . for the family, we want that house for the family, [we want to] live a certain way [together]." We started out [with] different rules, with [different] family meeting times. [We ended up] adjusting all kinds of stuff. [Ultimately], even the cars we drove were geared around our kids.

Steven also addressed the unifying influence his children had on his marriage. He said: "[Y]our kids help you stay together. . . . T]hey help you form a bond, 'cause you always got the kids [pulling you] together, saying, "Let's go here, let's do this, [let's] do that." [It pulls you together]." One father believed that his children helped him drop his pride and reunite with his wife following a formal separation. He reflected:

> My children influence [me and] my marriage every day. One Christmas, [my wife and I] were separated, I was living somewhere else at the time. . . . [But] I came over, dropped my pride a little bit. . . . [Even though I was living somewhere else at the time], my daughters still got me something for Christmas. I felt really awkward; good, but awkward. Well, it made me want to come back. [They] had that kind of influence. When I realized what I was messing up here, in terms of the marriage, [I thought], "Maybe everything I have and need is right here." I knew that I had to get back here.

A final reflection from Earl captures a frequently expressed feeling among the fathers that children "deepened the commitment" in the fathers' marriages. He said:

I think that having [children] just deepened the commitment that we had made to each other through getting married. It was a responsibility that I feel that we both took very seriously. . . . My kids influenced my marriage in so many ways. I just couldn't see nobody else raising them. I thank God for my kids and I thank God for my family. They've been my strength [and] they've been my joy. They've been my happiness. [My kids and wife] have been my life.

However, the above happy and helpful reports regarding children and marriage only capture part of the complexity involved. Many fathers, like Larry, could recall times when their children added strain to their marriage:

Sometimes [kids] play both sides of the parents. [T]hey know you, [just] like you know them. They know you and they push your buttons and play off the parents. . . . I think kids can impact marriage and they can impact them positively or negatively, just depending on what they got going on in their own lives. . . . [S]ometimes [a kid] brings out the dysfunction or any holes in the relationship between the parents. . . . The other side of that coin, it's been things that they've done that made us gleeful and happy and [makes us feel] like we did a good job [as parents]. [Those times] made it feel closer [in our marriage], so it goes both ways: [kids stress you and they bless you].

This final point that "kids stress you and they bless you" seems to capture the reported influence of children on their fathers' marriages as a complex and mixed bag. However, there were other influences children exerted on their fathers that were more personal and reflective.

PERSONAL CHANGE, IDENTITY, AND "BEING" A DADDY. The personal influences of children on men often involved a father foreseeing the bright promise of the next generation in his own child—with the simultaneous awareness of a long and potentially eclipsing shadow from the past, the shadow of his own father's failure. Andre, for example, commented:

[T]oo many of [us] have come into a situation where their Mama and Daddy [aren't together] when they come up. [That's the life] they have seen. [Then] hey, you just have a vicious circle. And until somebody breaks out of it . . . it's just gonna keep on continuing. [Someone's gotta] break out of here, and say, "I don't want this. I don't want the same thing. I don't want to grow up like this. I don't want this same thing happening to m[y kid one day]." [*I'm* gonna stay around].

Andre's desires reaffirm research that emphasizes that many Black men want "to be the kind of father they [have] not experienced" (2006:83). Several of our fathers offered messages and examples that resonated with Coles's (2002) work that found

> many of these [black] men found their lack of a nurturing father to be a consciously motivating factor in their own parenting experience. The pain of abandonment gave birth to a narrative of negation; that is, the men expressed strong desires to be unlike their negative role model, to not reproduce the abandonment experience, and to avoid having their children feel toward them the way they felt toward their own fathers.
>
> (422)

The difficulty of converting the desire to be a highly involved father into behavior can be acute, however. Even so, as mentioned in our first theme, many of the fathers we interviewed wrestled to overcome the "bachelor mindset" and succeeded in their efforts. In many cases, their child or children was a critical factor in their positive choices. In this and other ways, these fathers' experiences seemed to echo Coles's (2006) African American fathers who "attested to the fact that if not for their children . . . their lives would have taken a turn for the worse" (83). For example, a father in our study named Michael referred to stopping drug use after becoming a father:

> Well, [after having kids I focused on] keeping away from those things that are of the world. You know, not having any wine in the refrigerator [after] 23 years [of having it] and . . . I used to keep beer in there, and then I became who I am now, and that doesn't exist anymore. So, [I try to provide] examples of *not* having those things . . . not smoking, not using drugs [ever again].

Michael was not alone in making daddy-related changes. Frank, Luther, and Maurice—men who have lived through tough experiences and have some shadows from the past—all explained how children helped to change them personally as well. Frank:

> [Being a daddy], it's a great job. It's a job I've always wanted to have. Without kids, [life] wouldn't be as much fun for me. I like the idea of being a father. I think it's the best thing a man can do. I think it's the best . . . more important than a job, more important than your friends. There is no greater ego trip than [to] walk in the door [after a day at work] and three little young girls [run to you]. Even if you're poor . . . that makes you rich.

For Frank, being a Daddy is the "great job" that he has "always wanted to have." His children are his treasure; they make him "rich." Luther similarly explained: "I would not be happier [without children]. I'd just have more [money] to spend and waste. [Being a good father, a good husband] . . . it's why are you a man. You get married so you can work and provide for your family." Luther sees his fatherhood as a core part of his identity, as his purpose. Being a Daddy is, in his view, "why you are a man."

Maurice discussed how being a father "changes everything" and how it "allowed [him] to grow" "tremendous[ly]." He stated:

> I experienced a lot of change as a result of being a parent that I don't think I would have experienced had we not decided [and] agreed to have children. [Becoming a father] allowed me to grow. . . . [When you become a father], you have to adapt, you have to become [stable and strong] for someone else that's *not* an adult and that's a whole new dynamic. It changes everything! I'm blessed in the fact that I'm a parent. . . . It was a source of a tremendous amount of growth on my part, 'cause I just know looking back on it now, those [giving, unselfish] areas would be so undeveloped in me had it not been for the children.

The fathers we interviewed were often men whose fathers had not been actively involved in their formative years, and for many of them those "shadows" remained. Even so, the fathers we interviewed had determined to actively parent and to see that opportunity as "a great job," the reason "why you are a man," and "a source of tremendous growth." Being a daddy changed these men—it was not just something they did, it was something they *became*.

The reflections of these fathers are very similar in tone to fathers in Palkovitz's (2002) book-length study, which included several fathers who admitted that they made changes in their lives for (or because of) their children that they would not make for their partners or wives, including quitting drinking, smoking, or drug use or making other significant lifestyle changes. Sometimes men claimed that their child not only changed their lives but *preserved* their lives. In our study, although no question addressed the topic, some of the fathers we interviewed mournfully recounted the high mortality and incarceration rates among the men of their generation. It is fair to wonder whether some of the fathers we interviewed would still be alive were it not for the stabilizing, settling influence of marriage and children. Not only do these family relationships help preserve some black men, they also benefit the rising generation. One father we interviewed, Marcus, commented:

> [L]et's just face it, a lot of these kids out here are getting killed because of the fact that there is no [family] structure. You know, there's nobody there to know what time they come in, nobody to know if they're going to school, they don't know any of those things . . . so what's happening? A lot of kids are left to take care of [themselves], they're bringing themselves up. . . . And more likely than not, they're gonna get into some kind of trouble. And as you know and I know, the trouble out there now [is that] a lot of times they're dying. A lot of times, [those boys] die.

Fortunately for Marcus's sons, he *is* there for them. Most others are not as fortunate. To close our discussion on this idea of father-child relationships as a buffer from inner-city street life and violence, it is poignant to note that both a black man with a wife and child(ren), and a young black man with a residential, biological father are more likely to have better financial lives (e.g., Nock 2003), and both are more likely to stay alive, period (Gallagher 2003; Connor and White 2006).

Thus we see, in this third theme, that in addition to the well-documented influence that fathers have on children (Peters et al. 2000), children can also influence their fathers' personal lives and marriages (cf. Palkovitz 2002). Fittingly, the last theme we will discuss is based on fathers' descriptions of their relationships with their wives.

Depth of Relationship and Commitment with Wife

While the men we interviewed loved talking about their children (and in some cases their grandchildren), their narratives, thoughts, and comments were never richer, deeper, or more reflective than when these fathers discussed their wives. As a result, it seemed appropriate to us that our final theme in this chapter should illustrate the depth of relationship and sense of commitment to their wives that these fathers share. Some of the fathers discussed how their wives had been there for them, as they had vowed to be, in times of "sickness and in health." Charles reported:

> My wife has been a source of strength for me. I had a grand mal seizure and it came out of nowhere and I think it was the true test of commitment and true test of strength for her to step up to the plate. We had four children . . . and for a mother who was going to school and [me] having been hospitalized, on life support for 16 hours and hanging in the balance between life and death. . . . She withstood all that and nursed me back to health. If it wasn't for her stepping in and really [working hard to do all] she did to keep us together. . . . [S]he could have abandoned me in that moment, but she didn't. She trusted God and I'm sitting here today [because of] her commitment to walk through that with me.

J.D. similarly appreciated his wife's support and concern:

> [Awhile back] I went to the doctor [and] found out that I was a diabetic. I came home, and I needed her then to help me out. She keep[s] me straight now. Make[s] sure I get my medicine and everything. Before I leave [for] work in the morning, she'll be 'woke . . . before I leave . . . we pray. [Then] before I leave, she'll always say, "You got your medicine, you got your medicine?" Sometimes I will forget the medicine. I could forget them [pills if it wasn't for her reminding me]. . . . I love her [for] takin' care of me.

Many other husbands similarly reflected on their wives' support and strength during thin financial times. The fulfilled vow here seemed to be "for richer or for poorer," as Karl's words reflect.

> [My wife], she has been there throughout [my life and has always been a] very supportive, very giving person. I can remember times coming home from working two jobs and she'[d be] there waiting for me, and encouraging me. [W]hen I wanted to quit at times, [she'd be] there to say, "Honey, we don't have much more to go, if you hang in there for

a couple more months, I think our finances will be better . . ." Working two jobs, doing what [I] had to do to make ends meet at [an] early age, I think that [took] a significant toll on me . . . [but she was there for me].

For several of the fathers, like Brandon and Jason, their reflections on their wives were not especially dramatic, but indicated a steadiness, security, and a sense of support. Brandon: "I always remember that [my wife is] on my side. She's my advocate . . . [she's my best friend]." Jason:

I think [my wife is] a woman born out of due season. There's a wealth of knowledge and wisdom that is inside of her. If I can get her in the room with a Cornell West or if I can put her on the platform of the Black State of the Union . . . I [feel] my wife can stand with the best of them. Oh, she can run with the best of them. Part of my desire to move to Atlanta is so that she can have her moment. It is more about her than it is about me. I would sacrifice for her to have her moment. [To give her] an opportunity just to live out what God has breathed inside of her because it would touch so many people's lives.

As Jason's narrative reflects, the tide of commitment, strength, and support did not only flow from wives to husbands. The support of husbands was mentioned by most of the wives and mothers as well. Sarah recalled:

I appreciate the active love that he has shown me. Where he's always told me that he's loved me. He's always done things and he always gives me cards. Sometimes its *five* cards on my birthday. . . . It's always the consistency of loving me. I don't ever remember a time when I thought, "Okay, we're in trouble!" . . . I never have thought that he didn't love me.

Although several years had passed, another mother, Annie, still remembered her husband's tenderness and support when she had their first baby. She recalled:

He was so attentive and caring about how I felt while I was in labor which was about 26 hours or so. [He let me know], "I'm concerned about you, how are you feeling? How is it going?" And he'd hold my hand for contractions and stuff. And I'm squeezing his hand and he says he never thought he'd play the piano again. But I mean, I saw the real concern for me personally. Not so much [like], "You're going to have my baby and I can't wait until my baby comes." No, it was like, "I want to know how you are doing, and how's it going [for *you*]. I really saw his real love for *me*, for who I was as his wife, and not just the producer of his kids. [That] really strengthened our marriage a lot, cause I thought, "He *really* cares! Well, this man really love[s] me, oh my gosh!"

Another mother and wife similarly emphasized, "I've always appreciated the fact that he [has truly] loved me. It's a wonderful thing to be just loved. It's a gift to be loved like that. It is."

In sharing these sentiments from the mothers and fathers, we must not paint a challenge-free picture. In many cases, these are married couples that struggled early on with the "bachelor mindset" and wrestled to become interdependent, as discussed earlier. However, in many instances this struggle and many others that arose were *resolvable*. That is one of the key messages these couples seem to offer. Indeed, as seen in the preceding examples, an array of challenges and struggles involving sickness, financial hardship, multiple jobs, and childbirth often provided the context for marital closeness.

As individuals who had overcome challenges on their way to establishing enduring marriages, many of the fathers and husbands offered some counsel, guidance, and encouragement to the rising generation. Two examples include Nate and Joseph. Nate: "[A critical challenge in a marriage is] to learn how to work together as a team. . . . I am her number one supporter; she's my number one supporter. . . . [An important part of that support is to] never . . . *never*, ever say anything negatively about your spouse to anyone else." Joseph:

> Marriage is sacred. Marriage is wonderful. [I want to tell young black people] that there is nothing better. You . . . treasure your mate, and you get to know your mate. Don't be selfish, don't be in the world. Make God above all. God will glorify your marriage. . . . Be forgiving, be loving, [as a father and husband] be tender and be strong. Take care of your family. *Love your family. Love your kids. Honor your wife.* Don't be in the world.

For some, however, motivational guidance might be better drawn from stories than from direct counsel. We conclude our findings section with two such stories. William, a fifty-three-year-old husband married for three decades, shared this:

> Sometime[s] Jane will say, "Uh oh, I'm forgetting something." . . . This kind of bothered me. [We're afraid.] It's almost like she . . . has Alzheimer's or . . . something else. I said [to her], "Well hun, it don't matter. I'll still be with you 'till the end." . . . [Other times, she'll] talk about her vision [failing]. I said, "You know, I'm [still] going to be there [for you] . . . but [if you go blind] then you gonna accuse me of looking at some woman [*both laugh out loud*]; [some woman] that you can't [even] see . . . that I might not even be looking at." I said, "Okay, okay, [come disease, blindness, whatever], I'm going to suffer with it [right beside you], but *I'm going to stay with you to the end.* I'll just take care of you to the end, so don't [you] worry about it.

J.D., even more than William, knew what it was like to see his wife struggle physically. J.D.'s wife, Betsy (age forty-eight), mother to five foster children, was struck by a drunk driver and lost her legs, mobility, and ability to communicate clearly, after an extended coma. After both of them explained that they didn't have time to "hate nobody" and had forgiven the drunk driver, J.D. turned from the interviewer to Betsy . . . sensitive to a comment she had made that she wouldn't blame him if he "ran away" from her and their difficult situation. J.D. told Betsy:

> You know, like I told you, I said 'til death do us part. I'm going to be here, I want you to be here for me too. That's what my Mother told me. [She] said before we got married, "*[You've] got to listen to the words.*" That's what my Momma said, "If you [are] truly, really, ready to get married . . . you got listen to the words." That's what I did, I listened. That's what I want it to be, 'til death do us part. That's where I want the relationship to be. I'm always going to have [your] back and I want you to have mine.

Conclusion

In this chapter we have had the rare opportunity to hear the voices of married fathers (and, to a lesser degree, mothers). What have they told us? Some of the fathers confessed that it took them a few years to make their marriages priority one. "Hangin' with the boys," selfishness, and difficulty opening up and communicating with one's wife were frequently mentioned obstacles that these fathers identified. Even so, all of the couples we interviewed eventually found ways around these obstacles. Key assets included a shared family vision, a patient and loving (but firm) wife, and the support of other family-centered men.

Marital success has some unique accompanying long-term challenges for black fathers and mothers. Namely, while none of the couples we interviewed was upper-middle class, all of them were wealthy poor—resource rich compared with many in their extended kin and fictive kin networks. As a result, these couples frequently received knocks of need, calls for financial, temporal, emotional, or housing support. The collectivist nature of African American culture tries to insure that no one goes hungry but consequently makes "getting ahead" difficult. Many of the families for example, housed temporary children for extended periods of time. This help-focused emphasis is an important but often overlooked reason that "Black married couples earn 80% as much as White married couples but have only 27% as much net worth" (Mincy and Pouncy 2003:57). While the challenge of the "bachelor mindset" tends to be temporary, the challenge of "helping" is often perennial and permanent.

The importance of the father-child bond is further illustrated by two central ways in which children influence their fathers. Children indirectly affect married fathers by influencing the marriage relationship. Fathers discussed how children kept things "lively," enriched their marital lives, "brought the marriage together," and fostered spousal communication. However, fathers also described how children caused anxiety, worry, and conflict and reported that as children grow older they learn how to play parents off each other in ways that "brought out holes" and "dysfunction." On a marital level, "kids bless you and they stress you." On an individual level, the fathers reflected on introspective and personal changes their children had motivated in them. As in Coles's qualitative research with single black fathers, many of the fathers in our study did not have the benefit of a positive father themselves, but they vowed to do things differently and made changes in lifestyle, drug and alcohol use, and priorities. These were fathers who made "being a daddy" a core part of their identity.

The fathers also told stories of challenging times—of sickness, poverty, frustration—and recalled how their wives had "been there for them." Mothers similarly reflected on difficult times, including childbirth, when their husbands had shown love, concern, and support. Additional narratives portrayed what the marital therapist Bill Doherty (2001) has called "commitment-no-matter-what" (21).

The reader will note that the first two themes explored in this chapter portrays challenges these fathers and their wives faced and overcame. The third theme illustrates how children can both challenge *and* benefit fathers and marriages. The fourth theme captures, to some degree, the depth and meaning of the marital relationship itself for these fathers and their wives. In this chapter as a whole, our design has been to convey some of the obstacles, challenges, and costs associated with marriage-based fatherhood—as well as to provide insiders' insights regarding why the outcomes are worth the costs. We would argue that these fathers embody and exemplify noble (but often overlooked) elements of black manhood. Many of us know men like these. However, this group's voice is too rarely heard and represented. Their voice is not loud, brash, and brutal like that of the gangster rappers that perpetually pulses in urban streets. The voice of these fathers is strong, *but it is often quiet*, and if we do not listen carefully, we will miss it.

Notes

Loren Marks is appreciative of grant support from the LSU Council on Research. He would also like to thank Justin Wax, Tanya Davis, and Allison Rayburn for their help with qualitative data collection and analysis.

1. In opposition to (or at least in addition to) Wilson's thesis regarding marital decline, some scholars have presented explanations that involve cultural and familial issues *inside* the black community (for examples, see Dash 2003; Hymowitz 2005).

2. The participants' names have been replaced by pseudonyms.

References

Allen, W. D., and M. Connor. 1997. "An African American Perspective on Generative Fathering." In *Generative Fathering: Beyond Deficit Perspectives*, ed. A. J. Hawkins and D. C. Dollahite, 217–27. Thousand Oaks, Calif.: Sage.

Amato, P. R., and F. Rivera. 1999. "Paternal Involvement and Children's Behavior Problems." *Journal of Marriage and the Family* 61:375–84.

Blankenhorn, D., and O. Clayton. 2003. Introduction to *Black Fathers in Contemporary American Society: Strengths, Weaknesses, and Strategies for Change*, ed. O. Clayton, R. B. Mincy, and D. Blankenhorn, 1–5. New York: Russell Sage Foundation.

Bobo, L. D. 2003. Foreword to *Black Fathers in Contemporary American Society: Strengths, Weaknesses, and Strategies for Change*, ed. O. Clayton, R. B. Mincy, and D. Blankenhorn, xx. New York: Russell Sage Foundation.

Chapman, A. B. 2007. "In Search of Love and Commitment: Dealing with the Challenging Odds of Finding Romance." In *Black Families*, 4th ed, ed. H. P. McAdoo, 285–96. Thousand Oaks, Calif.: Sage.

Christiansen, S. L., and R. Palkovitz. 2001. "Why the 'Good Provider' Role Still Matters: Providing as a Form of Paternal Involvement." *Journal of Family Issues* 28:84–106.

Clayton, O., R. B. Mincy, and D. Blankenhorn, eds. 2003. *Black Fathers in Contemporary American Society: Strengths, Weaknesses, and Strategies for Change.* New York: Russell Sage Foundation.

Coles, R. L. 2002. "Black Single Fathers: Choosing to Parent Full-Time." *Journal of Contemporary Ethnography* 31:411–39.

Coles, R. L. 2003. "Black Single Custodial Fathers: Factors Influencing the Decision to Parent." *Families in Society: The Journal of Contemporary Human Services* 84:247–58.

Coles, R. L. 2006. *Race and Family: A Structural Approach.* Thousand Oaks, Calif.: Sage.

Coley, R. 1998. "Children's Socialization Experiences and Functioning in Single-Mother Households: The Importance of Fathers and Other Men." *Child Development* 69:219–30.

Coley, R. 2001. "Invisible Men: Emerging Research on Low-Income, Unmarried, and Minority Fathers." *American Psychologist* 56:743–53.

Comer, J. P. 1988. *Maggie's American Dream: The Life and Times of a Black Family.* New York: Penguin.

Connor, M. E. 2006. "My Dad, My Main Man." In *Black Fathers: An Invisible Presence in America*, ed. M. E. Connor and J. L. White, 73–86. Mahwah, N.J.: Erlbaum.

Connor, M. E., and J. L. White. 2006. *Black Fathers: An Invisible Presence in America.* Mahwah, N.J.: Erlbaum.

Cowan, C. P., and P. C. Cowan. 2000. *When Partners Become Parents.* Mahwah, N.J.: Erlbaum.

Dash, L. 2003. *When Children Want Children.* 2nd ed. Chicago: University of Illinois Press.

Doherty, W. J. 2001. *Take Back Your Marriage.* Guilford Press: New York.

Dupree, A., and W. Primus. 2001. *Declining Share of Children Lived with Single Mothers in the Late 1990s.* Washington, D.C.: Center on Budget and Policy Priorities.

Edelman, M. W. 2007. "A Portrait of Inequality." In *Black Families.* 4th ed., ed. H. P. McAdoo, 319–27. Thousand Oaks, Calif.: Sage.

Franklin, J. H. 2007. "African American Families: A Historical Note." In *Black families*, 4th ed., ed. H. P. McAdoo, 3–6. Thousand Oaks, Calif.: Sage.

Gallagher, M. 2003. "The Marriage Gap: How and Why Marriage Creates Wealth and Boosts the Well-Being of Adults." In *Black Fathers in Contemporary American Society: Strengths, Weaknesses, and Strategies for Change*, ed. O. Clayton, R. B. Mincy, and D. Blankenhorn, 71–83. New York: Russell Sage Foundation.

Green, C. 1997. *Globalization and Survival in the Black Diaspora: The New Urban Challenge*. New York: State University of New York Press.

Green, C. 2001. *Manufacturing Powerlessness in the Black Diaspora: Inner-City Youth and the New Global Frontier*. Walnut Creek, Calif.: AltaMira.

Herbert, B. 2003. "Locked Out at a Young Age," *New York Times*. October 20.

Hymowitz, K. S. 2005. "The Black Family: 40 Years of Lies." *City Journal* (Summer 2005). http://www.citycity-journal.org/html/15_3_black_family.html. Accessed September 26, 2007.

Kunjufu, J. 2004. *Countering the Conspiracy to Destroy Black Boys*. Chicago: African American Images.

Lassiter, S. M. 1998. *Cultures of Color in America: A Guide to Family, Religion, and Health*. Westport, Conn.: Greenwood.

Livingston, J. N. and J. L. McAdoo. 2007. "The Roles of African American Fathers in the Socialization of Their Children." In *Black Families*, 4th ed., ed. H. P. McAdoo, 219–37. Thousand Oaks, Calif.: Sage.

Marks, L. D., and C. Chaney. 2006. "Faith Communities and African American Families: A Qualitative Look at Why the Black Church Matters." In *Religion and Psychology: New Research*, ed. S. D. Ambrose, 277–94. Hauppauge, N.Y.: Nova Science.

Marks, L. D., and D. C. Dollahite. 2007. "Fathering and Religious Contexts: Why Religion Makes a Difference to Fathers and Their Children." In *Why Fathers Count*, ed. S. E. Brotherson and J. M. White, 335–51. Harriman, Tenn.: Men's Studies Press.

Marks, L. D., K. Hopkins, C. Chaney, O. Nesteruk, P. Monroe, and D. Sasser. 2008. "'Together, We Are Strong': A Qualitative Study of Happy, Enduring African-American Marriages." *Family Relations* 57:171–84.

Marks, L. D., O. Nesteruk, M. Swanson, M. E. B. Garrison, and T. Davis. 2005. "Religion and Health Among African Americans: A Qualitative Examination." *Research on Aging* 27:447–74.

Marks, L. D., and R. Palkovitz. 2004. "American Fatherhood Types: The Good, the Bad, and the Uninterested." *Fathering* 2:113–29.

Marks, L. D., M. Swanson, O. Nesteruk, and K. Hopkins-Williams. 2006. "Stressors in African American Marriages and Families: A Qualitative Study." *Stress, Trauma, and Crisis: An International Journal* 9:203–25.

McAdoo, J. L. 1993. "The Role of African American Fathers: An Ecological Perspective." *Families in Society: The Journal of Contemporary Human Services* 74:28–35.

McAdoo, H. P., ed. 2007. *Black Families*. 4th ed. Thousand Oaks, Calif.: Sage.

Mincy, R. B., and H. Pouncy. 2003. "The Marriage Mystery: Marriage, Assets, and the Expectations of African American Families." In *Black Fathers in Contemporary American Society: Strengths, Weaknesses, and Strategies for Change*, ed. O. Clayton, R. B. Mincy, and D. Blankenhorn, 45–70. New York: Russell Sage Foundation.

Nock, S. L. 1998. *Marriage in Men's Lives*. New York: Oxford University Press.

Nock, S. L. 2003. "Marriage and Fatherhood in the Lives of African American Men." In *Black Fathers in Contemporary American Society: Strengths, Weaknesses, and Strategies for Change*, ed. O. Clayton, R. B. Mincy, and D. Blankenhorn, 30–42. New York: Russell Sage Foundation.

Palkovitz, R. J. 2002. *Involved Fathering and Men's Adult Development: Provisional Balances*. Mahwah, N.J.: Erlbaum.

Palkovitz, R., L. D. Marks, D. W. Appleby, and E. K. Holmes. 2003. "Parenting and Adult Development: Contexts, Processes, and Products of Intergenerational Relationships." In *The Handbook of Dynamics in Parent-Child Relations*, ed. L. Kucynski, 307–23. Thousand Oaks, Calif.: Sage.

Peters, H. E., G. W. Peterson, S. K. Steinmetz, and R. D. Day. 2000. *Fatherhood: Research, Interventions, and Policies*. New York: Haworth.

Popenoe, D. 1996. *Life Without Father*. New York: Basic.

Stack, C. B. 1974. *All Our Kin*. New York: Harper and Row.

Staples, R. 2007. "An Overview of Race and Marital Status." In *Black Families*, 4th ed., ed. H. P. McAdoo, 281–84. Thousand Oaks, Calif.: Sage.

Stewart, P. E. 2004. "Afrocentric Approaches to Working with African American Families." *Families in Society: The Journal of Contemporary Social Services* 85:221–28.

Sudarkasa, N. 2007. "African American Female-Headed Households: Some Neglected Dimensions." In *Black Families*, 4th ed., ed. H. P. McAdoo, 172–83. Thousand Oaks, Calif.: Sage.

Testa, M., and M. Krogh. 1995. "The Effect of Employment on Marriage Among Black Males in Inner-City." In *The Decline in Marriage Among African Americans: Causes, Consequences, and Policy Implications*, ed. M. B. Tucker and C. Mitchell-Kernan, 59–95. New York: Russell Sage.

Tucker, M. B. 2000. "Marital Values and Expectations in Context: Results From a Twenty-one-City Survey." In *The Ties That Bind: Perspectives on Marriage and Cohabitation*, ed. L. Waite, 166–87. New York: Aldine de Gruyter.

Veroff, J., E. Douvan, and S. J. Hatchett. 1995. *Marital Instability: A Social and Behavioral Study of The Early Years*. Westport, Conn.: Praeger.

Wilson, W. J. 1996. *When Work Disappears: The World of The New Urban Poor*. New York: Knopf.

CHAPTER TWO

Poverty and Parenting Style Among Black Married Couples

Ronald E. Bulanda

Until the late 1990s, the proportion of children residing in two-parent (married or unmarried) households had been declining for most demographic groups in the United States (Mincy and Pouncy 2003). This decline had been especially significant among black children. Whereas two-thirds of black children under the age of eighteen lived with two parents in 1960, by 2004 this was down to just over a third (Lugaila 1998; Bureau of the Census 2006). Although this decline translates into more than 2 million fewer children residing in two-parent structures, the fact remains that nearly 4 million black children currently reside with two parents.

The primary factors contributing to the substantial decline in black two-parent families are the relatively high divorce rates and low marriage and remarriage rates in black families today. Recent data show that little more than one-third of black men are married (Kreider and Simmons 2003). The low rates of marriage obviously contribute to the high numbers of unmarried black fathers, and especially to *nonresident* black fathers. In turn, much of recent research on parenting in black families has shadowed that trend, focusing almost exclusively on either single mothers or nonresident fathers. Consequently, the relative exclusion of assessments of black married fathers overlooks a reduced but persistent context of parenting in black families today.

Married black fatherhood is distinct in several ways from nonresident fatherhood. As previous research indicates, fathers' involvement and contact with children tend to diminish when fathers reside outside of the home of the child (Casper and Bianchi 2002). More specifically, fathers who never married often have tenuous connections to their children, particularly when relations with the mother are conflicted (Casper and Bianchi 2002). Additional research indicates that fathers often focus their parental involvement on the children of their current, rather than former, partners (Furstenberg 1995). Hence, the parenting involvement and style of nonresident fathers is clearly influenced by factors not present in married-parent households. Regardless of circumstance, married resident fathers parent in a context that is both more stable and more conducive to greater involvement.

Earlier research suggests that married parents are generally in a better structural position to provide supervision for their children and to promote higher aspirations in the children (Mincy and Pouncy 2003). Compared to unmarried nonresident fathers, resident (married) fathers are more likely to possess greater authority in child-rearing decisions and to have more contact with their children (Casper and Bianchi 2002). Furthermore, families in which the two parental figures are married to each other generally exhibit greater structural stability—that is, they are more likely to remain together than unmarried cohabitors—which, in turn, promotes greater consistency and support between parents. Research shows numerous advantages among children of parents who exhibit parental consistency (Lindsey and Mize 2001) or demonstrate high-quality relationships with each other (Amato 1998).

An assessment of parenting in married-parent families is also warranted given the important implications it likely has for child outcomes. Much of the social concern regarding the low marriage rates in black families stems from a wealth of evidence showing that children living in one-parent families experience more disadvantages than those in married parent families (Wilson 2003). Comparing outcomes of children raised in married versus single parent households, the former are less likely to become teen parents or drop out of high school (Mincy and Pouncy 2003). Similarly, Blackman and colleagues (2005:6) assert that black children of married parents are "less delinquent, have fewer behavioral problems, have higher self-esteem, are more likely to delay sexual activity, and have moderately better educational outcomes."

Family structure may not explain these outcomes, however. Many of the benefits enjoyed by children reared in married-parent households stem from the relative economic advantage of this household type (McLanahan and Sandefur 1994; Blackman et al. 2005). Indeed, socioeconomic status is of central concern regarding *single*-parent homes primarily because children living in households headed by single mothers are identified as the poorest demographic in the United States (Wilson 2003). However, less is known about whether and how socioeconomic status influences the parenting of married fathers (Bulanda 2004; Nelson 2004). Although research shows marriage is generally correlated with men's economic well-being (Nock 1998), it is unclear how the economic variability *within* black married families may influence parenting. Given the relatively higher poverty rates among black families in the United States, it is important to better understand whether and how poverty status influences the parenting styles of black married fathers.

Ultimately, this chapter is intended to provide a simple descriptive portrait of parenting among this overlooked population of black married fathers. More specifically, it illustrates what fathering looks like within this select group in terms of parenting styles, parent-child relationships, and monitoring. In addition, it is important to show the relative similarities or differences between black married fathers and their wives on these same dimensions. However, these comparisons are not (and should not be) used to reflect benchmarks or deficiencies in either parent's approach to parenting but will instead be used as points of reference. For example, these comparisons will illustrate whether and how children observe one parent versus the other to be the primary source of support or monitoring.

In addition to the basic portrait of parenting among black married fathers, this chapter also assesses whether and how parenting varies according to poverty status. The existing parenting literature commonly identifies poverty (or income) as having a significant influence on parenting. Specifically, scholars advocate for studies of parenting to account for socioeconomic status because of its potential influence on parents' sense of efficacy (Menaghan 2003). Based on earlier research reflecting how poverty sometimes influences mothers and fathers in different ways (see Bulanda 2004), it is necessary here to illustrate whether the parenting of black married fathers is more or less susceptible (if susceptible at all) to the influence of poverty than the parenting of black married mothers. Hence, this chapter also examines whether and how poverty status correlates with both maternal and paternal parenting in black married families.

The data used in this analysis are from the National Longitudinal Surveys of Youth 1997, designed to be representative of U.S. residents in 1997 who were born during the years 1980 through 1984 (Center for Human Resource Research 2002). The NLSY97 cohort of 8,984 respondents includes a supplemental sample of black youths. The measures of parenting used in this portrait are derived from adolescent reports of their perceptions of their mothers and fathers. For the purpose of the analyses presented here, the overall sample is restricted to only black married families, resulting in a sample of 505. This sample is used to assess parenting styles in black married families with adolescent children. A second analytic sample, reduced by missing data on the remaining parenting dimensions, contains 320 respondents. Due to the select nature of this sample, the portrait provided in this chapter will not reflect the parenting of young children in black married families. The samples used to provide this descriptive portrait of parenting are black married parents with at least one adolescent child.

Parenting Styles

Although the term "parenting styles" is somewhat common in daily discussion of parenting, this phrase actually reflects a scholarly conceptualization of parenting. Specifically, the term represents a parent's combination of support and control, the two primary dimensions of parenting. Indeed, these are straightforward. Parents are generally charged with the responsibility of providing their children with guidance and regulation, or, more simply, control. Parents are also generally charged with the responsibility of providing their children with love and nurturing, or support. The concept of parenting style accounts for both of these dimensions and includes four specific categories based on a parent's level of support and control.

Figure 2.1 diagrams the classification of parenting styles according to parents' levels of support and control. Although there has existed concern regarding the applicability of this scheme across family structures, social classes, and race, evidence has clearly identified the most- and least-beneficial parenting styles (Amato and Fowler 2002). Research illustrates many positive outcomes highly correlated with an authoritative parenting style (Demo and Cox 2000). For example, children with authoritative parents demonstrated higher levels of psychological well-being and lower levels of psychological and behavioral dysfunction compared to children of parents with an uninvolved style

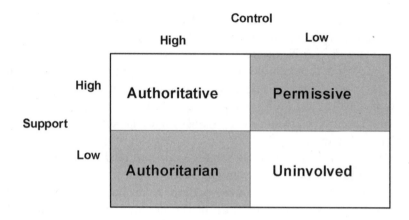

Figure 2.1 Conceptualization of Parenting Styles

(Lamborn et al. 1991). The academic competence of adolescents is also associated with authoritative parenting (Gray and Steinberg 1999). Related research illustrates an uninvolved style (also often termed a "negligent style") is negatively related to many outcomes, including academic achievement, sexual experience, and pregnancy history (Pittman and Chase-Landale 2001). Both sets of research findings underscore the important points that children are likely to benefit from parents who provide sufficient levels of both support and control (authoritative), while some negative implications are more likely among children with parents low on these dimensions (uninvolved).

The remaining two categories of parenting style are less straightforward. Overall, permissive and authoritarian parenting may be observed to be more beneficial than an uninvolved style, yet not as beneficial as an authoritative style. Lamborn et al. (1991) indicates children with authoritarian parents may exhibit greater conformity with rules yet suffer from a poorer self-concept. In contrast, a child with a permissive parent is likely to possess a positive self-concept but is more likely to engage in delinquent acts (Lamborn et al. 1991).

In terms of race/ethnicity, research has demonstrated that compared to white parents, black parents are more likely to exhibit an authoritarian style of parenting (Hofferth 2003). It has been suggested this style may occur more commonly among minority parents because racial discrimination (and related factors) may make it more difficult to exhibit high levels of warmth, while contextual factors more common among minority parents (such as poor neighborhoods) may make high levels of control more necessary. Moreover, Jackson-Newsom, Buchanan, and McDonald (2008) discuss the possibility that an authoritarian style may correlate with less negative child outcomes if it is more culturally normative among some minority groups. However, existing research is mixed in this regard (see Jackson-Newsom et al. 2008 for a review).

The measure of parenting styles used in this chapter is based on only two items: one dichotomized item reflecting the adolescents' evaluation of how supportive the parent is and one dichotomized indicator of adolescents' evaluation of the parents' strictness. In terms of the former item, responses of "very supportive" are categorized as high support, while responses of "somewhat" or "not very supportive" were coded as low support. In terms of control, responses of "very strict" are categorized as high control. The remaining responses were classified as low control. This specific measurement strategy of using two dichotomous indicators of support and control has been identified in previous research as a valid indicator of parenting style (Moore et al. 1999). Each parent is then classified in terms of one of the four parenting styles that emerge from the interplay between the support and control dimensions (see figure 2.1).

In terms of parenting styles, figure 2.2 indicates there are not substantial differences between mothers and fathers. Most importantly, it is clear mothers and fathers do not differ at all in the likelihood of employing either an uninvolved or an authoritative style ($\chi^2 = 0.12$, df = 1, p = .73). This lack of a difference is significant because it suggests mothers and fathers are equally likely to exhibit the least and most beneficial parenting styles. Moreover, the least popular parenting style for each parent is an uninvolved style, which as indicated earlier in this chapter, is associated with a number of negative child outcomes. In contrast, the most popular parenting style for each parent is the authoritative style, which is associated with a wide variety of positive outcomes.

The only difference between mothers and fathers in terms of parenting styles involves a small but real disparity in the employment of permissive and authoritarian styles. Specifically, figure 2.2 illustrates that mothers are more likely than fathers to be perceived as high in support but low in control (that is, permissive). In contrast, fathers are more likely than mothers to be perceived as high in control and low in support (that is, authoritarian). This difference is not especially

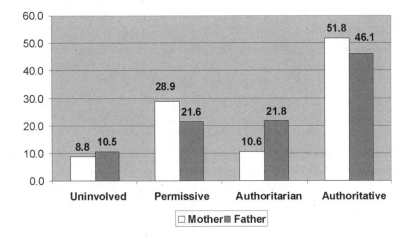

Figure 2.2 Mother and Father Parenting Styles

surprising given traditional gender norms, which generally entail the perception of women as more nurturing and supportive than men.

In fact, a closer assessment of the components used to measure parenting style reveals this traditional gendered perception. Although the overwhelming majority of adolescents identify their mother and father as "very supportive," this is slightly truer regarding perceptions of the mother. And in terms of strictness, while the overwhelming majority of adolescents identify their mothers and fathers as "very strict," this is slightly more prevalent in the characterizations of fathers than mothers. These trends give rise to the one difference in parenting styles observed in figure 2.2. Overall, fathers are more likely to employ an authoritarian approach, whereas mothers are more likely to employ a permissive style.

Given the relatively greater likelihood that fathers will employ an authoritarian style, it is important to take a closer look at the complete parenting context in the homes of these authoritarian fathers. Although these fathers exhibit high levels of control, their style gives the appearance of an absence (or low level) of support. However, a subsequent examination shows that in 60 percent of the situations where the father is authoritarian, the mother is actually high on support (either permissive or authoritative).

The importance of fathers' parenting styles goes beyond the 21.8 percent of black married families with adolescent children in which the father exhibits an authoritarian style. For instance, in well over one-third of the situations where the mother is permissive (only high on support), black married fathers employ a parenting style with high levels of control. These fathers ultimately contribute to a cumulative authoritative parenting style within the household. In a similar manner, black married fathers exhibit a style characterized by high support (permissive or authoritative) in nearly one-third of the situations where the mother is only high in control. Here, too, black married fathers contribute to a cumulative authoritative parenting style within the household. Ultimately, when accounting for the parenting styles of both black married mothers and fathers (of adolescent children), more than two-thirds of these households include some combination of high-support and high-control parenting.

Poverty and Parenting Styles

The assessment of the relationship between poverty status and parenting styles shows that paternal styles are more susceptible than maternal styles to the influence of poverty. Specifically, the results of this assessment show fathers who are poor are more than three times as likely to employ an uninvolved style rather than an authoritative style compared to fathers who are not poor. The implication here is that black married fathers in poverty are far more likely to exhibit low levels of both support and control, whereas black married fathers who are not poor are more likely to exhibit the opposite style. This finding is especially salient given the significant contrast between an uninvolved style and an authoritative style. In contrast, poverty status appears unrelated to the parenting styles exhibited by black married mothers. Specifically, the results do not support the notion that the parenting styles of black married mothers differ on the basis of poverty.

These results raise the question of why poverty is correlated with paternal but not maternal styles. Perhaps, because of traditional gender roles, men who are poor feel less confident about their parenting abilities, primarily in terms of their own expectations of providing financially for their children. An earlier study of black resident fathers found they were more likely to identify being a provider as more important than being either a "husband" or a "father" (Cazenave 1979). The conditions of poverty and disadvantage have the potential to convey a message "of reduced opportunity to exert personal influence in many facets of life" (Coleman and Karraker 1997:71). This may be truer for black fathers than mothers given the greater salience of being an economic provider to the identity of black fathers (Cazenave 1979). Earlier research has shown similar types of withdrawal from domestic duties based on male difficulty fulfilling the role of provider (Greenstein 2000). It is possible that poor fathers, primarily because of their economic circumstances, experience less confidence or more anxiety, making it more difficult to provide higher levels of support and control. Further research is needed to test this possible explanation.

Parent-Adolescent Relations

The quality of the parent-child-relationship often reflects the levels of warmth, nurturing, responsiveness, acceptance, and affection that parents show their children. Frequently, one or more of these specific indicators is used to measure, to some degree, a qualitative component of parenting. It is apparent that parental relationships that are more warm and accepting are beneficial for children. Parents who fail to be accepting and warm find that their children are less likely to be concerned with conforming to parental standards and values (Patterson, Reid, and Dishion 1992; Simons, Johnson, and Conger 1994). These children are also more likely to engage in delinquent activities and exhibit maladjusted behavior. Furthermore, adolescents who perceive their parents as having a rejecting nature are at greater risk for depression (Robertson and Simons 1989). Hence, poor relations with parents have consequences on the behavior *and* psychological well-being of children.

The measurement of parent-child relations assessed in this chapter sums the adolescents' responses to five items. These items are scored on a five-point scale with responses ranging from 0 "never" to 4 "always." Three of the items were reverse coded so that higher scores indicate greater parental support. The items inquire how often the parent praises you for doing well, criticizes you or your ideas, helps you do things that are important to you, blames you for his/her problems, makes plans with you and cancels for no good reason. The responses to the five items are summed for a composite relationship score ranging from 0 to 20.

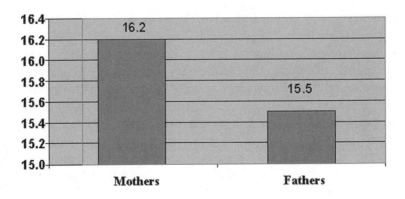

Figure 2.3 Quality Relations

The descriptive data for this measure of parental-child relations shows the average scores for black married fathers is 15.5, while the average score for black married mothers is 16.2 (see figure 2.3). Although from simple observation these numbers appear quite similar, a statistical test of this difference suggests the disparate scores are indeed significant ($t = 2.32$, $p < .05$). In other words, these numbers reflect what is interpreted as a social reality in this sample of black married parents: black adolescents generally perceive more warm and nurturing relationships with their mothers than their fathers. Two points must be made clear in assessing this difference. First, the difference, while significant in a statistical sense, is actually small in magnitude. Second, this difference in no way indicates the relationships black married fathers offer their children are deficient or ineffective but only that they do not match the adolescents' perceptions of their relationships with mothers.

The next stage of the analysis examines the relationship between poverty status and parent-child relations for black married fathers and mothers. This examination indicates that poverty status is unrelated to the adolescents' relationship quality with each parental figure. Hence, the quality of relations adolescents have with poor black married fathers does not differ from the quality of relations adolescents have with non-poor black fathers. The same is true for maternal relationships.

Parental Monitoring

Frequently, research uses measures of monitoring that include an ambiguous combination of parental rules and parental knowledge (Menaghan 2003). This chapter uses a knowledge-based measure derived from adolescent reports. Since parents may be unaware of how much they do not know about their children's behavior, this measure has the advantage of using youth reports of parental monitoring. Although some measures of monitoring may be used to reflect parental control, it is important to note that this knowledge-based measure of monitoring is a distinct construct compared to the more common dimension of strictness/control used in the measure of parenting style. The degree of parental monitoring is measured in terms of four summed items, with higher scores reflecting greater monitoring. The four items were scored based on five response categories, ranging from 0 "knows nothing," to 4 "knows everything." The questions asked the youth how much the parent knows about your close friends, who they are; your close friends' parents, who they are; whom you are with when you are not at home; and who your teachers are and what you are doing in school. This index has a potential range of 0 to 16 and is based only on reports of adolescent children ages thirteen to fifteen.

The descriptive statistics for these monitoring measures indicate the average score for black married fathers is 8.1, while the average for black married mothers is 10.5. Statistical tests support the notion that the disparity in monitoring scores for black mothers and fathers are indeed significantly different. Based on youth reports of how much their parents know about their friends, whereabouts, and activities at school, it is apparent that black married fathers engage in less monitoring than black married mothers. Again, this difference does not reflect a deficiency but only a difference. Further analyses show that poverty status is unrelated to levels of parental monitoring for both parents. Specifically, there is no difference in the degree of monitoring between poor and non-poor black married fathers or their maternal counterparts.

Subsequent analyses reveal the difference in monitoring between mothers and fathers is consistent across the knowledge arenas. In other words, this additional assessment seeks to uncover if the overall measure of monitoring is higher for a mother because she is more aware of one (or more) area of her adolescent's life. Figure 2.4 illustrates the

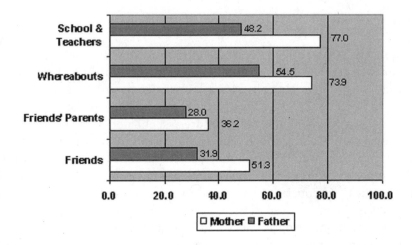

Figure 2.4 Parental Monitoring Percentage of parents who know most or all, by category.

percentages of black married mothers and fathers who, according to youth reports, know most or all of the various kinds of information. It is clear from this chart that mothers are significantly more likely than fathers to know most or all of their children's friends, friends' parents, school activities and teachers, and general whereabouts. Hence, the parental disparity in terms of monitoring is consistent across each of these domains.

Overall, these findings are at odds with other recent findings. Simons et al. (2006) do not find a significant difference between black mothers and fathers in terms of monitoring, although they assessed families with slightly younger children. Perhaps the disparate findings between studies reflect a divergence in monitoring behaviors once children reach adolescence. Future research will be needed to explore if black married fathers lessen their degree of monitoring as their children progress through adolescence or if mothers increase their monitoring.

Adolescents' Perceptions of Their Fathers

Although the assessments of the aforementioned parenting dimensions are important to understand, it is also important to better iden-

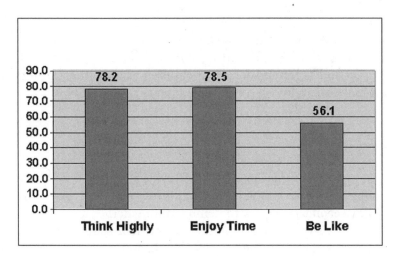

Figure 2.5 Adolescent Perceptions of Fathers

tify how black adolescent children perceive their married fathers in a broader sense. Figure 2.5 illustrates the level of adolescent agreement with the following statements: I think highly of him; I really enjoy spending time with him; and he is a person I want to be like. Reponses ranged from 0 "strongly disagree" to 4 "strongly agree." Figure 2.5 reflects the percentage of adolescents who agreed or strongly agreed.

This figure clearly illustrates the high regard with which adolescent children hold their married fathers. The vast majority of adolescents, more than three out of four, demonstrate a tremendous respect and admiration for their fathers and express great pleasure in spending time with them. These results take on a greater significance given the nature of adolescence, a time when children are expected to individuate and separate in their transition to young adulthood. In addition, a lesser majority (56 percent) claim they wish to be like their father. This statistic becomes clearer considering the gendered nature of role modeling. Subsequent assessments indicate nearly 70 percent of male adolescents agreed with this statement while less than half of female adolescents agreed. In this sense, the overall numbers in figure 2.5 are largely consistent—and offer ample evidence of the extremely positive parent-child relationship dynamics involving black married fathers.

Analyses further reveal that these attitudes toward fathers do not vary according to poverty status; the favorable perceptions of fathers are the same regardless of poverty status. This finding supports the notion that even in situations where poverty does appear to influence fathering behaviors (i.e., parenting styles), it does not seem to change the respect and affection adolescent children have for their fathers, nor does it make them less of a role model (particularly for boys).

Discussion

The primary aim of this chapter is to provide an initial descriptive portrait of parenting for a largely understudied population: black married fathers. A secondary aim is to demonstrate whether and how parenting style for this special group differs from their spouses' and according to poverty status. In these ways, the chapter ultimately serves the purpose of providing clearer details and contexts of the parenting of black married fathers.

An examination of parenting styles reveals several important trends among black married fathers. First, it is clear the most prevalent parenting style among these fathers correlates with most positive child outcomes (authoritative). In contrast, they are least likely to employ the negligent style of parenting, which we know to be associated with more negative child outcomes. Taken together, the parenting styles of black married fathers represent an overwhelming strength within these families.

A second trend reflected in these fathers' parenting styles is their greater likelihood, relative to mothers, to employ an authoritarian style. However, this trend is not unexpected given traditional gender norms, which would lead us to anticipate men's being more likely to exert control in the absence of high levels of support. Perhaps a more intriguing trend is that poverty status increases the likelihood that black married fathers will employ an uninvolved style versus an authoritative style, which does not correlate with the mothers' chance of doing so. In one regard, it is expected that poverty status would be more significantly related to paternal parenting than maternal parenting. Indeed, earlier literature (Cazenave 1979) and literature reviews (see Taylor et al. 1990) support the notion that black fathers' perceptions of themselves as providers is a significant correlate of their overall life satisfaction. Hence, poverty status may be especially consequential for the parenting morale and efficacy of black fathers, thereby making it more closely associated with paternal style than maternal style. However, given the age of this literature, combined with emerging norms regarding greater father involvement, it is possible these data represent the last remnants of an old cultural standard of black fatherhood. In other words, it may be the provider role is becoming less central to paternal parenting and therefore less consequential to the overall parenting of black fathers. This may explain why poverty status was unrelated to the other measures of fathering assessed in this chapter.

Assessment of parent-child relations and monitoring among black married fathers illustrates that neither dimension varies according to poverty status. One possible interpretation of the consistent levels of paternal relations and monitoring is a resiliency within the fathers themselves or resiliency contributed by the presence of an additional parental figure in the household. In either case, it is encouraging to observe stability in parenting across poverty statuses.

The assessments presented in this chapter do illustrate variability in parent-child relations and monitoring between black married mothers and fathers. It is clear that adolescents report higher-quality relations with their mothers and also report that mothers are more fully aware of their social and academic lives. Again, this is consistent with much of the existing research on parenting, which indicates that mothers' influence usually is stronger, even within the context of paternal influence (Amato 1998).

John McAdoo (1988) once observed how black fathers tend to be characterized in the literature as absent, if not aloof. It appears from the results of the assessments presented in this chapter that many black fathers are neither. Perhaps the most salient component of the figures presented is the graphic illustration of how black adolescents perceive their married fathers. They are held in high regard, appreciated for the time they spend with their children, and serve as role models. The latter appears especially true for black adolescent males. Yet this positive portrait of parenting may elicit more questions than it answers. Still to be investigated is how the parenting of black married fathers compares to nonresident fathers or how quality of parenting varies for children of all ages. How does the current portrait compare to years past, and is there reason to expect stability in the coming generations of fathers? Indeed, more research will be needed in these areas.

As a final note, it is extremely important to reiterate that it is inappropriate to interpret differences in parenting between mothers and fathers as representing a particular deficiency in one parent or strength in another. The analyses discussed in this chapter do not include any assessments of how these differences in parenting can or do influence the children's outcomes. Furthermore, the presentation of mothers' parenting scores and comparisons to fathers should not reflect a form of benchmarking, whereby one parent's score represent some "standard" of parenting. In fact, the goal of this chapter is to provide what has been lacking in both the academic and general literature: a portrait of parenting for *black married fathers*. The married status of this special group of fathers reflects an important contextual element: an additional parental figure, with biological ties to the child, resides *and* parents with these fathers. Hence, their parenting does not exist in a vacuum and is likely to complement and supplement the parenting of black married mothers. To best understand the parenting of black married fathers, we must also be aware of maternal parenting.

References

Amato, P. R. 1998. "More Than Money? Men's Contributions to Their Children's Lives." In *Men in Families: When Do They Get Involved? What Difference Does It Make?* ed. A. Booth and A. C. Crouter, 241–78. Mahwah, N.J.: Erlbaum.

Amato, P. R., and F. Fowler. 2002. "Parenting Practices, Child Adjustment, and Family Diversity." *Journal of Marriage and Family* 64:703–17.

Blackman, L., O. Clayton, N. Glenn, L. Malone-Colon, and A. Roberts. 2005. *The Consequences of Marriage for African Americans: A Comprehensive Literature Review*. New York: Institute for American Values.

Bulanda, R. E. 2004. "Poor Parents, Poor Parenting? The Influence of Poverty." Ph.D. diss. Bowling Green State University.

Casper, L. M., and S. M. Bianchi. 2002. *Continuity and Change in the American Family*. Thousand Oaks, Calif.: Sage.

Cazenave, N.A. 1979. "Middle-Income Black Fathers: An Analysis of the Provider Role." *The Family Coordinator* 28:583–93.

Center for Human Resource Research. 2002. *The National Longitudinal Surveys NLSY97 User's Guide*. Columbus: Ohio State University.

Coleman, P. K., and Karraker, K. H. 1997. "Self-Efficacy and Parenting Quality: Findings and Future Applications." *Developmental Review* 18:47–85.

Demo, D. H., and M. J. Cox. 2000. "Families with Young Children: A Review of Research in the 1990s." *Journal of Marriage and Family* 62:876–95.

Furstenberg, F. F. 1995. "Changing Roles of Fathers." In *Escape from Poverty: What Makes a Difference for Children*, ed. P. L. Lindsay Chase-Landale and J. Brooks-Gunn, 189–210. New York: Cambridge University Press.

Gray, M. R., and L. Steinberg. 1999. "Unpacking Authoritative Parenting: Reassessing a Multidimensional Construct." *Journal of Marriage and the Family* 61:574–87.

Greenstein, T. N. 2000. "Economic Dependence, Gender, and the Division of Labor in the Home: A Replication and Extension." *Journal of Marriage and Family* 62:322–35.

Hofferth, S. L. 2003. "Race/Ethnic Differences in Father Involvement in Two-Parent Families: Culture, Context, or Economy?" *Journal of Family Issues* 24:185–216.

Jackson-Newsom, J., C. M. Buchanan, and R. M. McDonald. 2008. "Parenting and Perceived Maternal Warmth in European American and African American Adolescents." *Journal of Marriage and Family* 70:62–75.

Kreider, R. M., and T. Simmons. 2003. *Marital Status: 2000*. Washington, D.C.: U.S. Census Bureau. http://www.census.gov/prod/2003pubs/c2kbr-30.pdf. Accessed February 23, 2006.

Lamborn, S. D., N. S. Mounts, L. Steinberg, and S. M. Dornbusch. 1991. "Patterns of Competence and Adjustment of Adolescents from Authoritative, Authoritarian, Indulgent, and Neglectful Homes." *Child Development* 62:1049–65.

Lindsey, E. W. and J. Mize. 2001. "Interparental Agreement, Parent-Child Responsiveness, and Children's Peer Competence." *Family Relations* 50:348–54.

Lugaila, T. 1998. "Marital Status and Living Arrangements: March 1998." *Current Population Reports*, Series P-20, No. 514. Washington, D.C.: Government Printing Office.

McAdoo, J. L. 1988. "Changing Perspectives on the Role of the Black Father." In *Fatherhood Today: Men's Changing Role in the Family*, ed. P. Bronstein and C. P. Cowan, 79–92. New York: Wiley.

McLanahan, S. S. and G. Sandefur. 1994. *Growing Up with a Single Parent: What Hurts, What Helps*. Cambridge, Mass.: Harvard University Press.

Menaghan, E. G. 2003. "On the Brink: Stability and Change in Parent-Child Relations in Adolescence." In *Children's Influence on Family Dynamics: The Neglected Side of Family Relationships*, ed. A. C. Crouter and A. Booth, 153–169. Mahwah, N.J.: Erlbaum.

Mincy, R. B., and H. Poucy. 2003. "The Marriage Mystery: Marriage, Assets, and the Expectations of African American Families." In *Black Fathers in Contemporary American Society: Strengths, Weaknesses, and Strategies for Change*, ed. O. Clayton, R. B. Mincy, and D. Blankenhorn, 45–70. New York: Russell Sage Foundation.

Moore, K. A., S. M. McGroder, E.C. Hair, and M. Gunnoe. 1999. *NLSY97 Codebook Supplement Main File Round 1. Appendix 9: Family Process and Adolescent Outcomes Measures*. Washington, D.C.: U.S. Department of Labor, Bureau of Labor Statistics.

Nelson, T. J. 2004. "Low-Income Fathers." *Annual Review of Sociology* 30:427–51.

Nock, S. L. 1998. *Marriage in Men's Lives*. New York: Oxford University Press.

Patterson, G. R., J. B. Reid, and T.J. Dishion. 1992. *Antisocial Boys*. Eugene, Ore.: Castalia.

Pittman, L. D., and P. L. Chase-Landale. 2001. "African American Adolescent Girls in Impoverished Communities: Parenting Style and Adolescent Outcomes." *Journal of Research on Adolescence* 11:199–224.

Robertson, J. F. and R. L. Simons. 1989. "Family Factors, Self-Esteem, and Adolescent Depression." *Journal of Marriage and the Family* 51:125–38.

Simons, L.G., Y. Chen, R. L. Simons, G. Brody, G. Cutrona, and C. Cutrona. 2006. "Parenting Practices and Child Adjustment in Different Types of Households: A Study of African American Families." *Journal of Family Issues* 27:803–25.

Simons, R. L., C. Johnson, and R. D. Conger. 1994. "Harsh Corporal Punishment Versus Quality of Parental Involvement as an Explanation of Adolescent Maladjustment." *Journal of Marriage and the Family* 56:591–607.

Taylor, R. J., L. M. Chatters, M. B. Tucker, and E. Lewis. 1990. "Developments in Research on Black Families: A Decade Review." *Journal of Marriage and the Family* 52:993–1014.

U.S. Bureau of the Census. 2006. "Living Arrangements of Black Children Under 18 Years Old: 1960 to Present." Table CH-3. Current Population Survey, March, and Annual Social and Economic Supplements, 2006 and earlier. http://www.census.gov/population/www/socdemo/hh-fam.html. Accessed April 29, 2008.

Wilson, W. J. 2003. "The Woes of the Inner-City African American Father." In *Black Fathers in Contemporary American Society: Strengths, Weaknesses, And Strategies For Change*, ed. O. Clayton, R. B. Mincy, and D. Blankenhorn, 9–29. New York: Russell Sage Foundation.

CHAPTER THREE

Rearing Biracial Children

The Experiences of Black Married Fathers

Erica Chito Childs and Heather M. Dalmage

Interracial marriage rates between blacks and whites remain relatively low, yet within black-white unions, the overwhelming majority is between black men and white women. While interracial relationships often receive significant media and scholarly attention, less emphasis is placed on the experiences of parents of black-white biracial children. As the number of black-white biracial children born to white women continues to grow, the perspectives of the black men who father these children are rarely heard. The history of challenging and dismissing black men as fathers has its roots in the foundation of America and still exists in contemporary American society; therefore the experiences of black men fathering biracial children are particularly important to consider for their intersection of lines of race and gender.

Historically, the treatment of black men, white women, and their multiracial offspring was intimately connected to the laws that regulated family formation along race lines and the images of black males as over sexualized "beasts" or as sambos (Hodes 1997; Ferber 1998). Stories of racial formation under U.S. slavery often focus on the role of mulattoes or mixed-race offspring. The regulation of interracial relationships has a long, complicated, and often violent history in the United States (Rogers 1945; Davis 1991; DaCosta 2004; Wallenstein 2004). At stake in the regulation was the very system of racial, gender, and class stratification upon which race, family, and property relations were built in the United States (DaCosta 2004). Among whites, interracial sex was constructed as deviant within the institution of slavery of black Africans, and from the beginning this notion of deviancy was primarily aimed at preventing black male slaves from engaging in sexual relations with white women. Numerous historical incidents have been documented where those who engaged in interracial relations were formally and informally punished through fines, whippings, banishment, or imprisonment.

The roles of white fathers throughout colonial times and slavery have been fairly well documented both in the United States and the many European colonies around the world. Moreover, the long history of white male rape and coercive sex with black women, particularly slave women, has been acknowledged as well (Spickard 1989). When laws allowed, some white slave-owning fathers freed the children and the mothers of such "unions" (at times this happened after years of servitude or when the white man bequeathed their freedom), yet in many other instances, cruel treatment was bestowed on mixed-race slave children by the white men who fathered them. In other words, through slave narratives, biographies, and historical texts we know that white fathers of multiracial children had myriad ways of responding to their roles as slave masters, patriarchs, and potentially active fathers.

To a lesser extent, historical texts reveal the hardships faced by white women who crossed the color line and gave birth to children of color (see, for instance, Hodes 1997). Yet we get only fleeting glimpses of the black fathers. We know these fathers, especially freedmen, were numerous enough to be regulated by law, and we know that some of these fathers remained in the lives of their children. For instance, Higginbotham and Kopytoff (2000:103), explain that

> free black men were required to support their free bastard children in the same manner as were white men. In 1663, John Johnson, a free black property owner, has a child by Hannah Leach, a white servant on a neighboring plantation. Aside from posting bond to ensure the child's support, and his future good behavior, Johnson has to "pay and sattifie all . . . damages." Presumably, that included payment to the woman's master for time she lost from work. Johnson also had to get a wet nurse for the child. Hannah Leach escaped whipping only because her master agreed to pay 1,000 pounds of tobacco. Philip Morgan, another free black, had a child by Margery Tyler, a white woman. Like Johnson . . . , Morgan had to post bond to save her from corporal punishment.

In other words, these black fathers and partners were compelled to maintain their obligations, and yet the history of their relationship to their children and their role in the "family" remains undocumented. Unfortunately, we do not know what black fathers—free or enslaved—of multiracial children contended with as fathers or how they understood the world or negotiated resources on their children's behalf.

Moreover, shifting definitions of whiteness worked to exclude more black men from the possibility of parenting their mixed-race children (Wallenstein 2004: chapter 9). Even if it was desired, the ever changing laws and regulations often made interracial marriage illegal, and extralegal violence made marriage, even cohabitation, dangerous (Ferber 1998). Records show that many black fathers and white mothers took great risks to stay together. Perhaps one of the most popular stories is that of "Irish Nell." While we know from the scarce details of her life that she and her husband, a black slave, broke the law in order to stay together and raise their children (although some were apparently sold away), we only know of his role in the family through the details of Nell's life. Historians and legal scholars, such as Randall Kennedy (2003), have documented "blocked interracial parenting," citing numerous incidents up until the 1960s where white women who had children by black men either tried to pass the child as white or gave up the child for adoption. Still, the study of parenting in multiracial families has continued to focus on white mothers, and we learn about black fathers only through the scattered details and perspectives of the white women and multiracial offspring who tell the stories.

While there is a growing and more recent body of literature exploring the issue of multiracial families from a variety of perspectives, remarkably absent is any in-depth exploration of the experiences of black fathers of biracial children. Most often we hear about black fathers of biracial children through others' perspectives. For example, there are a number of autobiographical accounts by white women, such as Jane Lazarre (1996) and Maureen Reddy (1994), who discuss their experiences married to black men and raising black children, using feminist theory and literary studies. The children's perspectives can also be found. James McBride (1996) and Lisa Jones (1995) document their experiences with their white mothers and black fathers and their own experiences growing up in interracial families. Research studies have also focused on the specific experiences of white mothers of biracial children (Luke 1994; Luke and Luke 1998; Hill and Thomas 2000; Karis 2000; O'Donoghue 2004). These studies focus on these women's negotiation of race and racial identity after having biracial children. They highlight the personal transformations these women undergo through these relationships, particularly their understandings of whiteness, white privilege, and racism. Even in the body of research that looks at the experiences of interracial couples and multiracial families in negotiating racial issues and parenting choices, there has been virtually no attention to the unique experiences of black fathers.

Therefore, in our study we conducted in-depth interviews with six heterosexual black fathers of white-black biracial children. The men were identified through convenience samples in Chicago and New York City. The men ranged in age from late thirties to early sixties, and all were middle-class professional black men. All of the men were married and living with their wives and children at the time of the interview. The men and their families lived in racially diverse middle- to upper-middle-class neighborhoods, yet they were close to and often interacted in predominantly black areas of a lower socioeconomic status. The interviews lasted approximately thirty to ninety minutes and were conducted in person or by phone. The interview schedule consisted of questions about parenting strategies, experiences with each man's partner/mother of the child, and stereotypes of black fathers. Based on these interviews, as well as previous research we have conducted with multiracial families, we present key findings on parenting strategies, the role of race and gender, parenting against societal stereotypes, and the extra burdens carried by black fathers in multiracial families. For the fathers we interviewed, the main themes that emerged were the different parenting strategies of discipline, racial socialization, and affirming blackness because they had a white partner and biracial children.

Parenting Differences: Gender and the Intensity of Racist Images

Like all couples, most interracial couples negotiate childrearing decisions and strategies about identity, friends, schools, and discipline (Dalmage 2000; Chito Childs 2005). For black men married to white women, parenting choices are complicated by the negative racial images of black men as violent, the images of white women as unable to address race issues, and broad differences between middle-class whites and middle-class blacks around acceptable behavior for children.

When we listen to the concerns and experiences of black men as they attempt to adopt the best practices for interacting with and disciplining their children, the weight of racist images in their choices becomes painfully clear—especially as they interact with their daughters. William, a minister, was a stay-at-home father when his three children were young. He discusses how he dealt with these stereotypes and how through his experiences of fathering he helped his children move beyond the stereotypes of black men while teaching them to think critically about destructive constructions of masculinity.

I guess the stereotype I have dealt with is that Black men don't cry. I have said to them, you *can* cry—not just about anything and everything, but it is okay to cry. My kids have seen this, I show them that I can be nurturing, my father was not nurturing, so I am trying to do that for my kids. My son used to tell me that when he grew up he wanted to be a stay-at-home dad [laughs]. Okay . . . I don't want my daughter to be stay-at-home mom either. I have since realized it was a compliment. My first thought was, "what kind of wimp am I raising" but, no, he's seen me doing it. So it shows how we have stereotypes too.

Nevertheless, in this sample, concern over the role the fathers play in relationship to shaping their daughters' identity and future relationships seems to rise above that for their sons'. James, a public school teacher, married with two children, speaks about the stereotypes of black men and his desire that his daughter learn that she can expect respect from men. He confided:

I also struggle with the stereotypes about black men—that they kind of "plant their seeds wherever they choose," "lazy," "don't want to do this or that" financially not viable. It could be violence. It's not just my kids see this, but all people. I have grown friends who think the same way. I have had girlfriends who think that's the way men should treat women—with violence and disrespect. They seem to seek it out. But I want my daughter to know that she should seek out men who care for her.

Similarly, Vincent, a forty-two-year-old father of two girls living on the far south side of Chicago and working as a supervisor of social workers, reveals concern about rearing a daughter who will have high expectations for the men in her future. He hopes that his example of being a caring and respectful man in her life will teach her to expect the same of her partner:

> I bring distinctive differences to my role as father that influences my consciousness as a father and a man. I have girls and I am trying to influence their selection of partners in life. I am the father figure, the male figure, so I have a responsibility to influence their future choices in men. If I have to run an errand, I bring my oldest daughter [eight years old] with me. She always goes with me; she wants to be with me. She is influenced by the first few years in life, I was the primary caretaker. Taking her with me, I have a sense of responsibility that I am influencing her relationship with men—black men. I make a big deal of treating her like a princess, I always do. I have this belief that someday there will be a guy that will want to take advantage of her and she won't put up with it because she will expect someone to treat her well. And, I think the images of black men are so soiled. The girls already see the images: gangbangers and crime and they see the images of criminals and the images they are seeing are black men. So I need to counter these images in their lives.

Despite a supportive wife and a shared parenting strategy, it is Vincent who must guard against racist images and thus carries a burden that his wife (and all white parents) is freed from and a burden that black men in same-race relationships can share with their partners.

Marlon, a forty-something stay-at-home dad in Harlem who recently began graduate school for social work while his wife works as a school administrator, also felt that burden. He works to foster a positive image of blackness for his young daughter despite the racial inequalities that plague their community.

> We live in Harlem . . . nothing I love more than walking with my daughter past . . . Langston Hughes's house, and our neighborhood has a real community feel . . . but I got to be truthful that there is not always the cultural, social, economic diversity I want, which really hit me with my daughter and being at [the social work program he is in]. . . . I don't want her seeing all the negative images and looking back at me, you know what I mean? [Interviewer asks to give an example] . . . Let me put it this way, we are bombarded with negativity from everywhere about black men not doing what they supposed to do, or black

men out doing what they not supposed to do, right? Just look on the news. But then where we live there are also brothers out here struggling, and I know it's not easy but I guess I worry about being that example for my girl.

Marlon not only felt that he needed to be a strong male role model, but he also worried about whether he could counteract the negative images of black men with which they are confronted every day. Since his daughter is biracial, he was concerned more about how negative images of black people, in particular, may cause his daughter to not embrace her black identity and even reject him on some level.

In addition to shaping their daughters' expectations for the type of men they would allow in their lives, the fathers also wanted to make "strong black women" of their daughters, though fathers chose various routes to achieve that end. Marlon discussed the seriousness of his role in raising his daughter and how an important piece of his parenting involved developing his daughter's identity as a strong black woman.

> For me . . . I knew this going in . . . I had to be the one who shows her about being a black woman, I mean, my wife really can't, and we discussed that beforehand, but I see it now, and I'm like, "This is on me, because she isn't going to get it anywhere else," and I feel fortunate that I am home with her every day, and a big part of my decision to go back to school when I did was about being able to be there for my daughter. Now I tell my mom, because you know she raised my brothers and I on her own, she raised a strong black man and I'm going to raise a strong black woman [laughs].

William, a minister and father of three children, addresses similar concerns that significantly affect the fathering decisions he makes. While he has two sons and one daughter, the extra parenting burden becomes clear as he explains the constraints that mediate his relationship to his daughter in particular.

> I have been very intentional about *not* making my daughter a daddy's girl—my daughter will not have a strong black female role model around all the time, so I have to be very intentional about having her get together with black female friends who can truly show her and help her to understand what it is to be a black woman. We haven't

done that with the boys, because they have me;,we don't have a need for that. I teach them. I realized when Angela was young that she needed to experience, on regular basis, a bond with a black woman to see, "to learn that she is a diva in training," and to strengthen her as a black child and black female to be a strong black woman. That's been the biggest difference. I try not to baby her—and it's difficult because it is tempting. . . . If I had a black spouse, I would be a lot more relaxed and at ease with Angela, letting her mother teach her about being a black woman. It would be a lot more [pause] then she could be daddy's little girl. . . . I think there'd be less tension because we'd have the same expectations about how to raise the boys. The blessing is that my wife realizes that she needs help and that she doesn't understand everything and is willing to follow. I have seen some white mothers with black children who assume they know, they say, "Well, I am just raising a child!" and I say, "No, you are raising a black child and that makes a big difference."

William's decision not to raise his daughter as a "daddy's little girl" was based on race. He comments that if his wife was black then he could "baby" her, yet since his wife is white he does not see her as capable of raising a strong black woman. Hence he must make his daughter strong through his parenting. His choice to bring her around other black women highlights the intersection of race and gender: not only is he concerned about his daughter being raised "black" but he emphasizes the particular socialization that he sees only a black woman being able to provide. These fathers' particular concern for their daughters likely reflects their feeling that although the mothers are of the same gender as the daughters, the particular junction of race and gender create a unique need that white women may not be able to fulfill.

Some previous studies indicate that some white mothers in interracial partnerships may feel that lack themselves. For instance, studies by Rosenblatt, Karis, and Powell (1995); Dalmage (2000); Karis (2004); and Chito Childs (2005) found that most white partners followed the lead of their black partner, not only in the way they discussed race but also in regard to choices about parenting strategies, neighborhood residence, and so on. For example, as part of an earlier study, Chito Childs (2005) discussed that many white women married to black men acknowledged that they adopted the same racial strategies as their black partners, whether race conscious or color-blind, especially in terms of cultivating their children's racial identity. Yet even when the white mothers agreed with the fathers' parenting approach, some acknowledged that they did not feel capable of socializing their children in terms of race. As some of the fathers indicated above, this may suggest a supplemental role for black women who are family or friends of black fathers of biracial children.

Patricia Hill Collins argues, "The birth of biracial and mixed-race children to so many White mothers raises new questions. . . . Black women remain called upon to accept and love the mixed-race children born to their brothers, friends, and relatives. By being the Black mothers that these children do not have, these women are expected to raise biracial children" (2000:165). These views highlight the overlapping realms of racial and gender socialization where black fathers report heightened concern about raising their daughters and even sometimes suggest that as black men they cannot raise their daughters to be strong black women without the help of other black women.

While each of these fathers is mindful of the stereotypes of black males and actively work against them in parenting, the path they choose is quite varied. Each father felt that he carried a much greater responsibility than fathers in same-race families. Each father viewed his role as more burdensome in light of the pervasive racist images against black men and their own beliefs that their white wives could not address "blackness" as they or black women could. Furthermore, when situated around questions of gender, these men expressed the great desire to be exceptional fathers and role models to their daughters.

Affirming Blackness

The fathers' discussion of their parenting strategies show how much they think about socializing their children in terms of "race" and black culture. Previous research on multiracial families has highlighted how these families negotiate race and racial identity within their relationships, as well as their need to navigate the response of "outsiders" to their families (Dalmage 2000; Chito Childs 2005). Relying on informal "teaching moments" within the family, as well as local community resources, fathers discussed the strategies they use to foster a strong black identity in their children. William describes how he uses conversation around the dinner table:

Each night at dinner we do "black facts," which includes black history and culture. We also made it that—we had a chance to do day camp in a nice white community but decided to do the Chicago Park District, Kenwood, to make sure the kids are connected to blacks. We have a membership at DuSable Museum [a museum that celebrates African/African American history and culture] and we make sure we get them there.

The oldest father we interviewed, Earl, a sixty-six-year-old black man with one twenty-nine-year-old son and two daughters, thirty-eight and forty-two, also discussed the importance of raising his children firmly grounded in black culture, which he felt he had done successfully through informal family traditions and nurture.

It is about traditions, my mother's family from Georgia, my father's family from Alabama, strong black people with traditions, just real grounded, especially when we moved from Hartford to [a predominantly white suburb in Connecticut]. I led by example and just filled them with self-esteem, pride about themselves as black people. . . . [Interviewer asks did you discuss this with your wife] . . . No there was never any sitting down, not something planned but I knew my children were black people.

Vincent explained that he and his wife have a "like-mindedness" and have spent many years thinking through their planned approach to parenting. He is quite clear about the approach they are taking.

The plan is to protect and educate. We have not been shy about letting them know that the world is a harsh place. I have specific conversations with her and she is very curious. In church they discussed the Jena 6 case along with a handout. So at home I shared with her the situation that happened between black and white people. I gave her the information, in child-friendly way—she knew about the noose, she had been to the Amistad at the DuSable [an African American museum].

A topic of concern that arose several times was the issue of friendships, how peer relations may shape one's racial identity and what friendship choices signify about children's developing identities. Fathers expressed some uncertainty as to how much to control those choices as a way of affirming their children's blackness. When asked what parenting choices he makes around the aspect of friendship concerns, James stated:

> With my daughter, we've had a lot of conversations, "I noticed most of your girlfriends are white." But, we keep talking around it. I have to wonder if it's because her mom is white; she has that comfort level. My son, we have lots of conversations, say, about boys in the classroom. He's drawn to Asian boys; he had a good friend in preschool that was Asian and maybe that set a pattern. He has black friends, but I see him trying hard with his Asian friends.

William, similarly, struggles with his children's choice of friends and his desire for his children to have a positive identification with blackness. Speaking of his eldest son, William explains:

> One of my frustrations is that he tends to gravitate toward being with white kids, not black kids, and part of that is the schools we've had him in. So we put him in a school that's 90% black, because that's what he needed, so he could figure out how to deal with being with black kids. The hard thing for me is that I have not exposed him to some of the traditional black kid stuff . . . but, now he is coming home with more black friends and listens to hip hop. I love hip hop! [laughs]. We also make sure the kids attend church with me so they have the black church experience.

This emphasis on friendship choices does not necessarily reflect opposition to their children's having white or Asian friends but represents concerns about the children's identity choices and connection to black communities. To these fathers, choosing predominantly non-black friendship circles symbolizes a potential rejection of blackness, which is particularly problematic since they view themselves as the primary person responsible for raising their children in terms of racial socialization.

These concerns are complicated by the fact that many interracial couples, particularly those of a middle-class status often reside in predominantly white neighborhoods or their children attend mostly white schools. The views of outsiders who presume that black men are unlikely fathers, particularly when the children have lighter skin tones, affect their desire to affirm their children's blackness and affirm their own black fatherhood.

For example, Marlon felt that many people, particularly whites he met while caring for his daughter in New York City, where they live, were surprised that he was such a good father:

> Now this happens a lot, in Barnes and Noble's, in parks, I see this group of white women, mothers, and they look at me like "who is this man of color taking care of this little girl," they look but then usually when they see how I interact with her, they ask her name or make some comment about how beautiful she is and how great I am with her, but you can tell I am like an oddity to them . . . they are trying to figure out first why am I with this child, should they be frightened, but then really trying to wrap their minds around that I am a black man, a father taking care of my daughter just like them. I know this because it just doesn't happen with other black people, like the nannies I see too, they smile because they know I am the father.

Earl also recounts this type of misunderstanding and negative stereotyping, even now in his role as a grandfather. For example, one day he took his eighteen-year-old granddaughter and her young baby to the emergency room because the baby was sick. The doctors were dismissive to his granddaughter but also immediately assumed he was a "neglectful father who wasn't working" despite the almost fifty-year age difference, rather than recognizing him as a caring grandfather. As a father, and even as a grandfather, he felt "his worth was constantly being challenged."

Heightened Parental Differences

Finally, reading through these narratives, the reader may see an underlying story—the potential for interparental disagreement about racial socialization. Even for their daughters, fathers perceive an inherent inability in their white spouses/partners to capably socialize their children when race is a salient aspect. Although, as indicated above, many white mothers of biracial children choose of their own accord to defer to the fathers in terms of racial socialization, sometimes there is disagreement about the import and effect of emphasizing race at all. For example, James is in the process of figuring out how to negotiate his children's choice of friends, his wife's lack of concern about the race of their children's friendship choices, and his own ambivalence about self-consciously "doing race."

> I have an issue with my kids not knowing who they are. They have never been in a predominantly African American area. I am concerned that I need to be more intentional about helping them have particular friends. That's not fathering, per se, but I think that's important. My wife doesn't see it as an issue at all. She doesn't want to push them one way or the other, but I am not sure about that. I am struggling with that right now.

Occasionally, parental style differences that may or may not be directly related to race are nevertheless interpreted within that framework, as each parent becomes the representative of his or her own race. Once again, James describes the tension between his disciplinary methods and those of his wife.

> I am kind of the guy in the house that puts the kids on a straight path and holds them accountable. My wife is different. When I say something it tends to be very authoritative and because of that I have certain struggles with the kids and my wife has struggles because of her style. . . . So, that becomes a barrier between me and my kids. . . . I wonder how my kids view me as this more authoritative figure—as the guy in the house who yells and that concerns me. I sometimes I think I need to learn to communicate in different ways, but we haven't gotten there yet. There is a fear that I don't want my children to be abused in the way I was, so when I discipline them—the loudness or strength of my voice, there is something else going on there and they are too young to understand that, I don't always understand it.

Conclusion: Learning and Growing as Black Men and Fathers

The history of challenging and dismissing black men as fathers has its roots in the foundation of America, yet in contemporary American society, as the numbers of black men fathering biracial children continues to grow, their experiences reveal the complex negotiations of race, gender, and sexuality that occur in parenting biracial children. For black fathers, like all fathers, choices about parenting are affected by intersecting locations. Race certainly matters, and it may be central to the "tensions" that parents in multiracial families experience.

The black fathers we interviewed struggled with how to raise their children against the backdrop of race and gender stereotypes, which they confronted in myriad ways. While these fathers certainly emphasized the importance of their role in racially socializing their children, they also discussed contributing to their development in every way, even raising their daughters to be strong women. Spending time with their children was a top priority, especially considering that four of the six fathers in this study chose to be stay-at-home dads while their children were young. These findings point to the importance of looking more closely at the experiences of black fathers in multiracial families, as their experiences reveal the different ways that the intersections of race, gender, and even sexuality complicate parenting, and fathering in particular.

References

Chito Childs, E. 2005. *Navigating Interracial Borders: Black-White Couples and Their Social Worlds*. New Brunswick, N.J.: Rutgers University Press.

Collins, P. H. 2000. *Black Feminist Thought*. New York: Routledge.

DaCosta, K. 2004. "All in the Family: The Familial Roots of Racial Division." In *The Politics of Multiracialism: Challenging Racial Thinking*, ed. Heather Dalmage, 19–42. Albany: State University of New York Press.

Dalmage, H. 2000. *Tripping on the Color Line: Black-White Multiracial Families in a Racially Divided World*. New Brunswick, N.J.: Rutgers University Press.

Davis, F. J. 1991. *Who Is Black: One Nation's Definition*. University Park: Penn State University Press.

Ferber, A. 1998. *White Man Falling: Race, Gender, and White Supremacy*. Lanham, Md.: Rowman and Littlefield.

Higginbotham, A. L., Jr., and B. K. Kopytoff. 2000. "Racial Purity and Interracial Sex in the Law of Colonial and Antebellum Virginia." In *Interracialism: Black-White Intermarriage in American History, Literature, and Law*, ed. Werner Sollors, 81–139. New York: Oxford University Press.

Hill, M., and V. Thomas. 2000. "Strategies for Racial Identity Development: Narratives of Black and White Women in Interracial Partner Relationships." *Family Relations* 49 (2): 193–200.

Hodes, M. 1997. *White Women, Black Men: Illicit Sex in the Nineteenth-Century South*. New Haven, Conn.: Yale University Press.

Jones, L. 1995. *Bulletproof Diva: Tales of Race, Sex, and Hair*. New York: Anchor Books.

Karis, T. 2004. " 'I Prefer to Speak of Culture': White Mothers of Multiracial Children." In *The Politics of Multiracialism: Challenging Racial Thinking*, ed. Heather Dalmage, 161–74. Albany: State University of New York Press.

Kennedy, R. 2003. *Interracial Intimacies: Sex, Marriage, Identity, and Adoption*. New York: Pantheon.

Lazarre, J. 1996. *Beyond the Whiteness of Whiteness: Memoirs of a White Mother of Black Sons*. Durham, N.C.: Duke University Press.

Luke, C. 1994. "White Women in Interracial Families: Reflections on Hybridization, Feminine Identities, and Racialized Othering." *Gender Issues* 14 (2): 49–72.

Luke C., and A. Luke. 1998. "Interracial Families: Difference Within Difference." *Ethnic and Racial Studies* 21 (4): 728–54.

McBride, J. 1996. *The Color of Water: A Black Man's Tribute to His White Mother*. New York: Riverhead.

O'Donoghue, M. 2004. "Racial and Ethnic Identity Development in White Mothers of Biracial, Black-White Children." *AFFILIA* 19:1:68–84.

Reddy, M. 1994. *Crossing the Color Line: Race, Parenting, and Culture*. New Brunswick, N.J.: Rutgers University Press.

Rogers, J. A. 1945. *Sex and Race: A History of White, Negro, and Indian Miscegenation in the Two Americas*. St. Petersburg, Fla.: Helga M. Rogers.

Rosenblatt, P. C., T. Karis, and R. D. Powell. 1995. *Multiracial Couples: Black and White Voices*. Thousand Oaks, Calif.: Sage.

Spickard, P. 1989. *Mixed Blood: Intermarriage and Ethnic Identity in Twentieth-Century America*. Madison: University of Wisconsin Press.

Wallenstein, P. 2004. *Tell the Court I Love My Wife: Race, Marriage, and Law—an American History*. New York: Palgrave Macmillan.

PART TWO

Single Resident Fathers

CHAPTER FOUR

Single Custodial Fathers

A Narrative Tour of Their Parenting

Roberta L. Coles

Black fathers, some have conjectured, are an endangered species. The veracity of this statement depends, in part, on how one defines "father." American society, as is well known, frequently uses the phrase "to father a child" to refer only to the act of conceiving a child who is eventually born (while "mothering" tends to connote parenting of varying degrees of quality). When a father also parents his children, this often requires an additional descriptor, such as "*involved* father" or "*hands-on* father." Sometimes in the black community, the two types of fathers are distinguished by employing the term "father" for the conception or biological father, and reserving the title of "daddy" for a father who parents to one degree or another.

In 2000, 65 percent of adult black men had had a biological child; that was the same percentage as white men and just slightly under that of Hispanic men (68 percent) (Halle 2002). However, the percentage of African American fathers residing with their children, particularly in a two-parent household, has experienced a steep decline. Table 4.1 indicates that since 1960 the percentage of black children living with both parents declined by nearly half. Although the percentage of children living only with a father doubled over the same time period, the percentage was so small that it doesn't begin to account for the decline of two-parent households. Obviously, there was a concomitant rise in mother-only households, a significant proportion of which subsisted below the poverty line and frequently on welfare. Based on those

Table 4.1
Living Arrangements of Black Children Under 18 (%)

Year	Two parents	Mother only	Father only	Neither parent
2006	34.6	51.2	4.8	9.4
2000	37.6	49.0	4.2	9.2
1990	37.7	51.2	3.5	7.5
1980	42.2	43.9	1.9	1.2
1970	58.5	29.5	2.3	9.8
1960	67.0	21.9	2.0	11.1

Source: Data derived from Current Population Survey 2006a.

trends, the assumption was that if the fathers weren't coresiding, they weren't parenting; that is, they weren't daddies.

In response to this trend, in the mid- to late 1990s government policy tightened welfare dollars in hopes that a "stick approach" would deter unmarried women from having children. As commonly happens, scholarly research followed suit, producing a slew of studies on single mothers and secondarily on "absent" or teen fathers, and studies of married black fathers became even more scarce. While the unmarried-teen birth rate has declined, particularly for African Americans, since the early 1990s, the percentage of nonmarital births has maintained or continued to rise (Hamilton, Martin, Ventura 2007). Unable to stem the tide of nonmarital births generally, the policy focus then turned to the fathers with the presumption that black men were "fathering" children left and right (though note that the percentage of black men who become fathers is no higher than for men of other races) but no longer parenting in any substantive or financial sense of the word. Therefore, for the past decade, government dollars have been funneled into "responsible fatherhood" programs that were primarily intended to secure child-support payments and secondarily to encourage men to marry the mothers of their children. The 2006 budget alone provided $100 million per year for five years for responsible fatherhood programs (Minoff, Ooms, and Roberts 2006). Simultaneously, a number of studies (Taylor, Leashore, and Toliver 1988; Danziger and Radin 1990; Seltzer 1991; Stier and Tienda 1993; Wattenberg 1993) began to take a more nuanced look at the levels of nonresident fathers' involvement with their children and found that while nonresident fathers usually exhibit less involvement than resident fathers, and too often no involvement, they are frequently not *absent*. As mentioned in the introduction, nonresident black fathers are more likely than men of other races to visit more and care for their children in some nonfinancial manner.

Nevertheless, until the early 2000s, no one had bothered to look at black single fathers who parented full-time on their own, despite the fact that census data indicated that the percentage of households with children headed by black men was about the same as, or higher than, that of households with children headed by white men. For instance, in 1996, the percentage of black children living with only their fathers was 5.9, and it was 4.5 for white children. In 2006, it was 4.8 for both black and white children (Current Population Survey 1996: table 11, 2006a).

Indeed, it seemed implausible that such unmediated fathering could occur. Even longstanding scholars of fatherhood were unable to conceive of the possibility. For instance, Ron Mincy (2002) of Columbia University, argued that "unwed parents have four options to choose from: no father-child contact, some father-child contact, cohabitation, and marriage." The option of father-child custody doesn't make the list.

I take no credit here for being any more enlightened; it didn't occur to me either until Rubin, a slightly older (than traditional students) black man—looking something like Sidney Poitier in a dashiki and sunglasses—enrolled in my Race and Family class and confided that he was the custodial father of his nine-year-old son. He as well was aware of his apparent rarity and proud to be telling me that he was at odds with the prevailing stereotypes. For me, the encounter with Rubin was akin to stumbling upon a diamond in the middle of the sidewalk. Fully aware that he embodied a chasm in the cultural landscape and probably a similar gap in the scholarly literature, I immediately asked him if I could interview him about his experience. He was happy to oblige, and his response has been fairly typical of many of the fathers in the study I discuss here. Most of them were grateful for the recognition and glad to be able to tell their stories to someone who was eager to listen.

My study asked the fathers about aspects of their families of orientation and of procreation, as the two families dovetail in a number of ways. Three aspects of their parenting experience stood out: the choice to parent, parenting roles and goals, and outcomes for the father. I intend here to provide the reader with the main narrative themes of each of these as a means of giving a context to this section of the book. (For an in-depth account of this study, see Coles 2009.) I will begin with

my own story of the methodology and the full description of the fathers; these capture the situation of single black fathers both individually and within the cultural mindset.

How the Project Developed

Rubin's story so fascinated me that I began reviewing the scholarly
literature on black single custodial fathers; that endeavor took only a
short time since there was no such literature. (Even since my study, I
am only aware of three more small studies on single black full-time fathers (Hamer and Marchioro 2002; Green in this volume; and Osgood
and Schroeder in this volume). Instead, I read the findings of the dozen
or so small, qualitative studies conducted on white single custodial fathers (some of the largest are Greif 1985, 1990; and Greif and DeMaris
1990). While my intention was not to compare the two racial groups,
this was the only comparable literature available.

Simultaneously, I began calling local churches, neighborhood centers, daycare centers, and fatherhood programs and Web sites, and I
announced my search in my classes. My students and the fatherhood
programs turned out to be the most fruitful sources of respondent contacts. For a fleeting time, it seemed that everyone knew a single black
custodial father, but always only one. A couple of the fathers pointed
me toward other fathers, but most did not know anyone else; most felt
as if they were alone in the wilderness. I took a hiatus to seek grant
funding and publish a few preliminary findings based on the first ten
interviews. The latter led to a few more contacts, and that's how I
put together my respondent pool. In methodological terms, it would
be called a nonproportional purposive sample. The interviews of these
twenty men occurred over a five-year period, from 1999 to 2005.

Fathers were admitted to the study based on their racial identity
and custodial status. Race was a self-identified status. "Custodial"
was defined as the child residing with the father at least four nights
per week for most of the year, though, as it turned out, all fathers had
sole custody. Custody could have been arranged formally, that is, legal-
ized through the court, or informally, arranged by the parents or family without the courts' intervention. All fathers were of majority age
at the time of the interview. Most of them were from southern Wisconsin (Milwaukee and Madison); four were from other states (New
York, New Jersey, Michigan, and Arkansas).

This qualitative study was based on a "grounded-theory" approach, which means that I entered the study with no hypothesis to test and instead intended to describe the fathers' experiences and derive questions for future research from the narrative data. The fathers first filled out a questionnaire that gathered demographic information about them, their children, and the children's mothers. Other sections of the questionnaire addressed the father's family background, parenting style and philosophy, the existence and proximity of a support system, the distribution of household labor and childcare, and a limited number of measurable outcomes for child and father. Upon completion of the questionnaire, I interviewed most of the fathers in person, usually for two to three hours and usually in their homes. Two interviews were conducted online, and one was conducted by phone. The interview questions, which developed largely from a symbolic interactionist approach, were designed to explore the motivations of the father, his definitions and enactment of parenting, and the effects he perceived parenting had on his identity and well-being. In the analysis, narratives were repeatedly read to identify reoccurring concepts and patterns. These then were developed into meaningful thematic categories related to the father's sense of self, parenting choices, and roles.

Father Profiles

As fascinated as I was by Rubin's story, his experience appeared straightforward by comparison to the fathers I later interviewed. Rubin had married in his early thirties, had a son, divorced relatively amicably, and then without much ado, by agreement with the mother, took custody of their nine-year-old son, Kyle. Rubin said it seemed the natural thing to do. He and his son were "kindred spirits. We're the same." Four more fathers had been married and divorced, and, like Rubin, most of them had taken sole custody of their children immediately following or soon after the divorce. But in some of these cases custody was complicated by the reasons for divorce (extramarital affairs or nervous breakdowns, for instance). One of the most complicated cases was that of Dominic. Dominic and his wife married after their first son was born. They had previously cohabited and had split up once before. They had had an on-again, off-again relationship, in part because his girlfriend was white and her family was not supportive. After marrying, they stayed together for about two and a half years until his wife became pregnant with a daughter by another man. Dominic left for a few months, but then his wife called and said her extramarital relationship had ended. So they got back together and eventually had a third child. However, right before his daughter was born, Dominic received a kidney transplant, which failed. During the failure, when he was so sick he could hardly walk, his wife left him, taking the two daughters with her. Two days later, she returned the girls, the youngest of whom was still only being breastfed. With help from his mother, uncle, and oldest son, they got through that period, and four years later, he's still the custodial father of three children, one of whom is not biologically his.

Other fathers also took less traditional routes to custody. One father, who was gay, adopted a six-year-old boy. Three of the fathers were made widowers by the unexpected and premature deaths of their wives. In these cases, finances, employment, child care, and residence became more complicated, but custody was fairly straightforward. However, one never-married father, James, who had previously cohabited with the mother for some time, took custody of his two youngest daughters (he had three older children with two other moms) when their mother died of a heart attack. Although the daughters had been staying with him regularly and he had declared paternity at the time of their births, he had to resort to court battles to fight "in-laws" in order to obtain custody. James describes it this way:

> All her sisters and brothers, her mother and father. I was in court with them on this issue. When the judge ruled in my favor . . . you know, he said, "you can't take these kids away from him." They didn't want me to have the kids, because they said I didn't have a wife and I wasn't able to raise two daughters by myself, but I was determined not to give up and I didn't. I didn't give up, and I didn't miss a day from work, and I never missed a court date.

Just over half of the fathers had never been married to the mother of their custodial children, though some, like James, had cohabited for some time. And a couple of fathers had been married to or cohabited with other women at some point. These circuitous routes led to what are now being called "complicated" or "complex" paternity; that is, some of this group of fathers had children by one or more mothers and had custody of some but not all of their biological children. Moreover, some were also caring for nonbiological children of girlfriends (not always current girlfriends) or of other family members.

More specifically, five of the fathers had other biological children whom they did not have custody of. In three of those cases, the noncustodial children were older children of different mothers, and in the other two cases, the noncustodial children were the younger, more recent children of different mothers. Seven of the fathers were caring for, in some capacity, other nonbiological children. In three cases, these children were residing with them, and in the remainder of cases the fathers were spending time with them or helping them financially. It's tempting to either romanticize these men because they are among the minority of men who parent full-time, even children who are not their own, or to excoriate them for creating those complicated situations. But to do either oversimplifies life in general and certainly the lives, options, and decisions of these men in particular.

Most of the men had paid child support, at least sporadically, or had been involved with these earlier noncustodial children, usually by taking them to or coaching their sporting events, enrolling them in extracurricular activities, or paying for various necessities. Some of the men were still paying child support arrearages that were being garnished from their wages and tax returns from the time the mothers were on welfare. In fact, two of the fathers were continuing to pay child support for children whom they currently had custody of. This occurred when custody had been arranged informally between the mother and the father. The fathers were afraid to stop child-support payments for fear that either the mother would get angry or the courts would intervene and reverse the custodial arrangement.

Table 4.2 lays out the major demographic characteristics of the fathers in this study. At least in terms of age, education, and income,

Table 4.2
Demographic Characteristics of Fathers, by Number and Percent, at Time of Interviews

Age	#	%	Education	#	%	Income	#	%
Through 29	3	15	High school only	7	35	Less than $15,000	3	15
30–39	8	40	AA or some college	2	10	$15,000–24,999	3	15
40–49	4	20	Bachelor's degree	8	40	$25,000–34,999	6	30
50 or higher	5	25	Graduate degree	3	15	$35,000–49,999	2	10
						$50,000 or more	6	30

these men are far from the stereotypical teenaged fathers on which much of the literature on black single fathers is based. While their ages ranged from twenty-two to seventy-six at the time of the interview, most of the fathers were in their thirties and forties. In addition, the vast majority of the dads were at least majority age when their first child was born. Only one was a minor, and four were eighteen or nineteen years old at the time of their first child's birth. (However, because men tend to pair with younger women, more of the children's mothers had been teen mothers.) It's quite likely that the fathers' older ages, especially at the time of the birth of the custodial child, played a role in their inclination and ability to take custody.

All of the fathers had at least a high school degree. Those with a terminal high school degree tended to be those who were at either end of the age range. Eight had a bachelor's degree, and three had a graduate degree. Several fathers had experienced a period of time as a nonresident single father and had completed a college degree during that interim before requesting custody. A couple of fathers completed degrees while a custodial father. Overall, they represent a more highly educated group than black men nationally.

At the time of the interview, three fathers had incomes below $15,000. One of those fathers was disabled; one was retired; and one had a previous felony record and was having difficulty finding sustainable employment. However, six had incomes over $50,000, which put the group's average income higher than the national average for black men. However, for seven of the fathers, their higher income results from working more than one job. Five of them work a full-time job *and* at least one part-time job (James worked one full-time and three part-time jobs). In fact, the fathers' juggling of multiple jobs and parenting responsibilities posed the single most important hurdle in the scheduling of their participation in this study. It was not uncommon that the scheduling of interviews might require a half-dozen or more calls to find a suitable time.

The Custodial Children

These twenty fathers had a total of thirty-six custodial children, twenty-one girls and fifteen boys. The plethora of girls appears to be somewhat unusual, compared both to the literature on single fathers generally and to census data. According to the 2006 Current Population Survey, girls account for 46 percent of all children under eighteen living in black father-only households (CPS 2006b). This might be explained by the high rate of widowhood among this sample of men— 20 percent of these fathers had experienced the death of a spouse or girlfriend—as all the widowed households contained girls. Five of the children were in the infant through preschool age range, seventeen were five to eleven years old, ten were teenagers, and four were young adults living at home.

Half of the fathers had custody of one child; six fathers had custody of two children; two had three children; and two had four. The length of custody ranged from half a year to sixteen years, but the majority of the fathers had had custody for five years or fewer. Four had had custody less than a year. The majority of fathers (twelve) had custody of their children through court appointment. In some cases, this was with the mother's agreement. In a few cases, the fathers fought against the mother or other family members to obtain custody. Five fathers had taken custody informally without going to court, usually with little to no resistance from the mother. Three of the widowed fathers "inherited" sole custody.

When I first began the study, I attempted to gather information, such as grades and behavioral characteristics, about the children in an attempt to measure their outcomes. However, many of the children were so young and the length of sole custody for a few of the fathers was so short that the data did not seem to be able to reveal anything substantive about the effect of father custody on the children, so I eliminated that section from the questionnaire. I can say that I met and talked casually with about half of the children, all of whom appeared well adjusted. However, five fathers each had a teenaged child who had experienced some behavioral problems. In two relatively minor cases, the teens were boys. One had left home without explanation, and another had graduated high school but was neither going to college nor seeking employment. One teen daughter had experienced temporary eating disorders; another had committed one case of credit card fraud; and the most severe case was a teen daughter who had gotten into drugs and been court-ordered to a detention facility.

The fathers represented a fairly diverse group of men, exhibiting a variety of previous marital statuses and a wide range of education, income, age, and custodial-child characteristics. Nevertheless, as one might suspect, the shared experiences of being black, male, and a parent imbued their narratives with many common themes.

Choosing to Parent

As I noted, these fathers differed from most of the literature on white fathers in the complexity of their previous marital status and multiple-partner fertility. That is, they had a higher rate of never-married and widowed status, a higher rate of having children by more than one mother, and a higher rate of having custody of or responsibility for children who were not biologically theirs. These trends affect the perception of choice not just for the men but for others, too.

Many people assume that fathers who are divorced or widowed have no choice but to take their children and that those who never married don't have to, and likely won't. There is some truth to these notions, but what seemed to crystallize in the narratives of these fathers that I didn't find as much in the literature on white fathers was the fact that even widowed and divorced fathers were offered, or considered, substitutes for their own parenting. That is, family members offered to take the children or suggested that the fathers give the children to other family members. Fathers were also aware that the state might step in as a parental substitute, and all of them wanted to avoid that possibility. The possibility of foster care, in particular, is not as frequent in the literature on white fathers.

Practical considerations, such as having a residence, being employed, and having family support, appeared to play a role in their choice to parent, as all of the fathers were employed at the time custody began. Several of them waited to seek custody until they had completed college, and several sought better residences before seeking custody. Most of them said their families supported them in their choice to take custody, but more than half of them did not seek or receive practical support from family members. Those who did receive regular child care or help around the house from family members tended to be younger or had young children. The fact that this is a somewhat older set of respondents who are, on average, economically better off probably accounts for the majority not receiving much practical support. (See Coles, forthcoming, for more analysis of this.)

However, none of those factors played a conscious motivating theme in their narratives about deciding to seek custody. Instead, some of the fathers pointed to individual emotional reasons, such as they had a stronger bond or connection with the custodial child (this was usually said in comparison to that of the mother's bond with the child, not in comparison to the father's bond with his other children).

Some of the men said they wanted to be a role model for the custodial child. This was more often said in reference to sons, that is, that they wanted to help their sons learn how to be men, but occasionally it was said for daughters as well. In these cases, it usually meant that they wanted to teach their daughters what good men are like and how their daughters should expect to be treated by men.

However, the theme that predominated related to their own fathers. That is, many of the men desired to be the kind of fathers they themselves had not had—a father who was more nurturing and a father who was *there* physically and emotionally for the child. This was not unlike the findings of Allen and Doherty (1998), who found similar language in the narratives of black teen fathers, and John Snarey (1993), who found that among white single fathers, those whose own father had been a negative role model were more likely than those whose father was a positive role model to desire to exhibit more nurturing parenting. (Also see Fox and Bruce 1996.)

For instance, Calvin's father was murdered when he was five. He fought for custody of his daughter and in the process decided to become a lawyer. He said of his choice to rear his daughter after he and his girlfriend separated,

> She's my only child. I was raised in a single parent home, I was raised without a father. And very early on I had made a promise, I think even as a boy, that if I ever had a child I will always be there. And ultimately, she's my responsibility. Whether she's with her mother or whomever, she's my responsibility. So, I wanted her with me, particularly when I realized that her mother was not going to allow me to be in her life the way I wanted to be. My father was taken from me and my sister, and there was no way that I was not going to be in my daughter's life. So it was just pure emotion, I think, that commitment and the promise that I had made to myself that was driving everything.

These fathers wanted to break what they saw as a cycle or trend. This was mentioned most frequently among those whose own fathers had not been present or were rarely present in their childhoods. However, even some who had had coresident fathers mentioned that they hoped to be more nurturing than their fathers. Antoine is a widower with custody of his middle-school-aged daughter. He grew up in a two-parent family, but he was nevertheless distant from his father, an experience he didn't want replicated with his daughter:

I would say, umm, I guess I'm the man that kind of defied the odds, tried to break the cycle, to do things differently than were I guess presented to me by my father. So I guess I'm not going to go that route or run away or not be there for my child. I am going to be there and I'm going to do everything I possibly can to make sure that she has everything that she needs. And I guess do the best that I can while I am here. I always know that nothing is guaranteed so if you want something you have to go after it.

A number of the fathers had struggled with delinquency as teens or young adults. They sometimes attributed those experiences or the nonmarital births to the absence of their own fathers. They speculated that maybe they would have made better choices had their fathers been present in their lives. While it is impossible to know what they would have done, and their statements overlook macrolevel factors, such as income, it is clear they wanted to eliminate any effects of father absence in their children's lives.

Parenting Roles

In the questionnaire, fathers were presented with a list of six possible parenting roles—provider, nurturer, teacher, disciplinarian, authority figure, and friend—and asked to prioritize them according to their own fathering experience. The interviews asked them to explain what those roles meant to them and to give examples of how they enact them on a day-to-day basis.

Not unexpectedly, most of the fathers ranked provider as first in importance. Other scholars, such as McAdoo (1993), have found the provider role to be an important part of African American male identity. Nevertheless, these fathers viewed provider as necessary but not sufficient, which explains why "nurturer" competed for first place. For instance, Tracy, a social worker and custodial father of nine-year-old Train (and noncustodial father of two-month-old Tracy Jr.) explained why he ranked provider first:

Because if you can't provide, you won't be here. They won't be here. Neither one of us would be here. So I had to put that number one. And I think the nurturing—I think you must nurture kids. I mean, they always need that affection, tell them that you love them. I tell him everyday I love him. That's part of me nurturing him. I hug him before he goes to school. I hug him when he goes to bed. You know, give him a kiss on the cheek. He kiss me on the cheek. And that's something I want, you know, until one of us dies.

"Friend" and "authority figure" ranked low overall. Fathers appeared to want to avoid what they viewed as polar ends of the continuum; they didn't want to be too chummy or peerlike to their children, as a "friend" might, nor did they want to be too rigid and distant from their children, an image generated by the term "authority figure." Interestingly, fathers who ranked authority figure higher were those who had children who were more difficult to handle.

"Teacher" and "disciplinarian" were generally ranked in the middle and were sometimes seen as overlapping, depending on how the fathers defined disciplinarian. When they defined the term as someone who teaches a child to be self-disciplined and reliable, for instance, as in teaching them to brush their teeth daily or practice a musical instrument regularly, then disciplinarian was viewed as overlapping with teacher. When defined as executing punishment of some sort, disciplinarian was seen as more overlapping with authority figure. A few fathers said they used spanking regularly, and a few said they never used spanking. Most used it rarely or on occasion. Several said they tried to avoid it because they themselves felt they had been spanked too much as a child.

The gender of the children appeared to play a role in the fathers' ranking of parental roles. Fathers of daughters were more likely to rank provider higher than were fathers of sons. Many fathers of daughters feared that they could not provide the kind of nurturing that they perceived their daughters needed. Instead, these fathers worried that they would not be able to play "girly" games (such as dress-up) with their daughters and would not be able to understand and counsel them about female experiences (usually menstruation). For instance, Don, a divorced father who had custody of two young girls, said,

I worry about not having a mother or female figure in the home for them to learn from. I will never be able to talk to them about what it is like growing up as a lady—from a lady's point of view. How do I talk to them about periods in a way that they'll understand? I can't play dress-up like they will want to do.

This impression of not being able to talk with or play with their daughters as they think a mother would do probably also explains why fathers of daughters also ranked friend significantly lower than did fathers of sons.

Behavioral Goals

In the questionnaire, fathers were given about a dozen behavioral goals, such as "respect their teachers and other authority figures," "obey me," "be creative," "be polite and considerate of others," "succeed academically," and "get along with others." They were asked to rank them as "very important," "somewhat important," "not so important," or "not important at all." This method did not produce much variation, as most fathers ranked most goals as very important; only a few goals were ranked somewhat important by a few dads. In other words, fathers wanted it all for their children.

The goals that were more likely ranked as somewhat important included: creativity, willingness to try new things, and getting along with others. In the narratives, fathers indicated that while they wanted their children to try new things (as most parents can appreciate, food was the most common item they wanted their children to try) or be creative and get along with others, they could also see the possibility of negative outcomes associated with those. For instance, being too willing to try new things or being too concerned about getting along with others might make their children more susceptible to problematic behaviors. Being creative was associated with not being taken seriously, having their ideas discredited, and leading to unstable careers.

Fathers were given the option of adding goals, and the one that most often came up in the interviews was "independence." However, fathers defined independence in a variety of ways. Most fathers thought of independent as self-reliance, their children's being able to stand on their own two feet by the time they reach majority age. Fathers of girls wanted their daughters to not need a man. However, one father, the son of a minister, thought of it as *thinking* independently: "That was something that I wanted to make sure—I don't believe in forcing religion on people, forcing them to believe something that you believe, simple because you believe it. . . . Because I think that has to be his choice, his belief, his faith in God."

Outcomes for Fathers

Overall, the fathers claimed to be doing pretty well. Some fathers were downright ecstatic about having the opportunity to parent. James said, "It's been a big challenge and rewarding. I feel like it's just filled a void in my life, having them in the household with me. . . . We all used to live together . . . , and then they moved out. I missed them a lot, just having them in the household. Once they came back to live with me, I felt I had been rewarded very highly. . . . So once I got custody, I felt great. I'm being rewarded right now."

Several fathers felt that parenting had rescued them, detouring them from paths of self-destruction. Tracy, father of two young boys, probably expressed that best:

> These two guys, they are the reason I live, you know. Because I feel without them ain't no telling what I'd be doing. There's no telling, because I mean so much stuff, so much damage has been done to me, as far as an individual goes, you know. People using you and abusing you and all that. And I just think that if it weren't for those two, I probably wouldn't even be here myself. You know, I'd probably be in jail somewhere or probably dead, you know. So—they inspire me . . . I'm just hanging strong because of those guys.

Parenting often produces those paradoxical outcomes: satisfaction despite frustration, reward despite worry. Therefore, while a number of fathers expressed some frustration, a feeling of being misunderstood, or uncertainty about the future, most of them also felt that these negative feelings were far outweighed by the reward. As in a number of studies (Hong and Seltzer 1995; Hong 1996) of women in multiple roles, these men who are workers and primary caregivers felt "blessedly stressed," deriving satisfaction from their successful fulfillment of numerous responsibilities.

Still, despite their satisfaction, it is unlikely that most of these men will always be single custodial fathers. Family lives are dynamic. Members move through various developmental stages or they come and go of their own accord or because others intervene. Many of the fathers will marry or remarry or, for whatever reason, return their children to their mothers. Society's response should not be to move men into one parental category or another—married or single, good dad or bad—but to facilitate their doing the best parenting possible no matter what category they are in.

References

Allen, W. D., and W. J. Doherty. 1998. " 'Being There:' The Perception of Fatherhood Among a Group of African American Adolescent Fathers." In *Resiliency in African American Families*, ed. H. I. McCubbin, E. A. Thompson, A. I. Thompson and J. A. Futrell, 207–44. Thousand Oaks, Calif.: Sage.

Coles, R. L. 2009. *The Best Kept Secret: Single Black Fathers*. Lanham, Md.: Rowman and Littlefield.

Coles, R. L. Forthcoming. "Just Doing What They Gotta Do: Black Single Fathers Coping with the Stresses and Reaping the Rewards of Parenting." *Journal of Family Issues*.

Current Population Survey. 1996. "Household and Family Characteristics (P20-495)." March. http://www.census.gov/population/www/socdemo/hh-fam.html.

Current Population Survey. 2006a. "Living Arrangements of Black Children Under 18 Years Old: 1960 to Present." CH-3 Current Populations Survey. http://www.censusbureau.biz/population/socdemo/hh-fam/ch3.xls.

Current Population Survey. 2006b. "American Families and Living Arrangements 2006." Table C2: Household Relationship and Living Arrangements of Children Under 18 Years, by Age, Sex, Race, Hispanic Origin: 2006. U.S. Government Census. http://www.census.gov/population/www/socdemo/hh-fam/cps2006.html.

Danziger, S., and N. Radin. 1990. "Absent Does Not Equal Uninvolved: Predictors of Fathering in Teen Mother Families." *Journal of Marriage and the Family* 52 (3): 636–42.

Fox, G. L., and Bruce, C. 1996. "Development and Validation of Measures of Parenting for Low-Income, High-Risk Men." In *Proceedings of the NCFR Theory Construction and Research Methods Workshop*, ed. A. Acock, 221–32. Minneapolis: National Council on Family Relations.

Greif, G. L. 1985. "Children and Housework in the Single Father Family." *Family Relations* 34 (3): 353–57.

Greif, G. L. 1990. *The Daddy Track and the Single Father*. Lexington, Mass.: Lexington Books.

Greif, G. L., and A. DeMaris. 1990. "Single Fathers with Custody." *Families in Society: The Journal of Contemporary Human Services*. 71 (5): 259–66.

Halle, T. 2002. "Charting Parenthood: A Statistical Portrait of Fathers and Mothers in America." U.S. Department of Health and Human Services. http://fatherhood.hhs.gov/charting02/index.htm.

Hamer, J., and K. Marchioro. 2002. "Becoming Custodial Dads: Exploring Parenting Among Low-Income and Working-Class African American Fathers." *Journal of Marriage and the Family* 64:116–29.

Hamilton, B. E., Martin, J. A., Ventura, S. J. 2007. "Births: Preliminary Data for 2006." *National Vital Statistics Report* 56, no. 7 (December). http://www.cdc.gov/nchs/data/nvsr/nvsr56/nvsr56_07.pdf.

Hong, J. 1996. "Are They the Blessedly Stressed, Too? A Study of Multiple Roles and Psychological Well-Being Among Older and Caregiving Women." Ph.D. diss., University of Wisconsin–Madison.

Hong, J., and M. M. Seltzer. 1995. "The Psychological Consequences of Multiple Roles: The Nonnormative Case." *Journal of Health and Social Behavior* 36:386–98.

McAdoo, J. L. 1993. "The Roles of African American Fathers: An Ecological Perspective." *Families in Society: The Journal of Contemporary Human Services* 74 (1): 28–35.

Mincy, R.B. 2002. "What About Black Fathers?" *American Prospect* 13 (April): 58.

Minoff, E., T. Ooms, and P. Roberts. 2006. "Healthy Marriage and Responsible Fatherhood Grants: Announcement Overview." Center for Law and Social Policy. http://www.clasp.org/publications/marriage_fatherhood_rfp.pdf.

Seltzer, J. 1991. "Relationships Between Fathers and Children Who Live Apart: The Father's Role After Separation." *Journal of Marriage and the Family* 53 (February): 79–101.

Snarey, J. 1993. *How Fathers Care for the Next Generation: A Four-Decade Study.* Cambridge, Mass.: Harvard University Press.

Stier, H., and M. Tienda. 1993. "Are Men Marginal to the Family? Insights from Chicago's Inner City." In *Men, Work, and Family*, ed. J. C. Hood, 23–44. Newbury Park, Calif.: Sage.

Taylor, R. J., B. R. Leashore, and S. Toliver. 1988. "An Assessment of the Provider Role as Perceived by Black Males." *Family Relations* 37 (4): 426–31.

Wattenberg, E. 1993. "Paternity Actions and Young Fathers." In *Young Unwed Fathers: Changing Roles and Emerging Policies*, ed. R. Lerman and T. Ooms, 213–34. Philadelphia: Temple University Press.

CHAPTER FIVE

Single Custodial Fathers and Mothers Meeting the Challenge

A Comparative Note

CHARLES GREEN

> It is admirable taking care of one's child but nothing can take the place of a
> loving couple working together.
> —PERRY, A CUSTODIAL FATHER OF TWO BOYS

Adjusting to change, whether at the microlevel of individuals and
small groups or at the macrolevel of large-scale institutional change,
is not something that occurs overnight (Giddens, Duneier, and Appelbaum 2007:412–16; Kornblum 2008:xix–xxi). A break with con-
vention and the way things have always operated is often met with
resistance and pressure for the supporters of change to demonstrate
its merit. The rise in the number of households across America that
are currently headed by single fathers represents a significant change
in the structure of families and family life in the United States. This
shift has encountered resistance from women as well as men who are
uncomfortable with this family type and are skeptical about a man's
ability to meet the challenges associated with single parenting.

Throughout most of the twentieth century we learned that a woman's place was at home with the children. Perhaps it was correct to assume that a man occupying the status "single head of household" was
either a widower or someone whose spouse or partner was the victim
of some physical or mental incapacitation. But this no longer seems to
be the case, as U.S. Bureau of the Census data show a steady decrease
in widowhood in the general population since 1960, thereby eliminating it as a major explanation for the rise of fathers as single heads
of household (Marriage and Family Encyclopedia 2003). As questions
about the nature of the shift and its implications for the larger society
grow, that which appears foremost on the minds of many Americans

is whether men, who are not recognized for their domestic skills, are capable of carrying out the tasks and meeting the challenges that have historically been assigned to mothers.

A combination of quantitative data and narratives based on the parenting experiences of single black fathers and mothers have been gathered for this chapter. It is not the aim of this study to tender comparative data for the purpose of declaring that one gender versus the other is more effective at fulfilling the single parent role. Rather, this chapter is intended to explore single fathers' and mothers' perceptions of one another, given the dominant cultural associations of good parenting and single parenting with mothers.

Certain fundamental questions arise when people are presented with the reality of an increasing number of single-father-headed households. Chief among these are, "Who is the better care provider and, specifically, nurturer?" and "Who has it easier?" These are not merely terms of a competition; the former has implications for child wellbeing and placement and the latter has implications for policy and programming. In keeping with this focus, I discuss parents' perceptions of who is the better care provider, their definitions of nurturing, whether nurturing is instinctual or learned, how their social life is subsidiary to their nurturing, and their perceptions about whether single dads or moms have it easier.

The Demographic Picture

By the 1990s, the number of single fathers across America began to rise sharply. But the shift had already been in motion since the 1970s with the rise of the feminist movement and women's quest for liberation. After 1995, the number of single mothers (approximately 9.8 million) remained constant for the next three years. However, during that period the number of single fathers increased 40 percent, from 1.5 million in 1995 to 2.1 million in 1998, at which time men constituted one-sixth of the nation's 11.9 million single-parent families (U.S. Census Bureau 1999; Bloir 2003).

In 2000, some 2.2 million single fathers were the primary custodians of children under the age of eighteen, a 62 percent rise since 1990 (Fritsch 2001). However, as Jason Fields, a family demographer with the U.S. Census Bureau pointed out, single-father families, at approximately 2.1 percent of all American households, are still far less numerous than single-mother households, which are at 7.2 percent (J. Fields in Fritsch 2001). One explanation for the increase of father-only households is offered by James A. Levine, director of the Fatherhood Project at the Families and Work Institute in New York City. He believes that the increase has something to do with the change that is taking place in men's aspirations. Increasingly, men are defining success not only in terms of career but also in terms of their success as fathers. Earlier research indicates that many single fathers want to be the type of father that their own fathers failed to be. Many of these men also reported that their fathers were more distant than their mothers and less nurturing. But there is noticeable change taking place among women and mothers. As Levine reports: "We are seeing some weakening of constraints on women to feel that they can only be successful if they are successful mothers. As a result more women are willing to concede primary custody of children to fathers without a fight—and we are seeing this across all races" (cited in Fritsch 2001).

A summary of the factors that have contributed to the rise in father-only households might be helpful at this point: family court judges, following a gender-neutral approach over the last ten years, are increasingly realizing that dads are capable of nurturing the children as well as or, in some cases, better than moms. With more women continuing to focus on the workforce and developing their careers, the number of single custodial fathers will continue to rise. Men, the traditional "climb the corporate ladder" crowd, have begun to put their careers on hold or alter their career plans to dramatically enhance their kids' lives. And there is less social stigma attached to women who don't pursue or are not awarded custody of their children. It's now acceptable to our larger society that being a mom doesn't automatically equate with being a custodial parent. (Associated Press 2001; Paniccia 2002; Bloir 2003). Concerning the latter point, one should be cautious not to run away with the idea that society has completely absolved women of their role as the primary caretakers for their children. In fact, if a mother does not have at least joint custody, criticism and raised eyebrows are certain to follow as the assumption will be that something is seriously wrong with her. Finally, it merits exploring whether the increase in single-father households and how they are counted might be influenced by other factors. For example, the rise in the number of father-only households has not necessarily increased their proportion of all households, and a rise in the percentage of children living in father-only families in part reflects a decline in the number of children in other types of households, for example, mother-only and married-couple. It is also likely that the increase in cohabitation between unmarried partners could lead to them being counted as single moms or single dads in demographic studies.

Background to the Problem

Persistent reservations about single-father families and the view that mothers provide the best living environment for children have roots that can be traced back to the very construction of gender and gender inequality. It is variously argued that because of women's reproductive role, they have been viewed as being closer to nature than men. Nature is generally interpreted as subordinate to culture and, moreover, subject to the constraints of culture (Hurst 2007:110–11). Since men lack certain natural and creative functions such as pregnancy and breast feeding, they must assert their creativity externally and artificially through the medium of technology and cultural symbols. In doing so, the man creates relatively lasting, external, transcending, not to mention important objects while the woman creates only "perishables or human beings" (Ortner 1974).

Particularly useful are theories that point out the unnatural origins of gender inequality. They inform that early in human history people lived communally and engaged in tasks together to produce goods principally for their own use. Since all resources were communally owned, individuals worked for the group as a whole. Rather than being "wives" within separate families, women were members of society. The work of both sexes was considered equally valuable. Albeit there was a division of labor based on sex, each sex was a master in its own sphere of work (Engels 1973; Sacks 1975; Sanday 1981; Hurst 2007). This situation was destined to change. Sweeping economic changes began to take place with the development of privately owned productive resources in the form of domesticated animals and land. Herding, which was taken over by men, made possible their control of surplus goods. Consequently, they became the primary holders of private property, which led to the change in the status of women from contributing adults equal to men to wives and daughters in a subordinate domestic position. Men became preoccupied with procreation and having children, chiefly male children, to whom they could pass along their wealth. Collins (1988) and other theorists would also argue that other structural and environmental shifts such as warfare and men's belief in their physical strength versus women's could inspire their need to dominate women.

The Dilemma for Women

The above glance at the literature underscores the patriarchal system and the history of exploitation that women have endured and also reinforces that it is through the socialization process that members of society learned to accept women's domestication or concentration around devalued housework. From that history would emerge the feminist movement, whose primary objectives were to liberate women from their marginalized status and to help them realize themselves as capable of achieving well beyond the boundaries constructed for them by men. (The feminist movement is not monolithic and differentiates along several themes including race. Leith Mullings, Bell Hooks, and Patricia Hill Collins are a few scholars who have carefully argued the position of black women vis-à-vis the interests of white feminists.) A contradiction arose whereby some women in pursuit of an equal playing field with men soon found themselves in a dilemma. Their socialization around the homemaker role left them torn between the desire to make it to the top professionally and the felt obligation to attend to the traditional activities of housework and child care. Sociologists have coined a new concept, "opting out," to refer to the present phenomenon whereby highly successful professional women are walking away from their careers to spend quality time with their children at home (Stone 2007). Unsurprisingly, the desire to return home that is observed chiefly among elite white working women has led some scholars to wonder whether this represents a form of neo-traditionalism (Welter 1973). The history of women as domesticians may explain in part their reluctance to share parenting with men and the public's uneasiness about father-only families.

Today we are witnessing men in greater numbers who are expressing an interest in becoming more involved in the lives of their children (Yeung, Duncan, and Hill 2000; John 2002; Weaver 2002). As I will discuss later in this chapter, many men are expressing their desire to "be there" for their children emotionally and in other supportive ways, unlike their experience with their own fathers growing up. It is no longer a sign of weakness or an erosion of their masculinity for men to weep openly or greet each other with a hug. This is anchored by a growing body of literature in sociology and related disciplines where attention is drawn to nonresidential fathers exploring various strategies to strengthen themselves and the bonds between them and their children (Daniels 1998; Barras 2000; Hamer 2001).

Warren Farrell, who defines himself as a male feminist and was elected three times to the board of directors of the New York chapter of the National Organization for Women, believes that the feminist movement failed to the extent that it increased options and emphasized fulfillment for women but did not do the same for men. In other words, the feminist movement had the opportunity to be a gender-transition movement but did not seize the moment (Avins 2000).

The Study Group

Given the growth of single-father households between the 1990 and 2000 censuses, there is every reason to predict that this growth will continue in the 2010 census. In light of this demographic trend and the uneasiness that continues to accompany this family structure, data from single fathers and single mothers who are heads of households were gathered and compared.

Beginning in 2006, single custodial fathers and single mothers were identified by word of mouth, outreach to churches across denominations and community based organizations, and announcements about the project to students in my sociology classes. Fathers and mothers were selected based on the following criteria: they were at least twenty-one years of age; they self identified as black/African American; they were the primary or custodial parent for their dependent child/children (up to eighteen years old) for a minimum of one year; and they resided solely with their child/children. Because fathers were being compared to single mothers, who are widely perceived as the traditional domesticians, it was felt that a strict selection criteria would increase the chances of gathering a sample of committed single fathers who were most comparable to the single mothers. Therefore, fathers who live part of the time with relatives or nonrelatives who help them with their children, and fathers who held custody of their child/children for less than one year were not included in the present study.

In light of its overarching importance, the nurturing factor provided the framework for the data gathering. Subjects were asked to complete a questionnaire that took approximately thirty minutes and included items concerning their perceptions of themselves and one another as nurturers, how they became a single parent, their use of support systems, and problems with their children and their resolution. Following that, subjects were asked to participate in a face-to-face audiotape-recorded interview lasting approximately sixty to ninety minutes that encouraged respondents to elaborate on items in the questionnaire.

A total sample of twenty-four single parents, thirteen fathers and eleven mothers, emerged, with a mean age of forty-eight years. Breaking it down by sex, the mean age of the fathers was forty-nine and the mothers, forty-four. These twenty-four fathers and mothers were the custodians of a total of forty-five children with an average of two children per family. The mean age of the fathers at the birth of their first child was 25.3 and for the mothers it was 26.8. A couple of fathers and mothers were in their late thirties and early forties at the arrival of their first child, and one father and one mother were eighteen years of age at the birth of their first child. The sample comprised a mixture of mainly working-class and middle-class people representing a variety of occupations and professions. They included a mother who works through the state workfare program, a university professor, a registered nurse, a high-school teacher, bankers, public administrators, a telephone installer, a social-agency caseworker, and a child specialist at a neighborhood daycare center. Subjects hailed from three New York City boroughs (Brooklyn, the Bronx, and Harlem in Manhattan), also Nassau County on Long Island, New York; New Jersey; Baltimore, Maryland; and as far away as Toronto, Ontario.

Twelve of the thirteen fathers had been married to their children's mother, and seven of the eleven mothers had been married to their children's father. Respondents' current relationship with the other parent tended to be mixed, but a majority of the fathers and mothers reported that they have a civil relationship with the other parent. In a few cases, however, the relationship with the other parent was described as disconnected.

Three fathers were widowers. Of the remaining ten fathers, six settled the matter of custody through the legal system while four gained custody through an agreement with the mother outside of court. None of the mothers was widowed. One mother became a single parent following her spouse's arrest and sentence to a twelve-year prison term. Of the remaining ten mothers, two settled the matter of custody through the court system and eight entered an agreement for custody with the father outside of court. A majority of single fathers and mothers expressed either abandonment by the other parent or the other parent's desire to uproot to pursue a new career as the main reasons for the family breakup and their seeking custody of their dependent child/children. Finally, it should be noted that at the time these interviews were conducted, two fathers and two mothers had remarried and started new families.

Among the single fathers, ten reported that their children were young adults and presently in college or working (though still living at home) and, in one case, married. Three fathers had children who were teenagers or younger and still residing at home. In the case of the mothers, five had young-adult children currently away attending college or working and still living at home, while the remaining six had teenage children or younger residing at home. Because a number of the children of these parents were adult and out of the house, some of these single parents were responding from hindsight. What these parents stressed at the end of their interviews was that their experiences as single parents remain fresh on their minds and that participation in this study allowed them the opportunity to revisit that important period in their lives.

What the Data Tell Us

Based upon data gathered from the individual interviews and questionnaires administered to twenty-four subjects, this section of the chapter will report on some of the similarities and differences between fathers and mothers in carrying out their role as single parents. Toward that objective, several factors are considered, all of which can be linked directly or indirectly to nurturing and subsequently guide the analysis. I begin this discussion with the parents' perceptions of who is the better care provider. I then explore some of their definitions of nurturing and whether it is instinctual or learned. This is followed up by a discussion of parents' interest in dating without jeopardizing their commitment as nurturers of their children. Finally, I examine the parents' perceptions about whether single dads or moms have it easier.

The Best Care Provider?

Whether single mothers and fathers each perceive the other as having it easier or as basking in "societal sympathy" leads to another more fundamental query that strikes at the heart of nurturing, namely, who is the best care provider for children, fathers or mothers? Care provision in this instance is defined as a parent caring for a variety of his/her child's needs including domestic, fiscal, social, emotional, and disciplinary. This question, when posed to the twenty-four single fathers and mothers in this study, revealed some interesting findings that are presented in tables 5.1 and 5.2.

Table 5.1 indicates that six fathers agree that fathers are best, while seven fathers disagreed. Three mothers agreed that fathers are better care providers, but eight mothers disagreed. Table 5.2 shows that six fathers believed that mothers are the best care providers, whereas seven disagreed, and nine mothers believed that mothers are the best care providers for their children, and only two disagreed.

In summary, the data reveal that among the fathers, as many agree that they are better equipped as feel just opposite. Moreover, when

Table 5.1
Number and Percent of Men and Women Who Agree/Disagree with Statement "Fathers Are the Best Care Providers"

		Strongly agree	Agree	Disagree	Strongly disagree	Total
Male	#	5	1	6	1	13
	%	20.8	4.2	25	4.2	54.2
Female	#	3	0	7	1	11
	%	12.5	0	29.2	4.2	45.8
Total	#	8	1	13	2	24
	%	33.3	4.2	54.2	8.3	100

Table 5.2
Number and Percent of Men and Women who Agree/Disagree with Statement "Mothers Are the Best Care Providers"

		Strongly agree	Agree	Disagree	Strongly disagree	Total
Male	#	5	1	5	2	13
	%	20.8	4.2	20.8	8.3	54.2
Female	#	7	2	2	0	11
	%	29.2	8.3	8.3	0	45.8
Total	#	12	3	7	2	24
	%	50	12.5	29.2	8.3	100

we examine fathers' feelings regarding mothers, the same finding results, that is, as many fathers feel that mothers are the better care providers as disagree. The mothers, on the other hand, appear to be quite confident about their ability to provide the best care for their children and are less confident about men's. While these data appear to boost the maternal-instinct argument and point to reluctance on the part of fathers to take charge, they should not be interpreted to mean that change is not taking place or that fathers should become disillusioned.

The question of nurturing is essential to any study on parenting and to my specific effort to compare single fathers and single mothers. In its broadest yet simplest terms, nurturing suggests the capacity for expressing emotion, warmth, and sensitivity in parenting, but it also implies the ability to use sound judgment and to set limits in caring for one's child/children. In their study on parenting styles in depressed urban communities, Simons et al. (2005) define authoritative parenting as the outpouring of warmth, affection, and support for one's children combined with close monitoring and controls. This style that has been found to deter affiliation with delinquent peers and antisocial behavior (Sampson and Laub 1993; Simmons et al. 2005). Most of the single parents in this study acknowledged this as their preferred approach to parenting. As we will see, how parents come to define nurturing is critical to understanding and comparing role performance between single fathers and single mothers.

Parents' Definitions of Nurturing

Nurturing and the "maternal instinct" are an inseparable duo; it is difficult to speak about one without referencing the other. Because nurturing is viewed as a distinguishing marker of motherhood, this duo has contributed in no small measure to the lingering public reservation about fathers' effectiveness as single heads of households. Socialization theory has been chiefly used by sociologists and social psychologists in challenging the idea of human instincts, including such the "maternal instinct" (Mead [1934] 1971; Davis 1947; Harlow and Harlow 1962; Turnbull 1983; Blum 2002; Giddens, Duneier, and Appelbaum 2007). Despite the efforts by proponents of the learned-behavior school, the maternal-instinct thesis has thus far proven resilient. The complexity surrounding maternal instinct and nurturing was evidenced when subjects were asked to state their definition of nurturing and to explain its relationship to gender. They were also asked if they believed a man could learn to nurture. In presenting the narratives that follow I compare the definitions of nurturing expressed by some of the single fathers and mothers while highlighting the confusion that is associated with this concept.

Tim, a victim of spousal abandonment, works as a conflict analyst for a prominent law firm while completing a degree at one of New York's ivy league universities. This is how Tim addressed the question about nurturing:

> My boys were 10 and 3 respectively when I assumed responsibility for them. I just did it as the Nike commercial says. I got up every morning to make breakfast. I got them dressed and took them to school; the older boy was dropped off first, then the younger boy was dropped off to pre-k. Then I had to go to school until 12:20 p.m. and then go to work from 1 to 8 p.m. I got home to relieve the babysitter, who fed them and bathed them for me. I then double checked homework and lay in bed with them until they fell asleep. Then I had to do my own academic assignment which generally would go up until 3 or 4 a.m. Then it was up at 7 a.m. to start all over again. Other than the babysitter, I had no outside help at all. My father was supportive with special events and things, but day to day was my responsibility. As far as I am concerned, nurturing is the emotional part of parenting; [that is,] loving and being able to show it. Everyone is capable of nurturing; it is not something women are born with. Men do not nurture as a rule because society teaches them otherwise and forces women to be more nurturing.

Dwayne, who works in construction, married his high school sweetheart in the 1980s and together they had three daughters and one son. Dwayne admits that he was young and wild, which caused his family to break up. By the time he tried to turn it around it was too late, and the couple divorced. His wife moved to another state with the couple's two younger children. The two older girls (still in high school at the time) lived with him for three years. Dwayne vividly recalls those three years of being a single parent. According to him,

> Nurturing means being there and making life as comfortable for your children as you possibly can. It need not be hugging and kissing, but

there is compassion. It means going to PTA meetings and being the only man in the room. Maybe there is a gene for nurturing that is found in women, and maybe birthing brings out nurturing. A man can nurture but differently from women. It can be learned; society directs our path.

Ken, a university professor, became a widower in 1999 after his wife succumbed to cancer. Ken assumed custody of the couple's nine-year-old daughter and seventeen-year-old son. At the time of his interview in 2006 he was remarried and the father of a newly born son. As far as Ken is concerned, "Nurturing is not a female instinct; culture dictates this. Women seem to know what to do because they have been immersed into those tasks from a very young age. Men are capable of being nurturers, but they are not taught to be so."

Nick is a secondary-school social-science teacher. He was a college freshman in 1988 when his girlfriend became pregnant and gave birth to their son. The young unmarried couple soon grew apart and the relationship ended. At age five, Nick's son came to live with him after his mother's marriage to an abusive man. At the time of his interview Nick had recently married, and his son was a second-year student at college. Nick believes that his experience has taught him something about nurturing which he defines as "being able to hold a child and say 'I love you'. It is being there when they are sick and taking them to the doctor. It is being supportive meaning you must go to baseball games and sit in the bleachers in the rain."

Paul is an installer for a Baltimore, Maryland, cable and telephone company. His wife decided to leave when their daughter and son were one year old and three years old, respectively. At the time of the interview both children were doing extremely well in school. His daughter was a high-school sophomore, and his son was about to graduate high school and move on to college. A gentle man of strong will and determination, Paul saw himself as more nurturing than his children's mother: "I know about nurturing. My kids' mother was never interested in that stuff. I was present at the birth of both my children"— proudly pointing to a wall in the living room and two separate photos of himself in the delivery room dressed in full surgical greens holding the newborns—"At home, I always changed diapers and did the feeding; I really enjoyed that."

Mike married at twenty-three. His wife of the same age was an enlistee in the U.S. Navy and was more excited about seeing the world than being a wife to her husband and a mother to two small sons. Mike, the eldest child from a large family, learned a lot about child care helping out at home with his younger siblings. Thus, taking care of his sons did not present a problem for him. The young couple argued constantly about her priorities, and one day while his wife was on duty at sea Mike took off with the children. They fled first to Florida, then to Maryland, where his maternal grandmother, who volunteered to assist him with the children, resided. Mike believes that his wife did not really want the responsibility of raising the boys, as she never pursued legal action to contest Mike's crossing state borders with them. He eventually petitioned and won custody of their two sons. Mike concedes that maternal instinct might exist but that it can also be learned. He also suggests that men may express nurturing differently than women, in ways that are not societally acknowledged as nurturing. According to Mike,

> There is such a thing as maternal instinct, but I also think that part of nurturing is also learned. Sports and coaching [which a lot of men do] are forms of nurturing. Society dictates what is male and what is women's nurturing. A man can spank a child then turn around and hug him or her; that is also nurturing.

Perry's first and second sons were born with mild cases of cerebral palsy. His third son experienced normal development. Perry's wife complained that she was frustrated and one day in 1979 decided to leave home in pursuit of her real self and her career. Perry returned home that day only to find that she was gone. According to Perry, he and his wife had a few issues, but "I never saw this coming; the problems facing a single parent are tall but when children have disabilities, it is even taller." After three years, the couple's youngest son went to live with his mother, and Perry continued to care for the two other sons. Until both boys reached a sound age with sufficient self-confidence, a constant problem for Perry was making sure they got on and off the school bus safely. Because Perry worked in Manhattan and lived in the suburbs on Long Island, he called home and the school constantly. As Perry recalled, "I could not rest until I was assured that they were safe at home. When it snowed or the weather was bad it became even more difficult. This went on 5 days a week." In his view, "All that I was doing for my boys and continue to do falls under the heading of nurturing."

Nearly a decade ago Dean became a widower when his wife was murdered in broad daylight on the street where the family resided in Brooklyn, New York. Their two daughters were seven and eight years old at the time. In Dean's view, it was his maturity and the support he continues to receive from his family (mother, siblings, close friends) that guided him through all the pain and loss. Dean revealed:

I grew up surrounded by aunts and a lot of female family members. A lot of my younger cousins lived with me too. I saw a lot of what can be called nurturing taking place between all of my female relatives and their children and often I had to help out. I learned how to nurture. I guess I was being prepared for the future and what was to come later on in my life. It is not something one is born with; it is learned. That is why we continue to buy cars for boys and dolls for girls. I work in child care and I see women [who are supposed to be the nurturers] abuse their children just like men.

But Dean, a subscriber to the learned-behavior theory, might be seen by the human-instinct proponents as contradicting himself. Not long after his wife's death, his girls experienced early menstruation, which he learned might have been related to the trauma of their mother's homicide. This was not a problem for him as he immediately turned to his largely female family network, who were eager to assist.

Sharif's experience is somewhat similar to what Dean reported in his interview. Sharif was only eighteen when he married. After a brief stay in prison, he was released and vowed to get his life together. His two children were still young when he returned home. His wife was unable to deal with his positive outlook on life and no-nonsense attitude. The couple argued a lot. She left, and for the next three years, he was a full-time single parent. Sharif believes that a man can learn to be a positive nurturer which is how he perceived himself. However, as he explained, "During my time as a single father of a daughter and a son, when something came up pertaining to my daughter that I was unable to address, I sent her to my sister or other available women in the familial and friendship network. It was never a problem for my daughter or me." The contradiction that neither Dean nor Sharif seemed to realize, which human-instinct supporters might say buttresses their side of the debate, is that they learned how to nurture because they were surrounded by women. Simply put, the fact is that most men learn to nurture from women.

Cathy is an unmarried, registered nurse and mother of an eighteen-year-old daughter who is currently attending college away from home. Following her daughter's birth, an agreement was reached with the father that gave her custody. Both she and her daughter maintain a positive relationship with her daughter's father. In her view,

> Nurturing sounds like a feminine word, but I don't think women are born with maternal instincts. Granted, the mother has her role and she has things that only she can do like breast feeding and so on. But there are a lot of women out there who don't breast feed; for example, I did not breast feed my daughter. In the complex where I live all the men I see are involved with their children. I see fathers across racial groups who are very involved with their children. I see nurturing from both the father and the mother. I can't say that one parent is more nurturing than the other.

Pat, a public administrator, raised her son pretty much by herself after she and her son's father, a creative artist, were divorced. Certain of their values collided, and they came to the realization that they were better off living apart. Pat's perspective on nurturing is interesting:

> Nurturing is all about providing an environment that would allow children to grow. It is instinctive to women but some men actually have it. When men do it, it is different. My son's father is a good example. He was great at domestic things and he could even cook better than me. Nurturing is a combination of learning and instinct. Parents should allow their sons to cry and express their feelings; that is how men will learn to become nurturers.

When Pat was probed to explain how nurturing could be instinctive to women yet a man could become so competent at it, she admitted that she could not explain.

Susan's husband left her and her two daughters when the girls were only one and five years old. The younger daughter was born with cerebral palsy and has always required special services. Her elder daughter, who completed university and is a primary-school teacher, presently resides at home. Her second daughter, now twenty-one years old, also resides at home. It is Susan's belief that "nurturing comes with giving birth to a child. It is part of a women's nature. It is something unique to women. I guess it is possible that a man could learn to be a nurturer.

But from my experience, men, when put up against certain domestic challenges, fizzle out."

These narratives are revealing. They indicate a clear divide along gender lines regarding the parents' definition of nurturing. The fathers seem to reject the constructed/feminized definition of the term that limits it to an outpouring of emotion and sensitivity. Rather, they advance a broad definition that would include attending events at their children's schools, playing sports, coaching, or activities that might be labeled masculine. The contradicting responses from Dean and Sharif and also from Pat and Susan remind us that nurturing is an extremely complex subject that will continue to be debated well into the future.

Dating and Nurturing

Many fathers and mothers expressed an interest in having a social life and dating; however, none was prepared to compromise the primary function of nurturing the children. They all felt the need to protect their children from any emotional trauma related to bringing someone new into their lives. More fathers in the sample than mothers reported that they dated, albeit irregularly. Ten of the thirteen fathers indicated that they dated while a single parent. Two fathers got engaged during that period, but in both cases they broke off their engagements. One of these fathers, Paul, said the problem with his fiancée was that she tried too hard to replace the children's mother and the children did not like that. Similarities between fathers and mothers on the matter of dating were glaring. All believed that dating and parenting should be kept separate.

Pat, the public administrator raising a son, reflects this sentiment: "I was the one dating, not my son; therefore I felt it important to keep my dates at a distance from my home; we arranged to meet outside. Of course, if I felt that a stable relationship might develop that would be a different situation."

Mike, the father of two boys, was perhaps the most active dater in the overall sample. He admitted having his share of female friends; however, he expressed the same concern for his children's welfare as did Pat: "If a woman slept over at my place, I would make sure she was out by the time my boys woke up the next morning."

Tim, the father of two sons, expressed the need to be extra cautious because his spouse ran off with another man. His older son, then ten years old, seemed to be affected more than his younger son by his mother's departure. As Tim recalled, "One day he blurted out that his mother is a whore. I did not know where he heard that word, but he seemed to know what it meant. Ever since then I have been extra careful about dating and who I introduce to my children."

Who Has It Easier: Single Dads or Single Moms?

Because of their rarity, there is a persistent myth that single fathers receive more sympathy than single mothers and as a result receive more help from family and friends and other support systems (Coles 2003). As I noted earlier, such an outpouring of sympathy would help reduce some of the daily pressure and enable these fathers to become more effective nurturers. But what is interesting to note is that single fathers also perceive single mothers as disproportionately benefiting from what could be termed "societal sympathy." James Levine, a fatherhood advocate, discusses the matter of societal sympathy in terms of the "invisible dilemma." That is, fathers and mothers are beginning to demonstrate parity in fulfilling parenting activities; however, because women tend to talk about their daily challenges and experiences, they continue to receive an outpouring of sympathy (Conner 2001:1). Thus, an interview and questionnaire item posed to subjects was: "Do you believe that single fathers or single mothers have it easier"?

Liz is a divorced mother of one son, who is about to graduate from college. Her former spouse and the father of her son was not ready for marriage and the responsibility that comes with raising a family. That led to their eventual divorce. Liz is a college graduate with a steady income who has taken care of her son ever since, but she admits that it has been frustrating at times, especially during the teen years. Discipline issues, some disrespect, and peer pressure, all seemed to occur simultaneously. She sometimes doubted herself or for that matter a woman's ability to raise a boy. But eventually as she stated: "With the combination of firmness, love, and prayers things began to turn around." Liz talked to friends who were single mothers and single fathers. She was able to identify with their experiences and realized that she was not alone. Her response to the question of who has it is easier was: "I think that single mothers and single fathers have it about the same."

Cathy, the registered nurse, thought single mothers garner more social sympathy:

SINGLE CUSTODIAL FATHERS AND MOTHERS · 117

I feel it may be a little more difficult for a man because he may not have the same kind of support from the outside world as do women. People feel sympathy for women. Towards [the woman's former partner, they say,] "How could he do that to her, poor thing?" and so on. A friend of mine has five children that he had to take care of on his own and did a super job, braiding hair and all. This is the same thing that mothers go through.

Tim, the abandoned father of two boys, was extremely adamant in his response that single dads encounter more barriers:

From what I have experienced out there, the system is stacked against men. It is much more difficult for single fathers than single mothers. The assumption is that the man is the negligent one who abandoned his family. Even the tax structure is harder on men, taking a greater percentage of their gross income for child support. Perhaps men are being forced to pay the price for decades and decades of abuse of women. This is why I am forming a support network for Black single fathers to fight this unfair treatment against men.

Ken, a widower, acknowledged the fact of gender inequality and its implications for the circumstances women often find themselves versus men.

Overall men may have the edge on women when it comes to matters such as finance and employment. Because I am an associate professor with an okay salary, after my wife's death, I was able to maintain stability at our house and our standard of living which might have been more difficult for many women today.

Many of the eleven mothers took the position that men might have it harder only because of their unfamiliarity with or inability to carry out certain domestic requirements. Generally, they seemed to accept as fact men's helplessness and perennial dependency upon women when it comes to domestic matters. Sue's statement, which was presented earlier, sums up these single mothers' position: "Men, when put up against certain domestic challenges, fizzle out".

Dean, one of the three widowers, considers men's domestic frailness an obstacle to be eliminated if men are to assume their rightful role as caretakers of their children. He adds:

Society hears "single parent" and people still automatically assume it is a woman headed unit. Because men are still viewed as providers and the woman as "nurturers" men will continue to have it harder. Society says to a man, go find a job and support those children. For a woman, society assumes that they have been abandoned.

Mike is convinced that fathers experience a lot of frustrations that women do not have to go through. As an example he cited an experience at a Washington, D.C., public-assistance office that reinforces Dean's argument concerning single fathers' negative image in the eyes of staff and administrators at public agencies and the need for them to assert themselves and change that image. Mike recalled what happened during his visit to a social service office to enquire about assistance: "As I approached the desk I was immediately greeted by an intake worker with the question: 'Are you here to make a payment?' As other men entered the office they were immediately hit with that same question."

The experiences that Tim, Dean, and Mike report are not imagined or unique to them. Recent work by Hamer and Marchioro (2002) focuses on this very form of gender discrimination. As more men become single custodial parents, they will be forced to become more sensitive to the indignities and mistreatment that women have experienced for decades.

For many single parents the toughest part of the day after a long and tiring day at work is returning home to "the second shift," a cliché made popular in the 1980s (Hochschild 2003). That shift referred mainly to dual-career mothers (single and married) who left one full-time job only to return home to a second, which entailed getting supper started, supervising homework, and getting prepared for the next day. Whether single mothers or fathers receive more hours of outside assistance from relatives and friends is still debated (Santrock and Warshak 1979; Barker 1994). All of the parents from this study resided alone with their children and did not benefit from the services of a live-in nanny. One father, Tim, hired a part-time person to meet his kids from prekindergarten and kindergarten and to serve a lunch that Tim had already prepared. Surprisingly, while none of the other fathers (or, for that matter, any of the mothers) benefited from Mike's experience of having cared for younger siblings, they all expressed having learned how to cook, clean, and do laundry while growing up. Some fathers said that they actually enjoyed cooking; nevertheless, there were still days when they came home tired and would have preferred going straight to bed. Many fathers reported that after a while it all became routine.

Fathers and mothers from this study reinforced the crucial role that support systems played and continue to play in carrying out their roles as single parents. A questionnaire item asked subjects to indicate how frequently (i.e. daily, weekly, monthly) relatives and friends assisted them with various tasks. The findings did not reveal that fathers exceeded mothers in terms of their demand for help. Moreover, when they did seek help from parents, siblings, friends or the child/ children's other parent, it was mainly in the areas of child care and problem solving. Finally, when the need arose, fathers as well as mothers reached out to school counselors, teachers, religious pastors, and social fathers for help.

Gender and Nurturing

It is a generally held belief that single fathers are better nurturers of sons than of daughters and that in deciding whether to pursue custody, they choose sons over daughters. Moreover, it is also believed that single parents with a child or children of the same gender often have it easier. Although the findings are mixed, most studies have shown that the child's gender is a factor in fathers', more so than mothers', decisions to pursue custody (Chang and Deinard 1982; Greif 1990; Meyer and Garasky 1993). Earlier research found that fathers are often more involved with sons because of shared interests (i.e., fathers having more in common with boys than girls) and because mothers press for more father involvement with sons (Coles 2003).

The present study involved a total of forty-five children; 47 percent (twenty-one) were boys and 53 percent (twenty-four) were girls. Interestingly, as shown in table 5.3, when we look at how this breaks down

Table 5.3
Fathers and Mothers Caring for Children by Sex and Number of Children

Sex of Children	Fathers	No. of Children	Mothers	No. of Children
Girls only	5	10	4	6
Boys only	5	9	4	4
Boys and girls	3	7	3	9
Total	13	26	11	19

between the fathers and mothers, we observe an almost equal number of fathers and mothers supervising children of the opposite sex. A similar number of parents had a combination of sons and daughters in their care.

Only one single father in the sample expressed his preference to raise a boy. Sporty works in sales and is also a business teacher. He has raised his son since he was six years old when he worked out an agreement with his son's mother that made him the custodial parent. Sporty is still single and, at the time of his interview, his son was one year away from graduation from an out-of-state college. He firmly believes that it is easier to be father to a son than a daughter. In fact, he admits that if he had a daughter instead of a son he might have arrived at a different decision regarding full-time single parenting. Echoing some of the single fathers in Coles's study (this volume), Sporty says,

> I guess being a man it's easier to pass different things on to a son, those things that you have experienced as opposed to having daughters. Mostly with daughters you have not experienced a lot of the things they are going through so you can't totally relate to what they're going through. With a boy you have a better point of reference; you went through what they're going through.

Both fathers and mothers may have it easier with children of the same sex, but single mothers and single fathers don't always have a choice about the gender of their children.

Conclusion

As stated in the introduction, the aim of this chapter was not to ignite a gender war by declaring one gender more effective than the other in performing its role as a single parent. Through mainly qualitative methodology, the objective of the chapter was to increase awareness about single custodial fathers' perception of themselves and their roles as newcomers in an arena that has been the historical domain of single mothers.

The data is that single custodial fathers and single mothers have much more in common with each other than they are aware in terms of strongly held values, their demand for outside support, the problems they encounter with their children, and their personal frustrations, as well as their hopes and aspirations for their children. Nurturing is critical to the study of parenting, and it provided the backdrop for the comparison of single fathers and mothers. The persistent debate on nurturing between those from the learned-behavior school and those from the maternal-instinct school is a major factor in the reverse gender discrimination that single fathers continue to experience.

Not overlooked in this chapter are the perceptions single fathers and mothers have of each other, much of which is clouded by stereotypes and mythology. Several strategies can be considered in order to help minimize the competition between single fathers and single mothers. Forums can be held in the communities at the usual gathering places such as churches and community centers where these issues can be aired and where single fathers and mothers can meet and interact. Helping these parents to see how much they have in common is essential. If they are able to flush out the existing misconceptions held about one another then they will be in a better position to close ranks and help strengthen the quality life for all single parents and their children.

Interviews with fathers led to the identification of policies that could help cushion these men from the daily pressures of single fathering. If the local public schools, for example, could extend the after-school program beyond the standard six p.m. cutoff, that would give fathers sufficient travel time to pick up their kids, especially on those occasions of major transportation delays. Human resources departments and employers (in both the public and private sectors) should be persuaded to make certain policy considerations to accommodate single-father employees who from time to time might need to request a flexible schedule in order to attend to a school-related matter or an emergency. Some employers already have these policies in place for their single-mother employees (Conner 2001:2).

Public-school chancellors, district superintendents, and teacher unions should be encouraged to sponsor districtwide forums for teachers and staff on the emergence of single-father-only families. Children need to be informed that these families exist, which might help to lessen the awkward feelings some children living in single-father families may experience in their interaction with other children. Agencies to which single fathers have to reach out, for example the child-support division at the local family court or TANF (Temporary Assistance for Needy Families) centers, where men have experienced mistreatment because of their gender, should be called upon to offer special sensitivity-training workshops for their employees and staff conducted by consultants from father-centered organizations such as the Fatherhood Project and Responsible Single Fathers.

The present study is viewed as a preliminary step to a larger investigation. Future research should appeal for resources to support an expanded version of this study that would enable findings to be generalized across a wider population. Another proposal for future research might consider an outcome study that would generate either longitudinal data on the children from father-only families or identify adults who grew up in these families. It would be an important contribution to the literature to learn how the children from these families have fared vis-à-vis children and adults who grew up in mother-only households.

References

Associated Press. 2001. "Census Shows Single-Father Homes on the Rise." *Berkeley Daily Planet,* May 18. http://www.berkeleydailyplanet.com/issue/2001-05-18/article/4999?headline=Census-shows-single-father-homes-on-the-rise. Accessed March 22, 2009.

Avins, M. 2000. "Having His Say." *Newsday,* February 7.

Barker, R. W. 1994. *Lone Fathers and Masculinities.* Aldershot, U.K.: Avebury.

Barras, R. 2000. *Whatever Happened to Daddy's Little Girl?* New York: Ballantine Books.

Bloir, K. 2003. "Single Custodial Fathers." Ohio State University Fact Sheet. http://ohioline.osu.edu/hyg-fact/5000/5310.html. Accessed February 5, 2008.

Blum, D. L. 2002. *Love at Goon Park.* Cambridge, Mass.: Perseus.

Chang, P., and A. S. Deinard. 1982. "Single-Father Caretakers." *American Journal of Orthopsychiatry* 52:236–42.

Coles, R. L. 2003. "Black Single Custodial Fathers: Factors Influencing the Decision to Parent." *Families in Society: Journal of Contemporary Human Services* 84 (2): 247–58.

Collins, P. H. 1990. *Black Feminist Theory.* Boston: Unwin Hyman.

Collins, R. 1988. *Theoretical Sociology.* New York: Harcourt Brace Jovanovich.

Conner, M. 2001. "The Invisible Dilemma: An Interview with the Fatherhood Project's James Levine." *Line Zine* (Spring): 1–4. http://www.linezine.com/5.1/interviews/jltid.htm.

Daniels, C. R. 1998. *Lost Fathers: The Politics of Fatherlessness in America.* New York: St. Martin's Press.

Davis, K. 1947. "Final Note on a Case of Extreme Isolation." *American Journal of Sociology* 60:429–37.

Engels, F. 1973. "The Origin of the Family, Private Property, and the State." 1884. In *Marx and Engels: Selected Works*, 204–334. Moscow: Progress.

Fritsch, J. 2001. "A Rise in Single Dads." *New York Times*. May 20.

Giddens, A., M. Duneier, and R. P. Appelbaum. 2007. *Introduction to Sociology*. 6th ed. N.Y.: Norton.

Greif, G. L. 1990. *The Daddy Track and the Single Father*. Lexington, Mass.: Lexington Books.

Hamer, J. 2001. *What It Means to Be Daddy: Fatherhood for Black Men Living Away from Their Children*. New York: Columbia University Press.

Hamer, J., and K. Marchioro. 2002. "Becoming Custodial Dads: Exploring Parenting Among Low-Income and Working-Class African-American Fathers." *Journal of Marriage and the Family* 64:116–29.

Harlow, H. F., and M. K. Harlow. 1962. "Social Deprivation in Monkeys." *Scientific American* 207:137–47.

Hochschild, A. R. 2003. *The Second Shift*. New York: Penguin.

Hooks, B. 1981. *Ain't I a Woman: Black Women and Feminism*. Boston: South End Press.

Hurst, C. E. 2007. *Social Inequality: Forms, Causes, Consequences*. New York: Pearson.

John, S. 2002. "Today's Dads at Work and at Play." *New York Family* (June): 14–16.

Kornblum, W. 2008. *Sociology in a Changing World*. 8th ed. Belmont, Calif.: Wadsworth.

Marriage and Family Encyclopedia. 2003. "Widowhood—Demography of the Widowed." http://family.jrank.org/pages/1753/Widowhood-Demography-Widowed .html. Accessed June 6, 2008.

Mead, G. H. [1934] 1971. *Mind, Self, and Society*. Chicago: University of Chicago Press.

Meyer, D. R., and S. Garsky. 1993. "Custodial Fathers: Myths, Realities, and Child Support Policy." *Journal of Marriage and the Family* 55:73–89.

Mullings, L. 1997. *On Our Own Terms: Race, Class, and Gender in the Lives of African- American Women*. New York: Routledge.

Ortner, S. B. 1974. "Is Female to Male as Nature Is to Culture?" In *Women, Culture, and Society*, ed. M. Z. Rosaldo and L. Lamphere, 68–87. Stanford, Calif.: Stanford University Press.

Paniccia, P. 2002. "New Trends in Child Custody." *New York Family* (June): 26–28.

Sacks, K. 1975. "Engels Revisited: Women, the Organization of Production, and Private Property." In *Toward an Anthropology of Women*, ed. R. R. Reiter, 211–34. New York: Monthly Review Press.

Sampson, R. J., and J. Laub. 1993. *Crime in the Making: Pathways and Turning Points Through Life*. Cambridge, Mass.: Harvard University Press.

Sanday, P. 1981. *Female Power and Male Dominance: On the Origins of Social Inequality*. Cambridge: Cambridge University Press.

Santrock, J. W., and R. A. Warshak. 1979. "Father Custody and Social Development in Boys and Girls." *Journal of Social Issues* 35:112–25.

Simons, R. L. et al. 2005. "Collective Efficacy, Authoritative Parenting, and Delinquency." *Criminology* 43 (4): 989–1030.

Stone, P. 2007. *Opting Out? Why Women Really Quit Careers and Head Home.* Berkeley: University of California Press.

Turnbull, C. M. 1983. *The Human Cycle.* New York: Simon and Schuster.

U.S. Census Bureau. 1999. "Facts for Features: Father's Day 1999: June 20." June 10. http://www.census.gov/Press-Release/www/1999/cb99ff08.html. Accessed June 6, 2008.

Weaver, B. 2002. "Dad's Day in School." *New York Family* (June): 10–13.

Welter, B. 1973. "The Cult of True Womanhood." In *The American Family in Social-Historical Perspective,* ed. Michael Gordon, 224–50. New York: St. Martin's Press.

Yeung, W. J., G. J. Duncan, and M. S. Hill. 2000. "Putting Fathers Back in the Picture: Parental Activities and Children's Adult Outcomes." *Marriage and Family Review* 29:97–113.

CHAPTER SIX

Public Assistance Receipt

A Comparison of Black and White Single-Father Families

AUREA K. OSGOOD AND RYAN D. SCHROEDER

The number of single-parent families has increased dramatically over the past several decades, with the greatest growth occurring in single-father families. The U.S. Census Bureau estimated in 2003 that almost 12.5 million American families were single-parent families: approximately 10 million were single-mother families and just over 2 million were single-father families (Fields 2003). Between 1970 and 2003, the proportion of single-father families grew from 1 percent to 6 percent of American families. Although they also make up less than one-quarter of single-parent families, single-father families are the fastest growing family form in the United States (Simmons and O'Neill 2001). The dramatic increase in single-father families is clear evidence that increasing numbers of fathers are assuming responsibility for their dependent children.

The overall number of single parents has grown as a result of dramatic increases in unmarried childbearing, divorce, and delay in marriage. The recent increase in single-father families has resulted from a combination of these factors as well as a shift in custody awards from sole maternal custody to both paternal and shared custody arrangements (Seltzer 1994). The growth in this family type has sparked researchers and policymakers to look closely at the social forces driving this increase and the dynamics and consequences involved.

While single fathers and single-father families have received some attention in both popular media and academics, *black* single-father families have been largely ignored in this conversation. The black single father is often viewed as unattached or uninvolved with his biological children, and much of the academic research has focused on the governmental push for "responsible fatherhood" (Johnson and Sum 1987; Savage 1987; Pirog-Good 1993) and nonresidential fatherhood (e.g., Marsiglio 1987, 1991). This research will focus on custodial black single fathers in an effort to rectify this omission.

Looking at the research on single fatherhood, one might conclude that black single fathers are nonexistent. However, data suggest that there is a higher rate of black single fatherhood than white single fatherhood. In fact, by the mid-1990s, black custodial fathers made up 12 percent of all custodial fathers and 6 percent of all custodial parents within the black community (National Urban League 1998). This impression may be related to the complexity of the black single-father family. For example, research uses countless terms to identify single fathers: "unmarried father," "father only," "residential single father," "male-headed families" (Coles 2002). This confusion blurs our understanding of the prevalence and implications of the black single-father family.

Recent U.S. Census data suggest that by 2002, 4 percent of all white children and 5 percent of all black children were living with a single father (Fields 2003). Estimates for 2004 suggest that just over 2 million children were living with single fathers: 1.7 million white children and 359,000 black children (Kreider 2008). Because there has not been much representative research, we know relatively little about the functioning of single-father families, the well-being of children in them, and the dynamics characterizing this familial environment, and even less about the diversity within this emerging family form.

Recent research has only just begun to examine the outcomes of children living in single-parent families, including single-father families. Current research has focused almost exclusively on single-mother families and child outcomes in these family types. Such limitations are often the result of poor data collection on fathers as the primary respondent or, importantly, as primary caregivers. Little research has focused exclusively on single-father families, and even less on black single-father families (Coles 2002; Hamer and Marchioro 2002). In contrast, single-mother families have been the subject of extensive research (McLanahan and Booth 1989; Hogan, Hao, and Parish 1990; Thompson, Hanson, and McLanahan 1994; Hogan, Eggebeen, and Clogg 1996; McLanahan and Sandefur 1996). Perhaps the most influential debate surrounding single motherhood is its association with poverty. Researchers have amassed ample evidence to document the precarious economic conditions faced by many single mothers.

By comparison, few researchers have considered the economic context of single-father families. Single-father families are better off economically than single-mother families but are disadvantaged compared to married-couple families (Beller and Graham 1985; Demo and Acock 1988; Hogan, Hao and Parish 1990; Fox and Kelly 1995; Lino 1995; Eggebeen, Snyder, and Manning 1996; Hao 1996; McLanahan and Sandefur 1996; Edin and Lein 1997). Additionally, research suggests that black single fathers are more likely than white single fathers to have lower incomes and are more likely to rely on relatives for social and economic assistance (Edin and Lein 1997).

Notably, economic well-being appears to influence parenting. Studies show that single parents who reported financial problems also felt less competent as parents and reported less satisfaction in their role as parents (George and Wilding 1972; Katz 1979; O'Brien 1982). Given the linkages between family economic resources, parenting, and child well-being, it is important to examine these processes in understanding such family forms as the single-father family.

United States Census Bureau data suggest that single fathers are diverse in their characteristics (Fields and Casper 2000). Among all single-father families, less than 10 percent include infants, compared to 11 percent among black single-father families and less than 8 percent among white single-father families. Black single fathers are slightly more likely than white single fathers to have only one child but no more likely to have three or more children. These data show that nearly half (45 percent) of all single fathers are divorced, 34 percent are never married, 17 percent are separated, and 4 percent are widowed. Separating single fathers by race illuminates more diversity in marital status. Black single fathers are nearly twice as likely as white single fathers to be never married or separated from their spouse. White single fathers, on the other hand, are more than twice as likely as black single fathers to be divorced. What remains unclear are the differences between black and white single-father families and the functioning of these families.

This research will address the question: To what degree do black and white custodial single fathers use public assistance programs? The goal of this research is to advance our understanding of the economic strategies used by single-father families. Current public policy focuses on single mothers and their children but overlooks the increasing population of single-father families. Research on single-mother families has consistently shown that support networks and public assistance enhance parenting and child well-being (Edin and Lein 1997). Further research suggests that single mothers are more likely than single fathers to use formal assistance programs, such as cash assistance or in-kind assistance (Osgood 2003). In a national sample of single parents, Osgood (2003) found that among single parents earning less than 200 percent of the federal poverty line, single-father families are significantly less likely to receive formal cash and formal in-kind assistance than single-mother families. This research will attempt to focus our assistance agendas on the increasing population of single-father families, who may present unique characteristics relative to single-mother families.

Basic descriptive information on black and white single-father families will be presented in this research, as well as a portrait of the economic circumstances of black and white single-father families. Using survey data from the National Survey of America's Families (NSAF), this research will address the extent of use of public assistance programs (cash and in-kind) among single-father families, focusing on the differences between black and white single-father families.

Economic Challenges and Strategies of the Single-Parent Family

Research suggests that fathers with custody face considerable economic hardship, compared to married fathers (George and Wilding 1972; Hipgrave 1981), mostly because of an increase in familial responsibility and the resulting career and social changes: shifts to less-demanding career, loss of overtime, a decrease in social networks with professional associates, and an overall increase in the time spent at home with children. These shifts in roles and responsibilities may cause some anxiety among single fathers. Single fathers, however, are more prepared *economically* for the parenting role than are single mothers. On average, single fathers have better paying, more stable jobs than single mothers and are less likely to have to quit. This added buffer allows single fathers more flexibility in their schedules as well as more aid from childcare providers, housekeepers, and other domestic assistants.

Approximately 22 percent of all single-father families are near poor, and 16 percent are living below the official federal poverty line (Fields and Casper 2001). National estimates suggest that among white single fathers, 10 percent live below the poverty line, compared to 25 percent of black single fathers. However, recent research shows that only 7 percent of all single-father families use means-tested cash-assistance programs (U.S. Bureau of the Census 2002). Research has not addressed the racial differences in assistance receipt among single fathers, but given their disadvantaged economic standing compared to white single fathers, a higher rate of benefit receipt among black single-fathers would be logical.

Research on single-mother families has consistently shown that support networks and public assistance enhance parenting and child well-being (Stack 1974; Edin and Lein 1997; Sudarkasa 1997). Single mothers often rely on several sources for economic assistance, including child support, public assistance (Aid to Families with Dependent Children, Temporary Assistance to Needy Families), in-kind programs (food stamps, Medicaid), kin support, and community resources. Single fathers also rely on these networks and programs for assistance (Rosenthal and Kershet 1981), although few researchers have focused on these families and their receipt. Out of necessity, the focus of the review that follows will be on single-mother families and their use of assistance. Information on single fathers will be included as available.

Strong support networks provide single parents with relief from the stress related to solo parenting (Gersick 1979); however, current research suggests that fathers are disadvantaged by a lack of sufficient access to public assistance programs (for example, advertisements for services and programs are typically not directed to fathers) as well as a lack of informal support (Hamer and Marchioro 2002), such as parenting support groups, same-sex friends with sole custody, or supportive educators. Specifically, low-income men and men of color are less likely than their white middle-class counterparts to use such support and are less likely to have opportunity to relax their work schedules and other work commitments (Hamer and Marchioro 2002). Similarly, middle-class fathers and low-income, working-class fathers use different types of support networks. Middle-class, white fathers are more likely to date and have intimate relationships, creating additional support, and are more likely to marry than low-income fathers (Hamer and Marchioro 2002). Black single parents are more likely to rely on relatives and kin for support and resources including childcare, emergency shelter, and economic assistance (Stack 1974; Edin and Lein 1997). Even within poor and near-poor single-parent families, single fathers are less likely to receive public assistance than single mothers (Meyer and Garasky 1996), creating further strain on themselves and their children. Low-income single fathers, according to Hamer and Marchioro (2002) often do not realize that they qualify for public assistance such as cash assistance and food stamps. When these fathers do apply for assistance, they are often met with negative responses and general distrust (Hamer and Marchioro 2002). In our research, we explore the differential economic strategies employed by single fathers of different racial backgrounds.

Formal Cash Assistance

Many single mothers rely on some type of economic assistance following a separation or divorce. However, only 22 percent of single mothers receive cash assistance (AFDC or TANF) a year after a separation, and welfare payments are generally low (Seltzer 1994). In 1995, the U.S. Census Bureau reported that single-mother households were five times as likely to participate in major means-tested programs as married-couple households (Tin and Castro 2001). In addition, more women than men receive benefits (23 million women versus 16 million men) (Tin and Castro 2001). Hispanics are three times as likely as white non-Hispanics to receive benefits for at least one month and have participation rates more than three times that of white non-Hispanics (Tin and Castro 2001). Literature on single fathers' use of public assistance, however, remains unavailable.

Formal In-Kind Assistance

In-kind benefits (for example, food stamps and Medicaid) have grown in importance over the past thirty years as instruments of transfer in the United States (Slesnick 1996). In-kind transfers have roughly the same impact on the poverty rate as cash assistance. The limitation of these programs seems to be the manner in which benefits are distributed to recipients. Individuals were more likely to participate in Medicaid than any other program, but they were more likely to participate in housing-subsidy programs for longer durations. In-kind programs, such as food stamps and Medicaid, do not, however, bring children in single-mother families into parity with children from intact, two-parent families (Garfinkel and McLanahan 1986; Seltzer 1994). Again, literature on single fathers' use of in-kind support programs is unavailable.

Importantly, these formal and in-kind assistance programs have been cited as racist by both academics and politicians (Gordon 1994; Quadagno 1994; Neubeck and Cazenave 2001). These critics have suggested that the welfare system has systematically excluded blacks from its programs. For example, through the New Deal era, domestic servants and agricultural workers were denied entitlement, disproportionately denying blacks assistance (Gordon 1994). Blacks therefore may come to the welfare system with this historical discrimination in mind, viewing its use as a handout or pity rather than entitlement or as being need-based. Kenneth Neuback and Noel Cazenave (2001) remind us that at the same time black mothers were being blamed for many of society's problems—from rampant drug use to the decline of the American family—"race" and "welfare" became synonymous for politicians and scholars alike. Further, public-opinion surveys (Neuback and Cazenave 2001) suggest that white welfare recipients are viewed with compassion and black recipients with contempt. Early assistance programs—from Mothers Pension to Aid to Dependent Children—have discriminated against black mothers or were implemented in a discriminatory manner, typically by providing states with the power to execute policies based on their own agendas (Neuback and Cazenave 2001). Given this historical mistreatment, we believe that although black single fathers are in a more disadvantaged economic position in our society than white single fathers, their odds of receipt of formal of in-kind assistance will not be significantly higher than white single fathers.

Data and Methodology

This study is designed to advance our knowledge of the well-being and functioning of black single-father families and their relationships with formal economic-assistance programs using current, nationally representative data. The focus of this study is on the economic well-being of black single-father families and will attempt to highlight the strategies of economic security used by these single fathers. Specifically, we provide a descriptive portrait of black single-father families, and we assess the degree to which children in black single-father families use public assistance programs, as compared to white single-father families. We use the 2002 National Survey of America's Families (NSAF), a large-scale national survey of economic, health, and social characteristics of children and nonelderly adults. We use white single-father families as the main comparison group to delineate the similarities and differences between these two key populations.

Unlike much of the previous research, the current study will contribute to the growing base of knowledge about families' economic well-being and structure by using a large, nationally representative data set to focus on the economic well-being of black single-father families, in terms of their use of public assistance programs. Previous studies of economic-assistance strategies have focused primarily on single-mother families, while single-father families have remained at the margins. In addition to redirecting the focus to single-father families, this study offers a more comprehensive understanding of formal assistance receipt, opening the door for future research to look at the relationship between formal assistance receipt and dimensions of family well-being in single-father families.

The National Survey of America's Families

We use data from the National Survey of America's Families (NSAF), a nationally representative survey of the economic, health, and social characteristics of children, adults under the age of sixty-five, and their families (Converse et al. 1999). The NSAF is particularly useful because it includes several measures of economic security, program participation, and informal assistance networks. Three rounds of these cross-sectional data were collected: the first in 1997, the second in 1999, and the third in 2002. We use the third round of data because of its substantial changes to the earlier program-participation section and the recent collection of data. Information on more than 100,000 individuals (and nearly 40,000 households with approximately 35,000 children) was collected for the 2002 round. The NSAF gathered information from several respondents in each household. For households with children, different interviews were completed for children under the age of six and between six and seventeen. Interviews were conducted with the most knowledgeable adult (MKA). In most cases, the MKA is the child's biological parent. Results from the NSAF are representative of the civilian, noninstitutionalized population under the age of sixty-five in the United States.

As this study is looking at the difference between black and white single-father families, children in other living arrangements are excluded. Both extended and cohabiting family structures differ from single-parent families (Lerman 2003; Manning and Brown 2003), and thus these children are excluded, even though they may be living with a single parent. Since non-biological-parent families make up a small proportion of overall families, they are also excluded for the purpose of this study. These exclusions limited the restricted sample to 964 families. Because we are mainly interested in black and white single-father-headed households, we further restrict the sample to include only black and white families (N = 868). The sample was further limited to families headed by adults sixty-five years of age and younger (N = 849) to reduce the possibility of grandparent-grandchild households, and was limited to U.S. citizens (N = 831). Finally, we eliminated all families with missing values on the receipt of cash or in-kind benefit variables, as well as those families with missing information on the marital history variable. The final sample size for this analysis is 823 families: 694 (84 percent) of which are headed by white single fathers, and 129 (16 percent) are headed by black single fathers. Missing values on the independent variables were rare (generally less than 2 percent of all cases) and were recoded with the mean value for each variable.

Dependent Variables

Two individual measures of *formal assistance* are included. The first consists of major cash programs: TANF (sometimes asked as "AFDC"). A dummy variable is included as to whether (1) the family is receiving TANF currently or (0) the family is not receiving TANF. A second measure of formal assistance is designed to assess the use of food stamps, which is a formal in-kind assistance program. This variable is coded (1) for receipt of in-kind assistance through the food stamp program or (0) for no receipt.

Primary Independent Variable

For the purpose of the logistic regression, race will serve as the primary independent variable, as this study serves as an investigation into possible differences in assistance participation between (1) black single-father and (0) white single-father families.

Independent Variables

For the analyses, control variables will be included that have been previously shown to have an effect on participation in assistance programs among black single-father and white single-father families. These variables include characteristics of the single father and the number and general age range of children in the household. Parent characteristics include age, marital history, employment status, and education history. *Age* is coded in years. *Marital history* is dummy coded to indicate whether the respondent is (1) ever married or (0) never married. *Employment status* is coded as a dummy variable indicating whether the respondent was at any point in the past year working (2), looking for work (1), or not working (0). *Education* is dummy coded to indicate whether the parent has completed less than twelve years (0), a high school education (1), or more than twelve years of education (2). The number of children in the household is grouped into two different variables indicating the *number of children in the household less than five years old* and the *number of children in the household ages six to seventeen.*

Analytic Strategy

First, a table of means and standard errors is produced for both black and white single-father families to provide a descriptive portrait of the two groups. Second, logistic regression analyses are completed for each of the two measures of formal assistance to assess the differences in odds of receiving cash or in-kind benefits by race. For each of the two dependent variables, two logistic models are estimated. The first model includes only race to establish the bivariate relationship between the racial classifications of the single-father families and receipt of financial assistance. The second model controls for the effects of relevant family (number of children in the two age groups) and individual father characteristics (age, educational history, marital history, and employment status). Because the dependent variables (receipt of cash and in-kind assistance) are coded as binary variables (1 = receipt, 0 = no receipt), logistic regression is used to analyze the odds of receipt.

As standard errors generally assume a simple random sample, additional steps were taken to correct for the complex sampling design of the NSAF. Using replicate weights to correct for oversampling, subsampling, and clustering design, corrected standard errors are reported in all analyses. Results of this analysis are generalizable to American single fathers.

Results

The weighted means and standard errors of the variables included in this study are shown in table 6.1. Of the final sample size of 823 single-father families, approximately 16 percent are black single-father families and 84 percent are white. For the total sample, approximately 8 percent of the single-father families receive formal cash assistance, and 13 percent receive assistance from the food-stamps program. While black single-father families receive these benefits at a slightly higher rate than white single-father families (17 percent versus 11 percent),[1] the difference in the proportion of these households receiving cash or in-kind benefits is not statistically significant.

In addition, black and white single fathers significantly differed in their marital status (64 percent of black single fathers are ever married; 87 percent of white single fathers are ever married) and age (black single fathers are, on average, thirty-eight years old; white single fathers are, on average, forty-one years old).

While both black and white single-father families enjoy familial incomes appreciably above the federal poverty level, with an overall average income of approximately 290 percent of the 2002 federal poverty line, black and white single fathers significantly differ on poverty status. As measured, black single fathers had incomes, on average, at 246 percent of the federal poverty level, and white single fathers have, on average, incomes at 302 percent of the federal poverty level. Specifically, black and white single fathers significantly differ in their likelihood of living below the federal poverty line: 10 percent of white

Table 6.1

Mean Comparisons Between Black and White Single Fathers

Variables	Total Sample		Black		White	
	Mean	Std. error[1]	Mean	Std. error[1]	Mean	Std. error[1]
Receiving cash (TANF) assistance	0.079	0.019	0.112	0.045	0.071	0.023
Receiving in-kind (food stamps) assistance	0.131	0.017	0.312	0.090	0.180	0.024
Father's marital history[2]	0.822	0.023	0.638	0.066**	0.868	0.023
Father's age	40.435	0.475	38.355	1.338†	40.946	0.452
Number of children age 5 and under	0.291	0.030	0.492	0.102*	0.241	0.028
Number of children age 6–17	1.290	0.051	1.078	0.115*	1.342	0.056
Percent of the federal poverty level	2.908	0.059	2.461	0.136***	3.018	0.066
Percent living below 100% federal poverty level	0.116	0.016	0.180	0.052	0.100	0.015
Sample N =	823		129		694	
Weighted N =	1,288.053		253,962		1,034.091	

† ($p < .10$), *($p < .05$), **($p < .01$), ***($p < .001$) indicates significant differences between black and white single-father-headed households.
[1] Standard errors presented are adjusted using jackknife procedures to represent true population parameters.
[2] Marital history is coded (1) for ever-married (including divorced, widowed, separated) and (0) for never married.

single fathers and 18 percent of black single fathers are living below the poverty line.

Furthermore, black single-father families have significantly more children under age five living in their homes, but white single-father families include significantly more children between the ages of six and seventeen. So, even though the average number of children in black and white single-father-headed households are very similar (1.58 for black single-father families, 1.57 for white single-father families), black single fathers have substantially younger children in their custody, in addition to lower familial incomes.

Table 6.2 provides a distribution of black and white single fathers' employment and education statuses. As expected, white single fathers are more likely to have completed a bachelor's degree (22 percent, compared to 11 percent for black single fathers). White single fathers are also less likely to have not finished high school (12 percent, compared to 14 percent for black single fathers). White single fathers are also more likely to be currently working (81 percent, compared to 70 percent for black single fathers).

In sum, black single fathers are significantly younger, less educated, less likely to have ever been married than white single fathers, and more likely to be in poverty. Although black single-father families appear to be in situations of greater need to receive cash and in-kind benefits to support their families than white single fathers, the bivariate data show that black single fathers are not pursuing this option at any greater rate than white single fathers.

The logistic regressions predicting the odds of receiving cash and in-kind benefits are shown in table 6.3. The baseline model estimating the odds of receiving cash benefits by race of the single-father family confirms the findings of the bivariate results reported above, as race does not significantly influence the odds of receiving cash benefits. The multivariate model predicting receipt of cash assistance further shows that race is not a determinant factor in using cash benefits as an

Table 6.2
Sample Distribution for Education and Employment Status

	Black	White
Education Status		
No high school diploma or GED	14.0%	11.7%
High school diploma or GED, but no college degree	75.2	66.3
More than a bachelor's degree	10.9	22.0
Employment Status		
Not in the labor force	14.0	11.8
Currently looking for work	16.3	7.1
Currently employed	69.8	81.1

Table 6.3
Logistic Regressions Predicting Receipt of Cash and In-Kind Assistance

Variables	Cash Assistance		In-Kind Assistance	
	B	B	B	B
Racial classification	0.504	0.079	0.724+	0.094
Poverty level		−0.535		−1.230***
# Children age 5 and under		0.358		0.342
# Children age 6–17		−0.074		0.078
Father's age		−0.021		−0.041
Father's level of education		−1.038		−0.157
Father's employment status		−0.982†		−0.782***
Father's marital history		0.444		0.080
Model X^2 =	0.654	4.454***	2.841†	10.336***

† p < .10, *p < .05, ** p < .01, ***p < .001

economic strategy. In fact, none of the variables included in the mul-tivariate model influence the use of cash assistance programs except employment status, with the families where the single father is em-ployed being significantly less likely to receive cash benefits. It must be noted, however, that this effect is marginally significant and should be interpreted cautiously.

The baseline model for estimating the odds of receiving in-kind benefits by race show a slightly different pattern than the bivariate re-lationship. Black single-father families are significantly more likely to receive in-kind benefits, in the form of food stamps, than white single-father families in this model, but again this relationship is marginally significant (p < .10) and should be interpreted with caution. The effect of race, however, diminishes to insignificance once the other relevant family and individual father characteristics are controlled (such as fa-ther's economic characteristics). Employment status again emerges as a significant factor influencing the odds of receiving in-kind benefits, as does familial income as a percentage of the federal poverty line. Whatever small effect that race exerts in the odds of using in-kind ben-efits as an economic strategy is accounted for by the lower economic and employment standing of black single-father families.

Overall, the data indicate that black single-father families use economic strategies similar to those of white single-father families, despite the greater economic challenges faced by black single-father families.

Discussion

This study contributes to the growing body of research in the area of economic well-being among single fathers and their families. In this study, the economic strategies of black and white single-father families were compared, using the 2002 round of the National Survey of America's Families. The purpose of this study is to explore the possible racial differences in receipt of formal cash and in-kind assistance among custodial single fathers.

Although black and white single fathers differ substantially in terms of income, age, age of children, marital history, educational attainment, and employment status, black and white single fathers do not significantly differ in their limited use of formal assistance programs. This suggests that black and white single fathers are using similar strategies to maintain economic well-being for their families. Specifically, the data show that the majority of black and white single fathers are employed and earn incomes above the federal poverty line. Perhaps this combination of employment and income allows single fathers of all racial backgrounds to avoid formal assistance through lack of necessity. However, it must be reiterated that racial discrimination in the welfare system is widely cited and that this lack of assistance use among black single fathers may also be a direct or indirect result of discrimination or discouragement from within the system itself.

While national data suggest that only 22 percent of eligible single mothers are receiving formal cash assistance (Seltzer 1994), it remains interesting to note that less than 8 percent of our nationally representative sample of single fathers receive such support, even after controlling for eligibility (poverty status). While research tells us that single fathers are earning higher incomes, we speculate that single fathers are also seeking less supplemental support for themselves or their children (specifically in the form of formal cash assistance and food stamps, as this study suggests). It remains interesting that we continue to see general differences in receipt between blacks and whites (and between single mothers and single fathers). Loveless and Tin (2006) report that in 2003, 13 percent of whites and 41 percent of blacks were participating in means-tested programs, and 26 percent of male-headed households and 48 percent of female-headed households were participating in such programs. Perhaps these racial differences in receipt reflect the higher percentage of single mothers among blacks and their higher poverty rates. Future research would benefit from an extensive study of the racial difference not only for single fathers but for single mothers and single parents more generally.

The goal of this study is largely descriptive, aiming to better understand the economic differences between black and white single-father families. As such, we are unable to explain why black and white single fathers differ in some areas or how these differences might play out for children in such families. However, this study does advance our understanding of economic strategies of single fathers and suggests that while many black single fathers are eligible to receive assistance, few are receiving it.

We must note, however, some of the limitations to both our data and to the possible conclusions that can be drawn from such a study. First, our data only examine the usage of formal cash assistance and in-kind programs rather than focusing on all possible sources of support (financial or otherwise). It would be wise for future research to address informal strategies (religious organizations, community assistance programs, private charities, and family support) that single fathers might use to maintain their economic well-being. Second, because of additional data limitations, lifetime economic well-being cannot be measured. Rather, this study uses a point-in-time estimate of economic well-being. Using a measure of duration of poverty spells and of parental employment may better estimate economic well-being. It may also be beneficial to understand a family's full history of assistance receipt. For instance, Hipgrave (1981) found that while single-father families are less likely to use public assistance than single-mother families in general, single-father families are more likely to receive public assistance earlier rather than later in their single-parenthood experience.

Furthermore, this study is limited in its inability to control for selection into single-father families. Earlier research suggests that single-father families are unique in their composition and in their development (Seltzer 1994). For instance, single-father families may have resulted from a difficult custody battle, causing additional strain on the economic stability of the family. Also, single-father families may be formed after a court decision concludes that a child's mother is unfit to parent or that a child's mother declines responsibility to parent. Fathers may also be chosen as the primary custodial parent because of relative financial stability of the family.

This research suggests the need for additional research to focus on single-parent families and their economic well-being. A key direction of future research should be to expand the current analyses to include more complex family structures and additional economic strategies. Specifically, future research should conduct separate analyses for in-kind assistance programs and expand analyses to include additional types of single-parent families (such as lone parent, cohabiting, extended, or those preceded by divorce, widowhood, or never-married status). Future research would also benefit from discussions of single fathers' receipt of formal cash and in-kind assistance in the context of welfare-reform policies, specifically those encouraging employment and discouraging long-term program use. Additionally, future research should expand the current study by focusing on informal and kin support among single-father families, focusing on differences between single mothers and single fathers in assistance receipt, and adding controls for poverty spell duration and duration of family structure.

Notes

An earlier version of this paper was presented at the annual meeting of the Population Association of America in Boston, Mass., April 2004. The authors thank Meredith J. Porter and Susan L. Brown for their assistance on this manuscript.

1. In a separate analysis, we found that among black single-father families living below 100 percent of the federal poverty level (18 percent), 50 percent received cash assistance and 60 percent received food stamps. Among white single-father families living below 100 percent of the federal poverty level (10 percent), 23 percent received cash assistance, and 52 percent received food stamps. This equated to 31 percent of the total sample receiving cash assistance and 54 percent receiving food stamps, among those below 100 percent of the federal poverty level (12 percent).

References

Beller, A., and J. Graham. 1985. "Variations in the Economic Well-Being of Divorced Women and Their Children." In *Horizontal Equity, Uncertainty, and Economic Well-Being*, ed. Martin David and Timothy Smeeding, 471–510. Chicago: University of Chicago Press.

Coles, R. 2002. "Black Single Fathers: Choosing to Parent Full-Time." *Journal of Contemporary Ethnography* 31:411–39.

Converse, N., A. Safir, F. Scheuren, R. Steinback, and K. Wang. 1999. *Assessing the New Federalism*. 1999 NSAF Public Use File User's Guide. NSAF Methodology Report No. 11. Washington, D.C.: Urban Institute.

Demo, D. H., and A. C. Acock. 1988. "The Impact of Divorce on Children." *Journal of Marriage and the Family* 50:619–48.

Edin, K., and L. Lein. 1997. *Making Ends Meet: How Single Mothers Survive Welfare and Low-Wage Work*. New York: Russell Sage Foundation.

Eggebeen, D. J., A. R. Snyder, and W. D. Manning. 1996. "Children in Single-Father Families in Demographic Perspective." *Journal of Family Issues* 17:441–65.

Fields, J. 2003. *Children's Living Arrangements and Characteristics: March 2002*. Current Population Reports, P20-547. Washington, D.C.: U.S. Census Bureau.

Fields, J., and L. Casper. 2001. *American's Families and Living Arrangements: March 2000*. Current Population Reports, P20-537. Washington, D.C.: U.S. Census Bureau.

Fox, G. L., and R. F. Kelly. 1995. "Determinants of Child Custody Arrangements at Divorce." *Journal of Marriage and the Family* 57:693–708.

Garfinkel, I., and S. S. McLanahan. 1986. *Single Mothers and Their Children*. Washington, D.C.: Urban Institute.

George, V., and P. Wilding. 1972. *Motherless Families*. London: Routledge and Kegan Paul.

Gersick, K. 1979. "Fathers by Choice: Divorced Men Who Receive Custody of Their Children." In *Divorce and Separation*, ed. G. Levinger and O. C. Moles, 307–23. New York: Basic Books.

Gordon, L. 1994. *Pitied but Not Entitled: Single Mothers and the History of Welfare, 1890–1935*. New York: Free Press.

Hamer, J., and K. Marchioro. 2002. "Becoming Custodial Dads: Exploring Parenting Among Low-Income and Working-Class African American Fathers." *Journal of Marriage and the Family* 64:116–29.

Hao, L. 1996. "Family Structure, Private Transfers, and the Economic Well-Being of Families with Children." *Social Forces* 75:269–92.

Hipgrave, T. 1981. "Child Rearing by Lone Father." In *Changing Patterns of Child-Bearing and Child Rearing*, ed. R. Chester, P. Diggory, and M. B. Sutherland, 149–66. London: Academic Press.

Hogan, D., D. Eggebeen, and C. Clogg. 1993. "The Structure of Intergenerational Exchanges in American Families." *American Journal of Sociology* 98:1428–58.

Hogan, D., L. Hao, and W. Parish. 1990. "Race, Kin Networks, and Assistance to Mother-Headed Families." *Social Forces* 68:797–812.

Johnson, C., and A. Sum 1987. *Declining Earnings of Young Men: Their Relation to Poverty, Teen Pregnancy, and Family Formation*. Adolescent Prevention Clearinghouse report. Washington, D.C.: Children's Defense Fund.

Katz, A. J. 1979. "Lone Fathers: Perspectives and Implications for Family Policy." *Family Coordinator* 28:521–28.

Kreider. R. M. 2008. *Living Arrangements of Children: 2004*. Current Population Reports, P70-114. Washington, D.C.: U.S. Census Bureau.

Lerman, R. 2003. "How Do Marriage, Cohabitation, and Single Parenthood Affect the Material Hardships of Families and Children?" Paper presented at the annual meeting of the Population Association of America, Minneapolis, May 2003.

Lino, M. 1995. "The Economics of Single Parenthood: Past Research and Future Directions." In *Single Parent Families: Diversity, Myths, and Realities*, ed.

S. M. H. Hanson, M. L. Heims, D. J. Julian, and M. B. Sussman, 99–114. New York: Haworth Press.

Loveless, T., and J. Tin. 2006. *Dynamics of Economic Well-Being: Participation in Government Programs, 2001 Through 2003: Who Gets Assistance?* Current Population reports P70-108. Washington, D.C.: U.S. Census Bureau.

Manning, W., and S. Brown. 2003. "Children's Economic Well-Being in Cohabiting Parent Families: An Update and Extension." Paper presented at the annual meeting of the Population Association of America, Minneapolis, May 2003.

Marsiglio, W. 1987. "Adolescent Fathers in the United States: Their Initial Living Arrangements, Marital Expectations, and Education Outcomes." *Family Planning Perspectives* 19:240–51.

Marsiglio, W. 1991. "Male Procreative Consciousness and Responsibility: A Conceptual Analysis and Research Agenda." *Journal of Family Issues* 12:268–90.

McLanahan, S., and K. Booth. 1989. "Mother-Only Families: Problems, Prospects, and Politics." *Journal of Marriage and the Family* 51:557–80.

McLanahan, S., and G. Sandefur. 1996. *Growing Up in a Single-Parent Family: What Hurts, What Helps.* Cambridge, Mass.: Harvard University Press.

Meyer, D., and S. Garasky. 1993. "Custodial Fathers: Myth, Realities, and Child Support Policy." *Journal of Marriage and the Family* 55:73–89.

National Urban League. 1998. *The State of Black America.* New York: National Urban League.

Neubeck, K., and N. Cazenave. 2001. *Welfare Racism: Playing the Race Card Against America's Poor.* New York: Routledge.

O'Brien, M. 1982. "Becoming a Lone Father: Differential Patterns and Experiences." In *The Father Figure* ed. L. McKee and M. O'Brien, 184–207. London: Tavistock.

Osgood, A. 2003. "Economic Strategies of Single-Father Families." Master's thesis, Bowling Green State University.

Pirog-Good, M. A. 1993. "In-Kind Contributions as Child Support: The Teen Alternative Parenting Program." In *Young Unwed Fathers: Changing Roles and Emerging Policies*, ed. R. Lerman and T. Ooms, 251–66. Philadelphia: Temple University Press.

Quadagno, J. S. 1994. *The Color of Welfare: How Racism Undermined the War on Poverty.* New York: Oxford University Press.

Rosenthal, K.M., and H. F. Kershet. 1981. *Fathers Without Partners.* Totowa, N.J.: Rowman and Littlefield.

Savage, B. D. 1987. *Child Support and Teen Parents.* Washington, D.C.: Adolescent Prevention Clearinghouse, Children's Defense Fund.

Seltzer, J. A. 1994. "Consequences of Marital Dissolution for Children." *Annual Review of Sociology* 20:235–66.

Simmons, T., and G. O'Neill. 2001. *Households and Families: 2000.* Washington, D.C.: United States Bureau of the Census, Census 2000 Brief.

Slesnick, D. 1996. "Consumption and Poverty: How Effective Are In-Kind Transfers?" *The Economic Journal* 106:1527–45.

Stack, C. 1974. *All Our Kin: Strategies for Survival in a Black Community.* New York: Harper and Row.

Sudarkasa, N. 1997. "African American Families and Family Values." In *Black Families*, ed. H. P. McAdoo, 9–40. Thousand Oaks, Calif.: Sage.

Tin, J., and C. Castro. 2001. *Dynamics of Economic Well-Being: Program Participation, 1993 to 1995: Who Gets Assistance?* Current Population Reports P70-77. Washington, D.C.: U.S. Census Bureau.

Thompson, E., T. Hanson, and S. McLanahan. 1994. "Family Structure and Child Well-Being: Econmic Resources vs. Parental Behaviors." *Social Forces* 73:221–42.

United States Bureau of the Census. 2002. *Current Population Survey.* Table 3: "Program Participation Status of Households—Poverty Status of Persons In 2001." http://ferret.bls.census.gov/macro/032002/pov/new03_001.htm. Accessed October 9, 2002.

PART THREE

Social Fathering

CHAPTER SEVEN

Fathering in Low-Income Black Families

Studying Father-Figure Flows

MANSA BILAL MARK A. KING

Today, academic and policy discussions about the American family often focus on nonnuclear families. Single-mother families, in particular, have been center-stage since the 1960s. The most common arrangement invoked by the term "single-mother family" consists of a biological mother and her biological children, all living in a household that does not include the biological father. The missing father is a salient feature in discussions of the single-mother family. For example, children in such families are often labeled as fatherless. Some analysts (Popenoe 1996) define such families by the missing element and call the entire family fatherless. Concerns about fatherlessness have helped to produce a body of empirical and theoretical research linking biological-father involvement to children's emotional, cognitive, and behavioral well-being (Lerman and Ooms 1993; McLanahan and Sandefur 1994; Popenoe 1996; Lamb 1997, 2004).

Rates of fatherlessness vary by race. In the 2000 census, 35 percent of African American family households reportedly were headed by a woman; had children present who were related to that woman by birth, marriage, or adoption; and also had no husband present. In comparison, only 22 percent of Latino and a mere 8 percent of non-Latino white family households reported single-mother headship (U.S. Bureau of the Census 2000).[1] The rate of fatherlessness in African American communities has stimulated several studies that explicitly examine the links between race and fatherlessness (Lewis 1966; Massey and

Denton 1994; Quadagno 1994; Wilson 1996; Anderson 1999; Moynihan [1965] 1999; Hamer 2001).

These studies attempt to explain the connection between race and fatherlessness, particularly in the case of African American families. For example, Anderson (1999) presents black men who seek sexual relationships with women and then allow peer pressure to push them away from meaningful family responsibilities. The result is a pool of young unwed black mothers whose behavior allows outsiders to invoke "ghetto culture" as the cause of "amoral behavior" in poor black communities. In fact, drawing on Frazier (1939) and Lewis (1966), Moynihan ([1965] 1999) argues that the high rates of fatherlessness in black communities had become culturally rooted by the 1960s. He expresses concern that the casual sexual relationships that produce nonmarital births are a more-or-less fixed part of black culture because of decades of forced impoverishment. Alternatively, Hamer (2001) and Wilson (1996) view the high rates of fatherlessness in poor inner-city neighborhoods as a more malleable product of social forces. Hamer uses a wide lens that links black fatherlessness to political, economic, and cultural forces under the control of dominant racial, economic, and political groups. Wilson focuses heavily on deindustrialization as the main driver of "ghetto-related" behavior patterns, of which fatherless families is just one form. Primarily by focusing on the salient "problem" racial group, then, research on fatherlessness has brought black fathers into the contemporary American family discourse.

As already mentioned, some call single-mother households "fatherless families." However, this concept (and the empirical data typically invoked to support it) may obscure the involvement of nonresident biological fathers and social fathers. Again, black children are among the most likely American children to have nonresident biological fathers. Many black children also seem to have social fathers. A social father is any man who acts as a father toward another man's biological child (Jayakody and Kalil 2002). Social fathers include grandfathers, uncles, stepfathers, and even family friends. Studies have found that anywhere from 20 to 50 percent of ostensibly fatherless black children have social fathers (Furstenberg and Harris 1993; Coley 1998; Black, Dubowitz, and Starr 1999; Jayakody and Kalil 2002; Simons et al. 2006).[2] This diversity in black children's paternal arrangements suggests a need for research on more than just black biological fathers. Rather, research on black father figures is needed.[3]

One aspect of the diversity in black children's father-figure arrangements is that men move into and out of the children's lives. A study (Mott 1990) using the National Longitudinal Study-Youth (NLSY) data from 1979 through 1983 found the pattern of movement of biological fathers in and out of black children's homes to be distinct from that of the nonblacks in his sample. In that study, 32 percent of black newborns lived with their biological fathers at birth, while 87 percent of nonblack newborns lived with their fathers. Data was collected once per year for the next four years. Every year some fathers became nonresident while others became coresident. Perhaps these findings were to be expected, but few would expect that more black fathers would become *coresident* than nonresident over the four years of the study. It was similarly surprising that more nonblack fathers became *nonresident* during the same period. Overall, 2 percent *more* black children had a biological father present when comparing the birth year to four years later. At the same time, 9 percent *fewer* nonblack children had a biological father present when comparing the birth year to four years later. Mott's data, which followed children born to mothers aged fourteen to twenty-five over four years, revealed something that needs further study: the distinct pattern by which father figures flow into and out of black children's lives.

Mott's study begs for complementary research. His data, based on a relatively disadvantaged sample, is now more than twenty years old. Those who were children at that time may now be parents. They grew up in an era when the "code of the street" described by Anderson (1999) was increasingly emitted to all Americans through primary agents of socialization (i.e., radio, television, and film). Arguably, the code has been presented as an acceptable way for black men to behave because "successful" black men have been the most visible bearers of the message. Since that time, changes in urban America's economic structure (Wilson 1987, 1996), continued racial segregation (Massey and Denton 1994), and increased incarceration rates (Pettit and Western 2004) may have also made it even more difficult for black father figures to maintain consistent involvement. Coresidence may misestimate paternal involvement (Day and Lamb 2004; Lamb 2004). Furthermore, Mott's study only follows the flow of *biological* fathers into and out of children's homes. Several studies of low-income Black families support the notion that some children with social fathers are doing just as well as some children with biological fathers (Furstenberg and

Harris 1993; Coley 1998; Black, Dubowitz, and Starr 1999; Jayakody and Kalil 2002; Simons et al. 2006).[4] Therefore, studying the flows of father figures (rather than just biological fathers) might be more appropriate. The goal of this chapter is to advance our understanding of black father-figure flows and demonstrate the need for a qualitative understanding of this phenomenon.

Conceptualizing Father Figures

Before moving forward, my use of fathering terminology should be clarified. As the second column of table 7.1 illustrates, family researchers use a consistent label to designate the man whose genes a child carries: "biological father." This man's place in the family as "the" father is typically taken for granted. As the third column of table 7.1 shows though, men who parent other men's biological children do not have a single accepted label, and by implication perhaps they also lack a clear place in our conceptualization of the family. A variety of terms are used, but "social father" and "father figure" are the most common. "Social father" seems the better label because the defining char-

Table 7.1
Typical Father Labels in Family Research

Author	Biological Fathers	Other Involved Men
Biller 1981	biological father role model	surrogate role model
Hawkins and Eggebeen 1991	biological father	social father
Furstenberg and Harris 1993	biological father	father surrogate or father figure
Coley 1998, 2000	biological father	nonpaternal male, nonbiological father figure, father figure, or social father
Jayakody and Kalil, 2002	biological father	social father; romantic-partner social father (e.g. stepfather, boyfriend); relative social father (e.g. grandfather, minister)

acteristics of the men in question are that they are not the children's biological fathers but are performing the *socially* recognized behaviors of a father toward the children anyway. "Father figure," on the other hand, is a term that I do not limit to social fathers. I use the term "father figure" when referring to any man—biological father or social father—who exhibits paternal behavior toward a child.

This provides a clear yet flexible language for the study of fatherhood. For example, in societies that are matrilineal and avunculocal (e.g., the Navajo), children's maternal uncles may perform activities expected of biological fathers in the United States (Burling 1958; Peoples and Bailey 1994). Biological fathers in such societies often treat their biological children more like American uncles treat their nieces and nephews. When a society is avunculocal, a newly married couple typically moves close to the bride's family. One might expect, then, that in matrilineal and avunculocal societies, paternal attention often comes from social fathers. For many Americans, social fathers are not the ideal father figures. Yet grandfathers and uncles are often seen as helpful social fathers who can take center stage when biological fathers are insufficiently involved. Boyfriends and stepfathers also spend a great deal of time with children sired by other men because of high divorce and nonmarital birth rates. Perhaps less frequently, men come from neighborhoods, churches, and mentoring organizations to provide paternal influence for children. Therefore, I use a language that accommodates the diversity of family life while minimizing confusion. Distinguishing biological and social fathers from each other but recognizing them both as father figures accomplishes these goals.

Notably, different kinds of social fathers can also be distinguished. For example, Jayakody and Kalil (2002) classified social fathers as either "romantic-partner social fathers" or "relative social fathers." For them, social fathers who are romantically involved with the mothers of their "social children" are romantic-partner social fathers. Relative social fathers are those who otherwise belong to their social children's blood, legal, or fictive kinship groups. Jayakody and Kalil (2002) published this classification scheme in their study of fathering in Fulton County, Georgia.[5] The last row of table 7.1 illustrates Jayakody and Kalil's father-figure typology.

Further study may yet determine better ways to conceptualize and label social fathers. For example, meaningful divisions among social fathers might follow kinship boundaries of blood, law, and social recognition. According to such a scheme, one group would be made up of blood kin, such as biological grandfathers and uncles. Affinal kin, like stepfathers, step-grandfathers, and older brothers-in-law, would constitute another group. Affinal social fathers are connected to children by legal relationships but not blood. For some in this group, the motivation to social father may be driven more by the desire to please a spouse or other affinal family members. Finally, social fathers of a third kind, fictive kin, may be informally recognized as "family," but no legal or biological links would bind them to their social children. The difference between this way of conceptualizing social fathers and that of Jayakody and Kalil is that legal institutions that buttress relationships are given prominence. As a result, stepfathers are differentiated from other kinds of maternal romantic partners. Their legal standing makes stepfathers affinal-kin social fathers. Meanwhile, unmarried partners are fictive-kin social fathers even if they are coresident, paying most of the bills, and involved in child care giving. It is possible that such divisions would influence social-father motivation. Many possibilities can be articulated, but data should guide the process. There are some data suggesting that Jayakody and Kalil's (2002) approach is valid, and therefore it is used in this chapter. Later research should use empirical data to evaluate the importance of blood, legal, and fictive-kin standing among father figures, though.

It is also possible for children to have multiple father figures, at least one of whom would be a social father. Few empirical studies seek to document multiple fathering. Yet, one study found that 10 to 20 percent of children with involved coresident stepfathers also had involved nonresident biological fathers (White and Gilbreth 2001). In this study, each father figure's behavior was found to be positively and independently related to child development outcomes. It should be noted, though, that children with multiple father figures might simply be in a temporary phase of family development. Cofathering arrangements involving the biological father and a stepfather have been specifically hypothesized as a transitional stage in which one father is "phasing out" as the other slowly assumes primary responsibility for the child (Hetherington and Henderson 1997). Alternatively, other research suggests that some children have close-knit extended families that provide them with several father figures (Stack 1974; Martin and Martin 1978; Lempert 1999). This chapter will document the presence of multiple black father figures in children's lives but lacks the data needed to resolve this debate.

Conceptualizing Paternal Involvement

Father involvement and *paternal involvement* are commonly invoked concepts in the study of male parenting behaviors (Pleck 1997; Amato and Gilbreth 1999; Amato and Rivera 1999; King and Heard 1999; Snarey 1996; Amato 1998; Coley 2000; Menning 2002; Day and Lamb 2004; Pleck and Masciadrelli 2004). It seems safe to assume that economic provision is the core duty envisioned when most people think of a father figure's responsibilities. Accordingly, father figures' economic support has been studied a great deal by family analysts. However, according to Pleck and Masciadrelli (2004), by the 1950s and 1960s the study of paternal involvement had increasingly focused on how biological fathers' absence affected the development of gendered thought and behavior in children. Then, over the next two decades, researchers began to study how a father figure's presence and direct involvement with children affects other domains of child development. Today, the study of fathering includes how father figures influence children's cognitive, social, and emotional development.

The current emphasis on noneconomic paternal involvement can be linked to critiques of child-development theories (Parke 1996) and the feminist effort to move fathers toward helping "reduce the child-rearing burden of employed mothers" (Pleck and Masciadrelli 2004:223). Looking at the paternal involvement literature, Lamb et al. (1985) first proposed a conceptualization of paternal involvement that delineated three elements of fathering: engagement, accessibility, and responsibility. Engagement refers to a father figure's direct interaction with a child. Nurturant fathering is another name for engagement. Engagement includes such behaviors as changing diapers, playing stimulating games, giving advice, and regulating behavior. Accessibility refers to how available a father figure is to his child when the child seeks him for advice or support. Responsibility reflects the extent to which a father figure takes the initiative to secure his child's general welfare and development needs. This emphasis on noneconomic involvement complements findings on low-income black fathers. This population of fathers may prioritize noneconomic involvement over provider behaviors (Hamer 2001). It is appropriate, then, that a measure of engagement was used to indicate paternal involvement in this chapter.

Study Design and Data

This project used data from a study that is being conducted in Boston, Chicago, and San Antonio called "Welfare, Children, and Families: A Three-City Study." The main goal of the Three-City Study is to gauge how the 1996 welfare reforms affected the well-being of children and families. Yet its data also allow analysts to study particular aspects of low-income urban American family life. For example, there are data on father involvement for the same children over time. The Time 1 data includes information collected in 1999 from face-to-face survey interviews of 2,402 respondents. Each respondent was a woman with primary responsibility for raising at least one child. The interviews were conducted in English or Spanish, according to the respondent's preference. Both the maternal caregiver and the child were able to provide some information on the biological father, but biological fathers and social fathers were not interviewed directly. Approximately sixteen months later, 88 percent of these caregivers and children completed a second interview (Time 2). Combining both waves of data on these same families yielded a longitudinal panel dataset. This name is commonly used among sociologists, who consider the respondents to be a panel of experts (on their own experiences) who provide data for analysis. Only families with usable data on father-figure involvement and racial/ethnic identification were included in the analyses presented in this chapter.

Families were randomly selected for screening, but final participation was constrained by the need to answer specific research questions. For example, of the households interviewed at time 1, 80 percent had to have incomes below the poverty line. Another constraint allowed for no more than 86 percent of the households in the sample to feature an unmarried female caregiver. The remaining 14 percent had a caregiver and her spouse. Ideally, the study was to also have an evenly divided sample in terms of racial/ethnic classification. Thirty-three percent of the families should have been African American with no Latino heritage. Another 33 percent should have been white with no Latino heritage. A final third should have been Latino of any race. However, low-income white families were too residentially dispersed in San Antonio for recruitment and interviews to be economically feasible. They were a little more clustered in Chicago and most clustered in Boston. As a result, most white families were recruited from Boston, but some resided in Chicago. Together, they represented far fewer than

Table 7.2

Racial/Ethnic Composition of the Sample

Race/Ethnicity	
Entire sample (n = 2153)	100%
Black (non-Latino)	42
Latino	48
Mexican	31
Puerto Rican	6
Dominican	4
Other Latino (or mixed Latino)	6
White (non-Latino)	5
Other race (or mixed/unknown)	5

Note: Errors are due to rounding. Also, the racial/ethnic classification was imputed based on the racial/ethnic classification of mother and child. If the respondent and the focal child had the same racial/ethnic classification then the father figure was assigned that classification as well.

33 percent of the sample (see below). Half of the focal children were zero through four years old and the others were ten though fourteen years old. The sample that was interviewed twice and had information on all variables needed for this study included 2,153 families.

Extensive baseline information was obtained on one child per household and his or her primary caregiver. Both child and mother provided information on the biological father. Only mothers provided information on the social father. Fewer questions were asked about social fathers in the survey instrument. The child is referred to as the "focal child" in the household. Only families in which the focal child's primary caregiver was female were included. Therefore, father figures in this study were never the sole care providers of focal children. Over 90 percent of the primary caregivers in the sample were the children's biological mothers, and 10 percent of them were social mothers (typically grandmothers or aunts). For convenience, "mother" refers to a focal child's female primary caregiver throughout this text.

The racial/ethnic classification of each father figure had to be imputed. If the maternal caregiver and the child were reported as being of the same race or of Latino origin, then the father figure (or potential father figure) was assigned that same classification. Based on imputed race, then, approximately 42 percent of the father figures were of African American race and non-Latino ethnicity. A slightly larger proportion of the sample, about 48 percent, was of Latino ethnicity (about two-thirds of these Latinos were of Mexican heritage). The remaining 10 percent were either non-Latino whites, or mother-child pairs of mixed racial/ethnic classification.

Measuring the Father-Figure Arrangement

A child's father-figure arrangement was determined by using the caregiver's answers to certain questions on the survey. First, it was determined whether the child had a father figure. If the child had a father figure, then the kin relationship between each father figure and child was ascertained. This relationship determined the type of father figure or figures a child had (e.g., biological father, relative social father, romantic-partner social father, multiple father figures). Finally, the level of paternal involvement was identified. This process is described in more detail later.

Each caregiver in the Three-City Study was asked if her focal child's biological father was still alive, had been in contact with the focal child in the past year, and also took some responsibility for the focal child's daily care. Wording of the question about daily childcare responsibility taken by the father was made appropriate to the age of the focal child.[6] Possible answers were: the biological father is dead or has not been in contact within the past twelve months; the biological father is alive but takes no responsibility; and the biological father is alive and takes some daily childcare responsibility. A dummy variable was created by collapsing the first two categories. Therefore, children were categorized as either having a caregiving biological father or not.

To determine whether children had social fathers, caregivers were asked to respond to the following: "Sometimes, there are other people who play a father-like role to a child. For example, a child might have a stepfather, a grandfather or uncle, or someone else who acts like a father to him or her. Is there someone who is more like a father to [CHILD] than [his/her] real biological father?" It was expected that men playing important roles in children's lives would be identified. If the caregiver identified a man as her child's social father, she was also asked about the kin relationship between the social father, herself, and the focal child. Finally, she was asked the same question about care giving that had been asked regarding the biological father. While caregivers were questioned about many aspects of biological-father involvement, only the question about daily childcare responsibility referred to both biological and social fathers. Therefore, this question was used as the indicator of paternal involvement for this study.

Discussing Father-Figure Flows

Sometimes analysts may assume stability over time once they have determined a father figure's presence or involvement level at one point in time. Yet this assumption is challenged by the literature on divorce and remarriage (Cherlin and Furstenberg 1994; McLanahan and Sandefur 1994; Hetherington and Stanley-Hagan 2000), nonmarital childbirth (Bell-Kaplan 1997; Mincy and Oliver 2003), and even just the movement of black biological fathers (Mott 1990). Indeed, there is reason to challenge the assumption of stable father-figure involvement as normative.

Father figures might flow in and out of children's lives more often (and in more ways) than is typically acknowledged. A child can have any number of father figures, and a different kind of connection to each man. These men can be involved in the child's life sequentially but with no overlap, sequentially with a period of overlap, or simultaneously. Further, any given father figure's tenure may be stable throughout a child's minor years, only during the early years, only during the later years, or cyclical. Documentation of these patterns may help researchers identify potentially important mediating factors when studying the connections between paternal involvement and child well-being.

Though this language is not in general use, father-figure *gain* and father-figure *loss* are already fundamental concepts in the study of father involvement. They are constantly invoked by those who study divorce and remarriage (Cherlin and Furstenberg 1994; Hetherington and Stanley-Hagan 2000). Father-figure loss accompanies divorce, and father-figure gain accompanies remarriage. In the typical situation, we focus on children who were born to married biological parents and therefore have an involved father figure at birth. Assuming the typical situation, in which mothers get physical custody of children, father-figure loss often occurs a few years after the parental divorce. Noncustodial fathers begin new romantic relationships, procreate with other women, or decrease their involvement for some other reason.

Father-figure gain can follow the preceding events, but it is normally discussed in only one of its forms: the father-figure gain that occurs when a child's mother remarries (Cherlin and Furstenberg 1994). Soon, however, the father-figure gain that accompanies a cohabiting partner (Graffe and Lichter 1999) will likely become similarly salient in the literature. Altogether distinct, though, is when father-figure gain follows divorce but precedes remarriage or cohabitation. This may happen when the child's custodial mother moves in with her parents and the grandfather becomes more involved (Hawkins and Eggebeen 1991) or when neither parent is available to take the child (Bullock 2005). In addition to (or in lieu of) the grandfather, there may be uncles, cousins, fictive kin, or institution-based mentors who assume the social father position (Lempert 1999). Despite these possible variations, the familiar narrative of father-figure loss and gain presumes biological-father involvement (and marriage) from conception. After marital dissolution, he may be followed by a relative social father, but most scholars focus on situations in which a romantic-partner social father replaces him.

Though this narrative allows for some diversity, it still omits potentially important father-figure arrangements. A different narrative can illustrate much of what's missing. Imagine a child whose biological parents were never married. The child's maternal uncle resides with her and her mother. The uncle helps with schoolwork, takes her to the doctor, and is generally an involved father figure. The child's biological father refused to acknowledge her before she was born but then accepted her after a couple of years. Sadly, the biological father was incarcerated a year after accepting paternal responsibility and remained in jail for three years. He might reenter his child's life during her late childhood or the early teen years. He is now willing to accept his parenting responsibility and can be seen as an involved father figure. This narrative could have featured employment or additional relationship difficulties in addition to incarceration (or as alternate events to incarceration). The uncle could have been replaced or joined by a nonresident boyfriend, resident boyfriend, stepfather, grandfather, step-grandfather, fictive kin, or institutional mentors. A third, fourth, fifth, and so on father figure could have entered or left the child's life at any point in time and for any period of time. All of the father figures could also have disappeared, leaving her totally fatherless for a time.

Family-studies analysts have little data on the prevalence of such experiences, but we do know that nonmarital birth is how most African American mothers become single parents. We also have little comprehension of what such experiences mean to children and how they influence child development over time. Each adjustment might present a distinct father-figure arrangement to those experiencing it. That is, just the sheer fact that the child's family structure is chronically unstable might negatively affect her (Cavanagh and Huston 2006). Alternatively, the prevalence of instability may have dulled its effect on black families. This would corroborate Stack's (1974) findings that black female caregivers try to rely on a network of real and fictive kin. The network includes father figures but does not solely depend on any one person. This might prevent father-figure flux from having such a powerful effect on children. Whatever the effect, father-figure instability may be common for children with black father figures.

Interrogating Father-Figure Flows

Tables 7.3 and 7.4 show the flow of father figures between two points in time among Three-City Study families. Table 7.3 shows nonblack father-figure flows. Table 7.4 shows black father-figure flows. Each child is identified as having a particular kind of father-figure arrangement: biological father, romantic-partner social father, relative social father, multiple father figures, or no father figure at all.

Table 7.3
Nonblack Father-Figure Flows (1251 = N)

Number at Time 1	Biological father	Romantic-partner social father	Relative social father	Multiple father figures	No father figure
Biological father: 562	80%	2%	1%	2%	16%
Romantic-partner social father: 84	4%	59%	10%	2%	25%
Relative social father: 97	5%	35%	20%	2%	38%
Multiple father figures: 59	32%	10%	19%	5%	34%
No father-figure: 449	22%	9%	8%	1%	60%

Status at Time 2

Note: Racial/ethnic classification of father figures imputed based on racial/ethnic classification of mother and child given by the mother. If the respondent and the focal child had the same racial/ethnic classification then the father figure was assigned that classification as well.

Table 7.4
Black Father-Figure Flows (903 = N)

Number at Time 1	Biological father	Romantic-partner social father	Relative social father	Multiple father figures	No father figure
		Status at Time 2			
Biological father: 269	66%	2%	5%	3%	24%
Romantic-partner social father: 96	2%	37%	12%	6%	43%
Relative social father: 122	11%	24%	15%	11%	39%
Multiple father figures: 30	49%	18%	1%	6%	26%
No father figure: 386	13%	14%	10%	1%	62%

Note: Racial/ethnic classification of father figures imputed based on racial/ethnic classification of mother and child given by the mother. If the respondent and the focal child had the same racial/ethnic classification then the father figure was assigned that classification as well.

For clarity, this is how to read the tables. In table 7.3, the raw numbers in the first column reflect father-figure status at Time 1. Therefore, at Time 1, of the 1,251 nonblack children in the sample, 562 (44.9 percent) had involved biological fathers, 84 (6.7 percent) had social fathers who were the romantic partners of their mothers, 97 (7.8 percent) had social fathers who were relatives, 59 (4.7 percent) had multiple father figures, and 449 (35.9 percent) had no father figures in their lives. By Time 2, of the 562 biological fathers, 80 percent were still involved, but about 2 percent had now been replaced by romantic-partner social fathers, relative social fathers (1 percent), or multiple father figures (2 percent), and the rest (about 16 percent) had left and not been replaced at all (no father figures). Similarly, 97 children started out with relative social fathers at Time 1, but by Time 2, only 20 percent of them remained, 5 percent of these relatives had been replaced by the biological father, 35 percent by the child's mother's romantic partner, and 2 percent by multiple father figures; 38 percent had left but not been replaced.

It should be noted that the percentages do not always add to 100 because of rounding, and the small cell sizes prevented reliable chi-square statistics from being calculated, so observed differences cannot be called statistically significant.

Findings

Comparing table 7.3 to table 7.4 reveals racial/ethnic differences that build upon Mott's (1990) father-figure-flows study. While Mott's study focused on biological fathers, this study broadens the scope. Social fathers are included among the father figures moving into and out of children's lives. Like Mott's study, though, this study investigates the notion that distinct racial/ethnic patterns characterize the flow of father figures. The most important finding of this study was the extent of instability that characterized black children's experiences with father figures over a time period that averaged sixteen months.

The racial/ethnic differences in father-figure flows are visible in tables 7.3 and 7.4. Note that the cells that form a diagonal line downward and to the right (from row 1, column 2) measure stable father-figure arrangements.[7] Across race/ethnicity, the most prevalent arrangements on the diagonal line were biological father stability and the stable absence of a father figure. Among nonblacks, 80 percent of the children with an involved biological father had stability in that relationship, whereas among blacks only 66 percent had the same. Among non-Blacks without a father figure, the rate of stability was 60 percent. This rate was 62 percent for Black children. There is a sizable racial difference in the former but only a minimal difference in the latter.

The tables show higher rates of involvement for black social fathers than nonblack social fathers. When one looks at all of the cells in which a father-figure was present at some time during the study (all cells but row 5, column 6), the differing experiences with social fathers become quite clear. Aggregating all of the involved father-figure cells, one finds that 76 percent of the black children had a social father at some point during the study (Time 1, Time 2, or both), but only 54 percent of the nonblack children had a social father at some point during the study. This suggests that low-income (and urban-dwelling) black father-figures are more likely to be social fathers than biological fathers. Because it was rare that social and biological fathers were simultaneously involved, black families seemed to rely more heavily on social fathers for paternal involvement.

One should not lose sight of the relative lack of stability in black social-father involvement, though. The tables show that involvement by romantic-partner social fathers was *less* likely to be stable among blacks (37 percent vs. 59 percent). That is, only 37 percent of the black children with romantic-partner social fathers enjoyed the stable involvement of that father figure. Among nonblacks, the stability rate was 59 percent. Relative social fathers were rather unlikely to be stably involved with children of any racial/ethnic group, but slightly more unlikely among blacks, where only 15 percent of children with relative social fathers enjoyed that father figure's stable involvement, compared to 20 percent of nonblack children. In a related vein, black father-figure arrangements that began with either type of social father were at a relatively high risk of having no father figure present at Time 2 (43 percent for romantic partners and 39 percent for relatives). Nonblack father-figure arrangements were less likely to evince this pattern (25 percent for romantic partners and 38 percent for relatives). All of this points toward greater paternal instability for black children with social fathers.

Multiple-father-figure engagement was not common for either group in this sample. For both racial/ethnic groups, children with multiple father figures rarely experienced father-figure stability (5 percent and 6 percent). The children's Time 1 coparenting arrangements reveal another racial difference, though. Black children with multiple father figures most often experienced a loss of the social father and retention of the biological father (49 percent), but nonblack children most often totally lost their father-figures (34 percent). Such a pattern among black father figures is encouraging, and in-depth interviews or ethnographies could reveal the conditions that give rise to this desirable result. Perhaps a clue lies in the finding that 11 percent of the black children with relative social fathers present at Time 1 experienced the return of their biological father (in a coparenting arrangement) by Time 2. Only 2 percent of the nonblack children with relative social fathers had the same experience. Considering the "it takes a village" rhetoric commonly used by politicians and activists, it is unfortunate that collecting data on cofathering is not a higher priority among funders.

Naturally, more quantitative study is needed to determine whether the black biological fathers tend to remain stably involved after the black social fathers pull back (or after they join the relative social fathers). However, qualitative research can tell us whether the participants experience this as a positive arrangement. If they do, then researchers could also identify which factors facilitate the formation and maintenance of such cofathering arrangements. Finally, we need to know the extent to which cofathering arrangements are similar across racial and ethnic groups. The success of any related public policies might depend on homogeneity in peoples' behavior or nuances in policymaking.

The experiences of children who were fatherless at Time 1 are quite important. Whether black or not, no more than 62 percent of these children remained fatherless. Yet black biological fathers were (again) less likely to be involved than nonblack biological fathers. While 14 percent (combining biological and multiple fathers) of the fatherless black children gained a biological father, 23 percent (combining biological and multiple fathers) of the fatherless nonblack children did so (including cofathering). Also, among those who began the study fatherless, black children with social fathers were more numerous than nonblack children with social fathers. Of the black children who began the study fatherless, 25 percent gained a social father. In comparison, 18 percent of the fatherless nonblack children gained a social father. Yet what is perhaps most important to remember about all children who were fatherless at Time 1 is that 38 to 40 percent of them gained some kind of father-figure involvement by the end of the study. More in-depth study of father-figure gain should be a priority for family-studies analysts. It is key that we learn how to facilitate father-figure gain, how to ensure that it has a positive effect, and how to keep these men stably involved in childrearing.

Conclusions

This chapter has provided new data for family-studies analysts, and fatherhood researchers in particular, that suggest some changes in perspective. A tentative language and typology that easily includes all men who father children beyond mere insemination was developed. Two distinct social-father typologies were proffered for evaluation in future research. Furthermore, the study of father-figure flows was expanded beyond a narrow focus on coresident biological fathers. It was shown that the study of father-figure flows can include social fathers. However, the fathering in low-income black families may be inordinately characterized by instability and social fathering. Research must address these possibilities if policy is to provide the needed supports. Such efforts would be complementary to the focus on single-mother households and stable biological-father involvement in low-income, urban black America (Stack 1974; Wilson 1987, 1996; Bell-Kaplan 1997; Moynihan [1965] 1999; U.S. Bureau of the Census 2000).

The finding that black father-figure involvement was generally unstable cannot be stressed enough. Black father involvement in this study could be best characterized as transient. Most romantic-partner social fathers (and even more relative social fathers) had ceased their involvement with children after sixteen months. In some cases they were replaced, but in other cases they were not. The Three-City Study data do not allow inquiry into why father figures ceased their involvement. However, classic and contemporary family research make "desertion" a plausible explanation (Anderson 1999; Frazier 2001). High rates of black male incarceration (Pettit and Western 2004) and death (Peterson and Krivo 1999) might also help to remove black father figures from children's lives. Finally, it must be stated that instability can include a father figure entering a child's life. In a significant minority of cases, a father figure came into the life of a fatherless child. If future research documents that such instability occurs often, then those who study black fathers should explore how black children are affected by the different kinds of instability.

Ultimately, though, the data presented here raise more questions than they answer. Little is known about black men's subjective experiences in the father-figure arrangements described above. The divorce and remarriage sequence has been studied well (Cherlin and Furstenberg 1994; McLanahan and Sandefur 1994; Hetherington and Stanley-Hagan 2000), but African Americans procreate while unmarried at much higher rates than most other American racial/ethnic groups (Goldstein and Harknett 2006). This probably creates a strong demand for social fathers. The dominance of nonmarital birth and social fathers in black families compels us to qualitatively study black fathers more. If we are to understand the long-term effects of black father-figure flows on children, then more quantitative data is also needed. While father-figure instability may generally be associated with child development problems (Forman and Davies 2003; Cavanagh and Huston 2006), some kinds of father-figure flows may have a positive effect (e.g., gaining a father figure after being fatherless). This notion is consonant with Pleck and Masciadrelli's (2004) conclusion that the positive effects of paternal involvement are probably contingent.

Policymakers and social activists can benefit from research on black father-figure flows. This research will probably reveal that some father-figure arrangements, though associated with instability, actually have positive effects on black child development. Such knowledge is especially important given the seemingly higher levels of instability in black father-figure arrangements. Research may also reveal the social conditions that maximize the beneficial effects of father-figure involvement. Based on this research, policies could be crafted that help black father figures enter children's lives and remain beneficially involved over time. In some cases, though, biological fathers are deceased, incarcerated, or unwilling to engage their children. In these cases, policies should target the identification of beneficial social fathers. The policy goals should be to recruit these men and to create supportive social conditions that will facilitate long-term and effective involvement. Resources will probably need to be distributed to organizations with rites-of-passage programs, fatherhood-training programs, and healthy-marriage programs, to mention a few. The applied research generated by program evaluations could help to refine our understanding of how public policies can support paternal involvement.

Notes

I wish to acknowledge core support to the Three-City Study from the National Institute of Child Health and Human Development through grants HD36093 and HD25936, as well as the support of many government agencies and private foundations. For a complete list of funders, please see http://www.threecitystudy .johnshopkins.edu. I also offer many thanks to my advisors, Andrew Cherlin and Katrina Bell-McDonald. Finally, I would like to thank Rebekah Levine-Coley, Robert Moffit, and others whose helpful comments improved my thinking and writing.

1. Though the link between marriage and paternal involvement is certainly not automatic, such data is an accepted estimate of fatherlessness rates.

2. Some children undoubtedly have both social fathers and a biological father.

3. In this chapter, the term "father figure" refers to both biological and social fathers. My use of the term "father figure" differs from its common usage in family studies. I explain my reason for doing this in the section on father-figure typologies.

4. I suspect, though, that certain subgroups in each category fit the national pattern in which children with biological fathers do better. As Pleck and Masciadrelli (2004) conclude after reviewing the general father involvement literature, the "positive effects of paternal involvement are likely to occur primarily or only in specific contexts." For example, the presence of biological fathers is highly correlated with married family life. There is no question that children of any race who live with married parents tend to be economically better off compared to children of the same race who live with single parents. Greater economic resources often translate into environmental advantages that facilitate better educational, behavioral, and long-term life outcomes.

5. Children whose social fathers are relatives but who are also romantically involved with their mothers do not fit easily into this typology. For example, a child's mother may begin dating a man who was a longtime family friend and even a father figure to her child before the romantic relationship began. Another possibility is that a child's mother may become romantically involved with one of the child's paternal blood kin, an uncle or grandfather, for example. Finally, a child's uncle by marriage is a relative, but romantic-relationship dynamics must still be considered.

6. The question asked: "How much responsibility does the focal child's biological father take in his/her daily care, such as . . . feeding, changing diapers, or bathing [for children < three years]? preparing food for [name of child], helping [him/her] get dressed, or giving [name of child] a bath [for children two through five years]? preparing food for [name of child], or making sure [he/she] goes to school [for children > nine years]?"

7. The meaning of stability here should not be confused with the meaning typically implied when the term is used in family studies. Stability typically refers to nuclear families and also connotes optimal well-being of the family members. Here, I use stability to refer to any family configuration that remains unchanged over time, and I presume no necessary links between family structure and family members' well-being.

References

Amato, P. R. 1998. "More Than Money? Men's Contributions to Their Children's Lives." In *Men in Families: When Do They Get Involved? What Difference Does it Make?* ed. Alan Booth and Ann C. Crouter, 241–78. Mahwah, N.J.: Erlbaum.

Amato, P. R., and J. F. Gilbreth. 1999. "Nonresident Fathers and Children's Well-Being: A Meta-analysis." *Journal of Marriage and the Family* 61:557–73.

Amato, P. R., and F. E. Rivera. 1999. "Paternal Involvement and Children's Behavior Problems." *Journal of Marriage and the Family* 61:375–84.

Anderson, E. 1999. *Code of the Street: Decency, Violence, and the Moral Life of the Inner City.* New York: Norton.

Bell-Kaplan, E. 1997. *Not Our Kind of Girl.* Berkeley: University of California Press.

Black, M. B., H. Dubowitz, and R. H. Starr Jr. 1999. "African-American Fathers in Low Income, Urban Families: Development, Behavior, and Home Environment of Their Three-Year-Old Children. *Child Development* 70 (4): 967–78.

Bullock, K. 2005. "Grandfathers and the Impact of Raising Grandchildren." *Journal of Sociology and Social Welfare* 32 (1): 43–59.

Burling, R. 1958. "Garo Avunculocular Authority and Matrilateral Cross-Cousin Marriage." *American Anthropologist* 60 (4): 743–49.

Cavanagh, S. E., and A. C. Huston. 2006. "Family Instability and Children's Early Problem Behavior." *Social Forces* 85 (1): 551–81.

Cherlin A. J., and F. F. Furstenberg. 1994. "Stepfamilies in the United States: A Reconsideration." *Annual Review of Sociology* 20:359–81.

Coley, R. L. 1998. "Children's Socialization Experiences and Functioning in Single-Mother Households: The Importance of Fathers and Other Men." *Child Development* 69:219–30.

Coley, R. L. 2000. "Invisible Men: Emerging Research on Low-Income, Unmarried, and Minority Fathers." *American Psychologist* 56 (9): 743–53.

Day, R. D., and M. E. Lamb. 2004. "Conceptualizing and Measuring Father Involvement: Pathways, Problems, and Progress." In *Conceptualizing and Measuring Father Involvement*, ed. Michael E. Lamb, 1–15. Mahwah, N.J.: Erlbaum.

Forman, E. M., and P. T. Davies. 2003. "Family Instability and Young Adolescent Maladjustment: The Mediating Effects of Parenting Quality and Adolescent Appraisals of Family Security." *Journal of Clinical Child and Adolescent Psychology* 32 (1): 94–105.

Frazier, E. F. 1939. *The Negro Family in the United States*. Chicago, Il: University of Chicago Press.

Furstenberg, F. F., Jr., and K. M. Harris. 1993. "When and Why Fathers Matter: Impacts of Father Involvement on the Children of Adolescent Males." In *Young Unwed Fathers: Changing Roles and Emerging Policies*, ed. R. I. Lerman, and T. J. Ooms, 117–38. Philadelphia: Temple University Press.

Goldstein, J. R., and K. Harknett. 2006. "Parenting Across Racial and Class Lines: Assortative Mating Patterns of New Parents Who Are Married, Cohabiting, Dating, or No Longer Romantically Involved." *Social Forces* 85 (1): 121–43.

Graffe, D. R., and D. T. Lichter. 1999. "Life Course Transitions of American Children: Parental Cohabitation, Marriage, and Single Motherhood." *Demography* 36 (2): 205–7.

Hamer, J. F. 2001. *What It Means to Be Daddy: Fatherhood for Black Men Living Away from Their Children*. New York: Columbia University Press.

Hawkins, A. J., and D. J. Eggebeen. 1991. "Are Fathers Fungible? Patterns of Co-resident Adult Men in Maritally Disrupted Families and Young Children's Well-Being." *Journal of Marriage and the Family* 53:958–72.

Hetherington, E. M., and S. H. Henderson. 1997. "Fathers in Stepfamilies." In *The Role of the Father in Child Development*, 3rd ed., ed. M. E. Lamb, 212–26. New York: Wiley.

Hetherington, E. M., and M. Stanley-Hagan. 2000. "Diversity Among Stepfamilies." In *Handbook of Family Diversity*, ed. David H. Demo, Katherine R. Allen, and Mark A. Fine, 173–96. New York: Oxford University Press.

Jayakody, R., and A. Kalil. 2002. "Social Fathering in Low-Income African American Families with Preschoolers." *Journal of Marriage and Family* 64:504–16.

King, V., and H. E. Heard. 1999. "Nonresident Father Visitation, Parental Conflict, and Mother's Satisfaction: What's Best for Child Well-Being?" *Journal of Marriage and the Family* 61:385–96.

Lamb, M. E., ed. 1997. *The Role of the Father in Child Development*. 3rd ed. New York: Wiley.

Lamb, M. E., ed. 2004. *The Role of the Father in Child Development*. 4th ed. Hoboken, N.J.: Wiley.

Lamb, M. E., J. H. Pleck, E. L. Charnov, and J. A. Levine. 1985. "Paternal Behavior in Humans." *American Zoologist* 25:883–94.

Lempert, L. B. 1999. "Other Fathers: An Alternative Perspective on African-American Community Caring." In *The Black Family: Essays and Studies*, 6th ed., ed. R. Staples, 189–201. Belmont, Calif.: Wadsworth.

Lerman, R. I., and T. J. Ooms, eds. 1993. *Young Unwed Fathers: Changing Roles and Emerging Policies*. Philadelphia: Temple University Press.

Lewis, O. 1966. "The Culture of Poverty." *Scientific America* 216 (4): 19–25.

Martin, E. P., and J. M. Martin. 1978. *The Black Extended Family*. Chicago: University of Chicago Press.

Massey, D., and N. Denton. 1994. *American Apartheid*. Cambridge, Mass.: Harvard University Press.

McLanahan, S., and G. Sandefur. 1994. *Growing Up with a Single Parent: What Hurts, What Helps*. Cambridge, Mass.: Harvard University Press.

Menning, C. L. 2002. "Absent Parents Are More Than Money: The Joint Effect of Activities and Financial Support on Youths' Educational Attainment." *Journal of Family Issues* 23 (5): 648–71.

Mincy, R. and Oliver, H. 2003. "Age, Race, and Children's Living Arrangements: Implications for TANF Reauthorization." *New Federalism Survey of America's Families*, Series B, No. B-53. Washington, D.C.: Urban Institute.

Mott, F. L. 1990. "When Is a Father Really Gone? Paternal-Child Contact in Father Absent Homes." *Demography* 27:499–517.

Moynihan, D. P. [1965] 1999. "The Tangle of Pathology." In *The Black Family: Essays and Studies*, 6th ed., ed. R. Staples, 7–17. Belmont, Calif.: Wadsworth.

Parke, R. D. 1996. *Fatherhood*. Cambridge, Mass.: Harvard University Press.

Peoples, J. P., and G. Bailey. 1994. *Humanity: An Introduction to Cultural Anthropology*, 3rd ed. Saint Paul, Minn.: West.

Peterson, R. D., and L. J. Krivo. 1999. "Racial Segregation, the Concentration of Disadvantage, and Black-White Homicide Victimization." *Sociological Forum* 14 (3): 465–93.

Pettit, B., and B. Western. 2004. "Mass Imprisonment and the Life Course: Race and Class Inequality in U.S. Incarceration. *American Sociological Review* 69 (2): 151–69.

Pleck, J. H. 1997. "Paternal Involvement: Levels, Sources, and Consequences." In *The Role of the Father in Child Development*, 3rd ed., ed., M. E. Lamb, 66–103. New York: Wiley.

Pleck, J. H., and B. P. Masciadrelli. 2004. "Paternal Involvement by U.S. Residential Fathers: Levels, Sources, and Consequences." In *The Role of the Father in Child Development*, 4th ed., ed. Michael E. Lamb, 222–71. Hoboken, N.J.: Wiley.

Popenoe, D. 1996. *Life Without Father*. Cambridge, Mass.: Harvard University Press.

Quadagno, J. 1994. *The Color of Welfare: How Racism Undermined the War on Poverty*. Oxford: Oxford University Press.

Simons, L. G., Y. F. Chen, R. L. Simons, G. Brody, and C. Cutrona. 2006. "Parenting Practices and Child Adjustment in Different Types of Households: A Study of African-American Families. *Journal of Family Issues* 27 (6): 803–25.

Snarey, J. 1996. *How Fathers Care for the Next Generation*. Cambridge, Mass.: Harvard University Press.

Stack, C. 1974. *All Our Kin*. New York: Harper and Row.

U.S. Bureau of the Census. 2000. *Households and Families*. Summary File 2 (SF-2) QT-P10. www.census.gov. Accessed: July 7, 2004.

White, L., and J. G. Gilbreth. 2001. "When Children Have Two Fathers: Effects of Relationships with Stepfathers and Non-Custodial Fathers on Adolescent Outcomes." *Journal of Marriage and the Family* 63 (1):155–67.

Wilson, W. J. 1987. *The Truly Disadvantaged: The Inner City, the Underclass, and Public Policy*. Chicago: University of Chicago Press.

Wilson, W. J. 1996. *When Work Disappears: The World of the New Urban Poor*. New York: Vintage.

CHAPTER EIGHT

Standing in the "GAP"

The Kinship Care Role of the Invisible Black Grandfather

AARON A. SMITH

Black grandfathers provide a special kind of "fathering," considering the fact that they have already reared their biological sons and daughters and, in their golden years, actively and consciously choose to rear their own grandchildren. These grandfathers do not fit the societal perception of black men who abandon and neglect their families with seemingly little regard for their young children. Instead, these black grandfathers possess generational integrity and make major sacrifices when they "claim" these children as their own, with all of the responsibilities that accompany such decisions to parent a "second time."

Black grandmothers have been historically and culturally identified as the primary caregivers to their families. Extensive research has already defined the multiple roles and responsibilities performed by these women and the attendant effects on the health and well-being of black families. However, black grandfathers have also been active participants in the creation of healthy families. Unfortunately, their contributions remain unacknowledged and underappreciated. Therefore, the intention of this work is to give voice to these men who, along side their spouses, provide guidance, safety, and nurture to the millions of children who are being reared in these "kinship care" families in the absence of their biological parents.

This chapter highlights an ongoing qualitative study documenting the experiences of grandfathers who are rearing their grandchildren.

These grandfathers are participants in an ongoing support group that has encouraged them to actively express their concerns, contributions, and needs as they continue in their designated roles in the lives of their grandchildren. They are currently being sponsored by a black family-service agency in south Florida. This qualitative, ethnographic study developed out of a four-year experience as a facilitator for a support group of thirty black grandfathers sponsored by the Grandparents Assistance Programs (GAP), a black community-service project in a metropolitan city in southwestern Florida.

The Emergence of Kinship Care

Conventional images of kinship-care-giving grandparents tend to focus on grandmothers as the primary providers of care and nurturing to the millions of children reared in their homes. This chapter will focus on the equally important role and filial responsibilities of black grandfathers as coparenting surrogates as they actively rear their grand and great-grandchildren. First, I will provide a brief overview of what has contributed to grandparents rearing their grandchildren.

Grandparents from diverse cultural groups are rearing their biological sons' and daughters' children because of parental alcohol and drug abuse, teen pregnancies, parental incarceration, homelessness, domestic violence, HIV-AIDS, emotional and physical illness and disability, poverty, parental death, abandonment, neglect, and other circumstances that render parents incapable of providing safe and nurturing environments for their children. Public child-welfare agencies have been unable to meet the increasing demand for nonrelative foster homes to provide this necessary care. Grandparents and other relatives recognized the need to come forward and claim these children as their own. In doing this, they realized the possibility of becoming surrogate parents in the absence of the biological parents. Consequently, child-welfare agencies endorsed relative caregivers' receiving appropriate financial and supportive services to lessen the burdens of taking on this new "parenting" responsibility. Under these conditions elderly grandparents emerged nationally as the extended family members most willing to take on this new "parenting" responsibility.

It has been noted that while grandparent care giving occurs in most ethnic cultural groups and all socioeconomic levels, black grandparents are disproportionately represented because of the effects of crack cocaine and parental incarceration on the lives of their adult children and ultimately the lives of their grandchildren (Joslin and Brouard 1995; Minkler and Roe 1996). According to Simmons and Dye (2003), the 2000 U.S Census Bureau data reported that 5.8 million children nationwide live with their grandparents in absence of their biological parents. This continues the trend identified in the 1970s as documented by Casper and Bryson (1998).

Child-welfare administrators and social workers acknowledge that kinship care is an important component of family preservation. This is a cultural strength within black families where surrogate parenting across generations has historically been a common practice involving grandparents, great-grandparents, aunts and uncles, and other extended kin (Burton 1992). However, maternal grandmothers are the most frequent surrogate parents.

Grandmothers and Grandfathers

A substantial body of research has explored the significant factors involved in the psychological dimensions of grandparent care-giving experiences. Demographics has identified the myriad outcomes for children reared by their grandparents and the effect of the care giving on the grandparents themselves. A review of this literature tends to most often imply that grandparent care giving is done primarily and almost exclusively by grandmothers, with an occasional reference to grandfathers in an adjunctive, ancillary, or attendant role. While many of the titles of academic and other scholarly works cite "grandparents" as the focus, an examination of the content reveals that most of these works typically focus on the grandmothers and their experiences as primary caregivers; the grandfathers are peripheral to the grandparenting experience or are not mentioned at all (Dressel and Barnhill 1994; Solomon and Mark 1995; Poindexter and Linsk 1999; Caputo 2000; Fuller-Thomson and Minkler 2000; Hanks 2001; Kelley et al. 2001; Edwards 2003; Musil and Standing 2005).

There are, however, some articles that do explore the experiences of grandfathers rearing their grandchildren. These articles confirm the reality of the presence of these men and also acknowledge the vital roles that they perform in the everyday lived experiences of the children they are rearing (Cath 1982; Kivett 1991; Bullock 2005).

Gendered Care Giving

Gendered care-giving ideology has often cited the apparent unequal distribution of work assigned to or acknowledged as being in the domain of women. Gerstel and Gallager (2001) document that women do more care giving than men, suggesting also that from an early age women feel responsible for nurturing while men are socialized early to be somewhat removed from such responsibilities. A statement heard occasionally about care giving is that "women get caught and men get away—that's just the way it is." The prevalence of this kind of thinking continues to dominate discussions about gender inequality in the area of employment outside the home and who does what in relation to care giving inside the home. Some studies have looked at the roles of women in terms of child and family care giving and continue to promote the idea that women are the ones who provide the majority of care for their children, their spouses, and their parents in the United States. Consequently, a range of services to assist them in their ongoing responsibilities are in place and continuing to be developed.

Black grandfathers are also important and vital members of kinship-care-giving families. They are especially important as partners to their spouses, yet it appears that they receive less attention and recognition for the contributions they make to their families. Parke (1995) and Pleck (1997) state that more gender-neutral, egalitarian views are needed to accommodate the fact that more fathers and grandfathers are presently participating in care-giving activities and other family responsibilities with their spouses.

Therefore, it would seem logical to assume that grandfathers as well experience stressors in their homes after taking in grandchildren. When we consider the magnitude of the stresses that grandmothers experience as caregivers, we can assume that grandfathers have their own experiences, influenced perhaps by the uniqueness of their own family position and the stigma regarding the role of the black family man in this country.

This chapter will focus on black grandfathers who are "standing in the gap" as the primary adult surrogate father figure in the lives of the grandchildren whom they are coparenting with their spouses. It will identify their active and positive participating presence and the extent to which they realize the importance of their care-giving role. It is also important to discover the dynamic that exists between the grandparent spouses and account for what appears to be limited use of black grandfathers by their spouses as in-home care providers. In response to these themes, a discussion of how society continues to ignore these and other care-giving black men while trivializing or minimizing their contributions to their families will be provided.

Collecting the Narratives from Members of the Grandparents Assistance Program

The grandfathers in this study met every two weeks for four years. The data were gathered by semistructured, audio-taped interviews designed to discover the specific experiences encountered by these grandfathers in their co-parenting responsibilities. The group intervention consisted of two-hour sessions facilitated by the author and assisted by one graduate student in social work who also recorded verbatim statements and dialogue. Unfortunately, toward the end of the project, four of the grandfathers' spouses who suffered from chronic illnesses died. These men slowly tapered off from active participation in the group. However, their experiences are presented in these research findings.

These grandfathers ranged in age from forty-eight to seventy-eight years; all were retired except the youngest, who was a junior-college counselor. Some grandfathers worked part-time jobs; all were receiving Social Security with some additional pension income. These men and their spouses were coparenting a total of 137 children, ranging in age from four-month-old twins to teenaged boys and girls. This chapter is enhanced by the voices of the grandfathers and their candid personal reflections, their in-depth life histories, and the conversations that developed within the group. Additional information was acquired from two home visits with the grandparents and their grandchildren.

An average of twenty men regularly attended the group sessions; some at times called in to indicate family emergencies, conflicts in schedules, and doctor appointments. Over time, these men gradually learned to trust one another and could then focus their discussions around specific content areas. This group of black grandfathers became the focal point for my grounded-theory qualitative research. Grandfathers were encouraged to continue to look at their roles and how those roles might benefit their families, themselves, and the children. I used active participant-observation strategy and extensive individual life-history reviews during home visits and interviews with both spouses. Occasionally I could observe interactions between the grandparents and the children when they were home during these visits.

Generated Themes

In this section, I will focus on the themes that emerged from the experiences of these men. Each theme will be defined by the voices and the stories that they shared in the group.

Transitional Timing of New Role

Role readiness or "unreadiness" to be a "parenting" grandfather was initially identified as a common concern. The timing of the actual move of the children into their homes was a moment the grandfathers were not prepared for; "caught off guard" and "knew it was coming, but didn't think so soon" were frequently used phrases. Most of the grandfathers agreed that they loved their grandchildren but needed more time to "get ready." As one grandfather said, "It's one thing to know it is gonna happen, it is another thing when it happens." Age was a factor for most of them as they had thought that "taking care of babies and children was over. This is supposed to be our time." Most admitted that their wives had been more involved with the grandchildren, knew them better, and had better relationships with them. It was quite an adjustment for these established relationships when the couple realized that these grandchildren would be staying full time and would not be going home to their parents. This required major adjustments in numerous spousal routines.

Many of the grandfathers were initially not as actively involved in the lives of the grandchildren as were the grandmothers, who had greater awareness and understanding of the problems of the biological parents and their lifestyles. When it became apparent that the grandchildren should be removed from their biological parents' care, the grandmothers understood that there were few options for their care. The choice was the "state" or the grandparents' home. The grandfathers' limited access to their grandchildren did not provide them with adequate preparation for the children's entrance into their homes so soon and on a permanent basis. The grandfathers never questioned their love for these grandchildren but were admittedly shocked that their own lives would become filled with new responsibilities and additional stress given their already compromised energies and resources.

The grandfathers became aware that the grandmothers had obviously discussed the situation with a child-welfare social worker but only mentioned this to them after the decision had been made. The grandfathers acknowledged that if they had been included in the original discussions, they may have discouraged their wives from bringing the grandchildren into the home because of their advanced ages and their continuing chronic health problems. While it has not been easy for them, the joy that they have received from the children now makes them feel guilty about their initial reluctance to take them in.

Becoming a Full-Time "Daddy" Again

Most of the men acknowledged that they took to the new role more slowly than they thought they would. Their wives had to show them how to do most things, how to relate to the grandchildren, how to talk to them, and so on. If they had done some of the things they were now required to do with their own children, they had forgotten them. Not being in control was a change for them. This added stress when they were supposed to have less of it in their lives. With the help of their wives, they learned how to be a "daddy" again. Most of the men admitted that as they gradually moved into the new roles, not only did it get easier, but they also did more. Their wives were pleased, and the men enjoyed being "an old daddy." This represented a significant change in the marital relationship, as the next theme demonstrates.

Coparenting Partnerships

Throughout most of the sessions, the conversations centered on the grandfathers' spouses. While the original purpose of the group was to hear from the grandfathers about their experiences and concerns about parenting a second time, the grandmothers' dominant presence in childrearing entered the conversations frequently. These men were focused on acknowledging the "patience and goodness of my wife, and all that she does for the children." Great energy emerged wherever these grandfathers reflected on the long-term commitment of their wives to caring for the children and how their newfound awareness of the sacrifices made by their wives made them more appreciative. It also made them aware that their wives really needed them "to be more helpful to her by being helpful with my grandchildren too." One grandfather stated with great passion, "My wife is the center of our family. I always knew it but now that I am home more, I see more, and I understand more. I get on her last nerves sometimes, but she knows that I respect her and what she does for all of us. I have helped her because I know why she is so tired every night; I am tired, too, but look how long she has been tired. I mess up sometimes with the diapers, but I'm trying." These grandfathers were clear that the role as helpers to their wives was also important to them.

These men acknowledge the centrality of grandmothers as primary caregivers, and by this recognition they become empowered to actively join their spouses in care giving to their grandchildren. As they actively become coparents, they share in the stresses and strains that they were shielded from by their spouses earlier in their marriage and initial childrearing years. This is an important discovery that was reiterated throughout the sessions.

Grandfather Involvement

The importance of being actively involved in everyday experiences with their grandchildren emerged in the data. These included becoming involved in the family life; doing things with the grandchildren; and participating in all aspects of their care, with the grandmothers and sometimes without them. As one grandfather illustrated: "Being there is not enough; there is work to be done and it should be done. Me and my wife, we are the only ones there, and my wife cannot do it all by herself." The grandfathers recognized that their presence in the homes meant more than "just being there." They learned that they had regained past parental responsibilities thought to be over. As one grandfather said: "We granddaddies got to be active with our kids. That is a good way to get to know them, and they need us to help them." Another grandfather said: "I got sugar [diabetes] and I get out of breath easy, but I take my three grandkids to the park down the street every day. They enjoy it, they expect it now, I like it. I'm slow but I get there. My wife says it gets me and the kids out of the house and out of her hair." Another states: "My wife has complained I spend more time with these children than I did with my own when they were growing up. True. Different time, different children. I got time now."

It is obvious that being involved with and having an active role to play in the lives of these grandchildren is important to these grandfathers. Even when their own health or other circumstances might be a problem for them, they persevere. Involvement with the children benefits everyone. Their past behaviors with their own children will be discussed later.

Grandfather Responsibility

These grandfathers consciously separated grandfather involvement from grandfather responsibility. This was one of the most poignant reflections between three grandfathers one year into the group's development: Mr. B stated,

> We are only doing what we are supposed to do. Our own grown sons and daughters left these children, not with us, but now we got them, and who else they got? Their momma's gone, daddy's gone, and it's just us. The street got our kids, but not these here. I done lost mine, not again. We all here worked too long and too hard to lose it all. So what me and my old lady do, we suppose to do, nobody else. We have to learn how to do it right.

Mr. C explained,

> I'm here because I didn't spend enough time with my children when they was little. Always worked two, three jobs, home just long enough to eat and sleep. God bless my wife, she put up with it and me, and it's hard to admit it here until now, but I didn't do right by my kids, and the streets got both my boys, and now I, we, got theirs. I agree, we got work to do so we don't lose these here. I got a new attitude now. I'm older and this is our chance to make it right.

Mr. A stated,

> I'm so full I could bust open. I'm seventy years old and I look back over my life—I'm a good man, good husband, but I wish I had been a better father. I had a heavy hand and I used it, and now I regret it because I wasn't there for my kids like I ought to—my wife said I did my best, but it needed to be better. I got a real responsibility to treat and love these kids I got now better than I did their mama and daddies. That's a big responsibility now, but we'll be ok, I swear.

Financial stability is an additional area of concern to these care-givers and their spouses. Most of the grandfathers had modest income from jobs that offered pensions or retirement benefits. Most of the grandmothers also worked in their younger years at menial jobs with low wages and limited pension plans. Not surprisingly, the majority of these grandparents live close to or below the national poverty thresh-old even though many of them own their homes. They are cash poor because of rising healthcare costs and Social Security depreciation.

Researcher's Reflection

At this point, it is critical that I stop and discuss what these conver-sations symbolized for me as a black grandfather. I had been hearing powerful, heartfelt reflections shared among strong men. At times there was complete silence and some tears shed. It was obvious that the group had reached an important juncture in its own process— complete honesty and open, genuine communication. But something happened to me as well. My first thought was that these are elderly black men talking with voices that most of society says do not exist, men who are able at this point in their lives to do some honest ap-praisal of their pasts and see the need to make restitution now in the lives of the young grandchildren they are rearing. Simultaneously, they are "letting go and taking on" not only new attitudes but also new identities—no longer victims of previous circumstances but truly em-powered to move forward with their spouses in treating themselves, each other, and their grandchildren differently. Now I will return to themes that emerged in the group.

"Pining" and Grieving

The majority of the men in the support group were very verbal and could become very emotional during their moments of sharing. Dur-ing one of their sessions, the men in the group were asked to share "your deepest regret." Mr. C stated that

> my regret is I will never be able to have my son back; he died of a drug overdose seven years ago. I regret all of those times when I rejected

my son's cry for me to help him. I tried to help him but the more help I gave, the more he wanted. He would come to the house, steal stuff to sell for dope. I remember him as a child, a good boy, one who would wait for me to come home every day from work. We was a team. Then he changed, wrong crowd, drugs, had babies, married but left after the second child. I loved him, and I want him back [began to cry]. Never a day that I don't think about him. Now I'm raising his two boys, me and my wife see him in them. A second chance. I want the first chance back, but I know I won't have him back, and that hurts.

Mr. W stated,

I know that's how I feel. I have a longing for my daughter; she's gone, never to come back, but if I could bring her back, me and my wife talk about it. It's been six years and I should be over it, but I don't know how to do that. I know my wife thinks about it. She keeps it to herself, and I know it bothers her when I try to bring it up. I don't go to the grave as much as I did before, but I still think about her and if I could have did something different she would be alive today and she could raise her own children.

Mr. T concurred,

I'm glad you all are talking about this, not glad about our kids. But I regret so much about my life before now, especially how I neglected my family, especially my kids. Their mother was always a good mom, always tried to get me to do right; I also wish I could have another chance with them, especially the son that overdosed in my house when he came to visit one time. We argued that time and that stays on my mind. If I could replay that day, I would be OK. If I could have a chance again, I would do better. Even though I know that I cannot go back, there are days when his image is right in my face. I just turned sixty-eight, and now his son and daughter live with me and his mom. I talk about him a lot, and that's OK. I never say anything bad about him to his kids.

Negotiated Coparenting Division of Labor

Grandfathers in the support group always identified their spouses as being responsible for helping them learn how to parent the grandchildren.

It was obvious that the men in a variety of ways were already helping with the grandchildren before they entered the group. Their wives validated that they were effective and good helpers. More than half the men and their wives had entered into negotiated coparenting relationships that they were finding supportive. Home visits that I made provided insight into how grandparents shared family responsibilities. Here are a few examples of how co-parenting divisions of labor emerged.

Mr. C explained, "Once I retired and was home a lot, I saw how busy and tired my wife was at the end of the day, so I asked her how I could help." Mrs. C then offered, "I was surprised at first because he had never offered before, but he had started picking up after himself and he had started dealing with the children more. When I saw how serious he was, I started helping and showing him." Mr. C replied, "She liked how I did things, and she told me so. Then we sat down and talked about who did the best in certain things." Mrs. C concluded, "It's working much better now, and I can leave the kids with him and not be concerned about them now."

Mr. D revealed, "I remember coming late to the group one morning because I had forgotten to iron the kids' clothes for school the night before, and I iron better than my wife." Mrs. D explained that "I cook better so we decided that if he ironed and I cooked, that would work fine for us. We both go to school visits together and doctors appointments together. Before that, I had to try to explain things to him that I didn't understand myself. It's much better this way now."

Achieving this negotiated division of labor required open and honest communication between the adults. Other couples acknowledged that building on their relationship made a difference in how they managed to work out a system of care that did not complicate matters further. Those grandfathers who were still tentative in getting involved with the care-giving responsibilities gained support from those in the group who were functioning better in their efforts. These problem-solving strategies continued to emerge over time, with the grandfathers becoming more active in their determination to be good "fathers" to their grandchildren and support resources for the grandmothers.

Putting Love on Hold, Waiting in the Wings

The men in the study were asked "to identify one thing that prevented them from bonding with the grandchildren as quickly as did the grandmothers." This was an area of concern that some of the grandmothers identified during the home visits, and we brought it back to the group. The wives had been complaining that the "men kept an obvious distance and the children were beginning to feel like Pop-Pop didn't care." One grandfather said: "I was still holding back, hoping that my daughter was going to come back through the door and take her kids home. If I got too close and started loving them and she came back, I wasn't ready for that." Another grandfather stated: "I thought that my wife gave them more so they didn't need mine, hers was enough." Another grandfather joined in with: "I was never that comfortable with my own kids, and these kids needed so much and I wasn't ready yet."

Most of the men admitted that they loved the grandchildren. However, they were aware that if the biological parents came back, the grandchildren would easily reestablish their bonds with their parents and might even forget the loving and care-giving functions that the grandfather had provided. After a great deal of open discussion, the grandfathers were reminded that they had already acknowledged that having kept themselves emotionally removed from their own children had created problems in those relationships and that this seemed a "repeat performance" of the same issue. This is one of the areas that required continued discussion. Three grandfathers eventually acknowledged to the group that they had been talking about "love on hold" with their wives. They stated that it was easier for them to show more affection toward their grandchildren because their grandchildren's parents were dead or "missing in action"—alive but not involved. When they accepted that the biological parents would not be coming back, they had to accept the fact that "we are parents now so we got to let that go and move on into the kids' lives. That was hard to accept but we got to accept it. Our wives already accept it."

This was another revelation: that these men are sensitive individuals, willing and able to discuss painful places in their lives and in their relationships with their spouses and with their grandchildren. This second chance will assist them in moving forward in enjoying and loving their grandchildren in ways they did not discover with their own children. These black grandfathers worry for and love their grandchildren, and after recognizing, acknowledging, and expressing these feelings among other men, the grandfathers find themselves able to share them with their wives. Their marriages then become more capable of providing care for their grandchildren.

Commitment and Dedication to the Family

In the support group, each man admitted that he and his spouse did not know what they were committing to when they agreed to have their grandchildren come live in their homes. One grandfather stated: "I thought they would stay a few days while their parents got their act together and then they would go back home." Another stated: "When the children was brought to us, the social worker said, a few days— two weeks at the most. It's been three years." Another grandfather was emphatic: "They could stay two months at the most because we had planned a real vacation, so we put it off for two months—it's been three years, a total surprise and shock."

Several grandfathers admitted that they thought that taking in their grandchildren would be a simple matter. However, they quickly discovered that once the novelty was over, the seriousness of the decision, the responsibilities involved, and the many changes their lives would undergo became clear. However, once the grandfathers became aware of the numerous problems that their grandchildren had experienced with their parents and in foster homes, their attitudes changed. Their commitment and determination to be better parents grew. One grandfather spoke for the others:

> These children needed a lot of attention, love, a lot of hugs and reassuring and understanding that they were children who needed me, needed my wife and the rest of our family; we are family and we cannot deny them the right to be loved, feel love, know that we care; they needed both of us, not just my wife. They needed me so I had to get a new attitude about me and about them. They are innocent ones, not their fault, sometimes our fault. We know and they know that we will do any and everything for them. All of us got our problems, I got prostate problems and diabetes, but they make me want to live for them. They make us all have a reason for getting up each day, aching knees and all.

These grandfathers recognize that they have multiple roles and a great deal of work to do, some of which they had thought they were already done with. The support-group process created special opportunities for these men to discover themselves and the many changes they had undergone since taking in their grandchildren.

Black Grandfathers and Generativity

The grandfathers in this support group were elderly black men, not wealthy and generally not physically well. By their own admission, they were not faultless or perfect, and yet they believed that they were making a major contribution to their families and to the world. At this stage of their lives, they and their spouses have taken on the major job of preparing their grandchildren and great-grandchildren for a social environment that has not really learned to value black children and their families. In particular, they found that imparting cultural imperatives to young people was a way to protect them in the future. Toward the end of the group's fourth year, the grandfathers began to experience some separation anxiety. The group agreed that it would begin to shift its focus toward closure. At some point in the future, the agency would determine if it would resume this group or begin another group.

These men had discovered new meaning in their lives, and much discussion focused on their ultimate reasons for doing what they were doing and what difference their relationships with their grandchildren would make. To further develop this, the group was asked about "your devotion to your grandchildren's and great-grandchildren's future in the world outside your homes." This inspired great sharing for several sessions.

The conscious focus of these grandfathers seemed to be on "generativity," described by Erikson and Erikson (1950) as the concern for establishing and guiding a new generation. These grandfathers saw themselves approaching the end of their own lives. Many of the grandfathers acknowledged concern about what would happen to the children when they, the grandparents, were no longer able to take care of them. While most of the grandparents had already filed permanent planning papers designating certain other extended relatives as the children's guardians once the grandparents died, they were still focused on how they could ensure that something of them would always be present in their grandchildren and on what their legacy for the children would be.

It was obvious that these reflections created moments of deep concentration as the grandfathers tried to find the meaning of their care-giving experiences. Bringing the group to closure after four years made many of the men raise questions about closure in their own lives. One grandfather, Mr. C, who was seen as their spokesman and anchor, raised a question that resonated with all of the other men. He said,

I need to know if all that we and our wives do will have meaning in our grandchildren's lives. I need to know that some of me will always be with them. How will I know that? When we are gone, who will know that we tried to do right by them? I don't worry but I am concerned that our black children will be able to meet life challenges and disappointments and still be OK and we won't be here.

Mr. M, one of the silent ones, joined in:

We all go to church and we are believers and we take our kids for spiritual guidance. We try to teach them to be good people, as young as they is, we teach them how to be kind to others in a world that might not be kind to them. The world of violence, drugs, and fast living got their mamas and daddies. How do we keep those things from getting to them? Is that the question? Giving our grandchildren our love and just wondering if that is enough to take them through the hard times we know that they are going to have.

The words that these men continued to use in their sharing—love, kindness, unselfishness, compassion, goodness, caring, honesty, and so on—were all used as buffers against negative messages that challenge the survival possibilities of their grandchildren. These discussions occupied a great deal of the remaining group sessions. It was important to these men that their grandchildren carry something of them over into the next generation.

Kotre's (2004) concept of generativity applies nicely to what these grandfathers wish to be: mentors who model actions, teach skills, provide guidance, and facilitate the advancement of others. Kotre further states that generative individuals are "keepers of meaning," concerned with preserving a family's traditions. Frazier (1939) referred to black grandmothers as "guardians of the generations" for the roles they played in caring for their grandchildren and families during the years of slavery in this country. Hill (1999) identified one of the important historical-cultural strengths of black families as the ability of extended families to sustain, support, and enhance the survival of the family in times of great need. These grandfathers in their own way manifest this determination to protect and preserve their families and especially their grandchildren, the future generation. These grandfathers acknowledge that their role as surrogate fathers is part of a cultural expectation within the dynamics of the black family.

On one occasion, Mr. D, a seventy-two-year-old grandfather rearing his grandson alone after the recent death of his wife of fifty-three years, made the following statement to the group:

We lived a good life together, and I miss her real bad. We took our fifteen-year-old grandson from our daughter when he was nine months old because she couldn't take care of him with a drug habit. When I look back over the years and how my parents and grandparents helped my mama and daddy take care of me, I'm doing what I am supposed to do. Black people long time ago took care of each other, we didn't throw each other away. Now with my grandson, I got a chance to give back, but I'm giving it to him. He's a good boy, loves me, loved his granny to death, but I promised her that I would take care of him for her and for me. I'm laying the foundation now for him to know right from wrong and how to survive. He don't like to hear me talk about dying, but I will, don't know when, maybe soon. But I pray to God that he let me stay here to see him become a man ready to be on his own. That's all I want because my wife is gone now and when I am gone, we will live on in our grandson Teddy. I know that for a fact. The way I love him is the way both my father and my grandfather loved me. When I teach him now right from wrong, when I tell him that we have strong black men in our family, he understands that. When I discipline him I tell him why so he don't do it again. Me and my wife, we laid the foundation with him. I did with his mama but she went the wrong way, but he won't. When I go, and he and his forty-five-year-old disabled uncle, who lives with us, when they are without me, they take care of each other. Me and my wife always said Teddy was God's gift to us, now this is his gift. When I am gone, he will miss me and he will think about me sometimes. What more can I ask for? I know that I can trust my son, his uncle, to take good care of him. We already talked about that. Me and my wife talked with our son years ago that when something happened one or both of us, he will always be there for Teddy. So that is done.

All of these grandfathers acknowledged the need to have alternative plans for the care of their grandchildren when they were no longer able to do so themselves.

Each of these black grandfathers began the process of reviewing his past, the good and the not so good. Through this self-empowering process within the support group, each man encountered himself and the others by talking openly and candidly. The reflections that emerged were sometimes painful, yet the men were encouraged to persevere. Thus they gained more understanding of their roles and the roles of their spouses as substitutes for their absent and unavailable sons and daughters. By their own admission, they began to realize that they might succeed in their mission to enable their grandchildren and great-grandchildren to encounter the world successfully and grow in independence and ability to survive as black children and black adults growing into adulthood. This became an important site of self-discovery for them.

Discussion and Conclusion

While extensive research has focused on the multiple and varied effects on black grandmothers of rearing their grandchildren, the research references of kin-care-giving grandfathers and other male relative caregivers is sparse. This small study of twenty-six black grandfathers was an effort to elicit self-reported reflections and information from men who are active participants with their spouses as coparenting surrogates for their grandchildren and great-grandchildren.

These men were able to express their numerous concerns about parenting a second time around when they least expected it, and during their golden years of retirement. They were able to connect with other men who were experiencing the same issues and as a consequence of sharing their reflections they also were able to find better ways of making their roles as father figures and coparenting spouses more effective.

Once the goals and objectives of the support group became clearer to these grandfathers, they became committed to open communication with one another. There was increased awareness and recognition of the needs of the grandchildren and the long-term toll that the caregiving responsibility had taken on their spouses. They also encountered some of their own confusion about their roles as men providing care to children; they quickly found themselves able to accept their responsibilities as the only adult male role model in their families.

These grandfathers debunked the myth that men, especially black men, do not talk, do not care, and do not share their feelings. On the contrary, these men talked candidly and with great emotion and expressed feelings of love and compassion and caring, especially toward their spouses and their grandchildren. Several acknowledged with amazement that they had disclosed things to one another in the group that they had never expressed even to themselves and certainly not to their wives. Yet having discovered their ability to discuss openly their experiences in this group setting, many acknowledged sharing this information with their spouses, who were similarly amazed and thankful.

By their own admission, these men had encountered life in all its variety and had survived, sometimes with emotional scars. They were able to embrace anger toward societal inequities that they and theirs had experienced in racism, discrimination, low income, job losses, and so on. However, they were able to recognize some strengths they did not know they had: being able to provide a living for their families; staying away from wrong crowds and bad influences; drinking occasionally but not being alcoholics; and being not perfect but also not totally flawed.

They also recognized that as fathers, they might have failed their own children sometimes without realizing it. They acknowledged that looking back was painful but necessary to avoid the same mistakes. I found these grandfathers to be truth-telling and truth-seeking men who, if given the appropriate supportive environment, were capable of sharing information and supporting one another when certain areas became emotionally charged and painful.

These black grandfathers know that they must conduct themselves as models of healthy masculinity and set an example that their grandchildren can look up to and emulate. One grandfather stated that "black grandfathers will have to set this model as our expectation that we have for ourselves and all other males. The ones you know and the ones you don't know. Image building is important but image behavior is vital." This kind of reasoning was common with these men, and again the negative myths about black men were challenged.

These grandfathers have many stories to tell that should be heard by all professional providers. The training to hear the strengths of black men is often lacking in mainstream professional-education programs. There are millions of black men of all ages who are willing to share the responsibilities and the work involved in rearing children. The men in this group recognize the need for positive interpersonal relationships between them and their wives; they recognized that the children needed to "see" and "feel" the emotional and spiritual connection, the mutual admiration and respect, between their loved ones.

STANDING IN THE "GAP" · 189

These grandfathers also have life lessons that they learned from their own parents and grandparents and other extended family relatives. They believe that grandmothers and grandfathers need to lead their families in prayer daily. They must instill values from their African heritage in the lives of their grandchildren. Black men should be awakened to take on their rightful family responsibilities and obligations. These black grandfathers feel they must document and dramatize for other black men appropriate behaviors and responsibilities to their families, teaching their children, grandchildren, and great-grandchildren how to be creative, caring, contributing, functional members of society.

While this is a small study of twenty-six black grandfathers and great-grandfathers, it is possible that it represents a much larger context of available, capable and responsible men who effectively joined their spouses in creating healthy, wholesome, loving home environments that will enhance the challenged lives of their grandchildren. The grandfathers in this study, while not highly educated, were articulate in identifying their concerns, fears, aspirations, intentions and needs. These black grandfathers possess important human longings that are grounded in cultural-historical and contemporary experiences as black men in the United States.

These men and their spouses create wholesome marital relationships that enhance the healthy growth and development of the next generation, their own grandchildren and great-grandchildren. These and all other relative caregivers prevail under challenging conditions, including their own aging process, limited financial resources, the emotional traumas that the children might have experienced before coming into their homes, and the absence and sometimes actual deaths of their own biological sons and daughters.

If care-giving relatives refused to provide homes for these children, the states would be overwhelmed by families needing multiple resources to sustain and nurture the children in their care. The social environment in which the grandparents in this study are rearing their grandchildren is very different from the world in which they were reared by their parents and grandparents. Yet these grandparents and other relative caregivers commit themselves and their meager resources for the betterment of their grandchildren, sometimes neglecting themselves in the process. It is the responsibility of child-welfare practitioners and policymakers to create services, programs, and legislative initiatives that will meet the needs of grandparents and the children they are rearing. It is critical that we respond to this national crisis.

References

Bullock, K. 2005. "Grandfathers and the Impact of Raising Grandchildren." *Journal of Sociology and Welfare* 32:43–59.

Burton, L. M. 1992. " Black Grandparents Rearing Children of Drug-Addicted Parents." *The Gerontologist* 92 (32): 744–52.

Caputo, R. K. 2000. "Second-Generation Parenthood: A Panel Study of Grandmother and Grandchild Coresidency Among Low-Income Families, 1967–1992." *Journal of Sociology and Social Welfare* 27 (3): 3–20.

Casper, L. M., and K. R. Bryson. 1998. *Co-Resident Grandparents and Their Grandchildren: Grandparent Maintained Families.* Population Division Working Paper No. 26. Washington, D.C.: U.S. Bureau of the Census.

Cath, S. H. 1988. "Vicissitudes of Grandfatherhood: A Miracle of Revitalization?" In *Father and Child: Developmental and Clinical Perspectives*, ed. S. H. Cath, A. R. Gurwitt, and J. M. Ross, 329–337. Cambridge, Mass.: Basil Blackwell.

Dressel, P. L., and S. Barnhill. 1994. "Framing Gerontological Thought and Practice: The Care of Grandmothers with Daughters in Prison." *Gerontologist* 34 (5): 685–91.

Edwards, D. W. 2003. "Living with Grandma: A Grandfamily Study." *School Psychology International* 24:204–17.

Erikson, E. H., and J. M. Erikson. 1950. *The Life Cycle Completed.* New York: Norton.

Frazier, E. F. 1939. *The Negro Family in the United States.* Chicago: University of Chicago Press.

Fuller-Thomson, E., and M. Minkler. 2000. "African American Grandparents Raising Grandchildren: A National Profile of Demographic and Health Characteristics." *Health and Social Work* 25 (2): 109–18.

Gerstel, N., and S. K. Gallagher. 2001. "Men's Caregiving: Gender and the Contingent Character of Care." *Gender and Society* 15 (2): 197–217.

Hanks, R. S. 2001. "'Grandma, What Big Teeth You Have!' The Social Construction of Grandparenting in American Business and Academe." *Journal of Family Issues* 22 (5): 652–76.

Hill, R. B. 1999. *The Strengths of Black Families.* 2nd ed. Lanham, Md.: University Press of America.

Joslin, D., and A. Brouard. 1995. "The Prevalence of Grandmothers as Primary Caregivers in a Poor Pediatric Population." *Journal of Community Health* 20:383–401.

Kelley, S. J., B. C. Yorker, D. M. Whitley, and T. A. Sipe. "A Multimodal Intervention for Grandparents Raising Grandchildren: Results of Exploratory Study." *Child Welfare* 80 (1): 27–50.

Kivett, V. R. 1991. "Centrality of the Grandfather Role Among Older Rural Black and White Men." *Journal of Gerontology* 46:S250–58.

Kotre, J. 2004. *Outliving the Self: Generativity and the Interpretation of Life.* Baltimore, Md.: Johns Hopkins University Press.

Minkler, M., and K. M. Roe. 1996. "Grandparents as Surrogate Parents." *Generations* 20 (1): 34–38.

Musil, C. M., and T. Standing. 2005. "Grandmothers Diaries: A Glimpse at Daily Lives." *International Journal of Aging and Human Development* 60:317–28.

Parke, R. D. 1995. "Fathers and Families." in *Handbook of Parenting*, 2nd ed., ed. M. H. Bornstein, 3:27–73, New York: Erlbaum.

Pleck, J. 1997. "Parental Involvement: Levels, Sources, and Consequences." In *The Role of the Father in Child Development*, ed. M. E. Lamb, 66–103. New York: Wiley.

Poindexter, C. C., and N. L. Linsk. 1999. "I'm Just Glad That I'm Here: Stories of Seven HIV-Affected African-American Grandmothers." *Journal of Gerontological Social Work* 32 (1): 63–81.

Simmons, T., and J. L. Dye. 2003. *Grandparents Living with Grandchildren: 2000.* Washington, D.C.: U.S. Census Bureau.

Solomon, J. C., and J. Marx. 1995. "To Grandmother's House We Go: Health and School Adjustment of Children Raised Solely by Grandparents." *The Gerontologist* 35:386–94.

CHAPTER NINE

African American Men Rearing Children in Violent Neighborhoods

BETHANY L. LETIECQ

Many studies have portrayed low-income African American fathers as deficient and irresponsible in parenting (Spencer 1990; Allen and Connor 1997). The "deficit-based" lens through which researchers have studied low-income African American fathering has been used largely because white, middle-class parenting practices and styles have been the standard by which parenting is measured (Fagan 2000). The research has also been systematically biased in favor of the traditional nuclear family in which married biological parents rear their children. Most studies of African American fathering have failed to consider the parenting practices and styles of these men *in context*. In other words, few studies examine how cultural variations in parenting are adaptations to "situatedness," the social, political, and economic environments in which African American fathers are rearing their children. However, as the work of Marsiglio, Roy, and Fox (2005) reveals, fathers' situatedness influences the ways in which they socialize, nurture, provide for, and protect their children. Context matters, especially when some contexts—such as those experienced by low-income African American families—are riddled with systemic and structural inequalities and unequal access to education, employment, political power, commercial goods and services, and resources (Lazur and Majors 1995; Coley 2001).

Researchers have long noted the disproportionate numbers of African American families experiencing poverty, violence, and other challenges resulting from economic and social disenfranchisement. For example, the percentage of African Americans falling below the poverty line is estimated to be 24.3 (compared with 8.2 percent for non-Hispanic whites, and 20.6 percent for people of Hispanic origin; see DeNavas-Walt, Proctor, and Smith 2007). African American families are ten times more likely than white families to live in neighborhoods where at least 30 percent of residents are poor (Duncan, Brooks-Gunn, and Klebanov 1994). African American families are also disproportionately represented in neighborhoods characterized by high levels of violence, crime, joblessness, and drug activity (Chase-Lansdale and Gordon 1996; Sampson, Raudenbush, and Earls 1997). Low-income African American families have the highest rates of criminal victimization (Hill 1993). And African American women have the highest rates of nonmarital births (Martin et al. 2006). Such statistics have led many to assume that African American fathers are absent from their children's lives and that these men are failing to provide for their families and protect them from violence.

However, some researchers examining African American fathering in context have suggested that these men may not "do family" the same way that the majority culture does family and that African American men—whether living in the same households as their children or living in separate residences—may be more "present" in their families and communities than previously understood (Smith et al. 2005). As Levine (1993) noted over a decade ago, fathers who are not officially living in the household may be "unofficially available" to young children. For example, in a study of fourteen Head Start programs located throughout the U.S., Levine and his colleagues found that a man, whether a father, boyfriend, or male relative, was residing in approximately 60 percent of Head Start households (Levine, Murphy, and Wilson 1992). Indeed, recent studies have found that unmarried mothers of young children often form new romantic partnerships early in their children's lives. Estimates suggest that 21 percent of unwed mothers are living with their child and a new male partner five years after their child's birth (Bzostek, Carlson, and McLanahan 2007). These men—referred to as social fathers—appear to engage with their partner's children in ways that are beneficial for child well-being (King 2006; Bzostek 2007).

What remains unclear is how low-income African American biological and social fathers parent their children, especially in dangerous contexts such as high-violence neighborhoods. Do social fathers employ the same parenting practices and styles as biological fathers with preschoolers? Are social fathers and biological fathers' perceptions of their ability to protect their children in violent neighborhoods the same? And how do their perceptions of power relate to their parenting practices and styles? To shed light on these questions, this study examined the parenting perceptions, practices, and styles of African American biological and social fathers rearing children in neighborhoods characterized by high rates of poverty and violence. Social fathers included both resident and nonresident stepfathers, mothers' romantic partners, grandfathers, uncles, and any other family associate who demonstrated parental behaviors and acted as a father to a child (Tamis-LeMonda and Cabrera 1999; Jayakody and Kalil 2002). This study is guided by a cultural-ecology framework (Ogbu 1981).

Theoretical Framework

A cultural-ecology model can be a useful framework for examining patterns of socialization and parenting competencies based on cultural contexts that are central to the attitudes, skills, and values of parents within a specific cultural milieu (Ogbu 1981; Hamer and Marchioro 2002). It is critical that researchers use a cultural-ecological lens to understand the myriad ways in which African American men and their families have adapted to their environments and the systemic and structural inequalities, institutionalized racism, discrimination, and segregation that characterize those environments. These adaptations may have yielded different family structures and more flexible roles and functions within families (Billingsley 1968). For example, scholars of African American family life discuss the role of the grandmother as being markedly more fluid and involved than that of white grandmothers (Billingsley 1992; Hill 1993; Ruiz and Zhu 2004). Scholars have also identified the role of fathers as more flexible than among other European American cultural groups and found that this role can be performed by biological and nonbiological fathers alike (Billingsley 1968; Jayakody and Kalil 2002). Recognizing the salience of African American social fathers in the lives of children, many scholars are now including these men in their studies to better reflect the true nature of African American family life (e.g., Black, Dubowitz, and Starr 1999; Jayakody and Kalil 2002; King 2006; Bzostek 2007).

Social Fathering

"Fictive" or social fathers have historically played an important role in African American families, reflecting a culture with strong traditions of role flexibility and concern for children (Billingsley 1968; Hill 1993). These social fathers are often involved with children who may lack daily contact with their biological fathers. Recent evidence suggests that researchers are beginning to explore social fathering in earnest and to examine the influence of these men on children's development. For example, in their study of the influence of African American low-income fathers on preschoolers' development and behavior, Black and colleagues (1999) included nonbiological social fathers in their sample and found that the biological relationship between the father and child did not appear to be a salient factor in explaining child outcomes (at least early in a child's life). Based on their findings, Black, Dubowitz, and Starr conclude that "preschoolers understand nurturance and care, but not necessarily distinctions related to biological status" (976).

More recent research conducted by Bzostek and her colleagues suggests that involvement by residential social fathers is as beneficial for child well-being as involvement by residential biological fathers (Bzostek 2007; Bzostek, Carlson, and McLanahan 2007). More specifically, Bzostek (2007) found that higher levels of engagement by resident social fathers with their partners' young children were related to fewer behavioral problems and better overall health for the children under their care. Bzostek concluded that the positive impact of father involvement may not be tied to the biological relationship between father and child. In another study of social fathering, Jayakody and Kalil (2002) suggested that the relationship of the social father to the child may matter for child development. The researchers found that the presence of male-relative social fathers was associated with higher levels of children's school readiness, whereas the presence of mothers' romantic partners was associated with lower levels of children's emotional maturity. While these emergent studies have examined the influences of social fathering on children's development, no studies to date have examined the parenting practices and styles employed by social fathers rearing preschoolers in neighborhoods characterized by high levels of poverty and community violence.

African American Fathering in Violent Neighborhoods

Darling and Steinberg (1993) suggest that researchers consider both parenting practices and parenting style in context in order to understand the ways in which fathers socialize their children. Parenting practices are the specific behaviors directed toward the child and can vary depending on the "situatedness" and cultural milieu of families (Marsiglio, Roy, and Fox 2005). African American fathers rearing children in underresourced, high-violence neighborhoods have been found to use a variety of protective parenting strategies, including monitoring their children closely, reducing their children's exposure to media violence, and teaching them about personal and neighborhood safety (e.g., avoiding eye contact with strangers and dialing 911 in an emergency; see Letiecq and Koblinsky 2003, 2004). Fathers residing in dangerous neighborhoods have also reported confronting drug dealers and "thugs" in the neighborhood and engaging in community activism to reduce violence where they live. While fathers residing in safer contexts likely use some of the same strategies (e.g., teaching children about personal safety), living amid violence appears to limit fathers' use of many practices considered "positive" and "proactive" by the standards of the European American majority. Allowing children to play on the playground to develop their motor skills, to walk to school to encourage autonomy, or to explore their environment to foster inquisitive minds may be too dangerous in violent neighborhoods and may place children at greater risk of harm. Thus, what is considered positive parenting in one context may not be positive in another.

Beyond parenting practices, the style of parenting used by fathers helps us to understand their attitudes toward their children. These attitudes are communicated to the child and create an "emotional climate" in which fathers' parenting behaviors are expressed (Darling and Steinberg 1993:488). Baumrind (1967) identified three parenting styles: an authoritative style, characterized by nurture, consistency, and reasoning; a permissive style, characterized by leniency and a lack of discipline and follow-through; and an authoritarian style, characterized by control, coerciveness, and strictness. Few studies have examined the parenting styles of low-income African American fathers; however, Taylor et al. (1990) suggested that African American parents are generally stricter and place a greater emphasis on obedience and self-control than do other parents. Fagan (2000), in his study of low-income African American and Puerto Rican parents of preschoolers, found

African American mothers and fathers to be significantly less nurturing, responsive, and consistent than Puerto Rican American parents.

A strict, less nurturing parenting style may be seen as necessary by African American parents who are socializing their children to cope with the harsh realities of racism, discrimination, poverty, and community dangers (Taylor et al. 1990). Indeed, in high-violence neighborhoods, fathers may not be able to rely on many of the authoritative parenting characteristics employed by parents in safer contexts because such characteristics may endanger children. Parenting children with warmth, nurture, reasoning, and a democratic style, for example, may not adequately prepare children for the harsh realities of life in violent communities and may not exert enough control over children if violence (e.g., a drive-by shooting) erupts around the family. Given their community context, these fathers may emphasize control and obedience to ensure their children's safety at all times (Letiecq and Koblinsky 2003).

While researchers are beginning to examine the parenting practices and styles of African American fathers generally, no studies to date have explored differences between social and biological fathers rearing children in unsafe contexts. Further, no studies have examined how fathers' perceptions of their ability to keep their children safe relate to their parenting practices and style. Thus this study explores the parenting practices and styles of low-income African American fathers as a function of their relationship to the focal child. This study also explores relationships between social and biological fathers' perceptions of parental power and control in high-violence neighborhoods and the practices and styles they employ to protect their children.

Sample, Community Context, and Child's Exposure to Violence

As presented in table 9.1, a total of sixty-one African American Head Start biological (n = 41) and social fathers (n = 20) were recruited to participate in this study. Social fathers self-identified as the child's uncle (n = 7), grandfather (n = 5), stepfather (n = 4), or men with other kinship or social ties to the child (n = 4). The majority of fathers (60 percent of social; 85 percent of biological) resided in the same household as the focal child. Ages ranged from 18 to 70, with a mean age of 36.2 years for the total sample. All fathers lived in the same low-income neighborhood as their child or within a five-mile radius.

Table 9.1

Demographic Characteristics of the Sample by Father-Child Relationship

Demographic Characteristic	Social Fathers (n = 20)[a]	Biological Fathers (n = 41)[a]
Father's Characteristics		
Father's age in years	40.80 (15.3)	33.95 (6.5)*
Father's education in years	12.95 (2.2)	12.59 (2.0)
Single	3 (15.0%)	13 (31.7%)
Single, living with partner	5 (25.0%)	9 (22.0%)
Married	7 (35.0%)	13 (31.7%)
Separated, divorced	4 (20.0%)	3 (7.3%)
Widowed	1 (5.0%)	0 (0.0%)
Other	0 (0.0%)	3 (7.3%)
Employed	15 (75.0%)	35 (85.4%)
Not employed	5 (25.0%)	6 (14.6%)
Number of children	3.26 (2.4)	2.95 (2.2)
Years of father involvement with target child	3.55 (1.1)	4.07 (0.8)*
Focal child living in household (Yes)	12 (60.0%)	35 (85.4%)
Focal Child Characteristics		
Male	9 (45.0%)	23 (56.1%)
Female	11 (55.0%)	18 (43.9%)
Child's Age in years	4.05 (0.7)	4.02 (0.8)
Heard gunshots in past year	13 (65.0%)	27 (65.9%)
Saw two teens/adults physically fighting in past year	16 (80.0%)	33 (80.5%)
Saw drug dealers on the street in past year	17 (85.0%)	24 (58.5%)
Saw a dead body in the street in past year	9 (45.0%)	16 (46.3%)

Notes: [a]Mean (SD) or number (%).
*p < .05.

The study took place in southeast Washington, D.C., and a Maryland county adjoining the District of Columbia. At the time of the study, southeast Washington, D.C., was experiencing high levels of community violence (Federal Bureau of Investigation 1998). In comparison to the fifty states, the District of Columbia had the highest teen violent-death rate and the highest child death rate from homicide since 1985 (Annie E. Casey Foundation 1999). The Maryland county also had high rates of community violence, with the fifth highest death rate from homicide, suicide, and violent deaths of all twenty-four Maryland counties in 1998 (Advocates for Children and Youth 2000). Targeted neighborhoods in Maryland had been identified as violent "hot spots" based on police data measuring murder/negligent manslaughter, rape, robbery, and aggravated assault.

Environmental scans of the study neighborhoods revealed the lack of institutions often found in more prosperous, stable, nonviolent communities. For example, there were no banking institutions nor ATM machines, no low-cost chain stores (e.g., Wal-Mart, Target), no grocery stores with a wide variety of fresh produce and other goods, and few restaurants other than fast-food establishments. There were many crack houses, check-cashing establishments, and buildings with boarded-up and barred windows covered in graffiti. Many of the Head Start centers visited during this study had bullet-proof windows, and nearby playgrounds were littered with drug paraphernalia (e.g., used needles) and discarded beer bottles.

When social and biological fathers were asked about their children's exposure to violence in the neighborhood, fathers reported that the majority of children had heard gunshots in the neighborhood, had seen teens or adults physically fighting in the streets, and had seen drug dealers near their homes (see table 9.1). Nearly half of all fathers reported that their children had also seen a dead body on the street.

Measures

BACKGROUND CHARACTERISTICS. Each participating father was administered a "Demographic Questionnaire" that ascertained his relationship to the focal child as well as his age, highest level of education attained, employment status, and residence (i.e., resides in same household as child, resides in separate household), among other variables. Information about the focal preschool child (e.g., age, sex, exposure to community violence) was also gathered.

PERCEPTION OF POWER. To measure fathers' perception of their personal power and control in protecting their children from neighborhood dangers, we asked them the following question: "How powerful or capable do you feel you are in protecting your child from community violence?" Response options ranged from 0 "not at all powerful" to 2 "extremely powerful."

PARENTING IN VIOLENT NEIGHBORHOODS. This study employed a forty-seven-item quantitative measure of protective strategies used to keep children safe from community violence, the Parenting in Violent Neighborhoods Scale (PVNS; see Letiecq and Koblinsky 2003 for details about scale development and factor analyses). This measure contains five subscales: monitoring and teaching personal safety (e.g., "I permit my child to play on playgrounds only when directly supervised by an adult"); teaching neighborhood survival tactics (e.g., "I talk to my child about safe routes for walking in the neighborhood"); reducing media violence exposure (e.g., "I keep my preschool child from playing video games that have a lot of violence"); fighting back (e.g., "I tell my preschool child to fight back in order to be safe"); and engaging in community activism (e.g., "I participate in neighborhood watch or other groups that try to reduce neighborhood violence"). Item response options were anchored by never (0) and always (4).

PARENTING STYLE. The Parenting Styles and Dimensions Questionnaire (PSDQ; Robinson et al. 1995) is a sixty-two-item measure that assesses global parenting typologies consistent with Baumrind's (1967) authoritative, authoritarian, and permissive typologies. In this measure, authoritative subscales include warmth and involvement, reasoning/induction, democratic participation, and easygoing styles. Permissive subscales include lack of follow-through, ignoring misbehavior, and lack of self-confidence. Authoritarian subscales include verbal hostility, corporal punishment, nonreasoning/punitive strategies, and directiveness. Each respondent was asked how often an item described him as a father of a preschool child using a five-point scale anchored by never (1) and always (5). The PSDQ was scored by summing the subscale items and dividing by the total number of items within each subscale.

Procedure

The current study was part of a larger effort examining the strategies low-income African American biological and social fathers use to protect their preschool children from violence in the neighborhood. Social fathers were included in the study to reflect the traditions of role flexibility and concern for children in African American family life (Billingsley 1968; Hill 1993). The study was funded by the U.S. Department of Health and Human Services' Administration for Children and Families (USDHHS/ACF) Head Start Research Scholars Program. Head Start is a comprehensive child-development program that serves children from birth to age five and has as its overall goal to increase the school readiness of young children in low-income families (USDHHS/ACF, n.d.).

A multiracial, multiethnic team of researchers (including graduate and undergraduate students) worked closely with Head Start teachers and staffs to recruit biological and social fathers of preschoolers for the study. The research team also worked closely with two community-based groups—the Significant Male Task Force and the Positive Men's Coalition—which were sponsored by Head Start to increase the involvement and visibility of significant males in Head Start programs in the Washington, D.C., metropolitan area. Working with Head Start professionals and the community groups was critical and placed this research effort within a context that was familiar to fathers and their families. The relationships built with Head Start teachers, staffs, and community leaders also facilitated the research team's ability to quickly build trust with fathers and establish our credibility in communities where, regardless of our team's racial/ethnic affiliations, we were outsiders because none of us grew up or resided in the neighborhoods included in the study.

In all, twenty Head Start centers located in high-violence neighborhoods were targeted, which resulted in the recruitment of sixty-one African American biological and social fathers to participate in one-on-one interviews. Once fathers consented to participate in the study, trained African American male interviewers conducted in-depth interviews. To determine fathers' relationship to the focal Head Start child, we inquired about their relational ties during the interview. For this study, social fathers were broadly defined and included stepfathers, mothers' romantic partners, grandfathers, uncles, and any other family associates who demonstrated parental behaviors and acted as a father to a child (Tamis-LeMonda and Cabrera 1999; Jayakody and Kalil 2002). Residential status of the fathers was not included in the inclusion/exclusion criteria for the study. The interviews took place at the father's home or the Head Start center and lasted approximately one and a half to two hours. Fathers received a small stipend for their participation.

Variation Between Social and Biological Fathers

Preliminary analyses revealed few demographic differences between biological and social fathers (see table 9.1). However, biological and social fathers differed on two variables: father's age and years involved with the Head Start child. Compared to biological fathers, social fathers were significantly older, an average difference of about seven years. Social fathers were also involved in the preschooler's life for significantly less time than biological fathers, by an average of about six months.

Next, this study examined differences in paternal perceptions of power, parenting practices, and parenting styles as a function of the father's relationship to his child. These analyses controlled for father's age and the number of years fathers were involved in their children's lives. Because of the small sample size used in the analyses, this study did not assess parenting practice and style differences as a function of the child's sex or the residential status of the fathers.

When fathers were asked how powerful or capable they felt they were in protecting their child from community violence, the majority (70 percent) of both biological and social fathers reported feeling powerful, and an additional third of the fathers reported feeling extremely powerful (see table 9.2). There were no differences in feelings of powerfulness or the capacity to keep children safe based on fathers' biological connection to their children.

This study compared biological and social fathers' parenting practices across five subscales: monitoring/teaching personal safety; teaching neighborhood survival tactics; reducing media violence exposure; fighting back; and engaging in community activism (see table 9.2). Results revealed few significant differences in the practices used by social and biological fathers; however, social fathers were significantly more likely than biological fathers to "fight back" by personally confronting drug dealers and thugs in the neighborhood or instructing children to stand up to bullies or other perceived threats. Additionally, social fathers were more likely to engage in community activism, such as joining Neighborhood Watch, than biological fathers.

To examine parenting styles, this study compared biological and social fathers across the authoritative, permissive, and authoritarian style subscales (see table 9.2). As with parenting practices, social and biological fathers employed similar parenting styles. There were no

Table 9.2

Parenting Perceptions, Practices, and Styles as a Function of the Father-Child Relationship

Demographic Characteristic	Social Fathers (n = 20)[a]	Biological Fathers (n = 41)[a]
	Paternal Perception of Power	
How powerful or capable do you feel you are in protecting your child from community violence?		
Extremely powerful	6 (30.0%)	11 (26.8%)
Powerful	14 (70.0%)	29 (70.7%)
Not at all powerful	0 (0.0%)	1 (2.4%)
	Parenting Practices in Violent Neighborhoods (PVNS)	
Monitoring and teaching personal safety	2.79 (0.84)	2.81 (0.63)
Teaching neighborhood survival tactics	2.83 (0.80)	2.59 (0.77)
Reducing media violence exposure	2.65 (0.77)	2.37 (0.75)
Fighting back	1.57 (0.75)	1.35 (0.74)*
Engaging in community activism	1.97 (0.96)	1.65 (0.73)†
	Parenting Style (PSDQ)	
Authoritative	3.75 (0.72)	3.79 (0.58)
Permissive	2.14 (0.46)	2.16 (0.49)
Authoritarian	2.24 (0.44)	2.32 (0.56)

Notes: PVNS scale anchored by 0 "never" and 4 "always." PSDQ scale anchored by 1 "never" and 5 "always."
[a]Mean (SD) or number (%).
† $p < .10$. * $p < .05$.

significant differences in the fathers' use of authoritative, permissive, or authoritarian styles. Overall, fathers were more likely to employ an authoritative style rather than a permissive or authoritarian parenting style.

Lastly, this study examined the relationships between fathers' perception of power and capability of protecting their children from neighborhood violence and their parenting practices and parenting style (see table 9.3). For social fathers, results revealed that the perception of greater power in protecting their children was significantly

Table 9.3
Relationships Between Social and Biological Fathers' Parenting Perceptions, Practices, and Styles

	1	2	3	4	5	6	7	8	9
1. Perception of power	—	.34	.18	.12	.46*	-.31	.20	-.37	-.18
2. Monitoring children	.30†	—	.79***	-.07	.41†	.51*	.73***	-.55*	-.54*
3. Teaching safety	.38*	.38*	—	-.23	.31	.52*	.75***	-.41†	-.53*
4. Reducing violent media	.16	.26†	.39*	—	-.02	-.23	-.24	-.34	-.37
5. Fighting back	-.10	.11	.05	-.23	—	.11	.51*	-.24	.08
6. Engaging in activism	.53***	.23	.54***	.26	.04	—	.35	.13	-.04
7. Authoritative style	.30†	.66***	.37*	.20	-.04	.38*	—	-.43†	-.44*
8. Permissive style	-.06	.06	-.25	-.06	.45**	-.15	.05	—	.58**
9. Authoritarian style	.12	.04	.16	.03	.45**	.16	-.14	.57***	—

Note: Social fathers presented above the diagonal; biological fathers presented below the diagonal.
† $p < .10$. * $p < .05$. ** $p < .01$. *** $p < .001$.

positively related to the strategy of "fighting back" (e.g., confronting drug dealers, teaching their children to fight back to protect themselves). However, among biological fathers, the perception of greater personal power was significantly positively related to teaching children neighborhood safety tactics and engaging in community activism. Additionally, biological fathers who perceived more power in protecting their children were more likely to employ an authoritative style.

Discussion

This study was guided by a cultural-ecology model (Ogbu 1981), which suggests that the cultural context of African American fathers residing in underresourced, high-violence neighborhoods must be considered when examining the parenting perceptions, practices, and styles used by these men. By including both biological and social fathers, this study attempts to capture the ways in which African American men have adapted their roles in family life in response to the historical, social, and economic challenges facing their families and communities. Consistent with the findings of a small but growing body of literature on social fathering (Black, Dubowitz, and Starr 1999; King 2006; Bzostek 2007), findings from this study suggest that social fathers are more similar to biological fathers than they are different from them. Indeed, this study found that biological and social fathers used similar parenting practices and styles to protect children from neighborhood dangers. Such findings suggest that future research with low-income African American fathers should continue to explore the contributions of social fathers to the development of young children. These fathers may be a "hidden" resource overlooked by practitioners and policymakers focused on promoting the salience of biological fathers only.

While few differences emerged in the data, social fathers were found to be more likely than biological fathers to fight back to protect themselves and their children from violence. These men were also more likely to engage in community activism than were biological fathers. Taken together, these findings suggest that social fathers may be more "social" in their expression of parenting. In other words, these men—who have clearly stepped in to perform a fathering role for someone else's biological children—may feel called to action. African American social fathering may be a manifestation of the larger cultural commitment to the well-being of children, irrespective of biological connection. Thus, social fathers may be actively engaged in meeting the needs of their "collective" communities, which includes performing the fatherhood role for children who may have limited contact with their biological fathers. However, it is also plausible that men who are involved in social parenting may be of a type more likely to volunteer (or be selected by others) to be a social father. Given that social fathers were older than biological fathers, it is also possible that social fathers felt more agency to fight for change or make a difference in a child's life. Although future research is needed to fully understand and explain differences between biological and social fathers, this research lends support to past findings suggesting that African American fathering is more fluid and flexible than fathering in other European American cultural groups (Billingsley 1968; 1992; Hill 1993).

Beyond comparing parenting practices and styles of social and biological fathers, this study also explored fathers' perceptions of power and capability of protecting their children from neighborhood violence and how such perceptions related to their parenting practices and styles. Here, fathers' relationship to their children may be meaningful in that social fathers who perceived themselves powerful to protect their children were more likely to fight back and teach their children to fight back in the face of personal and community dangers. It is possible that, for social fathers, perceptions of power gave them the courage to confront drug dealers in the neighborhood. Social fathers may have also believed that feeling powerful (or empowered) in the context of high-violence neighborhoods was an important characteristic to instill in young children. These men may have feared that their sons and daughters might be victims of bullying or lured into the drug culture by drug dealers if they did not know how to fight back to protect themselves. While such strategies may be essential to rearing children in unsafe contexts, future research might explore whether or not such strategies promote fear and mistrust in young children (in this study, aged three to five years) who developmentally may not understand why they have to protect themselves from others in the neighborhood.

When the relationships between perceptions of powerfulness and parenting practices and styles were examined among biological fathers, results revealed a slightly different picture. Biological fathers who perceived themselves as powerful in protecting their children were more likely to teach neighborhood safety tactics and engage in community activism. For biological fathers, perceived power seemed to translate into teaching children how to be safe in the neighborhood (e.g., teaching children safe routes to walk between home and school). Perceptions of power also appeared to be important in biological fathers' community activism. Fathers who felt powerful to protect their families from violence were more likely to join Neighborhood Watch or participate in voter registration drives in their communities. It is possible that, as compared to social fathers, biological fathers may have felt they had more to lose or that they may place their children in harm's way if they engaged in "fighting back" behaviors to protect their children. These men opted for safer, more active and positive parenting practices to keep children safe. Future research is needed to understand how perceptions of power in high-violence neighborhoods relate to the strategies fathers use to protect their children and, perhaps more importantly, how interventions focused on father empowerment may be important to promoting fathers' use of active parenting practices and positive community-engagement activities.

Implications for Researchers, Practitioners, and Policymakers

Clearly, additional research is needed on the complex ways in which African American fathers, particularly those residing in underresourced and violent neighborhoods, define their roles and responsibilities and contribute to the care and socialization of young children. Over a decade ago, Ahmeduzzaman and Roopnarine (1992) called for more research with African American fathers to identify within-culture variations in father-child relationships and to provide culture-specific information on father-child relationships to inform educators and policymakers about factors that may influence the socialization of young African American children. There continues to be a need for such culturally competent research that recognizes the situatedness of fathers and families and the macrolevel forces that influence different families in different and meaningful ways (Marsiglio, Roy, and Fox 2005).

Continued research is also needed to investigate the roles fathers and father figures play in high-violence neighborhoods to better understand how these men cope within this social context and how they understand their parental roles vis-à-vis their sons and daughters. Because of a small sample size, the current study was limited in its analyses and did not examine parenting practice and style differences as a function of the sex of the focal child. Future research should also examine differences within the "social father" category as mother's romantic partners, for example, may play a different role in children's lives than a male relative or stepfather (Jayakody and Kalil 2002). Moreover, future researchers should also consider the residential status of fathers or father figures as residence may be more salient in understanding parenting practices and styles than biological connection to the child.

Continued research with African American fathers (and mothers) is also necessary to inform the successful development and implementation of culturally sensitive violence-prevention and intervention programs designed to help parents and schools mediate the effects of community violence on preschool children and to empower communities to advocate for change. Consistent with the cultural-ecology model (Ogbu 1981), initiatives involving African American families in high-violence neighborhoods might draw on Afrocentric principles (e.g., communalism, spirituality, harmony) to help fathers and families restore some of the cohesion and mutual aid that has long sustained African American neighborhoods despite economic hardship (e.g., Nobles and Goddard 1993). Programs wanting to increase father involvement may find that focusing on how fathers or men in the community might best protect children from neighborhood dangers may be attractive to men who traditionally have played a protective role within their families and communities. Because African American fatherhood is understood to be an active, flexible relationship where families depend on both biological and social fathers to rear their children (Billingsley 1968; Black, Dubowitz, and Starr 1999), programs should consider defining "father" broadly and should include social fathers whenever possible. Such efforts may provide participants with an extended social family with which to share the tasks of tackling neighborhood problems, as well as the rewards and challenges of fathering young children.

References

Advocates for Children and Youth. 2000. *Maryland Kids Count Factbook*. Baltimore, Md.: Advocates for Children and Youth.
Allen, W. D., and M. Connor. 1997. "An African American Perspective on Generative Fathering." In *Generative Fathering: Beyond Deficit Perspectives*, ed. A. J. Hawkins and D. C. Dollahite, 52–70. Thousand Oaks, Calif.: Sage.

Ahmeduzzaman, M., and J. L. Roopnarine. 1992. "Sociodemographic Factors, Functioning Style, Social Support, and Fathers' Involvement with Preschoolers in African American Families." *Journal of Marriage and the Family* 54:699–707.

Annie E. Casey Foundation. 1999. *Kids Count Data Book: State Profiles of Child Well-Being.* Baltimore, Md.: Annie E. Casey Foundation.

Baumrind, D. 1967. "Child Care Practices Anteceding Three Patterns of Preschool Behavior." *Genetic Psychology Monographs* 75:43–88.

Billingsley, A. 1968. *Black Families in White America.* Englewood Cliffs, N.J.: Prentice-Hall.

Billingsley, A. 1992. *Climbing Jacobs's Ladder: The Enduring Legacy of African American Families.* New York: Simon and Schuster.

Black, M.M., H. Dubowitz, and R. H. Starr. 1999. "African American Fathers in Low-Income, Urban Families: Development, Behavior, and Home Environment of Their Three-Year-Old Children. *Child Development* 70 (4): 967–78.

Bzostek, S. 2007. "Social Fathers and Child Wellbeing: A Research Note." Working paper #2007-17-FF, Center for Research on Child Wellbeing, Princeton University.

Bzostek, S., M. Carlson, and S. McLanahan. 2007. "Repartnering After a Nonmarital Birth: Does Mother Know Best?" Working paper 2006-27-FF, Center for Research on Child Wellbeing, Princeton University.

Chase-Lansdale, P., and R. Gordon. 1996. "Economic Hardship and the Development of Five- and Six-Year-Olds: Neighborhood and Regional Perspectives," *Child Development* 67:3338–67.

Coley, R. L. 2001. "(In)visible Men: Emerging Research on Low-Income, Unmarried, and Minority Fathers." *American Psychologist* 56:743–53.

Darling, N., and L. Steinberg. 1993. "Parenting Style as Context: An Integrative Model." *Psychological Bulletin* 113 (3): 487–96.

DeNavas-Walt, C., B. D. Proctor, and J. Smith. 2007. *Income, Poverty, and Health Insurance Coverage in the United States: 2006.* Current Population Reports, 60-233, U.S. Census Bureau. Washington, DC: U.S. Government Printing Office.

Duncan, G. J., J. Brooks-Gunn, and P. K. Klebanov. 1994. "Economic Deprivation and Early Childhood Development." *Child Development* 65:296–318.

Fagan, J. 2000. "African American and Puerto Rican American Parenting Styles, Paternal Involvement, and Head Start Children's Social Competence." *Merrill-Palmer Quarterly* 46 (4): 592–612.

Federal Bureau of Investigation. 1998. "Uniform Crime Reports for the United States: 1997." http://www.fbi.gov/ucr/97cius.htm.

Hamer, J., and K. Marchioro. 2002. "Becoming Custodial Dads: Exploring Parenting Among Low-Income and Working-Class African American Fathers." *Journal of Marriage and Family* 64:116–29.

Hill, R. B. 1993. *Research on the African-American Family: A Holistic Perspective.* Westport, Conn.: Auburn House.

Jayakody, R., and A. Kalil. 2002. "Social Fathering in Low-Income, African American Families with Preschool Children." *Journal of Marriage and Family* 64:504–16.

King, M. A. 2006. "Father-Figures and Child Development: How Interchangeable Are Social Fathers and Biological Fathers?" *Dissertation Abstracts International* 67 (4): 1547.

Lazur, R. F., and R. Majors. 1995. "Men of Color: Ethnocultural Variations of Male Gender Role Strain." In *A New Psychology of Men*, ed. R. F. Levant and W. S. Pollack, 337–58. New York: Basic Books.

Letiecq, B. L., and S. A. Koblinsky. 2003. "African American Fathering of Young Children in Violent Neighborhoods: Paternal Protective Strategies and Their Predictors." *Fathering: A Journal of Theory, Research, and Practice About Men as Fathers* 1:215–37.

Letiecq, B. L., and S. A. Koblinsky. 2004. "Parenting in Violent Neighborhoods: African American Fathers Share Strategies for Keeping Young Children Safe." *Journal of Family Issues* 25 (6): 715–34.

Levine, J., D. Murphy, and S. Wilson. 1992. "Field Research for the Fatherhood Project." Unpublished data. New York: Families and Work Institute.

Levine, J. A. 1993. "Involving Fathers in Head Start: A Framework for Public Policy and Program Development." *Families in Society* 74 (1): 4–19.

Marsiglio, W., K. M. Roy, and G. L. Fox, eds. 2005. *Situated Fathering: A Focus on Physical and Social Spaces*. Boulder, Colo.: Rowman and Littlefield.

Martin, J. A., B. E. Hamilton, P. D. Sutton, S. J. Ventura, F. Menacker, and S. Kirmeyer. 2006. "Births: Final Data for 2004." *National Vital Statistics Reports* 55 (1).

Nobles, W. W., and L. L. Goddard. 1993. "An African-Centered Model of Prevention for African American Youth at High Risk." In *An African-Centered Model of Prevention for African American Youth at High Risk*, ed. L. L. Goddard, 115–29. Rockville, Md.: USDHHS/PHS/SAMHSA.

Ogbu, J. U. 1981. "Origins of Human Competence: A Cultural-Ecological Perspective." *Child Development* 52:413–29.

Robinson, C. C., B. Mandleco, S. F. Olsen, and C. H. Hart. 1995. "Authoritative, Authoritarian, and Permissive Parenting Practices: Development of a New Measure." *Psychological Reports* 77 (3): 819–30.

Ruiz, D. S., and C. W. Zhu. 2004. "Families Maintained by African American Grandmothers: Household Composition and Childcare Experiences." *The Western Journal of Black Studies* 28 (3): 415–23.

Sampson, R., S. Raudenbush, and F. Earls. 1997. "Neighborhoods and Violent Crime: A Multilevel Study of Collective Efficacy." *Science* 277:918–24.

Smith, C. A., M. D. Krohn, R. Chu, and O. Best. 2005. "African American Fathers: Myths and Realities About Their Involvement with Their Firstborn Children." *Journal of Family Issues* 26 (7): 975–1001.

Spencer, M. B. 1990. "Development of Minority Children: An Introduction." *Child Development* 61:267–69.

Tamis-LeMonda, C., and N. Cabrera. 1999. "Perspectives on Father Involvement: Research and Policy." *Society for Research in Child Development Social Policy Report* 13 (2): 200–219.

Taylor, R. J., L. M. Chatters, M. B. Tucker and E. Lewis. 1990. "Developments in Research on Black Families: A Decade Review." *Journal of Marriage and the Family* 52:993–1014.

U.S. Department of Health and Human Services/Administration for Children and Families. n.d. Head Start Bureau. http://www.acf.dhhs.gov/programs/hsb. Accessed November 9, 2005.

PART FOUR

Young Fathers

CHAPTER TEN

Caring for the Family Child

Kin Networks of Young Low-Income African American Fathers

KEVIN M. ROY AND COLLEEN K. VESELY

Sociohistorical shifts in recent decades, such as the rise and decline of the sole breadwinner role, declines in men's wages, and the entry of mothers into the paid labor force, have altered normative roles for generations of low-income men (Tamis-Le Monda and Cabrera 1999). In particular, with diverse patterns of household residence, union formation, and work histories, low-income African American men's interaction with family members has become increasingly transitory (Eggebeen and Uhlenberg 1985; Mott 1990). Expectations for fatherhood are less and less explicit, and the resulting ambiguity about what fathering means suggests that there is a need to understand how fathers' roles are constructed by low-income men and their families (Jarrett, Roy, and Burton 2002).

Men's efforts at making meaning are important for understanding how fathers make sense of these shifting roles (Marsiglio 1995). Identity, or the meaning of being a father, constantly shapes men's motivation and behavior as parents (Lamb 2000). However, father involvement relies on more than motivation alone; acting as a provider and caregiver requires access to resources, as does being a spouse, worker, or homeowner (Townsend 2002). Men from poor or minority communities may have limited access to the financial and human capital required for such involvement, and young men may lack necessary socialization into positive roles in poor neighborhoods. Therefore, it is important to examine the roles that kin networks play in the social construction of fathering roles within low-income families (Marsiglio et al. 2000).

In this chapter, we explore how the kin networks of thirty-five young African American men in Indianapolis helped to shape fathering roles. Learning about care giving was most explicit in kin networks with extensive resources, and some men indicated the availability of emotional, physical, and financial support, whereas for others these supports were limited or nonexistent. We examine how men used their kin networks through three processes: the creation of *norms of reciprocity*, which required exchanges of support that included young fathers; the *assessment of responsibility* as an indication of fulfillment of explicit obligations as fathers; and management of *control over access to children*, as a consequence of the need to place trust in family members and to secure a place as fathers and kin workers.

Transitory African American Fathers as Kin Workers

As likely targets of or participants in crime, limited job markets, and gang activity or police presence, African American fathers in low-income neighborhoods may be perceived as renegade relatives who can offer few contributions as parents (Stack and Burton 1993; Roy 2004). Most studies with national survey data on low-income minority fathers support the finding that low-income fathers are challenged to remain involved with their children (Coley 2001). Results from the Fragile Families study, based on national data from more than 4,700 unwed couples, show that most fathers were highly involved at the birth of their children (Carlson and McLanahan 2004) and that involvement was enhanced by men's positive attitudes toward fathering, committed couple relationships, and men's earnings in stable, full-time jobs (Johnson 2001; Carlson and McLanahan 2002). Twelve months after the birth of their children, however, multiple disruptions—including relationship conflict and financial instability—contributed to fathers' departures from households (McLanahan, Garfinkel, and Mincy 2001). Public discourse and social policies, as a result, tend to characterize poor minority fathers as invisible, irresponsible, and unmotivated parents (Burton and Snyder 1998).

However, the assumption of father absence may mask transitions of men in and out of residence, a modal pattern especially common for young black families (Mott 1990). Multiple sets of residential and nonresidential children complicate men's parenting responsibilities (Manning, Stewart, and Smock 2003). African American fathers often spend less time in residence with their biological children and more time in residence with nonbiological children, although some findings suggest that they become more involved with biological children as they age (Eggebeen 2002). These patterns point to role flexibility in dynamic family relationships and to cycles of engagement and disengagement with their children for low-income African American fathers (Jarrett, Roy, and Burton 2002). Nonresidential fathers may make efforts to provide and care for their children (Danziger and Radin 1990; Stier and Tienda 1993), but they commonly lack access to resources needed to successfully fulfill provider and caregiver roles.

Given these barriers to fathering, can low-income men participate in the work of maintaining kin systems, and if so, how? Extant research on kin networks has focused primarily on women and specifically women of color (Dominguez and Watkins 2003), although recent studies (Nelson 2000; Hansen 2005) find similar characteristics, including the importance of reciprocity, interdependence, and trust, in the kin networks of white families from diverse socioeconomic backgrounds. The kinscripts framework (Stack and Burton 1993) examines how family networks offer support for daily survival, social mobility, and care of children (Stack 1974; Jarrett and Burton 1999) and draws specific attention to interdependence among kin-network members (such as unmarried parents; see Roy and Burton 2007). Extended child-focused networks are maintained by parental figures who perform kin-work tasks "to regenerate families, maintain lifetime continuities, sustain intergenerational responsibilities, and reinforce shared values" (Stack and Burton 1993:160).

Within this framework, one of the most important processes in kin networks is the transition to parenthood over time. Kin systems may be resources by which fathers can give meaning to their roles and can secure involvement with their children (Hamer 2001; Waller 2002). Fathers tend to receive a significant amount of support during their transition to fatherhood, although they may not unanimously reciprocate (that is, both receive support from and provide support for another person) such support (only 38 percent of men—and less reciprocity among black than white fathers—in Hogan, Eggebeen, and Clogg 1993). Men often become dependent on female-headed households and networks (Scott and Black 1989; Roy, Dyson, and Jackson, forthcoming), but they generally engage in fewer intergenerational exchange relationships than women. Low-income fathers may also suffer from lack of role modeling from their own fathers, who may transition in and out of their lives during childhood and adolescence (Daly 1995; Roy 2006). In this way, researchers must discern between the availability of networks of kin and how these networks are used (Furstenberg 2005).

In this chapter, we explore how low-income fathers' close ties with kin members may be critical when the men themselves have few resources to secure positive involvement with their children. In this qualitative analysis we use participant observation and life-history interview data from thirty-five young, low-income African American fathers to consider how father involvement is shaped by the support and expectations of kin systems. Specifically, the following research questions were addressed in these analyses:

- How do young men learn about care giving from their kin networks?
- How do young men use kin networks to secure their place as fathers for their children?

Studying Young Low-Income Fathers

To build relationships with low-income fathers and their families, the first author worked with a research assistant in a young-fatherhood program in Indianapolis. More than fifteen noncustodial fathers, primarily African American, voluntarily enrolled in each eleven-week program session. To be eligible, their children were recipients of public aid. Their efforts to become more involved with their children and to access employment training and placement; parenting classes; educational, housing and drug treatment referrals; and parental counseling distinguished them in some ways from their peers who were not involved in such a program.

For this study, the project research assistant served as a facilitator of regular program sessions and worked with program staff and participants on a weekly basis. Research participants were recruited during these sessions. If they agreed to participate, they signed written consent forms.

These thirty-five men reflected the demographic variation of all fathers enrolled in the program. Men varied in age: eighteen were twenty-one years or younger, and another seventeen men were twenty-two years and older. Twenty of the thirty-five fathers (57 percent) were former offenders and twenty-four (60 percent) had completed high school or earned a GED. Eight of the fathers (23 percent) were employed in full-time jobs at the time of the interview, but the majority of participants were un- or underemployed.

The largest group of fathers, nineteen of the thirty-five (54 percent), lived with their own mothers or grandmothers, apart from their children. Only four of the fathers were living with their partners and their children. Six fathers were living with partners separate from their children. As a result, thirty fathers (88 percent) in the sample were nonresidential parents. Fathers had an average of 1.8 children. Nineteen fathers (54 percent) had only one child; eleven fathers (31 percent) had two children; and five fathers (14 percent) had three or four children. Nearly 30 percent of the sample (n = 10) had children in multiple households, and their paternal involvement varied from child to child.

We used three methods for data collection. First, we took detailed ethnographic field notes over eighteen months at the program site, and we constructed detailed genograms for each father's extended kin system. During two-hour sessions at the program site from December 2003 through December 2004, we used retrospective life-history interviews (Freedman et al. 1988) to gather more insight into social support systems and social construction of men's parenting roles. Protocol questions addressed the size of their extended families, reciprocity between members, and socialization to fatherhood. Credibility and dependability of the data were enhanced by the use of multiple sources of data and multiple methods of data collections, as well as prolonged engagement in the field (Lincoln and Guba 1995). In-person discussions with fathers some weeks after interviews (i.e., member checks) were used to validate initial understanding of the influence of kinship systems on men's parenting.

We eventually recruited and interviewed thirty-five fathers, after which point little new information about men's fathering was forthcoming (Daly 2007). Interviews were recorded on audiotapes and transcribed, and interview and field-note texts were coded using QSR NUDist software. Pseudonyms and ages were noted for participants. We adapted a constant comparative method of analytic induction from basic elements of grounded theory (Strauss and Corbin 1998). For this analysis, we paid attention to early socialization to fatherhood as an indication of the availability of potential resources in kin networks and to processes during early fatherhood, including reciprocal exchanges of support, assessments of responsible fathering, and issues of control over access to children.

Learning to Care in Various Kin Networks

Fathers' interactions with kin systems were complex and diverse across the thirty-five families in the study. We asked men to talk about a wide range of kin and non-kin who were part of their social-support network and to note which kinds of support they provided and if that support was reciprocal. We noted patterns in both quantity of family members and quality of support experiences. In general, fathers were embedded in one of three distinct types of kin networks: supportive, limited, or absent.

Some men participated in extensive, extremely supportive and dynamic kin networks, which played a major role in their abilities to remain involved with their children (n = 16, 46 percent). These networks featured a larger number of family members (three or more) with multiple examples of supportive behavior for young men. This family support was unique in that it was consistent from childhood through adolescence and into young adulthood.

There were fathers who mentioned having networks with only one or two family members they could turn to for assistance (n = 13, 37 percent). Although these family members also offered multiple examples of support, men felt that their families were "scattered." Some men in this group remarked that their networks had always offered strong support from only a few family members. Others noted that their networks were more extensive during their childhood but had attenuated over time because of death and illness.

Finally, a few fathers mentioned feeling as though they were not at all connected with their family and that there was no one who could provide support for them (n = 6, 17 percent). Most of these men also noted that their networks had appeared more extensive during their childhood but had dissolved over time. However, a few fathers were hard pressed to identify any supportive family members during childhood, adolescence, or adulthood.

What complicates our understanding of these three types of kin networks is consideration of how they change over time. By the time a young man became a father himself, a family network that began as extensive and highly supportive could have dissolved. Fathers further complicated this typology through personal decisions to participate more or less extensively in exchanges of support or to decline the support of family members who offered it. Ironically, a supportive network could be threatening to men's involvement with their children. In following sections, we examine what made each type of network distinct, in terms of men's early learning about care, and care-giving behavior, in families.

Supportive Paternal Kin Networks

Fathers who were embedded in extensive, supportive kin networks had a wide range of resources available to them and to their children, through family relationships that stretched across generations, geography, and time. Specific family members were actively engaged in providing support for young men throughout childhood and adolescence, and these extended networks shaped men's beliefs from a young age about how families contribute to the growth and development of children. Tyrese, a twenty-two-year-old father, realized the strength of his family system when he was a child, and he found his place in it through direct interaction with family.

> It's often as if, when everybody is around, you learn more as a youngster. You get to know everybody. I'd rather not say, "those are my children, they don't know my family. I don't know their uncles and aunties." So, if you're going to go to the family, you know your cousins, who you can depend on, who you can run to, talk to. You got that support, you feel more comfortable when you're around nothing but family.

Moreover, fathers embedded in supportive kin systems realized during their development that care for children was a family responsibility—not simply the responsibility of individual parents. Ben, a twenty-three-year-old father of four children with different mothers, described "the family child" approach.

> We'll rely on each other. It's like a circle. Everybody looks out for everybody. It's not just the mother, father, and child—it's the family child. My aunt was on drugs, and my cousins were in the worst state.

But nobody has been able to adopt anybody in our family, nobody out-side our family. If we had a problem, someone in the family steps up and takes them in.

Fathers with supportive kin networks were encouraged to be in-volved with and help care for younger family members. Ellis, an eighteen-year-old father of a newborn, noted that interactions with his preschool nephews prepared him for fathering:

> It comes with a child, knowing what I have to do before I become a father. I had no choice but to accept that role because their daddy is not here, he's deceased. It's up to the uncles to step up and try to show them the right way. Their mama, we're not blood, she "has family," but she really don't have family, so we make her family. We've been there for her, because she still has medical bills.

Supportive kin systems required young men to "do fathering" by hands-on, trial-and-error learning. Every family member had to lend a hand in rearing children. Jared, a nineteen-year-old father of a two-month-old baby, first became involved in his child's daily routine by simply "being there" with his family during the first weeks of his child's life. The support of his family, as well as their beliefs and ex-pectations, instilled in Jared the importance of keeping a connection with his child.

Socialization meant hearing and internalizing advice about how to fulfill parental responsibilities. For Tasheed, this advice was truly preparatory, so that he was quite confident about what was expected of him—and his girlfriend—as parents of a newborn.

> My mother taught me when I was younger, my brothers too. Since day one, she talked to me about taking it step by step and have your head on strong. You know what you got to do when you a father so you got to do it. She tried to teach me right from wrong. So me and my girl-friend just agree we got to do it. We both are going to become parents.

Other female kin contributed to men's experiences as fathers by providing physical, emotional, and financial support to the men's chil-dren or to the men themselves, in order to secure the fathers' place as responsible parents. Ben's sister supported her brothers when no one else in their family would offer assistance. She cautioned him when he was dealing drugs, and she offered money to Ben during periods of unemployment. During college, "she was there, it didn't matter, when I went to jail . . . for my brother in the pen, too, for parole violation." She noticed that his vocabulary skills were limited, so she taught him new words each day, "to substitute regular words for cuss words." Ben ran errands for her if she was too busy with her children. He declared that "to us, she is the backbone of this family. She is our mother, she takes care of me, no matter what."

Despite their level of embeddedness and the amount of resources available through their kin network, some men stressed the importance of assuming the majority of responsibilities for their children. Jordan, a nineteen-year-old with one unborn child, described the relationships among his family members as "very, very close knit," but when he was asked specifically about the support he received from his network, he stressed the importance of assuming responsibility: "I don't have anybody to rely on for anything like that. . . . I'm just basically relying on myself. It's all about what I can do for myself, and my child, right now. Can't rely on my mother no more. I'm a grown man now." Similarly, Allan was careful not to burden his family with child care: "Whenever they come over, you know. I'm not gonna put my burden on them. I'm not gonna have them watch my children because it's not their job. It's my job. It's my children. They raised their kids already. It's not their job. They already did they part, you know what I mean. So I respect that and I don't do it."

Scattered Paternal Kin Networks

For fathers with limited kin networks, childhood experiences with family members demonstrated the need for creating their own support systems for their children. These fathers identified few supportive family members in their lives, as illustrated in the following statement by Kareem, a nineteen-year-old father from Indianapolis.

> My relationships with other family are not real close. Nobody is really at the center. I was going through lots of moves and stuff like that when I was young: guardian's home, foster care, my mother's, my grandmother's. They don't stay in contact with each other. I just want to provide a new background for my kids and break the chain. My life's been kind of rocky. I feel like I have a new opportunity or something.

Young fathers, like Will, a twenty-two-year-old father of a one-year-old child, dubbed these kin systems as "scattered . . . the Three Musketeers was all for one, one for all, but my family and I are all for themselves. If I got money, then my cousin got money. But for the rest of them, we's like, 'To hell with them.'"

For some fathers, particularly those reared in single-mother homes, their early socialization provided them experience in child care and household chores. Taquan learned about parenting by default, as the oldest child in a house with a single working mother: "I was like the man of the house. At ten I was watching my little brothers. That's how I grew up, it's illegal, but I grew up faster than any other person. I was cooking at ten. I learned everything when she had to go to work, so I had to get up early and watch my brothers. I didn't have any help."

Not all men learned how to father through forced early maturity. Eric, a twenty-seven-year-old with three children, learned the importance of taking responsibility for one's family by observing his mother:

> That's how I was, my mother worked two jobs, sometimes three jobs. I remember one time it was thirteen of us in a three room house. You know, so, my mother never turned her back on our family. . . . Big Momma, that's what they call her. Keeps all the family together. Keeps everybody intact to make sure there's no arguing. See our immediate family, we've always been together all our life.

For all fathers in the program, their mothers' and grandmothers' presence, advice, and support were important in shaping ideas about their family and parenthood. However, this support was particularly critical for men in limited kin networks. Many of these men's grandmothers tried to socialize and teach them about family closeness and togetherness by providing a nurturing and stable environment. This was particularly true when adolescents could no longer live with their parents because of limited resources and when neighborhoods became too dangerous for young men. Fathers in scattered networks could form uniquely close bonds with their grandmothers. Tyrese was twenty-two with one child and still lived with his grandmother, referring to her as the "love of his life" and the "backbone" of his family. For men like Dion, a twenty-five-year-old father of one child who was extremely close to his grandmother and felt as though she was the only person who understood him, coping with the death of this important female figure was extremely difficult:

It was real hard, man, when she [his grandmother] passed. . . . When she was here . . . [she] was like the only friend I had in this world. . . . She the only person who ever understood me as a person. . . . Out of all the stuff I went through with my mother my father. I mean just going back and forth, back and forth, no type of stability or whatever, know what I mean? She the only one that really knew why. You know, she just understood me, you know. We had deep conversations. She was just my friend, man, my best friend.

Absence of Paternal Kin Networks

For the majority of fathers, the dynamics of their kin networks remained relatively stable throughout their childhood, adolescence, and the transition to parenthood. However, for a substantial minority of fathers, key kin in their networks died when these men were only adolescents. For fathers with already limited networks, this led to feelings of isolation and loneliness in relation to their families. Kevin, a nineteen-year-old with two toddlers, left prison only to find that his grandfather, who had raised him, had passed away. He said, "All the people I got attached to started dying . . . it messed me up inside. Truthfully, all I ever wanted was a role model, a male." Dramatic network changes could result from death of kin. Otis was twenty-three and had one child; he described how his network changed following the death of his grandmother, whom he considered to be the center of his kin network, as well as the person to whom he was closest as a child.

Everybody came apart [when grandma passed] . . . everybody used to meet up at my grandma house, all my family, my uncles, aunties. When she passed, everybody turning the enemies, turning back on each other. They just went they separate ways. [Q: So it was kinda like *Soul Food*?] Yeah. Except there wasn't no getting back together.

In addition to losing the support of his grandmother, he essentially lost his mother and her resources when she began to drink heavily and spiraled into depression.

Fathers' networks also dissolved if their needs were too great for the capacity of the network. Akida, a twenty-three-year-old father of one- and two-year-old children, lost his first son to a heart malformation. He became depressed and lost his job as well. Unfortunately, he could not turn to his large family for support. Akida felt that his brothers, sisters, and cousins avoided him, not knowing how to cope with the death of his infant son or how to help him work out of depression. He saw his extended kin system fade away around him, and he eventually accepted isolation from many of his once-close family members.

> I don't associate with none of my siblings, my brothers and sisters. I just don't. I prefer to be to myself. I just talk to my mother, that's it. After my son's situation I really stopped talking to my family. I mean I pretty much just shut down. I used to be more social, but after my son's death I felt like I had been cheated. Just my mother was supportive of me. My mother, my grandmother would just talk to me. But everybody else wasn't around.

Men's relationships with male kin in their networks tended to vary widely. Their own fathers could be positive figures to use as role models for parenting, while other fathers modeled certain behaviors (such as providing) but were deficient in their emotional availability. Some of fathers were completely absent from their sons' lives. In this circumstance, young men sought out "other fathers"—usually male relatives, such as maternal uncles or cousins, or family friends—to provide guidance. Kevin recalled how he responded to "other fathers" who watched out for him as a child and how he was called upon to watch out for his aunt's child, who similarly had no father:

> Every time somebody older, especially a male figure, came to me, ran me the law, put my mind right. I was the type of person who listened and took heed. You have a sense of comfort, they've been there, he knows. They're going to take care of me, going to show me some love. Looking for a little love, a little guidance. Put you on your feet. It can happen to anyone, not having a male around, and that is the downfall to most kids. I take my younger cousin, about four. My auntie, she's cool, but her baby's father is on drugs, so I just try to take them to the movies, out to eat, spend a little money on them.

Even in kin networks replete with resources, the majority of young men in this study could identify the involvement of their own biological fathers only for short periods during childhood and adolescence. Many asserted their intentions to be better parents than their own fathers, but they also expressed uncertainty about how to father because they lacked good role models. Allan, a father with two children, described being driven by his desire to be a good parent: "I never had a father-figure. So, I didn't know the first thing about being a dad. But what made me become a father is because I want to be a good father."

A lack or withdrawal of support from kin systems led some men to construct their ideas of fathering on their own. When asked, "Who taught you to be a father?" a majority of these fathers indicated that no one had taught them to be fathers. Latrell, a young father, was frustrated without direction, saying, "Tell you the truth, I don't have a father figure, so I don't know what fathers are supposed to do. I mean, I taught myself everything I know, so I'm living like I'm stuck, I'm very stuck here." Fathers who grew up without extensive kin networks experienced little to no early socialization, including fewer opportunities for learning how to parent by caring for siblings or cousins. As a teen father, Earl only reached a realization of the important changes that waited for him when talking with his best friend: "Me and my best friend was sitting there, it was maybe ten or eleven at night. He was like, 'Man, you know you ain't the only one now.' That's when being a father hit me. You can't just think of yourself no more. And being sixteen, that's a lot to swallow when it's always been just you."

Utilizing Paternal Kin Networks to Secure Fathering

In this section, we explore three processes related to young fathers' use of kin interaction and its consequences. First, we examine the norms of reciprocity that held kin networks in place for fathers. Second, we note how these obligations allowed kin and fathers to assess how they acted as "responsible" parents. Finally, we identify the salience of young men's control over access to their children, in the midst of taking part in kin relationships.

Norms of Reciprocity and Obligations

Young fathers in supportive networks often indicated how normative such support could be. As Jordan described, "It's like everyone's always happy to see each other no matter what. . . . It's the way it's supposed to be, and everyone just looks after each other." The idea of family members looking after one another was a casual reference to reciprocity, and highlighted a theme heard repeatedly from these fathers. Shawn, an eighteen-year-old father, talked about the impact his family support network had on him and how it would ultimately affect his daughter: "All I gotta do is say my daughter's name and my family jumps for joy. They all want to take her, so that's really helpful. We've got support behind. We share basically. Like my mom kept her last weekend, and she enjoyed that. As she grows up, she won't need support nowhere else. She has her family."

When these men could trust their kin networks, the rules for reciprocity were clear. First, family members shared a special bond with one another when they were in the same network, primarily because each individual understood the value of the investments made in him or her. It was clear to many of the young fathers whom to go to for financial assistance, emotional support, or life advice. As Jared said, "If you're going to go to the family, you know . . . who you can depend on, who you can run to, talk to. You got that support and you feel more comfortable too when you're around nothing but family. Everybody is out to take care of you."

More importantly, obligations in supportive kin networks offered more explicit expectations about nurturance of "the family child." Kin-network members made certain that young fathers understood the group's fundamental beliefs before they engaged them in network activities. Many fathers indicated that their family members shared common beliefs about childrearing, in terms of appropriate behavior, and that these beliefs were taken very seriously. Ben spoke about the high premium his family placed on children and the willingness of his family members to do whatever they could for children born into their network: "[In] my family, children are everything. It's always about the kids with everybody in the family. People in the family, when it comes to the children, people gonna do what they can do. If you need some help or something, you gonna get that help. Because it takes a village to raise our children. That's how we taught, that's how it was taught to us."

Some kin networks took risks in investing potential resources in young fathers in spite of precarious circumstances. Family members worked to help fathers deal with tangible and dangerous barriers to their education and employment in order to equip them with the stable resources that are precursors to father involvement. Ray, a twenty-four-year-old father, was incarcerated during the early months of his children's lives. Although many friends and some family members gave up on him, he found vital emotional support from key family members in order to put his experiences behind him: "My name was on the lips of my family. 'You know he ain't gonna be . . . he locked up again, he robbed.' I had a whole lot of soul searching to do, days in the cell, isolated to get my mind right. In a way to think about it, some of my family brought me back."

Male peers and family members who experienced similar barriers to employment and education played unique roles in helping the fathers through difficult periods. Amir, a twenty-seven-year-old father, recalled a friend who helped him during his time in jail: "My brother's best friend sent me money, called me, checked up on me, tried to get me a job, you know what I mean . . . I can call him anytime. He's genuine. He's so real." Likewise, low-income fathers from the same neighborhood realized that they shared common goals and needs. Will and his male cousins were incarcerated at the same time, and upon their release, they formed a reciprocal relationship that centered on sharing. "If I got money they got money, if they got money I got money," he explained.

Fathers in the study relied on their kin networks to assist with the childcare responsibilities as well. Brian, a nineteen-year-old father, discussed how his cousin watched his son during the day while he went to work. When asked how he reciprocated and if he felt that assistance was shared equally between him and his cousin, he explained his swap of money and time:

> I've only been able to give her money when I have it. Nowhere near what normal babysitters will receive on a weekly basis, but she's been watching him for the duration of these last four or five months and that's just been a great boost for me. Whatever I can do [to reciprocate]. Being around for her kids, taking them places, or watching them, whatever, it's pretty much give and take. That's how I want to be with my relations, with mostly anybody.

Stepping up to take care of a child in the family involved subtle negotiation and renegotiation of normative parenting roles. In particular, for this sample of young African American men, fathering roles were flexible, and they incorporated multiple complex meanings into their identities as parents. Responsible fathering of one's children, for example, meant entering into reciprocal obligations with not only paternal kin members but maternal kin members as well. Ramel, a twenty-year-old father of a newborn, noted that "my girlfriend's mom and my mom both encourage me to really take responsibility, because every child deserves to have a father."

As other studies have shown, conflictual relations between unmarried fathers and mothers likely lead to restrictions on men's involvement with their children. In contrast, comfortable, amicable relationships made reciprocal exchanges substantially less complicated. Through the establishment of trust and respect, mothers and fathers could communicate clear expectations for men's interaction with children. Taylor, another twenty-three-year-old father, reiterated this point when he discussed how his child's mother made him feel like a very important part of their son's growth and development:

> She [child's mother] encourages me. She wouldn't have it no other way. She would never keep my son from me, even if we weren't together or we done fell out. I got one of the best women I can have because I ain't never got no problems. She take good care of my son, she's a good mother. . . . She goes up and beyond, being a mother to my son.

To show his appreciation for her hard work with their son, this father said he reciprocated by "just giving her what she ask[ed] me for."

Integration of paternal and maternal kin networks led to fragile but critical supports for young men's fathering, and so these young men were careful to nurture quality relationships among family members. They made efforts to link their parents and grandparents to their friends, even to their intimate partners. Leonard, another young father, actively protected his family members from non-kin who might use or damage mutual support arrangements. "My mother's talking to my girlfriend, and she's talking to my best friend. They're all like really, really tight. My mom's friends with my brothers' friends, too. But I don't call people friends . . . people I call associates. I've been through a whole lot. That's why I'm careful about what I bring into the family, friends I mean."

Fulfilling the expectations of fair mutual exchanges among kin was challenging for young low-income fathers. With hard work men avoided becoming "drains" on their kin networks. However, they often faltered during times of transformation, such as drug use or incarceration, or when they had few resources (time or money) to offer in return to family members. Brian, for instance, listed all the people for whom he's not been able to reciprocate:

> I don't want it to be that way, but everyone gets to their breaking point at times and there are some things I just say no to. There's some things with my mom, some things I can't do. There are some things with my girlfriend I can't do. There are some things with my cousin Belinda I can't do, some things with my grandmother I can't do, my cousin Regina—it has its time. It's not an overbearing journey, but there are times that I can't do it.

In contrast to kin systems with ample or even limited resources and support, men without kin systems faced few if any normative expectations for involvement. These men spoke generally about the value of children and how to act as a responsible parent, but when asked about a family approach to child care, they spoke about vague assumptions. Earl could not give specific examples of kin care, but he asserted that "everybody in my family believes that a father should be part of [caring for kids]. I wouldn't say that it is necessary for them to be, but it was just thought of as good for the development of the child." Few family.members held these men accountable for learning parenting behaviors at a younger age or for acting as responsible parents at a later age.

Kin networks with fewer avenues of support also did not facilitate men's efforts to be involved with children. For some men, a sole family member tried to support their relationships with their children and mothers. Kareem lived with his great-grandmother, who stayed in communication with the mother of Kareem's child. Apart from looking out for the child's well-being, his great-grandmother did not offer consistent support for Kareem. He said, "My great-grandmother orders me and doesn't understand about my age. She thinks I just want to run around the streets. She goes off on a lot of assumptions. She's old—she supports me one minute, then turns around and talks about me."

Assessment of Paternal Responsibility

Men embedded in kin networks with opportunities for support perceived clear messages on responsibility and the sanctions for irresponsibility. A father's failure to understand and comply with maternal kin's desires and needs could result in a mother granting him limited time with his child. For some men, then, responsible fathering began early. Brian discussed his attempts to gain acceptance into the network of his child's mother while she was pregnant:

> I visited her at the hospital trying to make good relationships with her family, trying to vouch for the fact that I am presently in school, I am educated, I do have ambitions, I'm not out here trying to make babies all over the place. It's just, I'm going to do the right thing, I'm going to be responsible, I'm going to handle what I can, I'm going to build the relationship I need to.

As children aged, these fathers began to understand how reciprocal exchanges benefited many family members simultaneously. Amir discussed the notion of "forward passing" exchanges in promoting children's well-being. He was happy to support his child's mother when he knew that the child was benefiting. For example, he readily gave money to her for car repairs because "getting her brakes fixed, I look at like doing something for him [the child], because without that she can't get him where he need to be." In addition, his attention to their safety signaled to kin members that he could be a responsible parent for his son.

Young fathers understood that providing was a key element in acting as a responsible parent. However, there were barriers to being a good provider, and kin members often recognized these barriers. Instead of failing in the face of mainstream ideals for providing—as many fathers without supportive kin networks did—these fathers and their kin expected that providing did not refer exclusively to material goods or services but also to emotional, moral, and psychological support. As Ellis said with regard to his five-month-old daughter:

> The child has to be provided for. They didn't ask to be here. I mean, I can't just think about myself no more. Holding her, I am just showing her I love her. I know my father like, when I was growing up, he used to always give me stuff, but he never really got to like the father-son bond. . . . You know what I mean? There's a difference between providing and loving and you got to have both of them, a mixture.

These men integrated and prioritized the importance of care giving as a required activity of fathers in supportive kin systems. Mo, a twenty-two-year-old father of two preschoolers, echoed the notion of the package deal when he referred to fatherhood as a composite responsibility of a man: "If you are the father, you play the role of a provider. You also play the role of the caretaker, the caregiver. Umm, a father is just— you just taking off of your responsibility as a man. It's all wrapped in one. It's a big responsibility."

It is important to note that the supports offered by women in paternal kin networks went far in helping to secure the men's status as responsible fathers to their children. In addition to the work of their own mothers in maintaining fragile connections with and taking care of children, fathers turned to women to help them untangle confusing messages about their parental status during the process of establishing legal or informal paternity. Ben lived with his grandmother, who "refused to let any child born into our family disappear [outside of the family]."

> I got stories on top of stories. With my one-year-old, his mother sleeps around. I don't know if she's picking me to be the baby's father, she told everybody it was mine. It got to my grandma, and she said, "Look, did you have sex with her? Did you use protection? What's the odds of that being your baby? When the baby gets here, let me see it." My grandmother pointed it out to me, "How would you like it, a baby whose father didn't want anything to do with it?"

Young fathers without input from kin networks remained unclear about expectations as well as "responsible" fathering behavior. Along with the children's young mothers, they often crafted a poorly defined set of expectations with few effective sanctions. Parrish discussed how his baby's mother encouraged him to be involved, but such messages of encouragement were limited to her, as his family had withdrawn from influencing his fathering role.

> She tells me I should watch her more. I should play with her more. I should talk to her more. You know I should just be there more, period. Hold her, talk to her, play with her, feed her, wash her, clothe her, take her out, take her out for a walk in her car seat, just hold her now, feed her with her bottle. That's what she means. I should be there.

When expectations for fathering were left to negotiation between teen parents, fathers often had little to go on. Expectations were not enforced or supported, and as a result, the father role appeared to be very ambiguous and undefined. Denham, a nineteen-year-old father of a newborn baby, appeared indecisive about who he was to be for both his child and his girlfriend.

> I don't know—we were sex partners, and now we're going to be mom and dad together. What's the deal? To tell you the truth I really don't know. She can be my girl. But, right now I don't really know 'cause right now we still just talking like friends. But, so other than that we just like, I'm the baby daddy. That's all I can tell you.

These experiences suggest that fathers with limited kin systems were challenged to incorporate meaning into their role as parents. The meaning of being a caregiver, with all of the hands-on demands and years of advice behind it, could be lost on these fathers. In these circumstances, expectations for their roles as fathers emerged with a focus primarily on the young men's experiences and perceptions—and not their children's. Will, for example, was hesitant to build his life around his one-year-old son's need for care. "Every couple days, I go over to my cousin's, to stay with her two kids," he said. "Or, I go over to my grandma's house and watch the child for awhile. I'm always on the move, people can barely catch up with me."

Given the relative youth in this sample, construction of a positive father role seemed to be a daunting task. It became easier for fathers like Will—who had few resources to support a child, let alone himself—to deny the role and the relationship altogether.

> I can't play father. I don't believe he's mine. It is what it is. They call my mother and relay the message about him. They keep saying that boy is mine. I got a shaky feeling. I don't want to do anything. . . . I can't take him, one being that I don't got a crib [baby bed], and two being when you do come to my mom's crib [apartment], I don't got no food to feed. At my mom's with my brother, and I'm scavenging myself.

Control Over Access to Children

Finally, we noted that there may be unique challenges and even disadvantages for young fathers in supportive kin networks. Support from kin ultimately had consequences for control over resources and relationships within growing families. Extensive support often resulted in a tradeoff: young men surrendered control over the terms of their involvement to family members who managed their interaction with their children. This was especially important as it related to the men's mothers, who frequently controlled when, where, and how their sons became involved in reciprocal exchanges. Taquan talked about how the relationship between his mother and his girlfriend influenced his own interactions with his son. Through coresidence with his own mother, he allowed her to supervise his interactions, to make sure he was fulfilling his fatherly obligations, and to dictate the terms of his relationships.

> I'm [living] here, at my mom's, again . . . so it's really their [mother and girlfriend] arrangement and I just happen to be living here. So that's what allows me to see him [son] like that. It's not like I got my own place and that's the arrangement. So actually, I'm on someone else's time with him. I'm on my mama's time—his grandma's time—with him.

Ceding control over access and the manner of interaction with their children could be seen as a legitimate exchange for assistance in securing a place as fathers in the first place. The decision to cede control may be the best option for men who do not know where to begin as teen fathers, when the facilitation of appropriate fathering roles and provision of consistent care for children were important first steps. Graham, a twenty-five-year-old father, felt that the birth of his daughter brought the power of his family system to bear on potentially precarious circumstances: "It seems like the family just came together. My mom told me, 'Don't have my grandkids.' But she's going to do everything in her power, in her will, to keep them safe and teach them right from wrong, to let them know everything is gonna be alright."

Fathers also allowed their kin members leeway to express how family legacies could be created and recreated. For example, Akida had a child with his partner, Tina, who was half Asian American and half European American. He wanted his daughter "to understand where she comes from, where she is, and just never look down on someone because of their race." Akida's mother, however, actively socialized her to her African American heritage, in an effort to balance the child's multiple racial and ethnic backgrounds. "My mother views it as Quiana needs to be around us," Akida said. "She wants Quiana by her side, since the child's mother is white, and most of her friends are white or half white. She figures that she needs to be around her black side more."

However, ceding control of parenting roles to kin was a risk for many fathers who struggled to participate as legitimate providers or caregivers for their children. Family members, often men's own mothers and sisters, could decide that fathers were "renegade relatives" who endangered tenuous relationships and did not offer reciprocal assistance in taking care of children. Paternal and maternal grandmothers often took primary responsibility for child care, and they could withhold information on children's daily routines or whereabouts. After the close support of his mother for his two grade-school-age children, Devon, a twenty-three-year-old father, struggled to gain access for even short visits. His mother and the children's mother established joint custody apart from him, in response to his decision to move out and marry a new partner, of whom they disapproved. In this way, the crafting of fathering responsibilities could pit men against their own kin over valuable resources—their own children.

Future Directions in Research on Fathers and Kin Networks

Most fatherhood research has framed meaning making as the result of the agency of individual fathers. The ideal of a combination of provision, care, marriage, work, and home ownership sets up expectations for fathers as individual actors who succeed or fail on their own terms (Townsend 2002). Even low-income fathers of color aspire to this ideal, commenting that "it's on me" to succeed "as a man" and therefore as a father. However, success in these multiple but related fathering roles is almost impossible without adequate resources. In this study, we argue that supportive kin systems are some of the most vital resources for low-income fathers, particularly those who are young parents in transition.

We outlined a variety of processes by which families continue to shape young men's participation in kin networks. Young men learned to use networks to build shared understanding about their own roles as fathers. Moreover, family members confirmed and legitimized men's paternity status. They may facilitate a man's involvement with a child, or potentially with multiple children when the father attempts to bring together children from different households. In return, these family members helped to ensure fulfillment of a certain level of responsible behavior as fathers, which often involved renegotiation of mainstream ideals of providing. Kin systems also require shared control over the construction of fathering roles and men's involvement. Although loss of control may threaten some fathers, the decisions of central kin workers in families (paternal grandmothers, in particular) are deemed necessary to protect the viability of close reciprocal relationships around child care. They may also give age-appropriate patterns for responsible fathering behavior for young fathers who seek guidance in basic questions about parenting. Researchers can further articulate such processes by, for example, comparing fathering in different cultural contexts.

In future research on fathers and families in low-income communities, the conceptual framework of kinscription (Stack and Burton 1993) can offer new understanding of how kin develop shared expectations of when and in which sequence kin-work should occur. Typically, women and older children are recruited through a process of kinscription, and we offer evidence that fathers are also active participants in kinscription, connecting their children with family members and resources in their network (see also Roy and Burton 2007). Family members help to secure fathers' involvement with their children through contributions of time, money, guidance, and emotional support. However, young men without supportive networks of family members are forced to secure involvement with their children on their own.

Researchers can also explore how the forced early maturity of children and adolescents (Burton 2007) can be linked to learning about how to care for family members. Early socialization to fatherhood is one process by which kin systems can invest in young men as potential kin workers and in effect create new social capital. In the midst of transitory male involvement, such investments are important not just for fathers but for the continuity of families in low-income neighborhoods.

Finally, this study identified how the dynamics of fathers' kin systems change in important ways over time. Longitudinal research on kin systems and fathers could explore the changing structure of kin systems and the extent of social support obligations over time. Family members tailor commitments from kin systems to the ages and developmental needs of children, as well as to the ages and developmental needs of fathers themselves. As young fathers mature, their relations and roles within kin networks change. Potentially, they become integral kin in the networks upon which the next generation relies.

Note

This study was conducted with support from the National Institute for Child Health and Human Development under Project No. 5 R03 HD 42074-2, the W. T. Grant Foundation, and the Purdue Research Foundation at Purdue University. The authors would like to thank Megan Jakub, Omari Dyson, Sherri Brown, and Mary Schultheis for assistance in data analyses. Correspondence concerning this article should be addressed to Kevin Roy, Department of Family Science, University of Maryland School of Public Health, College Park, MD 20742. Electronic mail: kroy@umd.edu.

References

Burton, L. 2007. "Childhood Adultification in Economically Disadvantaged Families: A Conceptual Model." *Family Relations* 56:329–45.
Burton, L., and A. Snyder. 1998. "The Invisible Man Revisited: Comments on the Life Course, History, and Men's Roles in American Families." In *Men in Families: When Do They Get Involved? What Difference Does It Make?* ed. Alan Booth, 31–39. Hillsdale, N.J.: Erlbaum.
Carlson, M., and S. McLanahan. 2002. "Father Involvement in Fragile Families." In *Handbook of Father Involvement: Multidisciplinary Perspectives*, ed. C. Tamis-LeMonda and N. Cabrera, 461–88. Mahwah, N.J.: Erlbaum.
Carlson, M., and S. McLanahan. 2004. "Early Father Involvement in Fragile Families." In *Conceptualizing and Measuring Father Involvement*, ed. R. Day and M. Lamb, 210–38. Mahwah, N.J.: Erlbaum.
Coley, R. L. 2001. "(In)visible Men: Emerging Research on Low-income, Unmarried, and Minority Fathers." *American Psychologist* 56:743–53.
Daly, K. 1995. "Reshaping Fatherhood: Finding the Models." In *Fatherhood: Contemporary Theory, Research, and Social Policy*, ed. W. Marsiglio, 21–40. Thousand Oaks, Calif.: Sage.
Daly, K. 2007. *Qualitative Methods for Family Studies and Human Development.* Thousand Oaks, Calif.: Sage.
Danziger, S., and N. Radin. 1990. "Absent Does Not Equal Uninvolved: Predictors of Fathering in Teen Mother Families." *Journal of Marriage and the Family* 52:636–41.
Dominguez, S., and C. Watkins. 2003. "Creating Networks for Survival and Mobility: Social Capital Among African Americans and Latin American Low-Income Mothers." *Social Problems* 50:111–35.
Eggebeen, D. 2002. "The Changing Course of Fatherhood: Men's Experiences with Children in Demographic Perspective." *Journal of Family Issues* 23:486–506.

Eggebeen, D., and P. Uhlenberg. 1985. "Changes in the Organization of Men's Lives: 1960–1980." *Family Relations* 34:251–57.

Freedman, D., A. Thornton, D. Camburn, D. Alwin, and L. Young DeMarco. 1988. "The Life History Calendar: A Technique for Collecting Retrospective Data." *Sociological Methodology* 18:37–68.

Furstenberg, F. 2005. "Banking on Families: How Families Generate and Distribute Social Capital." *Journal of Marriage and Family* 67:809–21.

Hamer, J. 2001. *What It Means to Be Daddy: Fatherhood for Black Men Living Away from Their Children.* New York: Columbia University Press.

Hansen, K. V. 2005. *Not So Nuclear Families.* New Brunswick, N.J.: Rutgers University Press.

Hogan, D., D. Eggebeen, and C. Clogg. 1993. "The Structure of Intergenerational Exchanges in American Families." *American Journal of Sociology* 98:1428–58.

Jarrett, R., and L. Burton. 1999. "Dynamic Dimensions of Family Structure in Low-Income African-American Families: Emergent Themes in Qualitative Research." *Journal of Comparative Family Studies* 30:177–88.

Jarrett, R., K. Roy, and L. Burton. 2002. "Fathers in the 'Hood: Qualitative Research on Low-Income African American Men." In *Handbook of Father Involvement: Multidisciplinary Perspectives,* ed. C. Tamis-LeMonda and N. Cabrera, 211–248. New York: Erlbaum.

Johnson, W. 2001. "Paternal Involvement Among Unwed Fathers." *Children and Youth Services Review* 23:513–36.

Lamb, M. 2000. "A History of Research on Father Involvement: An Overview." *Marriage and Family Review* 29:23–42.

Lincoln, Y., and E. Guba. 1985. *Naturalistic Inquiry.* Thousand Oaks, Calif.: Sage.

Manning, W., S. Stewart, and P. Smock. 2003. "The Complexity of Fathers' Parenting Responsibilities and Involvement with Nonresident Children." *Journal of Family Issues* 24:645–67.

Marsiglio, W. 1995. "Fathers' Diverse Life Course Patterns and Roles: Theory and Social Interventions." In *Fatherhood: Contemporary Theory, Research, and Social Policy,* ed. William Marsiglio, 78–101. Thousand Oaks, Calif.: Sage.

Marsiglio, W., P. Amato, R. Day, and M. Lamb. 2000. "Scholarship on Fatherhood in the 1990s and Beyond." *Journal of Marriage and the Family* 62:1173–91.

McLanahan, S., I. Garfinkel and R. Mincy. 2001. "Fragile Families, Welfare Reform, and Marriage." Policy Brief No. 10. Washington, D.C.: Brooking Institution.

Mott, F. 1990. "When Is Father Really Gone? Paternal-Child Contact in Father-Absent Families." *Demography* 27:399–518.

Nelson, M. K. 2000. "Single Mothers and Social Support: The Commitment to, and Retreat from, Reciprocity." *Qualitative Sociology* 23:291–317.

Roy, K. 2004. "Three-Block Fathers: Spatial Perceptions and Kin Work in Low-Income Neighborhoods." *Social Problems* 51:528–48.

Roy, K. 2006. "Father Stories: A Life Course Examination of Paternal Identity of Low-Income African American Men." *Journal of Family Issues* 27:31–54.

Roy, K., and L. Burton. 2007. "Mothering Through Recruitment: Kinscription of Non-residential Fathers and Father Figures in Low-Income Families." *Family Relations* 56:24–39.

Roy, K., O. Dyson, and J. Jackson. Forthcoming. "Intergenerational Support and Reciprocity Between Low-Income African American Fathers and Their Aging Mothers." In *Social Work Interventions for Young African American Men*, ed. W. Johnson and E. Johnson. New York: Oxford University Press.

Scott, J. W., and A. Black. 1989. "Deep Structures of African American Family Life: Female and Male Kin Networks." *The Western Journal of Black Studies* 13:17–23.

Stack, C. 1974. *All Our Kin: Strategies for Survival in a Black Community*. New York: Random House.

Stack, C., and L. Burton. 1993. "Kinscripts." *Journal of Comparative Family Studies* 24:157–70.

Stier, H., and M. Tienda. 1993. "Are Men Marginal to the Family? Insights from Chicago's Inner City." In *Men, Work and Family*, ed. Jane Hood, 23–44. Thousand Oaks, Calif.: Sage.

Strauss, A., and J. Corbin. 1998. *Basics of Qualitative Research: Techniques and Procedures for Developing Grounded Theory*. 2nd ed. Thousand Oaks, Calif.: Sage.

Tamis-LeMonda, C., and N. Cabrera. 1999. "Perspectives on Father Involvement: Research and Policy." *Society for Research in Child Development Social Policy Report* 13 (2): 200–219.

Townsend, N. 2002. *The Package Deal: Marriage, Work, and Fatherhood in Men's Lives*. Philadelphia: Temple University Press.

Waller, Maureen. 2002. *My Baby's Father: Unmarried Parents and Paternal Responsibility*. Ithaca, N.Y.: Cornell University Press.

CHAPTER ELEVEN

Feuding Identities

To Be African American, a Father, and a College Athlete

JACQUELINE D. SMITH

Many identities—racial, familial, sexual, religious, and so on—garner private and public scrutiny. For any individual, one identity may be more salient than another, but at times several salient, competing identities combine to create a matrix. Within this matrix, each identity is inextricably bound to the others, compounding the issues that each singularly wrestles with. How does one navigate and negotiate these identities? Such is the dilemma with the young men in this study. They are African Americans, fathers, and college student-athletes.

To be African American remains a struggle in American society. A person's actions are scrutinized, and, if deemed positive, she or he is a credit to the race. If deemed negative, he or she affirms many stereotypes. For a father, societal expectations often emphasize dependability and solid economic provision. Fathers who do not exhibit these characteristics are labeled "deadbeats." Being a college athlete is another struggle. Unlike the nonathlete student, the athlete's academic and social lives are subordinated to the rigors of the athlete role. Student athletes, particularly football players at Division I universities, have a significantly different college experience than their nonathlete counterparts (Adler and Adler 1991).

Schools in Division I have the highest level of athletics sanctioned by the National Collegiate Athletic Association. These universities are collegiate-athletic powers operating with larger budgets, more athletic scholarships, and more elaborate facilities than non–Division I schools. Historically, the quality of the football program has dictated whether a university was given Division I status. Hence, Division I football players are simultaneously treated as valuable, protected commodities and exploited. Such treatment places the athletes in a unique position. They are both revered and resented by their classmates as well as faculty.

For Division I schools, athletics is a major source of revenue. The NCAA filters money into the athletic programs at these schools, and, in turn, these athletic programs generate money for the NCAA. Division I football teams gross enormous revenues for their universities. The average revenue generated by Division I football teams in 2001 was $10.4 million (Litan, Orszag, and Orszag 2003). This revenue is earned from bowl-game participation, television rights, ticket sales, donations, and other means. As such, the players who are recruited and subsequently become college athletes are valuable commodities. Unfortunately, certain athletic departments value their ranking over their athletes' academic well-being. As such, much of the athlete's college life is dictated by the athletic department.

College football players often arrive on campus to find their majors and classes chosen for them. Typically, freshman football players neither attend orientation nor live with nonathlete freshmen. They have limited free time, and what they do have is often dominated by the athletic department. As they navigate their college experience, these athletes express heightened sentiments of isolation and time constrictions (Adler and Adler 1991).

The perception and consequences of these restrictions are only compounded when the athletes are African American men and fathers. Negative stereotypes of athletes are exacerbated when they interlock with those of the African American man, and the restrictions of athletic life have more serious consequences for fatherhood.

To explore this identity matrix, I interviewed four black college football players at a Division I university. The complexities of these identities illustrate that it is impossible to examine one facet of these young men's lives without considering others. They are inextricably linked. And while the nature of these dueling identities makes it impossible to privilege one over another, it is also impossible for them to coexist harmoniously. The main issues identified by the participants were: struggling between combating and embracing the stereotypes of being an African American man; experiencing guilt from privileging football over their children; and feeling isolated in their academic, social, and personal lives.

Research Background

As an academic mentor for the football team at a midsized, private, Division I university in the northeast, I noticed that these young football players were a study in themselves. I was a master's student in the Department of Communication and Rhetorical Studies and interested in different aspects of identity studies. Before earning my master's, I was in an undergraduate major that was home to many student athletes and became intrigued with their multifaceted college experience. Admittedly, at one point I wished that I, too, could be privileged with a full scholarship and campuswide notoriety, but I soon realized that these fringe benefits came at great expense.

As a mentor, I was responsible for ensuring the academic wellbeing and integrity of players with learning disabilities as well as those on academic probation. During the two years that I served as a mentor, of the approximately twenty students needing mentors, on average, eighteen were African American. The team averaged fifty-five scholarship players, and approximately 75 percent of those players were African American.

I was required to attend monthly meetings with the academic coordinator and the other mentors. In these meetings, we were to discuss our students' progress and any issues stifling their academic success. However, these meetings often served as a safe space for the mentors to air their personal gripes about student athletes. Many of the mentors admitted to believing the athletes were undeserving of admission into this university. They believed these young men were inferior students who were both spoiled by the athletic department and irresponsible. One mentor stated, "I hope my students make it to the NFL because they will never earn a degree." Hearing these views made me push my assigned students, as well as any others who would listen, to strive for excellence. Unlike my fellow mentors, I saw these young men as deserving of their scholarships; they offered an invaluable service to the university. In many ways, athletes are akin to employees of the university. Whereas other scholarship students are allowed to focus on studies, athletes must learn to balance their sports requirements and academic requirements.

My frustration with my fellow mentors fueled my interest in the integration of academics and athletics for Division I football players. I began to engage my and other student-athletes in conversations about perceptions of athletes. The most interesting conversations were with the students who were fathers, as they presented additional and more complex issues. For them, time management was not merely about being able to go to a social function on the weekend; it was about the possibility of getting home to spend time with their children. Their inability to hold paid employment during the season led outsiders to deem them "deadbeat dads." Rather than praising them for being college students, they were labeled as selfish for ruining the children's mothers' lives while pursuing their own goals. The unearthing of these intertwined issues led me to formally interview four football players at the university. In addition to interviews, the participants were asked to write journal entries chronicling their most personal dilemmas.

On several different occasions, they spoke with me about the complexities of being student-athletes and fathers. They mentioned the difficulties in balancing academic, athletic, and family life. They talked about their emotional turmoil over leaving their young children behind in an effort to further their education and possible professional football career. And there was the inner and public debate over their motives: were they in school and college athletics to pursue their own dreams or to create a stable foundation for their children?

The four men who participated in this research were students at the university and football players hoping to one day secure professional football contracts. John is an eighteen-year-old freshman who completed high school early and entered college in January, a semester ahead of his freshman class. He became a father at the age of sixteen and has one son. Calvin, a twenty-three-year-old, fifth-year senior, grew up in the same city in which the university is located. He is the father of both a son and a daughter, who were born four months apart to two different women who were students at the university with him. The children were born during his sophomore year, when he was nineteen years old. Following the birth of the son, the mother was placed on academic probation and subsequently suspended from school. She returned to her home, four hours away, with their child. Like Calvin, the mother of his daughter continues to live in the university town. With Calvin's support and that of both her and his family, she was able to graduate from the university. Michael is a twenty-two-year-old senior and a new father. He and his girlfriend met at the university. This is the first child for both of them. Lastly, Kyle is a twenty-three-year-old senior and the father of a six-year-old daughter. His daughter lives three hours away with her mother, who is white.

These men were asked open-ended questions about their perceptions of being African American, fathers, and college athletes. Questions included, for example, "What are the difficulties you find being student-athletes and fathers?" "Describe a typical daily schedule." "What do you think are the cultural images of African American males?" "How do stereotypes shape the way you're perceived?" "How might these perceptions shape your own thoughts and behavior as African American men who are also college athletes and fathers?" In addition to the interviews, the athletes were asked to document any events or emotions that addressed the intersection of their identities as African Americans, fathers, and college athletes.

Racial Stereotypes Predominate

A man is expected to behave like a man, I was expected to behave like a Black Man.

—FRANTZ FANON, BLACK SKIN, WHITE MASKS

For African Americans, race is inextricably bound with identity. There is no escaping the fact that one is African American. Of the identities discussed here, the racial one is the most explicit. It's the one everyone sees first, as Calvin points out.

> No matter how you slice it, I am black first. That is what everyone sees. They don't see the fact that I'm a college student, they don't see the fact that I am a father, they see the fact that I am a black man and that is the biggest strike against me. That clouds everyone's judgment. And I'm not just talking about white people either. Black people judge me too.

Calvin clearly suggests that negative stereotypes adhere to being African American. Regardless of the racial or ethnic composition of the company one keeps, there are habits and actions associated with being African American. Depending on the environment or circumstance, one might be either admonished or praised for exhibiting behaviors associated with being African American. Navigating this identity and its many facets can be problematic. Considering that the actions of individual African Americans are often viewed as representative of the entire race, one wants to be neither a token nor a disgrace. John exhibits a reflexive awareness of the fact that his individual experience is in a sense a public debate.

> Man, being black is tough enough as it is. Then you add on the fact that I'm a man and that's a double threat. . . . But being black puts a lot of pressure on me because I feel like I am always representing for my race. Like when I became a father at sixteen, my parents were disappointed because they felt I was now the most common stereotype of a young black man. And sometimes I think about that. Like, I'll be in Soc [sociology] class and we'll be talking about stereotypes or something and I think about the fact that I'm a walking stereotype. I also think about that fact that a lot of black girls expect us to have children. It's like we believe all of the negative things about ourselves.

Like Calvin's, John's narrative indicates that being African American overshadows all of his actions. He feels pressured and sees that others look to him to fulfill or avoid the stereotypes associated with black men. John is aware of the complexities and contradictions he exhibits. Though he does not want to appear as a stereotype, that he is an African American male, a teenaged unwed parent, and an athlete affirms many stereotypes.

Michael also expresses similar frustration with the fact that his race seems to walk ahead of him on his college campus. Like John, Michael says his fatherhood status fulfilled a stereotype, yet he exudes pride that he has also resisted stereotypes by remaining with his girlfriend and son and graduating from college.

> You know, it's crazy because I grew up in a racially and ethnically mixed town in Jersey. I don't remember race being an issue. I feel like we all just got along. We had interracial couples and all that and no one really seemed to care. But I get to college and it's a whole 'nother ball game. Everything around here seems racially motivated. Especially when people found out that we were having a baby. They thought I was gonna dump my girlfriend. We met here at school. Why would I dump her now? There were people who made jokes about me and how all black men were good for is getting a girl pregnant. But who's

laughing now? Me and my girl have our son and we are both graduating . . . which is more than can be said for some of them. But the thing that makes me the most mad is that it's not just white people who say these things. It's black people too. I mean sometimes I would look at them and wonder if they even think before they speak. How could you think so negatively of your own people?

All three men express dismay over the realization that other African Americans have internalized these negative images. These young men believe it is enough of a struggle to have to prove oneself to other ethnic and racial groups and find it disheartening to have to prove themselves to their own racial group. Blake and Darling (1994:402) explain this phenomenon:

> Skin color evokes a number of negative perceptions. Blacks are frequently labeled as immoral, lazy, violent, and mentally deficient, along with being sexual superstuds, athletes and rapacious criminals. After years of interacting with these racist stereotypes, we have begun to digest them. . . . Men must realize that their success in the world is tied to their ability to assimilate into what white America deems appropriate.

Calvin, however, refuses to assimilate. He illustrates the conundrum that these men face. Exhausted by constantly resisting these stereotypes, and feeling unappreciated for it, he chooses to embrace them:

> As a sociology major, I have become tired of all the talk about controlling images and black women. Has anyone taken the time to talk about us [black men] and controlling images? People expect me to be hanging out on the corner, they expect me to be a delinquent, they expect me to be a deadbeat dad. They give me no credit for the positive things that I do. Instead, I am viewed as a rare exception. That's why there are times that I just give in and give them what they want. They expect me to come to class late, fall asleep, and leave early. So I'll do it. They expect me to be disruptive, so I am. I get tired of fighting the stereotypes.

Calvin is attempting to reappropriate these images. He further explains his reasoning for embracing the negative stereotypes that have defined him:

You see, if I choose to act this way and people talk about me, I laugh. Because I know that I am not stupid or lazy. I know that I am not a deadbeat. But I also know that if I do anything other than what is expected, people will just say I am having a good day or something. They'll think it's a fluke. So, if I act in a certain way . . . and the key word is "act," then I am in charge. They are not creating an image for me; I am creating it for myself. When I create the image for myself, it is not oppressive. I learned that in sociology too! That's more proof that I deserve to be here!

Some might view Calvin's reappropriation as counterproductive; however, the goal of reappropriation is to move from object to subject. By embracing these images, Calvin sees himself as simultaneously putting sociological theory into practice; debunking the myth of the dumb, underachieving black male; and giving himself legitimacy (Blake and Darling 1994).

While vehemently aware of the power of stereotypes to define him, Kyle finds humor in his situation:

I see myself as an outsider. Yes, I am an athlete and thus part of a team but I entered the U with a three-year-old biracial child at home. While many will expect me to go pro and marry that blonde-headed white girl, I did it early. Well, I didn't marry her, but you know we had our daughter when we were both sixteen. The only difference is that she is stuck at home and I am here. Sometimes I think it's funny when I hear about the abandoned black woman because I created an abandoned white woman, but no one has sympathy for her. So, I get here after my postgraduate year at a somewhat elite prep school. I'm not from the city or a broken home, and I am not illiterate. Interestingly, I feel discrimination from many of the other black guys on the team. They think I'm different. They say I'm crazy. But at the end of the day, I just want them to respect me.

In an ironic way, Kyle defies main elements of the stereotype of the black male athlete, but his doing so is viewed as odd by other black members of the team. There is a sense in which they just can't win, as the demands of each identity compete in often contradictory ways.

All four young men pinpoint stereotypes as one of the main difficulties in being an African American man. Race is the most visible aspect of their identity and colors all of their actions. As teenaged or unwed fathers, these young men have fulfilled one of the main stereotypes of both African American men and African American male athletes. As such, they seek to mediate scrutiny by pursuing their education through athletics. Yet their pursuit of higher education fuels the stereotype of the absent African American father. Their frequent absence from class because of athletic requirements supports the notion of the absentee student athlete. These outside issues hinder their ability to be "model" African American men, students, and fathers. Their situation can be appropriately summed up by Frantz Fanon (1967:116):

> I am given no chance. I am overdetermined from without. I am the slave not of the "idea" that others have of me but of my own appearance. . . . When people like me, they tell me it is in spite of my color. When they dislike me, they point out it is not because of my color. Either way, I am locked in the infernal circle.

The Student-Athlete's Father Experience

According to King, Harris, and Heward (2003), nearly half of the children in the United States will experience a period in their childhood of living without their biological fathers in the home. The fact that a father is noncustodial does not necessarily indicate parental noninvolvement (Coles 2002). Several factors can influence the type and range of a father's involvement in his child's life (Pleck 1997). Issues affecting parental involvement can range from geographic proximity, to the relationship with the mother of the child, to finances. For the men in this study, being a college athlete served to compound the many issues surrounding the ability to parent and parental involvement.

Being a teenaged father is a struggle. What happens when you are a teenaged father who happens also to be a high-school student and a top football recruit? Do you forego your dreams and opportunities to remain at home and assist in childrearing? Doing so may win kudos from others, such as the child's mother and some family members, in the short run, but the acquisition of a college education will help everyone in the long run. While the college education, particularly one accompanied by an athlete's notoriety on campus, may make the latter choice appear motivated by personal advancement, it, too, comes with costs. For John this dilemma was reality:

Now remember this is my first semester in college. I have never been away from home. My son is a year old. I didn't even really graduate high school yet. I mean I finished all of my coursework but I didn't walk across the stage yet. And here I am, clear across the county with nothing and no one. I talk to my son's mother every day on AOL [instant messenger]. But I don't have a cell phone, can't afford one. She sends me pictures of our son every day on e-mail. I call whenever I can and she calls me when she can. She is around more people, like family and all, so it's easier for her. All I know up here is my teammates, and the ones who don't have kids don't understand so I rather not get them involved. But it's hard knowing that I am missing a lot of my son's firsts. I'm going to miss his first steps, his first word, his first Thanksgiving, I might even miss his first Christmas if we go to a bowl game. I can look into the future and see all of the other stuff I am going to miss. And I know I can't blame anyone but myself because I made this situation, but that don't make it easy on me. I love my son to death.

Unlike the typical teenaged father, John's situation is complicated by the fact that he is attending college away from home. He and his son are on opposite coasts. His many athletic requirements constrain him from going home regularly. Though he acknowledges a desire to be a part of his son's life, he is contractually unable to do so.

An important aspect to father involvement in the child's life is the relationship that the father has with the mother. Johnson (2001) found that the lack of a romantic relationship between a mother and father was associated with a lack of interest on behalf of both parents in father involvement. John experienced similar sentiments from the mother of his son. He explained that, initially, both he and his son's mother had plans to go away to college. Once she became pregnant, she relinquished her dream but encouraged him to pursue his. John completed high school and enrolled in college a semester early. However, since he has been at school, his son's mother has expressed feelings of resentment. She says that it is not fair that she is the primary caretaker for their son and had to give up her dream. She was a promising student, and although she graduated from high school, she was unable to attend college. She tells John that it is unfair that he lives a carefree life. As an example, she points out that, unlike her, he is able to go to parties without having to arrange for babysitters. John has ambivalent feelings; he recognizes her loss but doesn't want to forfeit his own dreams either: "Sometimes I feel bad that his mom is stuck back there raising him by herself. I mean, she probably thought she was gonna go to school too. But I knew I was going to school, wasn't nothing gonna stop me. But at least she graduated, right? But, I mean, I know it's hard on her."

The relationship that Calvin has with the mother of his child vacillates as well. The mother makes sure he doesn't forget that their daughter is both their responsibilities: "Everyone knows, she thinks nothing of dropping my daughter off at my door. At first I had to adjust to that. I was used to the life of freedom, but my daughter's mother makes sure that I remember I have a child. Sometimes it's hard for me." However, Calvin also acknowledges that his daughter's mother frequently denies his requests to see his daughter whenever she is angry with him. This anger sometimes stems from his denying her romantic advances, but it also stems from her not believing that football consumes most of his time:

> Sometimes she gets all crazy when I tell her that she can't drop my daughter off. I mean she knows that I have breakfast check at eight in the morning and I have study table at night. Sometimes I really am there until ten at night. Then there are times that we have to do volunteer stuff on the weekends or go to dinner with the boosters. Man, I can't miss that stuff. She forgets that football is like my job; they just don't pay me!

John's and Calvin's experiences of conflict with the mothers are not unlike those of many single, nonresident fathers. However, their experience is further complicated by the fact that their desires to parent are mediated by their athletic and scholarly demands.

Only one of the fathers, Michael, has been able to escape the tension between his and the mother's competing goals. Michael's experience differs from the other three in that both he and his girlfriend are students at the university, and both are successfully completing their college career. Additionally, they are both twenty-two years old. Consequently, they can offer their child slightly more stability than can many teenaged parents, and they have a stronger interpersonal relationship that has allowed them to cooperate to the benefit of all three:

We met here in school. I am on my way out of here and so is my girl. Everyone thought she was gonna have to take a semester off or a leave of absence when she got pregnant but she kept on going and she is a nursing major, so it was rough. She had to go to the hospital for her [birthing] classes and be in the classroom but our son was born in December. So, we were able to adjust to being parents over the Christmas break, then be ready for school in January. I am happy that the baby didn't interrupt the flow of either of our lives. I think that is why we have such a good relationship now. Plus I think the fact that this is our last semester helps a lot too.

The parental cooperation required when two parents rear a child while they are building their own social capital is difficult to negotiate regardless of the age, race, and marital status of the parents. However, the demands of athletics and academics coupled with the effort of combating racial stereotypes only work to compound those negotiations.

A key aspect of parenting that the players cite as being manipulated by their status as an athlete is their finances. Paramount to being viewed as a "good" father is the ability to be able to provide for your child (Johnson 2001). All four of the men interviewed exhibited frustration over what they believed to be a ban on employment for Division I athletes during the academic year. For instance, John complains:

I can't work because of NCAA regulations, so I can't really support my child. I'm not there to help out with the day-to-day stuff, but I try to make sure he knows that daddy loves him very much and that I'm way out here trying to make sure he has the best life. I mean, I have to make it. It's not just about me, I have to do it for him. I believe that with all of my heart, but football makes that tough. I have already missed so much. I can't be there when he cries at night, and I can't give his mom a penny. What kind of provider am I right now?

Michael was the only respondent to address the issue of public assistance. He is embarrassed that his child has to live on funding from Women, Infants, and Children, a federally sponsored food and nutrition program: "It bothers me that she is on WIC. I mean here I am, a man who is about to become a professional athlete in a couple of months, and my son is receiving free milk and cheese from the government."

Calvin has actually circumvented the rules to fulfill his role as a provider:

Yo, I need a job. Coach don't know it but on the weekends, I work at a bar downtown as a bouncer sometimes. Man, I can't let my kids be out there with nothing. I think they keep forgetting that I have two kids. I don't get no Pell Grant like these other cats up here. So, I got to struggle with nothing. And I'm tired of my daughter's mom calling me and telling me how I'm no good. I keep telling her that I can't work. It's not like I'm really a deadbeat. Man, a deadbeat just *won't* work. I *can't* work. And then you know them little jobs they be getting us in the summer. What am I supposed to do with that little money?

All four of these athletes stated that, according to NCAA rules, Division I athletes are not allowed to maintain employment during the academic year. During the summer, when not enrolled in academic courses, they are allowed to hold jobs secured by the football department with an average salary of ten dollars per hour. Most of these positions are part-time. Perhaps this is the reason many of the athletes refer to football as a full-time job.

Interestingly, according to the NCAA Web site, the ban on academic year employment for Division I athletes was lifted in 1998 under Proposition 62 (http://www.ncaa.org/wps/portal), but all four athletes stated that the football department told them they were not allowed to work during the academic year. Consequently, they often expressed feelings of being modern-day slaves to the university. Universities receive revenue from ticket sales, merchandise, and television rights, yet the players are led to believe that they cannot work to support their families. Instead, they are told that those who are eligible must survive on Pell Grant refunds. The desire and need to work is central to the ability to provide for a child, but it is not in the best interest of the athletic department to encourage these young men to obtain employment.

The Father-Athlete's Academic Experience

Incoming athletes at the university quickly learn that their freshman experience differs from that of the nonathlete student. Football players usually enter the university with their majors chosen by the athletic department. Their class choices are limited to those that do not conflict with afternoon practices and evening team meetings. Though athletes are allowed to change their major, they are encouraged to privilege their team requirements (Adler and Adler 1991). Kyle is proud that he was able to choose a major that is viewed as harder than one most football players have.

> I'm well aware of the stereotypes that surround and follow me like a shadow. Notice that I am an information [technology] studies major, I am not one of those other majors typical for athletes. And I'm not trying to act like I'm better or smarter than anyone. But I know that I was smart enough to get out of the major that coach assigned me to. I wasn't gonna waste my time in some major and then not be able to get a job when I graduate. Or get a job where I wouldn't even be able to support my family.

In Kyle's opinion, the coaches place athletes in less-demanding majors that allow for sufficient time to be dedicated to athletics. However, his identity as a father motivates him to do more and, in his view, distinguishes him from many other football players:

> Cuz, you see I am different from these other guys. They take everything as a joke. They wanna be at every party and in the bars every Thursday and Friday but I don't have that luxury. I had to come in here focused because I know that when I leave I will still be a father and still have a family that I will be responsible for. Even though my daughter isn't here, I know that I am responsible for her.

John also is similarly motivated by fatherhood and likewise views himself as different from many of his teammates:

> Even though I don't like to think like this, even if I don't make it to the league, I'm definitely leaving here with a degree so I will be better than when I started off. I don't understand some of these dudes who come in here with nothing and leave with nothing. That's a waste of five years, man. Once you become a father, you can't live for yourself anymore. I'm young but the day I became a father my dad told me that my fun and free life was over. He said no matter what, my son was to come first.

Kyle's and John's focus on education is not uncommon for African American football players. According to Hyatt (2003), only 7 percent of African American college football players expect to become professional athletes, and less than 2 percent of NCAA senior football players are drafted by the NFL.

Another common sentiment among these athletes is a feeling of isolation. Being college athletes isolates them from both their families and fellow classmates. Adler and Adler (1991) state that college athletes are subject to "role engulfment." Because of the demands of athletic life, they have less time to dedicate to their families and friends at home. In addition, their status as athletes and the myths that accompany it often alienate them from their classmates. The fathers suggested that they often were viewed as intruders on the campus, undeserving of being there. Nonathlete students often are ignorant that many of the university's upgrades are financed by funds won through football bowl games. Being a college athlete bears the stigma of being privileged. There are those who resent the athletes for their perceived status and those who desire the athletes for their perceived status. As expressed by Calvin:

> You know what? I hate going to class. There are those people who want to sit next to me and be all friendly because I'm a football player. You know, they start off the conversation like, "Hey, that was some tackle you made on Saturday" or "I caught your interview on *Sports Center*." Or there are the times when no one wants me to be in their group if we have a group project. It's like I can't win. Then people always wonder why all the athletes hang together. Man, it's because we are the only ones we can really trust!

The alienation that these young men feel does not end with their classmates. Some of the players indicated their status as a father and their desire to fulfill that role also alienate them from their teammates when it comes to a social life. According to Kyle: "These guys up here don't understand me. They don't get that I'm not into the same stuff they are. All that running around is how I got to be a father at sixteen! I had to grow up quickly. I don't need to be at every party and at the bars every Thursday night." John also shares the same feelings:

> Sometimes it is a little strange. Like at night I just want to be at home and near the computer so that when my son's mom IMs me, I am there. I don't want to miss out on anything. These guys don't understand that. But when I became a dad, my son became my priority. Don't get me wrong, I still want to go out and have fun and all of that. After all, I

am still young, but I don't want to have any regrets about my son. But I can't explain that to my roommates, my teammates, my boys! They don't know how being a father changes a man. They can't understand.

Calvin's experience of alienation differs from that of John and Kyle. On the one hand, Calvin feels he doesn't fit expected African American stereotypes: his parents are married, and he attends church with them on a regular basis. On the other hand, he is also atypical compared to most college students: he had two children with two women within a four-month period, and many of his fellow students denigrate him for that.

Man, my story has got to be the most unique! Here I am a freshman and somewhat of a local, you know, home is only twenty minutes away. Every Sunday my parents come to pick me up for church, and, yes, I did say parents. And, yes, they had been married for over twelve years before I was born. So, I come from a stable, nuclear family . . . I learned those terms in class. Yet, I am the man that no one will forget! It seems like every time I walk into the locker room or the weight room guys are talking about me. And I'm sure that people will be talking about me long after I leave here! So here I am, freshman year, and honestly just happy to be out of my parents' house. You don't understand. There are only two black families where I grew up so there weren't tons of girls after me, but here at college I was a sex symbol. So, to make a long story short, I had a real girlfriend and then I had a couple on the side. The real girlfriend got pregnant, and then one of the ones on the side got pregnant, too. Can you believe that? So, I end up nineteen with two children that are born four months apart. How many guys can relate to that? Who can I really talk to about my situation? And to be honest, I would feel stupid trying to talk to someone. Most of the guys tell me that I am stupid for getting myself into this situation. But I felt that I had to own up to my responsibility. So, I am doing the best that I can.

Discussion

These young men present new issues for the study of parenting and fatherhood. They are not merely unwed parents. Their parental residential status and availability is mandated by their athletic and academic demands. Their employment status and financial contribution are also mandated by outside influences. They have three interlocking identities that simultaneously empower and hinder them.

As African Americans, they are judged against what is viewed as normal. Their behaviors are either a credit or detriment to their race. As fathers, they attempt to work within the confines of being both African American and college athletes. As college athletes, they are slaves to a system that simultaneously exploits and assists them. Unlike students on academic scholarships, athletic-scholarship football players create large amounts of revenue for their university. However, they are viewed as undeserving of their place in the university. For all of the revenue generated by their efforts, these young men are often struggling financially. To solidify their financial contribution to the university, these young men are often required to attend social functions and volunteer with various organizations. These appearances allow potential donors the opportunity to socialize with the athletes. These events take precedence over scholastic and familial endeavors. For college athletes who are also fathers, these constraints are too demanding. Unfortunately, too often, rather than attempt to negotiate the uncertainties of fatherhood, scholastics, and athletics by earning a college degree or an NFL contract or both, they falter, withdraw from athletics and school, and return home. Fortunately, the four young men who participated in this research persevered and were able to balance their multiple identities and responsibilities.

These young men seek to rebut the stereotype of the neglectful African American athlete who is also a father. They view their parental absence as a sacrifice made to fulfill the role of college athlete. Their parental role has sacrificed social relations with teammates and other students. Each role has its costs and benefits to the father-student-athlete, but the fathers see these as short-term costs that will produce long-term benefits, providing them with the resources and potential to become the fathers, caretakers, and providers.

References

Adler, P. A., and P. Adler. 1991. *Backboards and Blackboards: College Athletes and Role Engulfment.* New York: Columbia University Press.
Blake, W. M., and C. A. Darling. 1994. "The Dilemmas of the African American Male." *Journal of Black Studies* 24 (4): 402–15.

Coles, R. L. 2002. "Black Single Fathers: Choosing to Parent Full-Time." *Journal Contemporary Ethnography* 23 (4): 411–39.

Fanon, F. 1967. *Black Skin, White Masks*. New York: Grove Press.

Hyatt, R. 2003. "Barriers to Persistence Among African American Intercollegiate Athletes: A Literature Review of Non-Cognitive Variables." *College Student Journal* 37:260–76.

Johnson, W. E. 2001. "Parental Involvement Among Unwed Fathers." *Children and Youth Services Review* 23 (6/7): 513–36.

King, V., K. M. Harris, and H. E. Heward. 2003. "Racial and Ethnic Diversity in Nonresident Father Involvement." *Journal of Marriage and Family* 66:1–21.

Litan, R. E., J. M. Orszag, and P. R. Orszag. 2003. "The Empirical Effects of Collegiate Athletics." Commissioned by the National Collegiate Athletic Association. Washington, D.C.: Sebago Associates.

Pleck, J. H. 1997. "Paternal Involvement: Levels, Sources, and Consequences." In *The Role of the Father in Child Development*, ed. M. E. Lamb, 66–103. New York: Wiley.

PART FIVE

Fathers Through Children's Eyes

CHAPTER TWELVE

Daughters' Constructions of Connectedness to Their Nonresident Fathers

EUNICE MATTHEWS-ARMSTEAD

The issue of father absence and its impact on African American women has long been a concern of the African American community. Fatherless African American women are often perceived as troubled, damaged, and struggling with issues of abandonment, insecurity, and self esteem. Some research indicates fatherless women experience higher rates of promiscuity, teen pregnancy, high-school dropout, and delinquent behavior (Krohn and Bogan 2001; Flouri and Buchanan 2003). Although the research is clear about the possible challenges these women face as a result of growing up without a father in the home, their fate does not appear to be sealed. Fatherless women do succeed. Some African American women are able to avoid many or all of these pitfalls associated with their early developmental challenges. How might we explain these differential responses to father absence?

In recent years, with the breakthroughs in infant mental health and the introduction of attachment theory, the discourse regarding father absence and its impact on child development has shifted away from the discussion of simplistic indicators of father involvement to an examination of the quality rather than the quantity of the interactions. A focus on relational issues liberates us from the superficial distinctions of the father's presence or absence in the home and directs our attention to a more in-depth examination of the relational process (Coley and Chase-Lansdale 1999). The father's influence on the daughter's socio-emotional outcomes is said to be best understood in relation to the daughter's perceptions of closeness—an affectional bond of attachment—to her father (Benson, Harris, and Rogers 1992). It is within the context of the father-daughter relationship and the interactions that characterize that relationship that our understanding of female development will be enhanced and insight into the differential responses to father absence may be found (Coley 2003; Sobolewski 2006).

By focusing on the quality of the relationship, the examination becomes concentrated on the responsiveness of the father to the daughter, which necessitates an incorporation of her subjective experience of the relationship. A factor that is inherent in her subjective experience of closeness but missing in much of the research is the daughter's basic expectations of the attachment. Coley's (2003) study of African American father-daughter relationships found that young women who retained an intense emotional connection, either positive or negative, to fathers who themselves were unresponsive demonstrated high levels of negative internalized and externalized behaviors. Coley contends that such behaviors may be related to unfulfilled expectations. She goes on to suggest that a more in-depth examination of daughters' expectations of their fathers and how well they perceive their fathers fulfilling such expectations would support a greater understanding of the role of fathers in African American families. The issue of father absence then becomes more a matter of the daughter's *interpretation* of the experience and much less a matter of what fathers do or don't do. It is about how the daughters define their fathers in their fathers' absence.

In the biological father's absence, his role is often assumed by other men, such as grandfathers, uncles, brothers, or the boyfriend of the mother, or to some extent by the mother. Yet is it merely a matter of finding a replacement to fulfill the father's assigned task, or is there more to it? There are those who would choose to look at the role of father as a position, a set of tasks, a gendered role that could be filled by any willing man. The literature speaks of social fathers, father figures, men who were "like a father," as if the role of father is replaceable, as if biological fathers don't really matter because any man could do. Such narratives render biological fathers tenuous and insignificant in terms of life development.

Some research suggests little difference between the biological father and a father figure in terms of the influence on the daughter's development. Supposedly, only the quality and consistency of the interaction between the daughter and father or father figure is of significance (Khaleque and Rohner 2002; Coley 2003). However, it could be argued that what is being observed is not a lack of distinction between the father and social father but rather the empirically supported significance of responsive interactions between a child and another adult. Studies do support the notion that a responsive, caring relationship between a child and another adult can have positive effects on the child's development (Lansky 1989). Therefore, the positive influence of the social father does not in and of itself negate the value or influence of the biological father. To enhance our understanding of the influence of fathers, it is necessary to make a conceptual distinction between the biological father as an object of attachment and the acts of fathering, the latter referring to the interaction between the child and a male adult. This chapter will focus on the former, a qualitative examination of daughters' perceptions of and attachments to their fathers.

The narratives of the African American women in this discussion support the notion that biological fathers always matter. Their fathers, for better or for worse, represented the first man in their lives. For them, the term "father" meant the man responsible for bringing them into the world. Although they were exposed to social fathers, when asked about their fathers there was no question as to whom they were referring nor to the significance that he held in their lives separate from his physical presence. The differential responses to father absence demonstrated by these women highlight the complexities of the father-daughter relationship. It also demonstrates that our inquiry into the father-daughter relationship cannot overlook the influence of biological fathers.

This chapter integrates into the discussion of African American fathers the voices of their daughters to assist us in gaining additional insight into this dynamic relationship. The differential responses and interpretations of their fathers' behavior provides the literature with a more layered understanding of the phenomenon of absent biological fathers. The daughters' dyadic memories of their fathers direct us to an understanding that father absence is far more complex than a simple lack of physical presence. Emerging from an examination of both the content and coherence of their personal narratives, I organized a "typology" of absent fathers based on how daughters negotiated the gap between what they expected of the father-daughter relationship and what they think they received. The father-daughter interactions described by the women of this study were clustered together into three categories of absent fathers: the Shadow Father, the Powerless Father, and the Idealized Father. The following discussion will use the women's stories to illustrate how daughters create and shape and attach to fathers in their absence.

The characterization of absent fathers presented in this chapter can serve as an interesting starting point for the exploration of the effect of fathers' absence on their daughters by highlighting the importance of subjectivity. This discussion is inspired by the belief that the greater our understanding of this critical relationship, the better will be our ability to make the necessary adjustments to ensure a more positive outcome for the daughters and in turn the African American community.

The Profile of Daughters

This is a qualitative study of twelve African American women who grew up in homes without their biological fathers. The women ranged in age from nineteen to thirty-nine. None of them was a teen mother, and all of them graduated from high school, with six having attended college. All but one of the women came from economically challenged backgrounds, with three having spent much of their childhood in the foster-care system. However, today, all of them are high-functioning women with a positive work history who have avoided many of the pitfalls, such as mental issues, substance abuse, and early pregnancy, associated with growing up in low-income households without a resident father. Two of the women are married with children. The only other mother among the participants is in a long-term common-law relationship with the father of her child. Among the remaining participants, the four who were under the age of twenty-five were still living at home with their mothers but were contributing to the household. All of the women began employment when they were sixteen years old and continue to work.

These remarkable women shared their life stories, aspirations, and relationship histories. Because the effects of their experiences are believed to be a part of both their conscious and preconscious minds, the analysis involved both an examination of their conscious descriptions of their circumstances as well as the underlying meaning implied in those experiences. The general flow and content of their narratives, the tone in which they were delivered, and the language they used were all examined.

Daughters' Conceptions of Fathers

Building upon Coley and Chase-Lansdale's (1999) and Coley's (2003) work on father-daughter relationships, this study chose to examine more closely the women's perceptions of their biological fathers in the context of their perceived expectations of the relationship. Emerging from the women's descriptions of their biological fathers and the nature of their relationship was a pattern of perceptions indicating how they negotiated internally the differences between what they expected their fathers to be and what their fathers actually provided. Based on the similarities in the themes among the women's narratives, I clustered their characterizations of fathers and their dyadic relationships into three categories of fathers.

Again, I note that these characterizations were based on the daughters' active interpretive work and less on the fathers' actual behaviors. Although the majority of the fathers acknowledged the existence of their daughters and had made some effort to contact their daughters during their childhood, three fathers remained completely unknown to the daughters, and one was deceased, having been murdered when his daughter was a toddler. Only two of the fathers had been married to the mothers, and in those cases, they had divorced when their daughters were less than four years old. Most of the women had little knowledge about their fathers. But the limited knowledge they possessed indicated that the majority of the fathers were marginally functional, with sketchy work histories and limited economic resources. None of the women indicated having received regular financial support from her father.

The Shadow Father

The Shadow Father is just that to this set of women, a shadow, a vague image that lurks just beyond clear recognition but a presence just the same. For some he is a figure fed to them by their mothers and others in their lives who knew him; for other daughters he's a faint memory from a brief encounter, a man they saw in passing. Daughters of Shadow Fathers acknowledge their fathers, although they have little tangible evidence of his existence. Carrie states, "I know I have a father, I have no idea who the hell he is or where he is but I know I have one."

They speak of him as having "took off," "left," "disappeared." These women characterized their fathers as missing in action. Their evaluations of his involvement in their lives, as with all the women in the study, was clearly internal; it was not based on any objective evaluation of the frequency of contacts or the amount of concrete support. It was about something far deeper for them. Cathy states,

> My dad, he was around. I would see him a lot in the neighborhood. My aunt, my father's sister, would come get me when I was little, and I would stay at my grandmother's house for like the weekend. He lived there, too, so I would see him come in and out of the house. He might even stick around for a little while and watch TV. But, I never got the sense that he was there with me. It was just like we happened to be in the same room.

Cathy goes on to talk about how she never really got the sense that she could depend on him or that he would be there for her if she needed him. He did not inspire in her a sense of security or trust.

Although scant in number, the memories of their fathers appear to linger in a place of easy access. Without much effort, they recall them. Carol shares her one and only contact with her father.

> When I was nine, as a matter of fact on my ninth birthday, I met this man. I came home from school and he was sitting there and my mother said that that's your father, and I'm like Wow! She was like this is your father and whatever, so he says that he's going to take me to his mother's house, right—But then my mother is like wait until the weekend. He was supposed to come back and pick me up. He never did. So I never saw him again. I never saw him again in my life. That was the first and last time. His name is [father's name] I think.

For Carol, her father was a strange man sitting on the couch in her home. She couldn't really remember much of what he looked like or any real details about him. She wasn't even sure about his name. Yet, she held onto this memory of the fleeting interaction between the two of them as a representation of her father.

These daughters express a sense of loss; something is missing in their lives. That sense of loss suggests the existence of an expectation, even if not explicitly stated. The women were of the impression that fathers are supposed to "be there" for their daughters, particularly during such significant life events as graduation, getting a first job, and getting married. Carrie, who is married now with two children, talked about planning her wedding. Her comments again indicate that these women carry with them societal expectations of what a father should be and do in relation to his daughter. There is a sense of anger toward the father for not being there to help her fulfill society's expectations.

> When you get married your father is supposed to give you away, walk you down the aisle. What about me? It's like okay my father's not around to give me away. I had to figure out who should walk me down the aisle. I don't know, it seems wrong to me that I should have figure out something that should be so basic.

But for Carrie and the other daughters of the Shadow Fathers, their seemingly inconsequential contacts with their fathers had a long-lasting effect on them and how they constructed their sense of self. These women struggle with the question of what their fathers' absence means in terms of their own value. Is his absence a reflection of their lack of worth? But as their fragile walls of self-protection weaken from this kind of inquiry, they dismiss those thoughts and quickly redirect their thinking. They transform those life events into achievements and present them as testaments of how well they are doing without him, treating the open wounds created by fathers' absence with a light bandage of dismissal and denial. They profess for themselves that they didn't need him, that they are fine without him.

Although they try to present an impression of indifference about him, as if they couldn't care less, their internal struggle is revealed in their conversations and in their comments. In a tone of shame, the women would confess to thinking and wondering about their fathers: "What is he really like? How might my life have been different if he had stuck around or been a more dependable force in my life? How could he have abandoned me?" They recognize the lack of expected mutuality and reciprocity in their father-daughter relationships and feel ashamed for caring for someone who apparently doesn't return the feeling.

Feelings of anger and resentment emerge in their tone. Catlin, whose father struggles with substance abuse and left her mother when she was small, states, "He doesn't think about me so I don't think about him." But the validity of this position of indifference is immediately called into question by the daughters' ability to recall every contact, chance meeting, and missed opportunity with their fathers. They were able to reproduce from their memories with relative detail when and where the interactions occurred as well as some of the things that were said or not said. The women appear to be unaware of the apparent contradiction between their claims of indifference and their detailed recall. For example, one daughter, Cori, could not recall ever receiving a call or card from her father on her birthday. He had left before she was two, but in a "matter a fact sort of way" she describes an interaction with her father that took place about twelve years before, when she was around fifteen years old,

> I was outside playing when my mother called me into the house. She didn't say why. She just yelled out the window for me to come upstairs. When I got there she told me "your father's on the phone." I m not sure why, she didn't say that when she told me to come upstairs, maybe she thought I wouldn't come. But I would have. . . . But anyway, when I got to the phone I really didn't have much to say and neither did he. So I asked him did he know when my birthday was? He got the month right but did not know the day. I didn't have much to say after that.

We talked about the encounter. Cori didn't know why she had asked that question of her father, particularly because she knew how he would answer. Cori mentioned that maybe she had wanted to make a point but wasn't sure what point she was trying to make. Perhaps she had hoped she would be wrong and he would have redeemed himself, coming closer to her expectations. The daughters of the Shadow Fathers engage in this ongoing struggle between accepting the reality of their relationship with their fathers and desiring it to be different.

As the daughters of the Shadow Fathers shared their stories of painful incidents, the incongruence between the content of their stories and their emotions were startling. They frequently denied having any feelings at all, attempting to present an impression of acceptance. Although they mentioned the incidents of their fathers not knowing their birthday, never having sent a card or letter, standing them up at an arranged visit, or meeting them only one time in their lives, the daughters presented these potentially emotional stories with a flat affect, disconnected from any feelings, as if indifferent. However, in further discussion, they would betray themselves with flip, denigrating comments that revealed the anger and discontent just beneath the surface. For instance, they might end a story by saying "what a jerk" or "you see, isn't he worthless?"

The daughters of Shadow Fathers seemed to need to protect themselves from the emotional content of their experiences. By engaging in this sort of disconnection from lingering feelings of pain, sadness, confusion, and anger, it was as if they were trying, albeit unsuccessfully, to convince themselves that their fathers didn't matter and that their experiences of them had no effect. It was as if each needed to make her father dispensable, to present a kind of take-it-or-leave-it attitude about their relationship. In so doing, they hoped to insulate themselves from the source of their pain.

The attachment experience of daughters and Shadow Fathers is tenuous but not absent, as some researchers would suggest. Even if the daughters had never met their fathers, he seemed to have a place in their lives. He occupied their thoughts. Their fathers were unavailable and unresponsive, but the women expressed a sense of connection to them, evidenced in their struggle to resolve the contradiction between what they expected and what they got. The struggle was revealed in their anger and resentment toward their fathers. The inadequacy of this apparently fundamental relationship left the daughters of Shadow Fathers with an underlying sense of self-doubt and an exaggerated need to be independent. The daughters of Shadow Fathers were strikingly self-reliant and self-directed. They wore their independence like a set of armor.

The Powerless Father

Powerless Fathers, similar to the Shadow Fathers, were unavailable or inconsistent in terms of their contact with their daughters. What distinguishes the Shadow Fathers and the Powerless Fathers is not the fathers' actual behavior but their daughters' perceptions of the fathers' level of involvement and the intensity of the perceived connection to him. The daughters of the Powerless Fathers chose to temper their disappointment about their unmet expectations by redirecting focus away from their fathers' actions onto an indisputable connection existing between the two of them, which was merely the fact that they were the biological child of the father.

These daughters view their fathers as being within their sight but just beyond their reach. Because their fathers were not consistently around, these daughters express a sense of longing, an incompleteness created by his absence. However, unlike the daughters of Shadow Fathers, these daughters insert a mediating influence in the father-daughter relationship. They explain the lack of father involvement by an intervening variable. They suggest that "every time it seems like we had a chance to get to know each other, something happened." For example, Nancy, whose father had been in and out of prison all of her childhood, mentions one of the many times he returned home:

> I was so excited when he came home. I think I was around five. I'm not sure. I know I was young and I had started school. Well anyway, he came home, and I thought he and my mother were going to get back together. But, he started using again, and my mother threw him out. I'm not sure when he got locked up after that. But, I don't know, maybe my mother could have given him a little longer to get it together before she threw him out. I not sure she really got my dad.

These daughters perceive their fathers as being taken or driven away by something or someone else. They would say, "My Dad had to leave," "They took him," or "He had no choice." This perception of their fathers having been taken away rather than leaving of their own accord appears to protect them from feelings of rejection and abandonment.

Any anger that the daughters feel is displaced on the circumstances that they believe to be the cause of their fathers' absence. Such circumstances might include drug addiction, the criminal-justice system, or an abusive family history. The daughters of Powerless Fathers see their fathers as misunderstood, struggling with issues they are unable to manage or overcome. Rather than anger or resentment, this set of daughters feels a sense of sorrow for their fathers. They appear to accept the fact that their fathers are not great men or even good fathers. But, for them, that doesn't matter. They forgive all his shortcomings, they don't care who he is or what he may have done; they just want to be with him. It is that need for a sense of connection that dominates their narratives.

Daughters of Powerless Fathers are preoccupied with the need to have a "relationship" with their fathers. Although such a relationship is clearly difficult if not impossible to develop, they feel compelled to try. The women address their feelings of emptiness and incompleteness by exaggerating connections between themselves and their fathers. Neda's father was in prison, serving a long sentence for much of her childhood. She could recall only one time when she actually visited him. But she nevertheless felt connected to him: "I have everything he ever sent me. Every picture, every letter, every gift. You know what I mean. You know those things they make in prison by hand. He made me this wallet one time. I don't use it though. I don't want it to get messed up. I put it with the rest of my things from him in a special box."

These daughters desperately hold on to any sign of their father's acknowledgment of their existence. Any call, letter from prison, or brief visit supports not necessarily an image of him as a wonderful father but the existence of a bond between them. They find comfort in his recognition of them as their daughters. They still struggle with their desires for him to be more of a father, but they convince themselves that he would be, were it not for other circumstances.

Although the women report experiences of their fathers as being unresponsive and unreliable, they are quick to explain it away. Nelly's father divorced her mother and left the state before her fourth birthday. He failed to maintain contact after he left. It wasn't until her senior year in high school that she ever laid eyes on him again. Initially during the interview, though, she stated that he had maintained contact with her and her siblings even after his departure, but as the interview continued, she revealed that she had no direct contact with her father during most of her childhood and that it was only through her father's relatives who remained in the community that she was even aware that he was still alive and doing well. When we talked about her earlier misrepresentation of the relationship, Nelly explained, "I don't know. I thought you might misunderstand. I mean it really wasn't his fault, most of the time we didn't even have a telephone so he couldn't call us." Her explanation acquired a defensive tone in an attempt to protect his image. She feared that I might get the wrong impression about him. But as with daughters of Shadow Fathers, the line between the fathers' and daughters' image is blurred. Perhaps she was equally concerned that her father's absence might reflect her lack of value, that he didn't think enough of her to maintain contact. The daughters of the Powerless Fathers needed to believe that "if he could, he would be there," even though the evidence to support such a notion is sadly lacking. While these daughters find some solace in this perspective, just beneath the surface they continue to struggle with a lingering sense of loss, sadness, and emptiness created by his absence or inconsistency.

The daughter of a Powerless Father constructs what she perceives as a special connection between her and her father by presenting herself as the understanding person in his life. She sees herself as being different from everyone else who may have abandoned and rejected her father. She views herself as the only person who really tries to understand her father, who believes in him, and who wants to be there for him. Nelly explains,

> When I was growing up, times were really hard. My parents got married really young, and I guess he just couldn't take it so he left. My brothers and sisters, they don't talk to him. They say they don't want anything to do with him. But, I don't know, I kind of feel sorry for him. I mean he missed out on watching us grow up and really getting to know us. I look at his family. His father left when he was young, too.

In constructing this special role for themselves, the daughters in turn gain a sense of significance and purpose from their perspective. Their affirmation of this role as a special person is not found in their fathers' actions or affirmed in any expression of appreciation by their fathers but rather resides in their own minds. Creating a perception of themselves as special averts some of the feelings of unworthiness while simultaneously providing them with the motivation to be more tolerant toward and forgiving of their fathers and bolsters themselves against all the disappointments and pain. This sustains the connection with the fathers, who, "for reasons they can't help," are only partly able to reciprocate. The women have created for themselves a complex net of perceptions designed to protect their sense of connectedness to their fathers and to challenge their overwhelming feelings of loss and emptiness.

The daughters of Powerless Fathers appear to experience a real sense of insecurity in relation to their connection to their fathers, and they hesitate to place any expectations on the relationship. Their self-constructed role as the special people in their fathers' lives clearly rests on a shaky foundation. Though they are reluctant to admit it to themselves, they do acknowledge only tenuous involvement in their fathers' lives. From their perspective, their fathers may be one of the "most important people in their lives," but they exhibit lingering doubts about their own significance to them, which appears to be a source of great pain.

Perceptions of their marginality are manifested in their reluctance to "rock the boat," so to speak. They actively struggle not to present themselves as being too much trouble or an inconvenience to the fathers. Although they see their connection to their fathers as being important, they also see it as extremely fragile. So they are unusually accepting of their fathers' negative behavior, motivated by a paralyzing fear that if they cause too much trouble, upset him too much, he will disappear. For instance, Nancy described her graduation. She and her mother had argued because she only had a limited number of tickets, and Nancy wanted to be sure to save one for her father. On the day of graduation, her father didn't show. The next weekend she made the trip across town to see him, but during her encounter with him, she failed to hold him accountable. When asked what she did when she saw him after his failure to come to her graduation, she says, "I didn't ask him. When I got there he mentioned something about not having any money. I didn't really say anything but I figured that was it. I knew he would have come if he could." As was true of the other daughters of Powerless Fathers, Nancy overlooked ignored invitations, broken promises, missed visits, and gifts that were supposedly sent but never arrived. These actions, or lack thereof, are never questioned, explanations never sought. The women find comfort in the perception that "it wasn't really his fault." Disappointments are said to be forgotten, all in the interest of preserving what is most important, the father-daughter connection and the role she plays as that special, particularly tolerant, person in the life of her father.

Just as they see their fathers as unaccountable, these women see themselves as victims. Inherent in this perception of themselves is an underlying sense of being powerless. The daughters of the Powerless Fathers struggle between presenting themselves as the understanding people in their fathers' lives and their own feelings of emptiness, dissatisfaction, and unworthiness. Yet they remain afraid to take action. They remain locked into a painful scenario, compelled to play the part of the stable unconditional supporter that requires from them a strength and self-assurance that they lack. Like the daughters of Shadow Fathers, these daughters also begin to feel that their fathers' lack of consistent responsiveness must stem from their own inadequacies. These feelings of self-doubt and unworthiness created by their fathers' tenuous commitment to them are infused into their perceptions of themselves. They think if they were better daughters, then perhaps their fathers would have been more inspired to be better fathers.

Although reluctant to place blame on the fathers, these women seem to have no problem taking responsibility on themselves. Among all the women of the study, the daughters of the Powerless Fathers presented as the most dependent and least self-reliant. Their sense of security and stability appeared to be more dependent on external forces than those internally generated. They were the least likely to take risks, such as moving away from home, changing jobs, or being without a partner.

The Idealized Father

Idealized fathers represent the smallest group of fathers among the study participants. Only a few women expressed this perspective. Yet the way they talked about their fathers was so distinctive from the other women that it warranted a separate category. From objective standards, Idealized Fathers were no more or less involved than Shadow or Powerless Fathers, but there was a qualitative difference in the way their daughters experienced them.

The daughters of Idealized Fathers expressed a sense of stability and confidence in their relationships with their fathers that was clearly lacking in the perceptions of the other women. These women clearly did not see their fathers as being absent. They experienced themselves as being connected to them. They cherished their identification of themselves as their fathers' daughters. They expressed a feeling of belonging to their fathers even if only in spirit alone. For example, Beverly's father was murdered when she was just a toddler. She has no personal memories of him. But that doesn't seem to matter. Beverly states, "I know I am a daddy's girl. Everybody in my family says so. They are always telling me how when my father was alive he really spoiled me." Based on what she has been told by others, Beverly concluded that she was important to him. She has no concrete representation of him, not a piece of jewelry, a toy, not even his last name, only the passing comments of relatives and friends of her father. But the little that she has seems to be enough for her to think of herself as a "daddy's girl." Therefore, the attachment, the bond between the two of them, is established. And this affirmation is enough to support her perception of herself as worthy. For the daughters of Idealized Fathers, it is that sense of connection, however tenuous, that they focus on when talking about their fathers.

The daughters of Idealized Fathers did not express feelings of disappointment or share perceptions of themselves as being abandoned or rejected. They managed their expectations of the father-daughter relationship by virtually not having any. For them, mere biological connection—as evidenced through physical or personality resemblance—is sufficient. Beverly mentions with pride, "Everybody says I look just like him." Barbara also seemed pleased to point out, "I have a terrible temper just like my father." Whether such traits were positive or negative was irrelevant, as long as the traits were associated with their fathers. Such traits were symbolic of their inheritance and confirmation of the father-daughter connection.

Noticeably absent from the discourse about their fathers among the daughters of the Idealized Fathers was any discussion of negative experiences related to their fathers. There were no complaints of contacts that weren't made, life events that fathers may have missed, or gifts they may not have gotten. Instead, these daughters accepted and cherished whatever morsels their fathers provided, overlooking any shortcomings. Barbara talks about the time her father took her in: "I was little then, it was before I went into foster care. My mother had gotten evicted from our apartment and we had no place to go. My father took us in and we stayed there for a little while until my mother could find some place for us to live. I don't remember how long it was maybe a few weeks. But he took us in." To Barbara her father was the hero in this story. This one incident erased her father's numerous failures to act, to intervene. Barbara didn't complain that her father had not otherwise provided financial support, nor did she discuss the fact that he did not come forward to prevent her from going into foster care when her mother's substance abuse became unbearable. Those types of failures to act were inconsequential to the daughters of Idealized Fathers.

Like the cliché of looking at the glass half full, these daughters only focused on what they did receive, the times they did see their fathers, and the presents they got. These daughters appeared reluctant to question or look too deeply into anything in regard to their fathers' behavior, thus sustaining their fantasy of the wonderful father and protecting their perceptions about themselves as being valuable and worthy. For the daughters of Idealized Fathers, the smallest gesture or hint of recognition is transformed into an acknowledgement, used as affirmation that they are, in fact, his daughter, which in turn confirms for them their value. Betty talked about how she frequently saw her father: "My father was around a lot. Particularly, when I was young I would be at the playground and I would see him on the basketball court or I would be walking down the street and see him hanging out with his friends. He would always stop to give me a hug." It was only with further inquiry that Betty mentioned that her connection with her father was basically limited to these chance meetings. She had no memories of outings together or scheduled visits to the house. But that seemed not to matter; in fact, she appeared somewhat annoyed and defensive by the fact that the issue was even mentioned. For these women, no grand gestures are required, no overt sacrifices necessary; simple recognition from the father, sometimes only through a third party's statement that a father was proud to have a daughter, would serve to verify their connection with their fathers.

These daughters protected themselves from feelings of rejection and worthlessness by redefining their fathers. The passionate way in which they came to their fathers' defense underscored the reality of the intense connection they felt toward them. For instance, "I can't take it when anyone talks about my father," the women would defiantly say. The idea of having to entertain for even a moment that their fathers were not the "best fathers in the world" seemed intolerable. Any denigrating remark or subtle negative inference was clearly not welcomed and sometimes was met with a rather aggressive denial, "They don't know what they're talking about," or a swift dismissal, "Who cares what they think?" These women were able to creatively handle any challenges to their internalized image of their fathers so as to hold onto their idealized perceptions of them.

The Idealized Father is viewed by his daughter as being beyond reproach. Barbara says it all with her statement: "My father is the best father in the world." Their connections to their fathers were unconditional; they had few expectations and placed no demands on their relationships. They went beyond mere toleration, ascribing positive value and behavior to their fathers. They accepted and cherished whatever their fathers had to give. To the outside observer, these daughters may appear naive, patient, and understanding. But for them it is more an unconscious battle for survival. Their seemingly distorted vision of their fathers, which they were able to construct with the help of others through a combination of selective vision and defensive rationalizations, appears to them a small price to pay for their own well-being. The daughters of Idealized Fathers remain steadfast in their convictions about their fathers, diverting their attention only to those things that support their perceptions and ignoring or refraining from anything that may challenge it. The daughters of Idealized Fathers saw no need to test their perceptions of his attachment to them, thus protecting themselves from any potential disappointment. They saw themselves as being inseparably connected to him and, therefore, he could not truly be absent.

Although motivated by a different set of perceptions, the daughters of Idealized Fathers were similar to the daughters of Shadow Fathers in that they were also independent and self-reliant. The daughters of Idealized Fathers viewed themselves as capable and competent.

Discussion

These women's narratives give us insight regarding the influence of fathers on the psychosocial development of their daughters. We cannot overlook the impact of the biological father just because he is not around. Through the telling of their stories, these women help us see that biological fathers, even if they are not there in body, remain present in the minds of these women. The father-daughter relationship represents a fundamental attachment that they are unable to relinquish or dismiss. In fact, they often actively construct a father and a father-daughter relationship where it is lacking. Whether the attachment stems from societal expectations or from an inherent human need, these women's narratives confirm the significance of biological fathers.

The behaviors of the fathers toward the daughters were not distinctively different; instead, what varied was the way in which women defined their fathers and explained their behaviors in relation to their expectations. Daughters of Shadow Fathers felt that their fathers did not meet their expectations; it was their disappointment and resentment that maintained their attachment. Daughters of Powerless Fathers excused their fathers' inability to meet their expectations. Daughters of Idealized Fathers had few expectations so their fathers were easily able to meet them and the daughters escaped disappointment.

The narrative material presented in this chapter could serve as a framework for future study. Bringing to light these women's subjective experience reveals that the experience of father absence is something that is internally negotiated, demonstrating that a father is never simply absent. His absence has meaning and is defined and experienced by the daughter in significant ways. Women's differential responses to their fathers' absence can serve as a useful location to inquire about the impact of fathers on the psychosocial development of the daughter. Future studies could examine the factors that contribute to the women's differential interpretations of their father's absence. Such factors might include the influence of others, such as mothers, in shaping the way daughters construct nonresident fathers. Also, the effects of their constructions of father absence on their construction of self as well on other aspects of their lives, such as work, parenting, and other relationships, could assist in our understanding of women whose fathers are not an integral part of their lives.

References

Benson, M. J., P. B. Harris, and C. S. Rogers. 1992. "Identity Consequences of Attachment to Mothers and Fathers Among Late Adolescents." *Journal of Research on Adolescence* 2 (3): 187–204.

Coley, R. L. 2003. "Daughter-Father Relationship and Adolescent Psychosocial Functioning in Low-Income African American Families." *Journal of Marriage and Family* 65:867–75.

Coley, R. L., and P. L. Chase-Lansdale. 1999. "Stability and Change in Paternal Involvement Among Urban African American Fathers." *Journal of Family Psychology* 13 (3): 416–35.

Flouri, E., and A. Buchanan. 2003. "The Role of Father Involvement in Children's Mental Health." *Journal of Adolescence* 26:63–78.

Khaleque, A., and R. P. Rohner. 2002. "Perceived Parental Acceptance-Rejection and Psychological Adjustment: A Meta-Analysis of Cross-Cultural and Intracultural Studies." *Journal of Marriage and Family* 64:54–64.

Krohn, F. B., and Z. Bogan. 2001. "The Effects Absent Fathers Have on Female Development and College Attendance." *College Student Journal* 35 (4): 598–608.

Lansky, M. R. 1989. "The Paternal Imago." In *Fathers and Families*, ed. S. H. Cah, A. Gurwitt, and L. Gunsberg, 27–46. Hillsdale, N.J.: Analytic Press.

Sobolewski, J.M. 2006. "Nonresident Fathers' Contributions to Adolescent Well Being." *Journal of Marriage and Family* 68:537–57.

CHAPTER THIRTEEN

Where's Your Daddy?

African American Father Figures in Children's Story Books

Suzanne Lamorey

My daughter is a dark-skinned, East Asian, adopted teen who grew up in our single- parent family. As an early-childhood educator, I often wondered what she learned from the mainstream media about single-parent families, adoptive families, and even dark-skinned East Asian girls. When she was younger, I personally found it challenging to locate children's picture books that could speak to her in positive ways. Disney was rarely my friend, and stories about talking turtles, shiny fish, and baby bears provided limited insights about one's identity. As a consequence, my daughter and I created many books ourselves, and I invented diverse serial tales about her and other family members (i.e., the "Naughty Granny" saga, the "Perils of Poppa," the "Bothersome Brothers" series, and "The Night You Arrived") in order to tell her our family stories.

Spurred by these maternal experiences over the years, I have long been interested in making sense of the underlying themes portrayed about various families, identities, and values in children's picture books. There is nothing more motivating than your own parenting experiences and inquiries when it comes to pursuing a line of research. In "Stories I Tell My Daughter" (Lamorey 2006), I analyzed the themes and meanings inherent in family storytelling. I found that parents chose stories that informed their sons and daughters about appropriate social and cultural roles that reflected family values as well as community standards. These stories occurred in a vein similar to the

instructive lessons that spiritual elders might provide for their follow-
ers in the context of parables and allegories. According to Black (1991)
as well as Fiese and Bickham (2004), families tell stories in order to
create a sense of family identity, communicate family values, and enhance the bonds between family members. In other words, stories tell
us who we are in relation to others and what we believe in.

Building on the story-related approach to understanding family
experiences, one way to add to our understanding of African American fathers is to analyze the roles of African American fathers in children's story books. Like family stories, children's literature (or more
correctly, perhaps, literature aimed at children) can be understood as
cultural capital in terms of the attitudes, traditions, stereotypes, goals,
and morals that society encourages children to value and emulate.
What messages do young African American children receive about
their families in the stories that are read to them? What are African
American children told about the role of fathers, uncles, and grandfathers in the family and the community?

Story-book research has focused on topics such as gender stereotypes (Kortenhaus and Demerest 1993; Turner-Bowker, 1996; Valpy
1996; Sugino 2000), the commercialization (or as some say Disneyfi-
cation) of children's stories (Zipes 2001), and historical trends in children's literature (Hillman 1974). Gender stereotypes are one category
in which children's stories function as cultural instruction. According
to Turner-Bowker (1996), socially learned stereotypes are powerfully
communicated to young children in the books written for them. For
example, gender stereotypes in children's literature show that certain
behaviors, values, and attributes are appropriate for men, whereas different behaviors, values, and attributes are appropriate for women.
This research has indicated that female characters in children's stories
are commonly described as pretty, afraid, worthy, and sweet. Males, on
the other hand, are referred to as large, great, brave, proud, as well as
fearsome. Sugino (2000) has also found that in contemporary Japanese
children's books, males are depicted as energetic, adventurous, mis-
chievous, courageous, and honest, while females are described as caring, sweet, timid, as well as adventurous, curious, dependable, imagi-
native, mean, and self-centered, depending on whether the author was
a male or a female.

These gender stereotypes in literature have been shown to influence children's behaviors and attitudes (Anderson and Hamilton 2005).
According to Trepanier-Street and Romatowski (1999), children's at-

titudes about gender stereotypes can be manipulated by the choice of books presented to them. Narahana (1998) found that nonsexist books can have positive effects on children's self-concept, attitude, and behavior. Similarly, Ochman (1996) reported that young women who were exposed to stories with strong female characters subsequently demonstrated higher self-concept scores. When a preschool teacher is reading a story to a group of children, they are not only learning about emergent literacy but in essence receiving a powerful lesson about socialization beliefs and acceptable behavior from a person in a position of authority.

In examining story stereotypes relative to the characterization of parents, Valpy (1996) reports that fathers fare poorly in children's books while mothers are the main actors. He has found that mothers are portrayed as keeping order, protecting children from monsters, caring for children's aches and pains, finding lost children in the mall, and generally maintaining life as we know it. Fathers, according to Valpy (1996), are most often depicted as one-dimensional backdrops to family stories and are usually characterized as judgmental, aloof, outdoorsy, or nerdy. Disney also paints a variety of stories about parents and these include the wicked stepmothers in *Cinderella* and *Snow White;* the protective mothers in *Dumbo, Bambi, 101 Dalmatians, Lion King,* and *Tarzan;* and the nurturing, self-sacrificing fathers in *Beauty and the Beast, Mulan, Pinocchio,* and *The Jungle Book* (Tanner et al. 2003).

Quinn (2006) has examined the social construction of fatherhood in contemporary American culture in her content analysis of children's literature. Considering stories as cultural artifacts, she focused upon the themes of father involvement in Caldecott Award–winning stories over a span of fifty-four years. This research found that fathers are depicted as interacting with children 67 percent as often as mothers and showed fathers more often providing verbal affection, teaching children, and playing with children. These stories and their message of father involvement are viewed by Quinn as cultural scripts for children, portraying nurturing images of father behavior. Additional research on how fathers are portrayed in popular media, such as television advertisements, cartoons, and magazine and newspaper articles, also finds that various images of fathers contribute to our social expectations of the roles of fathers and serve as sources of role-identity formation for fathers and their families (LaRossa et al. 2000). Over time, these media images have shown fathers as providers and, more lately, as nurturers.

Beyond a basic analysis of father/mother stereotypes in children's story books, there has been a limited amount of research investigating meaning making in terms of racial and cultural issues as portrayed by characters, settings, and plot. If we believe that children's stories are instructive about cultural norms and expectations, then it would be particularly important to examine these stories for their messages to and about culturally, linguistically, and racially diverse children and their families. As this volume is focused on the roles of African American fathers in their lives of their children, a sociopolitical review and analysis of children's stories would seem to provide an interesting perspective. In this chapter, I investigate the context of paternal care giving in children's storybooks in order to understand the messages about fathers (including social fathers such as uncles and grandfathers) in the lives of young African American children. In the following section, I describe the selection of the stories in the children's section of a regional library and portray the demographics of the population served by the library. In the "Profiles" section, I have organized the stories into categories by parent role and have summarized the caregiver themes inherent in those stories relative to the meanings and messages imparted to young children about fatherhood, race, and family.

Selecting the Stories

In seeking out the messages about African American fathers contained in children's picture books, I reviewed a total of 4,334 available picture books including all authors in the children's section of an award-winning regional county library in a large Southeastern metropolis. The metropolitan population of the region served by the library totals almost 650,000 people and includes the twentieth-largest city in the United States. In this city, the median family income is $56,000, and 7.8 percent of families live below the poverty line. City racial demographics include 58 percent Caucasian, 33 percent African American, 9 percent Hispanic or Latino, 3.5 percent who self-identified as other, 3 percent Asian, and 1.7 percent who self-identified as mixed race (Census Scope 2000). I chose the public library for my compilation of children's books because the library is where parents, teachers, and other caregivers of various socioeconomic backgrounds would typically have the greatest access to reading materials for children without the cost prohibitions that accompany the purchase of children's books in stores.

My selection and review of the books included in this analysis focused upon fiction and nonfiction stories about the lives of young African American children. Over the course of several weeks, I tackled the shelves of picture books in the children's section of the library. I sat on the floor in front of each shelf and methodically removed a handful of books at a time. I immediately returned books whose cover illustrations featured children or other family members who did not obviously appear to be African American. In addition, alphabet books, counting books, and poetry that featured African American children were not included in the process. In reviewing the stories, I did not try to compare children's books across races, socioeconomic levels, or child gender. My goal was to examine the adult characters that appear in stories about African American children and their families and to explore the categories of caregiver themes that authors addressed in these stories.

Of the 4,334 children's stories available on the shelves of this regional library, over a two-month period I found 79 that featured stories about African American children and their families. In these 79 story books, 47 percent (n = 37) featured African American fathers as primary or secondary characters. Primary characters played an interactive role with the child as an integral part of the story, and secondary characters were pictured in the background. These secondary characters might be shown in illustrations but had minimal roles in the story. For example, a secondary character could be a father who is shown in a picture attending a child's birthday party, but the focus of the story is on the child's friends and birthday gifts. Almost 13 percent (n = 10) of the stories featured uncles or grandfathers as the primary male characters. In the remaining 40 percent of the stories (n = 32), there was no mention or picture of a father or male parental figure (uncle or grandfather) in the story. These thirty-two stories were focused solely on mother-child relationships, grandmother-child relationships, or children in the context of peer or sibling relationships.

Family Structure

Of the family structures in these seventy-nine stories, 29 percent (n = 23) featured two-parent nuclear families (e.g., mother, father, and children). Some 42 percent (n = 33) of the families could be categorized as extended families that included a mother, a child, and at least one other adult family member, an aunt, uncle, or grandparent. Single mothers or single grandmothers without other adult family members seemed to be the heads of the household in 22 percent (n = 17) of the stories. In the remaining 5 percent (n = 4), there was no adult mentioned. In addition, siblings were present in 33 percent (n = 26) of the time.

Census data from 2006 specific to family households indicates that 46 percent of African American family households were headed by a married couple, 45 percent by a female householder, and 9 percent by a male householder (U.S. Census Bureau 2006). There is no statistical way to determine specific comparative data differences between census data and the family structures in the stories. However, two-parent African American families were depicted in the stories less often than their actual prevalence in communities would suggest. Overall, the stories included significant numbers of female-headed households as well as extended-family situations (about 64 percent of the stories versus 45 percent in the census data). Because the census data does not break down into categories such as mother-headed, grandmother-headed, and father-headed households, or into extended family configurations, it is difficult to compare the families depicted by census data to those in the children's stories. However, it seems that these children's stories may not reflect the family lives of many African American children, focusing instead upon the lives of children in female-headed households.

Child Gender and Age

In terms of child gender, the main characters were girls in 59 percent (n = 47) of the stories, boys in 32 percent (n = 25), and both a boy and a girl in 9 percent (n = 7). The approximate age ranges of the children included 4 percent (n = 3) who appeared to be between three and five years old, 23 percent (n = 18) who seemed to be between five and eight years old, 48 percent (n = 38) who appeared to be between eight and ten years old, 20 percent (n = 18) who looked to be between ten and twelve years old, and five percent (n = 4) who seemed to be over age twelve.

Story Setting

In stories situated in the United States, the setting was rural (e.g., farms, plantations) in 31 percent (n = 23) of the stories. In 26 percent (n = 19), the story appeared to take place in a suburban or small-town environment, and in 22 percent (n = 16) the setting could be characterized as urban or inner city. Approximately 16 percent (n = 12) of the stories took place in a city or village in Africa. In four stories, it was difficult to identify the setting.

Profiles of the Stories

The seventy-nine stories portray a wide assortment of themes, including the need for security, the importance of friends, responsibility, parent sacrifice, freedom, self-esteem, and children's emotions such as fear, sadness, loss, disappointment, and loneliness. While some stories portrayed such celebrations as birthdays, holidays, and special family customs, others told of the importance of family memories and family histories, with many recounting events that occurred during and after the Civil War. Some stories focused on activities in the children's neighborhoods. Many stories focused on the struggles of growing up, including the birth of a new sibling, moving into a new neighborhood, the death of a family member, and divorce. There were also themes such as the role of ancestors, spiritual guardians, magic, and folklore.

The roles of fathers and other male adult family figures (uncles or grandfathers) ranged from silent backdrops in the home or neighborhood to significant individuals who cared for children during a time of need (e.g., when children were lost, disheartened, scared, lonely, jealous, or sad). Interestingly, there were few characters in the stories that portrayed teachers or preachers, which are considered to be historical professional role models within the African American community. Well-meaning, concerned neighbors were mentioned. In the following section, I will focus on the roles of fathers, uncles, and grandfathers in the story books. I will summarize several of the most powerful stories in some detail and then generalize the contexts of some of the related stories.

Grandfathers' Roles

Grandfathers' roles seem to focus upon preparing the way for future generations. The grandfather stories are about harvests and legacies. In *The Grandad Tree* (Cooke 2000), two siblings recall the childhood memories that they made with their grandfather as they played near the apple tree on his farm. The story portrays their interactions together under that tree that span the seasons and the years. Granddad is a consistent presence in the children's lives, working in his yard and playing with his grandchildren. When Granddad dies, the siblings remember him by planting a new young apple tree under that older family tree. They add their contribution to the family legacy of growing sturdy trees that last for generations and that provide for future memories, shade, and fruit. The story emphasizes the sense of continuity, care, respect, and nurturance. Similarly, *Grandfather's Orchard* (Ghazi 1994) portrays the grandfather as the family gardener, planting apple trees for the benefit of future generations. He plants the trees, and the rest of the family labors with him in the orchard to establish and nurture them. In this story, Grandfather comments that the fruit will not be ripe in his lifetime but will sustain his family when he is gone. As the family works together in the orchard, Grandfather tells stories of religious figures and the accompanying parables explain the ways to live one's life. The theme of Grandfather's legacy of spiritual and nutritive sustenance is portrayed in this story.

Grandfathers are also portrayed as the keepers of family stories, dreams, and folktales, particularly as the keepers of the stories and heritage related to Africa. In one story, a young girl dreams that she flies to Africa where her grandfather welcomes her home to his village. In her dream, she explores the market and tall stone buildings and meets the native animals. She dances to her uncles' drumming and visits with her cousins. Then, in the midst of her dream, she turns into a baby, and a long-ago grandmother holds her and rocks her to sleep. This is one of several dream-sequence stories in various children's books that seem to combine the perspectives of one's heritage (Africa, music, foods, plants, animals) with a sense of family faraway. That sense of family and cultural heritage is strongly represented by the grandfather.

Granddaddy's Street Songs (DeGross 1999) portrays the role of the grandfather as an active community participant and source of social networking. In this story, Granddaddy is a street-wagon vendor who calls out to the families with special individualized songs to let them know what's available for sale. He is pictured as an affectionate, joyful life force who sustains the relationships and care that hold together the community. From Africa to the United States, the grandfather figure provides sustenance, culture, and connections across the generations, continents, and neighborhoods.

Stories about the Underground Railroad and escapes from slavery are common in the children's story books about African American families. In *Ain't Nobody a Stranger to Me* (Grifalconi 2007), Grandfather tells his granddaughter about the family's escape from slavery. He, Grandmother, and their baby "set their hearts right and trusted the Lord" to help them escape via the Underground Railroad. The story chronicles their dangerous travels and their subsequent hard work as they farm their own fields and become successful landholders. Grandfather talks about planting his "memory seeds," apple seeds that he had carried with him from his slavery days. At the end of the story, the little girl and her grandfather plant his memory seeds together on his farm. Again, the recurrent elements of planting, apple trees, intergenerational continuity, memories, heritage, and family are represented by children's interactions with Grandfather.

Uncles' Roles

There was a strong showing of uncle stories in this collection of children's books. However, in these stories, there seem to be no consistent roles for uncles. In one story (Greenfield 1980), a girl's uncle plays the role of social father, her caregiver during her mother's absence. Throughout this story, the young girl observes her uncle and seems to learn about men and their various roles. She watches him shave, cook, play his guitar, and play games with her. The uncle also tries to comfort her when she misses her mother. The young girl eventually becomes less shy around him and has grown to know her uncle by the time her mother comes to get her. In another story, *Nappy Hair* (Herron 1997), the uncle celebrates his niece's hair, again acting as the social father as he attempts to raise her self-confidence and teach her about her worth. He is instrumental in nurturing her acceptance of who she is as an African American girl as well as a member of a family and community.

In some cases, the uncle is portrayed as a young man transitioning to adulthood. For example, in one story (Howard 1993) a popular young uncle leaves the family farm to move to the big city, where he gets an important job as a conductor on passenger trains that run up and down the East Coast. The uncle sends a message to his family that he will toss a special package to his niece and nephew one night as his train passes the family farm. The gift is a beautiful conch shell from

Florida. The young nephew dreams of growing up to emulate the uncle and travel to faraway places like Florida. The father in this story plays a minor role, and the young uncle seems to represent the new wave of adults leaving the farm and heading to jobs in the big cities. The young boy idolizes the man in the family who moves beyond his father's station in life.

One contemporary story (Dakari 1995) is about an uncle from Africa who visits his nieces in the United States. His nieces are trying to play jump rope on the sidewalk, but there are not enough children to turn the rope. The uncle gives the girls a magic jump rope from Tanzania, and suddenly several neighborhood children appear on the sidewalk wanting to play with the new jump rope. The uncle provides the girls with something more than familiar, everyday experiences; he provides something special and magical. Again, fathers play a minor and less powerful role than the uncle, who offers something extraordinary.

The final uncle story, *Little Lil' and the Swing-Singing Sax* (Gray 1996), features the theme of the uncle who makes a sacrifice to support his family, which consists of his adult sister and his niece. Told from the niece's point of view, Mom is very sick, and the uncle (a musician) pawns his horn to pay for her medicine. There is no mention of a father, and the uncle seems to function as a protective father in this household. In effect, he pawns his identity (by becoming a musician without an instrument) to rescue his sister. Interestingly, the niece finds a way to "buy" her uncle's horn back by drawing a beautiful picture which she "sells" to a very sympathetic pawnbroker. The child finds her own creative and instrumental power to cure the adults' problems in a magical format.

Fathers' Roles

In this collection of children's books, fathers have a variety of pivotal roles, including family caregiver, teacher, rescuer, freedom seeker, and sacrificer for his children. In several stories, fathers are portrayed as nurturing and wise champions for their children. For example, in two stories (Conway 2006), the fathers are the adults who search for and find their lost children. These children are hiding because fear (of displacement by new baby siblings and of disappointing the father), and the understanding father lovingly brings them back home to their family. To illustrate, in *Down the Road* (Schertle 1995), a young rural girl goes into town to buy eggs for the family. However, on the way home she falls and breaks the eggs. She hides in a tall apple tree, afraid to go home. Her father finds her there in the tree and tells her that she is more important than some eggs. They pick apples together, and Mother cooks a delicious apple pie, rather than eggs, for breakfast. Father is portrayed as a protective and understanding adult. He sends his child off to become independent and comforts her when she thinks she has failed.

In three additional stories, fathers have to leave their families for a time in order to fulfill their roles as providers and caregivers. One father leaves his wife and young son in order to care for Grandmother in *First Pink Light* (Greenfield 1991) and two other fathers have left their families in order to earn money in the city in *Tar Beach* (Ringgold 1991) and *The Tangerine Tree* (Hanson 1995). The children in these stories articulate the sadness and longing they feel as they deal with the missing father. These absent fathers return to their homes with their provider and caregiving roles accomplished, and they subsequently embrace their families. In one of these stories, Father asks his young daughter to take care of his tangerine tree while he is gone, and he tells her that when she learns how to read he will be home again. She tends the tree and learns to read and write. The story is about Father's sacrificing for his family and also about his expectation that his child will be productive while he is gone—will become educated and tend the family tree. In these stories, we see the themes of departure and reunion in the return of the father to his children when his work is done. His return is promised and then celebrated by his children.

In many of the father stories, the role of the father is to prepare his children for their future. One story, *Dear Mr. Rosenwald* (Weatherford 2006), tells of a group of rural southern African American fathers who construct a school as an investment in their children's future. Because they value their children, education, and an opportunity for a better tomorrow, the exhausted men work hard every day after their labor in the fields in order to build the school. As one of the fathers tells his son, "Tomorrow is in our hands." *Minty* (Schroeder 1996) is another "preparation" story and features the early years of Harriet Tubman's life, during which time her father teaches her how to make her run for freedom. Along with vivid illustrations, the majority of the story is about how her father taught her the ways of survival in the wilderness so that when she runs away from "master" she will be able to survive on her own. It was as though her father spent her childhood preparing her for a hard future. The story ends one night as she is contemplating her run.

In a modern story, *Boundless Grace* (Holtman 1995), Father helps his daughter process her parents' divorce, his relocation, and his remarriage. The young girl's father has moved to Africa and has started another family there. She wants what she calls a "regular" family. With her mother's blessing she goes to visit her father in Africa. He helps her learn that no matter where he is or whom else he loves, he will always be her father, and in a sense he gives his daughter the ability to wear her new African dress home to mom. She realizes that she can be loved by two different families. She is empowered to move between two cultures, two families, and she integrates a strong, positive sense of her own identity. This seems to be one of the most valuable lessons that a father can give to his daughter.

Implications

Children, particularly our youngest children, seek to discover themselves and their world in the books they consume in classrooms, libraries, bookstores, and their own homes. They look for themselves and their families in a search for their self-worth in those pages. They seek to understand their own identity in the world of relationships as demonstrated in stories. They draw on stories as they come to grips with the developmentally typical childhood fears of the unknown (new challenges at school, menacing situations in the neighborhood, struggles surrounding new siblings). They employ stories in their search for explanations and security when faced with the loss of parents or grandparents to divorce or death.

Stories and pictures are children's media for meaning making before they mature into the more abstract thought characteristic of adolescents. Young children are magical thinkers. They believe that clouds and trees have feelings, that cars are alive because they move. They scare themselves in the mirror when they wear a Halloween mask and do not understand that tomorrow is not the same as next week. When they cover their eyes, they believe that they are invisible. This magical thinking also extends to the ways that young children interpret stories and pictures. If a book is about flying with birds to Africa in a dream, young readers flap their arms and pretend they are on their way. If a book is about a father choosing a dress for his daughter, or a grandfather gardening with his grandchild, or an uncle entertaining his nephew with a musical instrument, children will clamor about their own fathers and grandfathers and uncles, recounting and embellishing their memories of similar interactions. And if the stories are about European American girls and their pink-colored dolls, children of other races will often buy into the pink-doll phenomenon, wanting those pink dolls to the exclusion of the brown or tan or African American dolls that match their own skin (Clark and Clark 1947).

The reality for large numbers of young African American children is that they will grow up in families that are different from the ones portrayed on television and in the library story hour or preschool circle time. African American children will have a difficult time finding their families in the books available at the library. As the most commonly accessible portal for children's story books, the public library in this typical metropolitan area contained 4,334 story books of which 1.8 percent (n = 79) featured African American families. Furthermore, only .8 percent (n = 37) of the total number of these book, or less than half of the African American family books, included African American fathers in either primary or secondary family roles. After reading enough books, African American children might as well stop anticipating the sight of an African American father character caring for his children.

Many of the stories portrayed in this small collection of books about African American families chronicle children's struggles with difficult episodes in life (births, deaths, divorce, parent unemployment, family financial problems, fears, and loneliness). In almost a third of these stories, there was neither a father nor father figure available to buffer the hard times or share the good ones. There is a potent lesson here for young African American children, that children should not always count on a protective father or father figure in times of need. In the majority of these stories, the family guardian was a mother or grandmother. What does this theme of the absent father mean in terms of African American children's lives today? Does this represent a demographic reality that many African American children can relate to, or does it shape future generations' images of how a father should be?

When fathers were present in the stories, they seemed to serve three main roles. First, fathers rescued lost children. They did this literally as well as figuratively. One divorced father rescued his "lost" daughter by helping her reconcile with his new family in Africa. Other fathers rescued their lost children when the children ran away from home due to jealously or fear. Second, some fathers' roles as provider and caregiver forced them to leave their homes and families for a period of time in order to earn money and afford a better life for their children. The temporarily absent father was explained to children as someone who departs to fulfill his role as the family's provider. Third, a father's role was to invest in his child's future. This occurred in terms of teaching his children to survive in the world as well as investing his time and muscle in constructing a school for his children's future educational opportunities.

One frequent finding seemed to be that the African American extended family was very much present in the children's story books. The grandfathers' roles are the ones that seem to be enduring, consistent, and supportive. Grandfather is often idealized as the child's social and cultural father, the one figuratively preparing the family for the future generations. Grandfathers are pictured as spiritual beings who are knowledgeable about dreams of the future and folklore that explains the past. The grandfather is the cultural connection between past, present, and future, and they support their grandchildren in their visions.

The roles of the uncles were meaningful, too, as these extended family members offer help to children as mentors and support as social fathers. In some stories, the uncle was a stand-in for the father. He demonstrated the care-giving attributes of fatherhood in the absence of a father. In one story, he seemed to represent the portal to adulthood and a bigger world than that of the father, who remained on the farm. In two of the stories (Dakari 1995; Howard 1993), the uncles were from a faraway place beyond the children's everyday world, and they brought the children beautiful and magical gifts from those places to which they traveled. It seemed that the uncles might represent alternative new worlds and new possibilities for children to imagine.

Conclusion

For hundreds of years, storytelling has been a way to convey significant family events, family history, family heroes, family values, and important lessons from one generation to another. Most families have stories about how Mom and Dad met, "day you were born" stories, stories about the best and worst summer vacations, and other highlights of family life that are individually significant for family members. There are stories about bravery and wisdom displayed by tribal members as well as patience or forgiveness epitomized by certain religious figures, and these stories compel us to identify with those groups and their characteristics. Stories invite us to belong, to identify, and to understand the script of the roles we learn to play.

Nowadays, reading to one's child has become a national passion in the United States, and many kindergarten readiness programs funded by No Child Left Behind require parents to spend a minimum of thirty minutes daily reading to their children. Reading stories to our children enhances their future literacy skills, vocabulary development, cognitive abilities and academic futures (Hart and Risley 2003; NICHD 2004). Yet, with the impetus to read to children, I wonder what we are teaching our children in addition to phonemic awareness.

In light of the connections among stories, attitudes, and behavior in terms of gender roles, cultural expectations, and family values, parents and teachers must thoughtfully select the story themes they want to portray to their children. Books and other media directed toward young children can be dangerous and disparaging as well as enriching and instructive. Why should it be so difficult to find a book about African American families? Where are the African American fathers in children's stories that can instruct young boys about an emergent identity as a provider and caregiver and support young girls in developing positive family and societal roles?

According to Zipes (2001), the major publishers of children's books are the conglomerates that also produce children's DVDs, toys, music CDs, and Harry Potter pajamas. Children's books have become a vital link in a media chain that extends to movies, toys, t-shirts, and breakfast cereals. Most publishing houses are now part of large conglomerates and are directed by business managers. Decisions to design and publish books are more often than not made by marketing people, and markets are now the ones driving the stories that shape children's attitudes and beliefs.

With the national emphasis on the importance of reading to children in order to promote literacy, it is important to recognize commercial and cultural contexts in terms of investigating the content of what is being read. If young African American children cannot find positive role models of significant adult family members in the stories they hear, early literacy and school readiness suffer as does early self-identity and socio-emotional readiness. In considering the more covert elements of the emergent literacy movement for young American children, it is important to ask all young readers, "Where's your daddy?"

References

Anderson, D., and M. Hamilton. 2005. "Gender Role Stereotyping of Parents in Children's Picture Books: The Invisible Father." *Sex Roles: A Journal of Research* 52 (3/4): 145–51.

Black, M. 1991. "A Phenomenological Case Study of Family Stories and the Relationship to Identity." *Dissertation Abstracts International* 51:6139–40.

CensusScope. 2000. http://www.censusscope.org. Accessed December 10, 2007.

Clark, Kenneth B., and Mamie P. Clark. 1947. "Racial Identification and Preference in Negro Children." In *Readings in Social Psychology*, ed. T. Newcomb and E. L. Hartley, 169–78. New York: Hold.

Conway, D. 2006. *The Most Important Gift of All*. Columbus, Ohio: Gingham Dog Press.

Cooke, T. 2000. *The Grandad Tree*. New York: Candlewick Press.

Dakari, H. 1995. *Magic Moonberry Jump Ropes*. New York: Dial.

DeGross, M. 1999. *Granddaddy's Street Songs*. New York: Hyperion.

Fiese, B., and N. Bickham. 2004. "Pin-Curling Grandpa's Hair in the Comfy Chair: Parents' Stories of Growing Up and Potential Links to Socialization in the Preschool Years." In *Family Stories and the Life Course: Across Time and Generation*, ed. B. Fiese and M. Pratt, 258–77. Mahwah, N.J.: Erlbaum.

Ghazi, A. 1994. *Grandfather's Orchard*. New York: Amica.

Gray, L. M. 1996. *Little Lil' and the Swing-Singing Sax*. New York: Simon and Schuster.

Greenfield, E. 1991. *First Pink Light*. New York: African American Butterfly Children's Books.

Greenfield, E. 1980. *Darlene*. New York: Methuen.

Grifalconi, A. 2007. *Ain't Nobody a Stranger to Me*. New York: Dial.

Hanson, R. 1995. *The Tangerine Tree*. New York: Clarion.

Hart, B., and T. Risley. 2003. "The Early Catastrophe." *American Educator* 27 (4): 6–9.

Herron, C. 1997. *Nappy Hair*. New York: Dial.

Hillman, J. S. 1974. "An Analysis of Male and Female Roles in Two Periods of Children's Literature." *Journal of Educational Research* 8:84–88.

Holtman, M. 1995. *Boundless Grace*. New York: Dial.

Howard, E. F. 1993. *Mac and Marie and the Train Toss Surprise*. New York: Four Winds Press/Maxwell Macmillen.

Kortenhaus, C. M., and J. Demerest. 1993. "Gender Role Stereotyping in Children's Literature: An Update." *Sex Roles: A Journal of Research* 28 (3/4): 219–32.

Lamorey, S. 2006. "Stories I Tell My Daughter." In *Writing the Motherline: Mothers, Daughters, and Education*, ed. L. M. O'Brien and B. B. Swadener, 55–64. Landham, Mass.: University Press of America.

LaRossa, R., C. Jaret, M. Gadgil, and G. Wynn. 2000. "The Changing Culture of Fatherhood in Comic-Strip Families: A Six-Decade Analysis." *Journal of Marriage and the Family* 62:375–87.

Narahana, M. 1998. "Gender Stereotypes in Children's Picture Books." ERIC Document Reproduction Service No. ED419248. East Lansing, Mich.: National Center for Research on Teaching Learning.

National Institute of Child Health and Human Development. 2004. *Report of the National Reading Panel: Teaching Children to read: An Evidence-Based Assessment of the Scientific Research Literature on Reading and Its Implications for Reading Instruction.* NIH Publication No. 00-4769. Washington, D.C: U.S. Government Printing Office.

Ochman, J. M. 1996. "The Effects of Nongender-Role Stereotyped, Same-Sex Role Models in Story Books on the Self-Esteem of Children in Grade Three." *Sex Roles* 35:711.

Quinn, S. 2006. "Examining the Culture of Fatherhood in American Children's Literature: Presence, Interactions, and Nurturing Behaviors of Fathers in Caldecott Award–Winning Picture Books (1938–2002)." *Fathering* 4 (1): 71–96.

Ringgold, F., 1991. *Tar Beach.* New York: Crown.

Schertle, A. 1995. *Down the Road.* New York: Browndeer Press.

Schroeder, A. 1996. *Minty: A Story of Young Harriet Tubman.* New York: Dial

Sugino, T. 2000. "Stereotypical Role Models in Western and Non-Western Children's Literature." ERIC Document Reproduction Service No. ED447502.

Tanner, L., S. Haddock, T. Zimmerman, and L. Lund. 2003. "Images of Couples and Families in Disney Feature-Length Animated Films." *The American Journal of Family Therapy* 31:355–73.

Trepanier-Street, M., and J. Romatowski. 1999. "The Influence of Children's Literature on Gender Role Expectations: A Reexamination." *Early Childhood Educational Journal* 26:155–59.

Turner-Bowker, D. M. 1996. "Gender Stereotyped Descriptors in Children's Picture Books: Does 'Curious Jane' Exist in the Literature?" *Sex Roles: A Journal of Research* 35 (7/8): 461–88.

United States Census Bureau. 2006. "The Black Population in the U.S.: March 2004 (PPL-186) Family and Nonfamily Household Type." http://www.census.gov/population/socdemo/race/black/ppl-186/tab4.html. Accessed April 20, 2008.

Valpy, M. 1996. "Fathers Fare Poorly in Children's Books." In *Only Connect: Readings on Children's Literature,* ed. S. Egoff, G. Stubbs, R. Ashley, and W. Sutton, 301–3. New York: Oxford University Press.

Weatherford, C. 2006. *Dear Mr. Rosenwald.* New York: Scholastic Press.

Zipes, J. 2001. *Sticks and Stones: The Troublesome Success of Children's Literature from Slovenly Peter to Harry Potter.* New York: Routledge.

PART SIX

Policies Affecting Black Fathers

CHAPTER FOURTEEN

Parenting on Parole or Probation

African American Fatherhood Under Community Supervision

AMY B. SMOYER, KIM M. BLANKENSHIP, AND TRACY MACINTOSH

I got the crazy history and that's not the way I want to live my life though. . . .
[I'm] really trying to be the best father. If you ask my kids anything about me,
they tell you I'm the best father in the world. I'm not saying I'm the best . . .
I'm not saying that . . . but that's what my kids think.

—KEVIN, 25

To understand men's capacity to parent, it is necessary to consider the
context in which they are fathering (Ogbu 1981; Cochran 1997; Letiecq
2007). This chapter focuses on one important contextual factor that
shapes fathering for many African American men: the criminal justice system, in particular, probation and parole (P/P). We use qualitative data from longitudinal interviews conducted in New Haven, Connecticut, from September 2005 through August 2007 with individuals
recently released from prison or jail to parole or probation. This study
design offered rich data about these men's experiences with fatherhood
and how this experience changes and develops over time.

These data were collected as part of a larger study funded by the
National Institute on Drug Abuse to analyze the effects of parole and
probation on HIV risk (R21 DA019186-0, PI Blankenship). Forty-eight
people on parole or probation were interviewed at six-month intervals
for one year, for a total of three interviews each, with each interview
lasting approximately two hours. Participants who were incarcerated
during the period when one of their follow-up interviews was due were
interviewed in prison or jail. The study included men and women who
were most recently convicted for a nonviolent drug offense, including
sale or possession of narcotics, or nonviolent property crimes related to
drug use. Eligible participants had been incarcerated for at least three
months before being released to parole or probation. Of the forty-eight
participants, thirteen were African American men with one or more

biological children. Although the study was not originally intended to concentrate on parenting issues, we found that parenting was a central concern for these men, one that they continually referenced when discussing a wide range of topics related to criminal justice, reentry, relationships, and health. This chapter discusses what we learned about the effects of parole and probation on the parenting intentions and identity of these African American men.

Characteristics of the Fathers

The thirteen African American fathers who participated in the study ranged in age from twenty-three to fifty-five, with an average age of thirty-eight. They were primarily non-Hispanic from the United States, except for two men of Jamaican descent and one with Puerto Rican parentage. All the men identified as heterosexual. Participants' lives reflected high levels of poverty, instability, and addiction. Seven of the men had histories of homelessness (defined narrowly as sleeping on the street, in a shelter, or in a car). All thirteen had both used and sold drugs (primarily cocaine and marijuana) as their main source of income during at least one point in their lives. On average, the men had been incarcerated four times and, at the time of the baseline interviews, eight were on parole and five were on probation. Seven of the men were re-incarcerated during the study period. Six had never been married, two were divorced, and five were married. Three of these married men got married during the study period, two for the first time. (See table 14.1.)

In the full study, there were six additional African American men who were *not* fathers; their distinctions from the fathers are noteworthy. Two were middle-aged men with significant mental disabilities and low levels of social functioning that were readily apparent to the research staff. One of them claimed to have a son whom he had never met and who was being hidden from him by his relatives; it was not clear if this was true or not. At the time of the interview, he was living in an intensely supportive housing environment for people with mental illness. The other man had low communication skills and a deteriorating eye condition that made him partially blind. He had lived between homeless shelters and prison for the last twenty years, is a registered sex offender, and was re-incarcerated twice during the study time period. Two other nonfathers were young men who had been

Table 14.1

	Age	Age at first fatherhood	# of biological children (BC)	# of mother(s) of BC	Age of BC, in years	Were any BC born while father incarcerated?	Ever lived with any BC?	Social father	Location status	Marital Status
Darnell	23	21	2	2	3, <1	No	Yes	Yes	No	Never married
Kevin	25	21	5	4	3, 2, 2, 1, 1	Yes (2)	Yes	Yes	No	Married
Joe	29	17	2	2	11, 10	Yes (1)	Yes	Yes	Yes	Never married
Derrick	30	32	1	1	<1	Yes (1)	No	No	No	Married
Terrance	33	19	1	1	16	Yes (1)	Yes	No	No	Never married
Reggie	36	21	1	1	17	No	No	No	Yes	Never married
Curtis	41	21	4	4	22,17,17,17	Yes (1)	Yes	No	Yes	Married
Nathan	42	18	2	2	26, 20	No	Yes	No	No	Never married
Marcus	42	29	1	1	16	No	Yes	No	Yes	Never married
Chris	43	18	7	5	27, 25, 23, 22, 19, 19, 12	Yes (1)	Yes	No	Yes	Married
Dwayne	45	20	4	3	27,21,18,17	Yes (1)	Yes	No	Yes	Married
Darren	53	17	4	3	37, 36, 35, 23	Yes (1)	Yes	No	No	Divorced
Julian	55	19	6	2	38, 37, 32, 26, 25, 12	No	Yes	No	No	Divorced
Average	38	21	3	2.4	19	62%	85%	23%	46%	

receiving Social Security payments for physical or mental disabilities from an early age. These men reported having girlfriends, but their relationships were brief and did not involve cohabitation. One of these young men, who lived in a public housing project for people with disabilities, died in an accident that may have been a suicide in the time period after his second interview. In contrast, none of the men with children reported a serious mental-health diagnosis or physical disability.[1] These differences suggest that among African American men, *not having children* may be an indicator of higher services needs and instability (Flavin 2007).

Fathering Relationships

Fathering relationships for the men in our sample took a number of different forms. One participant, twenty-five-year-old Kevin, illustrates this well. As figure 14.1 shows, he was incarcerated for the first time, at the age of fifteen, for five years. Since then, he has been incarcerated four more times. Between February 2004 and December 2006, he

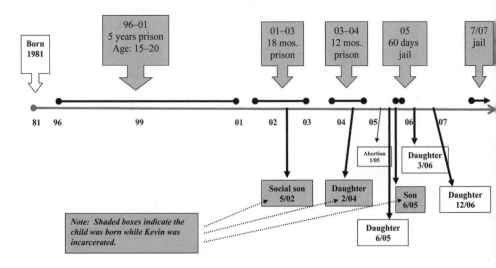

"The thing I'm most proud of? Being there for my kids. That's the most thing I'm proud of, being a father."

Figure 14.1 Fathering and Criminal-Justice History of Kevin, Age Twenty-five

had five children with four different women, the first one when he was twenty-one years old. During this same three-year period, a sexual partner, with whom he did not have a child, had a pregnancy that was terminated by abortion. He also has a social son (see figure 14.1) who was born in 2002. The mother of his social son is the mother of his two oldest children. Two of his biological children and his social son were born while he was incarcerated. At the time of his enrollment in the study, he was three months out of jail, and all of his children were living with their mothers. At the first follow-up interview, he had a new girlfriend, who was not the mother of any of his children; she later became pregnant but had a miscarriage. A year later, at the end of the study period, three of his children were in non-relative foster care, he was married to his girlfriend and had been re-incarcerated for a new crime.

Biological Fathering

Kevin's experiences reflect the multitude of relationships that constitute fatherhood among our study's participants (see table 14.1). The average age at fatherhood for the men in our sample was twenty-one, and they had, on average, three biological children each. Eight of the men had children who were born while they were incarcerated. Four of the men had only one child. Among the nine men with more than one child, all had children with more than one woman. Eleven of the men reported ever living with any of their children, but most cohabited with children for short, sporadic periods, interrupted by incarceration and breakups with the children's mothers. Only one man, Julian, lived consistently with his wife, the mother of most of his children, and these children, throughout their childhood. While eleven of the men have children under the age of eighteen, many of the participants' children are in their late teens. Only three men have children under the age of ten. As the father of young children (all five children are under the age of four), Kevin is distinct from the rest of the sample. The average age of the participants' children was nineteen.

Social Fathering

There is considerable discussion in the literature about nonbiological fathers (also known as social, step, kinship, fictive, "other fathers") and fathering (Coley 2001; Tripp 2001; Jayakody and Kalil 2002; Roy and Burton 2007. See also King's and Letiecq's chapters in this volume.). Here we use the term "social fathering" to describe participants' relationships to children who are not biologically related to them but whom the participant has willingly and enthusiastically chosen to father. (Later, we will describe another type of nonbiological fathering, "location fathering," which is not chosen but happens by default when men live with women who have children.) The three youngest fathers in our sample, including Kevin, each had a social child. That Kevin's social son was named after him speaks to his commitment to the child or the child's mother's perception of his commitment. Darnell has a social daughter and a biological son. Both have the same biological mother who, like Darnell, has a history of drug use and incarceration. Here Darnell (23) describes actively choosing to father his social daughter: "The little girl, she's not really mine but since I raised her—well, she knows me as her daddy, so I claim her." In a later interview, Darnell recounted meeting his social daughter's biological father and aggressively asserting his fatherhood authority:

> He's [the biological father] like, "Yo, thank you for taking care of my little girl." I'm like, "That's not your little girl no more. Your daughter, you ain't got one. . . . That little girl, that's me right there. I done birthed her, fed her, took care of her, changed her diaper. I'm there three, four o'clock in the morning when she get up . . . if you want to come through and see your little girl, whatever, you're not going to tell her that you're her father. Straight like that. You're going to wait 'til she get older and tell her that. 'Cause if you do tell her, there's going to be problems. 'Cause all she know is me as daddy. So, that's what she's going to know."

In all cases, the social child was the eldest child of the participant's biological child's mother. When the participant became involved with the child's mother, she either already had the young child or was pregnant. The social father had lived with his girlfriend and her young child, had a biological child or children with the girlfriend, and considered all the children as his own, even after his romantic relationship with the children's mother ended.

The fact that none of the older fathers reported social children may reflect a generational difference or, perhaps more likely, that these bonds fade over time, especially when the child grows older or if the social father's relationship with the child's mother ends. Even within the relatively short study period, all the bonds between the self-identified social fathers and their social children deteriorated as the participants' lives became increasingly complicated, they were unable to provide financial support, and their romantic relationships with the children's mothers ended. Nelson (2004) describes "selective parenting" as a phenomenon where parents focus on one child at the exclusion of others. When lack of time and money pushed these social fathers to make "selective parenting" choices, the social children were the first to go. Consider, for example, Darnell, whom we just quoted from his initial interview. At his third interview, he was living with a new girlfriend who was pregnant and scheduled to give birth in the next month. His older son and social daughter, who had been living with their mother and her parents, had moved into foster care. His son had been placed with a relative, and Darnell saw him twice a week. But his social daughter was in nonrelative care, and he had not seen her in five weeks: "I haven't seen her since last month, yeah, like the end, last week of . . . last week of January [interview in early March]. . . . [She's] five. I heard she is in school. I haven't like really like seen her . . . but my son I have, but I see my son at school . . . but she still has my last name."

Location Fathering

Participants reported another type of fathering relationship that we refer to here as "location fathering." During the study period, six of the thirteen men moved into homes with children who were not their own (neither biological nor social). These children, primarily teenagers, were the children of the girlfriend or female relative (sister, mother) with whom the participant was living: "My kids, my four kids, I want her [fiancée] to feel like they're hers. That's how I treat her kids. But it's different. I treat her kids and be around her kids more than I be around my own kids because I'm around her. She's my fiancée. I'm staying there...Her kids are not disciplined no" (Dwayne, 45). Dwayne's comments suggest he hopes that his fiancée will care for his children in the same way that he cares for hers. However, the fact that his children live elsewhere limits his fiancée's opportunities to parent these children and creates an unequal exchange of parental responsibilities. For the most part, participants reluctantly took on this role because there was no other male figure in the household:

> [I told the friend of my girlfriend's son,] . . . "Take your shoes off." He told me to wait. He said, "Hold up." Her son's like that too. . . . I was like, "Oh, my God," I think I almost look—I think I busted a blood vessel that day. I was like, "Man, are you crazy? You in my house." You know what I'm saying? . . . You a little kid . . . you don't disrespect nobody like that . . . my girl does not like nobody walking on the rug. I can't do it. I'm enforcing her rule. It ain't got nothing to do with me, but if I can't do it, he definitely can't do it.
>
> (Reggie, 36)

The men often had ideas about how to raise children that differed from those of the children's mothers, and it was not uncommon for their "location father" role to be a source of household conflict among the participants, their girlfriends, the children, or the children's friends. Still, the men took on this role, especially as it related to disciplining children who they felt were not showing appropriate respect to them or the children's mothers.

Fathering, Incarceration, Probation, and Parole

It is difficult to know the extent to which their histories of involvement with the criminal justice system account for the complicated fathering relationships these men have with children (Hamer 1998; Hamer 2001; Tripp 2001; Roy 2004; Pattillo, Weinman, and Western 2006). Undoubtedly, their movement in and out of the system contributes to instability in their relationships with female partners (Adimora et al. 2003; Blankenship et al. 2005), which may be one of several socioeconomic factors that result in a variety of different parenting relationships and arrangements. What is clear is that the men do not feel that their history of involvement with the criminal-justice system means that they cannot be good fathers. Nevertheless, incarceration, probation, and parole create a context within which it is difficult to meet many of the criteria typically associated with good fathering: serving as a breadwinner, providing a stable living situation, spending adequate time with children, and maintaining the patience, optimism, and energy that parenting requires.

Self-Assessments of Fathering Skills

Most fathers in our sample expressed confidence about their ability to be "good" fathers, especially during their first interview when they were just coming out of prison.

> It's natural. I've always been daddy . . . it's like I never missed a beat with them. I swear it's just so natural. . . . Nothing changed [laughs]. Nothing's changed. I'm still, it's me personally, they know me. Like the back of they hands. So, you know. Everything just fell into place like easy, it wasn't like the hard transition, nothing like that.
>
> (Joe, 29)

Kevin, quoted earlier and whose criminal justice and fathering histories are described in figure 14.1, claimed, "The thing I am most proud of? Being there for my kids. That's the thing I'm most proud of, being a father." Many of the men implicitly believe that their presence is, or would be, a positive force in their children's lives. For example, Curtis (41) has four children: the oldest is twenty-one, the other three are all seventeen, and every child has a different mother. Although he was incarcerated for much of his children's lives (ten of the last twenty years) and lived sporadically with each when not incarcerated, he reported speaking with the seventeen-year olds on a daily basis and was eager to play a central role in their lives: "It's harder to live in jail now and I don't want nothing else to do with it. Plus, my kids are older now, [they] need me out here with them." At the same time, Curtis and other participants discussed how difficult it could be to gain the respect from their children that they felt they deserved, especially from older children who might not be ready to accept their father's desire to be actively engaged in their lives. The previous quote from Curtis was from his baseline interview. In the second interview, he described the problems he encountered in attempting to realize this fatherhood role:

> My daughter's twenty-one. . . . I wasn't around and then I come home I'm trying to find out about her, she's telling me that you know, "How you gonna come home and just expect to get respect" when I was locked up again for her. . . . And we got into a conversation, and then we got into an altercation and . . . I grabbed her by the throat and I told her that you ain't gonna disrespect me, I slapped her a couple times.

The participants' eagerness to take on the role of father and their confidence in their ability to do so, in spite of past histories of noninvolvement, often because of incarceration, may be an attempt to claim an identity from which they can derive pride and respect. Existing literature suggests that for some African American men, fatherhood may be the only legitimate adult role available to them, given socioeconomic barriers to full-time employment, financial security, and marriage (Cochran 1997; Nelson 2004; Roy 2006). This may be especially true for men with criminal-justice histories that further impede access to economic and social success (Travis, Solomon, and Waul 2001; Nurse 2002; Petersilia 2003). As these men come out of prison and seek to rebuild their lives, it makes sense that fatherhood would trump the other, less desirable identities (parolee/probationer, ex-con, felon, recovering addict, unemployed, etc.) available to them.

Their confidence may also reflect a nontraditional definition of fatherhood that they *are* able to fulfill and that is not completely understood by social scientists. Consider the following quotation (emphasis added): "I try to draw myself away from that crowd. And they call me funny acting, whatever, but I'm a *family man* now" (Darnell, 23). When he made this statement, Darnell was not providing consistent financial or custodial support, the traditional markers of fatherhood involvement. He may, however, have been meeting other, alternative or modified criteria. Only six of the men report having a positive father figure as a child; many of them are building their own understandings of fatherhood from scratch. Further qualitative research is needed to better understand what being a "family man" means for low-income, nonresidential, African American fathers.

Fathering in the Context of Probation and Parole

For the men in our sample, the criminal-justice system, parole and probation (P/P) in particular, is a critical part of the context that shapes fathering and determines, on some level, their ability to successfully meet the demands of this role. If good fathers are men who provide economic and housing stability for their families, spend time with their children, and maintain the patience and energy parenting requires, parole and probation put them at a disadvantage in every regard.

Probation is a period of community supervision ordered by the sentencing judge either in place of or in addition to incarceration. Parole allows prisoners to serve some portion of their sentence in the community, under the supervision of a parole officer. Parole is granted by a parole board based on the criminal offense, community-based resources, and the inmates' behavior while incarcerated. While there are significant differences between parole and probation, especially in the sentencing processes and the powers invested in parole as compared to probation officers, the program requirements for nonviolent offenders are quite similar. P/P requirements are tailored to the offenders' needs and perceived threat to public safety. Stipulations may include some or all of the following: meeting regularly with P/P officers (PO), submitting to regular drug testing and home inspections, attending substance-abuse or mental-health treatment requirements (either inpatient or outpatient), taking educational classes (e.g., domestic violence, anger management, parenting), securing full-time employment or, in the absence of employment, doing unpaid community service, and complying with travel and social-network restrictions.

The African American fathers who participated in our study described the challenges they faced in attempting to balance the demands and restrictions of community supervision with their parental roles and responsibilities. These challenges may not be unique to African American male probationers and parolees; all parents on P/P may find that their relationships with their children are shaped to some extent by these community-supervision systems. However, African American men are overrepresented in all facets of the criminal justice system. In 2006, 4.8 percent of all black males were in prison or jail, compared to 0.7 percent of white males; 11.7 percent of all black males aged twenty-five to thirty-four were incarcerated, compared to 1.7 percent of white males in the same age group (Sabol, Minton, and Harrison 2007). Approximately one in three African American men in the United States is expected to go to jail at some point in his life (Bonczar 2003). This race disparity holds true for parole and probation as well. Although African Americans constitute only 13 percent of the total U.S. population, among the more than 4 million people on probation, 30 percent are black and 77 percent are male (Glaze and Bonczar 2006). There are 750,000 people in the United States under parole supervision: 40 percent are black and 88 percent are male (Glaze and Bonczar 2006). Because black men are disproportionately represented in the population of probationers and parolees, these issues are of critical importance to them and to society's understanding of African American fatherhood.

Conflicts Between Parole/Probation and Fatherhood

Money

The economic demands of P/P may reduce men's ability to provide financial support to their children. These economic demands can include:

1. *Restitution Payments*: Offenders who are convicted of larceny or burglary charges may be required to repay the victim (usually a store or bank, sometimes an individual). Installment plans are arranged that take into consideration the offender's income and the amount of time they will be on community supervision. The debt must be paid in full before the end of the P/P sentence.

2. *Drug Testing and Monitoring Devices*: Parolees and probationers may be charged for surveillance equipment or drug testing. These copayments are determined by the parole/probation officers, depending on the offender's income. While these charges were uncommon among study participants, some men did pay for these services, especially monitoring bracelets.

3. *Required Classes* (e.g. domestic violence, anger management, and parenting): Some classes that are required by P/P have a copayment (generally between $10 and $20). Participants cannot attend the class unless the copay is paid; not surprisingly, participants reported skipping classes and violating the terms of their community release because they did not have the money to pay this fee.

4. *Transportation*: Only one of the African American fathers we interviewed had his own car. All the other men relied on public transportation or rides from friends or family, who often requested money for gas. While the $2.50 that is required for a round-trip bus trip in New Haven may seem like a minimal outlay, these fares were a significant expenditure given the participants' limited incomes and the number of required weekly appointments.

Although parolees and probationers are expected to pay these expenses, P/P does not provide income support or job-placement assistance beyond motivational interviewing and requiring that men have full-time employment. (The one exception is among parolees who are released to halfway houses, where job placement assistance is often provided. These halfway-house positions, however, are generally minimum-wage, temporary jobs that end when they leave the program.) The State of Connecticut does offer food stamps (up to $155/month) for low-income single men and General Assistance, in the form of cash (up to $200/month), for certain individuals who are unemployable because they are in substance-abuse treatment. Most of the participants received food stamps, especially in the months right after their release from jail, and several also received General Assistance for a short period of time.

Two of the thirteen African American fathers were consistently employed throughout the study period in jobs that paid above the minimum wage. The others went back and forth between unemployment, temporary work, minimum-wage service jobs, and illegal hustles. None of the men had much discretionary income because those with relatively well paid jobs had higher expenses (e.g., rent, car, child support). Living on low incomes created a constant tension among personal living expenses and bills, expenses relating to their criminal justice status, and expenses relating to their children. For example, Marcus (42), who lived with a female relative and was unemployed, working occasionally at a temp agency, described trying to gather twelve dollars for the background check required to get his parole transferred to another state where his parents were living:

> I'm trying to get twelve [expletive] dollars, you know, twelve dollars, all I needed to get twelve dollars. And I couldn't get that. . . . I had it a couple of times, but, you know, I had more important things to do with it because I have a daughter and she's sixteen . . . and she calls me up, "Oh, Daddy, can you help me get some clothes for school?" and stuff like that. And I just said, "Okay, I have fifty dollars, so you can just come and get that."

Expenses relating to P/P and state-mandated child support were usually paid first, as nonpayment could result in reincarceration. These demands limited the fathers' capacity to offer direct financial support to their children and their children's mothers. Even without P/P expenses, many of these men may not have been able to provide economic support for their children, but P/P requirements exacerbated their poverty.

Parole assignments to halfway houses or residential substance-abuse programs can also affect the economic resources men have available to support their children. Offenders cannot be released onto parole unless they have a parole-approved "sponsor" who can offer housing to the parolee. For many parolees, this means coming out to a halfway house or treatment program. Halfway houses are a point of reentry paid for by parole, and they offer a welcome source of housing support for many who have nowhere else to go. As was described earlier, halfway houses also can facilitate employment for residents. At the same time, however, these programs require the men to save money and restrict the amount of money that participants can keep. These policies mean less is available to spend on children, as Dwayne explains: "You don't do with fifty-five dollars [a week], especially when you getting furloughs, you know, and try to spend time with your kids, and bus fare to get back and forth to work. . . . You have to use that fifty-five dollars." Given that fatherhood is often defined and judged by the man's ability to provide financial support to his children, these constraints on their economic resources constitute a barrier to successfully fulfilling the fatherhood role.

Time

In addition to these financial burdens, the requirements of P/P also consume a significant amount of time. These demands on the men's time reduce their ability to provide child care and spend time with their children. P/P requires all individuals under supervision, except those undergoing intensive substance-abuse treatments, to have full-time jobs. If probationers and parolees cannot show pay stubs to prove employment, they can be required to do full-time unpaid community service. It was not uncommon for fathers in our study to have a prework appointment with their PO, or for methadone treatment, and a postwork (afternoon or evening) appointment to fulfill treatment, counseling, or Narcotics Anonymous/Alcoholics Anonymous (NA/AA) requirements. These P/P obligations, combined with an eight-hour work day and bus transportation, can result in fourteen-plus-hour days and leave little room for children, especially for these fathers who, for the most part, did not live with their children.

When fathers were unemployed, working part-time, or working an evening/nighttime shift, they had more time to spend with their children. But this time was often less than ideal because they were looking for jobs, tired (in the case of nighttime workers), or bringing their children with them to required appointments. It was also short-lived because of P/P employment requirements and a policy that does not recognize "stay-at-home" father/caregiver as full-time employment. Sometimes, the conflicts between family obligations and probation can require men to parent at the P/P office: "There are plenty of times . . . I'll have my older daughter go knock on the [PO's] door and go in there and she's [PO] like: 'Little Kevin, what are you doing?' I can bring my kids there [to the Probation Office] because I don't be having a babysitter, know what I mean?" (Kevin, 25).

In addition to time conflicts between P/P and parenting, the "on-call" nature of P/P can make it difficult for fathers to manage their time or keep commitments to their children and their children's mothers. For example, some probationers are monitored by a random drug-testing scheme that requires them to call a preprogrammed message each morning that will tell them, based on their social security number, if they are required to come to the office for a drug test that morning or not. This arrangement creates a situation where family plans may be thrown off track at the last minute, depending on the testing schedule. In addition, parolees or probationers may be called and asked to report to the probation office at any time, usually in response to suspected violations or because of a missed appointment, creating a conflict:

Monday morning, she [PO] calls me, "Um, listen . . . I need to see you. Can you get in here? I need to talk to you." I said, "Well, I got my little nephew [location-father role] with me." He was a newborn at the time. I was babysitting . . . so I said, "I can't come right now. When his mother gets home," I said, "I'll be more than glad, I'll be there." "Well," [she said,] "just make sure you be there at one o'clock."

(Curtis, 41)

Housing and Travel

In addition to the restrictions on fathers' time that are directly associated with meeting the requirements of P/P, there are at least two other major ways in which P/P can make it difficult for fathers to have meaningful contact with their children: through its effects on housing and because of restrictions on travel.

As indicated above, halfway houses are a frequent option for men released back into the community on parole. However, halfway houses restrict men's ability to reconnect with children in several ways. For

one, halfway houses for men in Connecticut accommodate only offenders; children and other family members are allowed to visit at specifically appointed times. Of the 1,220 beds funded by the Connecticut Department of Corrections in community-based halfway houses,
treatment units, and work-release programs, there are thirty-one for
female offenders with children. As small as this number may be, it is
larger than what is available for men: there are no such places for male
offenders with children. Further, resident mobility is restricted; time
away from the halfway house, "passes" that may be up to seventy-two
hours, must be earned and strict curfew is enforced. This limits the
residents' ability to visit family and children in their homes. In this
context, visiting with a child is a privilege that must be earned, not a
right:

> I want to sit on the couch . . . and watch a good movie and play with
> [my son], and I don't know, kiss my wife. . . . [Living apart] really—it
> really pressures you further . . . when you're really trying to do the
> right thing. I'm just trying to be a good dad, a good husband. . . . So
> for me to be trying to do the right thing will be really nice for her to
> see that . . . to be able to feel the love that I'm reciprocating to her,
> and not just over the phone or walking down the street, or sitting in a
> lobby somewhere where we got an appointment.
>
> (Derrick, 30)

Finally, halfway house residents are not allowed to have cell
phones. A house phone is usually available to them, but access to this
phone is limited, which inhibits fathers' ability to communicate with
children, especially teenagers. For five of the participants with teenage children, their relationships with these nonresidential children
were built entirely upon telephone conversations. In other words,
when they were unable to contact them via phone, they did not talk to
them. For example, at all three time points, Chris reported calling his
twelve-year-old son every day at three p.m. At the baseline interview,
he was living in a homeless shelter and making money by taking on
odd jobs. He did not have a lot of money, but he had a cell phone with
a prepaid card that he used to build his relationship with his son.

For participants on probation and parolees whose stays at halfway
houses have ended, the most common types of housing included sober
houses or the homes of girlfriends or female relatives. (Only two men
lived on their own, one with a housing subsidy relating to a physical

disability and one with a relatively well paying job and financial support from his mother.) Sober houses are less restrictive than halfway houses, but curfews are enforced and children are not permitted. Residents can, however, control their own money and have cell phones. Housing with female relatives or sex partners is, on many levels, less restrictive than institutional forms of housing. However, in spite of the fact that most of the men contributed to the rent and household expenses or made in-kind contributions to the household economy, the leases were not in their names and so their stays in these homes were conditional; they had to deal with norms and expectations set by the leaseholder or risk being asked to leave and perhaps face reincarceration if they are unable to identify another parole-approved home.

One of the primary points of conflict between study participants and the women with whom they lived was children. As was described earlier, their relationships with the women's children were often problematic. In addition, the female partners often prohibited the men's children from visiting the home:

> [My girlfriend] doesn't want her [my daughter] in the house. . . . So they [my other children] never really got on either because they don't like how she [girlfriend] talks, she cusses a lot and all that type so they don't like that. So none of my sons, I got two sons, none of them like going over there; they don't come over there.
>
> (Curtis, 41)

When animosity existed between a man's housing provider and his children, his ability to rebuild relationships with his children was compromised. Finally, public policies that ban people on P/P or with histories of incarceration from federally subsidized housing (Carey 2004) kept one of the African American fathers in our study from living with his wife and teenage son.

Overall, the African American fathers who participated in this study experienced high levels of housing instability. The participants' places of residence were recorded at release from prison, baseline interview, follow-up one, and follow-up two. Four of the men lived in different locations at each of these four time points. Seven men reported three different residences. Only one man lived in the same place for the entire time period; one man reported living in two different locations. Most of these residences were homes where the men's children did not reside: only one of the men lived with one of his children and the child's mother for more than a few days at a time during this time period. This perpetual movement adds to the chaos of their lives and complicates the fathers' ability to reconnect and spend time with children.

Individuals on P/P also are not allowed to travel out of state without permission from their POs. Six of the African American fathers in our study had children who lived out of state. While some of these men were estranged from their out-of-state children and most did not have money to travel, P/P restrictions created additional hurdles for those who did want to make these visits. Intrastate travel was also complicated by the financial and timing restrictions associated with community supervision. The costs and possible delays associated with public transportation made many men hesitant to travel outside of New Haven. For example, several respondents described missing required P/P meetings or classes after being "stranded" in other parts of the state while visiting family, when rides back to New Haven from friends or family fell through and they didn't have money to pay for the train or bus. While these particular scenarios were not associated with visiting children, the insecurity around travel outside of the city definitely discouraged visitation with out-of-town children. The burden, therefore, generally fell on the children's mothers or guardians to transport the children to New Haven to see the fathers. Finally, because people on P/P are prohibited from visiting correctional facilities, the two participants with sons in prison were unable to visit them.

Spirit

On a psychological level, the quasi-incarcerated state of people on P/P creates a sense of insecurity that can build and grate on their nerves over time. The study participants constantly referred to the uncertainty of being neither incarcerated nor free. There was a sense among many of the men that their lives are not completely their own. This feeling of continued servitude to the system may shape how they see themselves, how they perceive themselves as fathers, and how willing they are to reinsert themselves into their children's lives: "I try to give him [my son]—I try to give him what I never had, which is freedom, so I got my freedom now. I really ain't even got it, because this parole, this probation thing, well, I'm still out on the street" (Kevin, 25).

P/P requires a certain level of mental attention that can be distracting and impair the probationers/parolees' ability to focus on their children:

> It's so many issues that a person coming out of jail is dealing with, like me, for instance, the whole immigration thing and no transportation, the baby's mother, employment. . . . It's just so many things that the father doesn't think, it's like shaky because you have to get right and stable yourself before you could deal with these children the way they're supposed to be dealt with.
>
> (Joe, 29)

In the following passage, a participant describes a sense of exasperation because his adolescent daughter was acting out and he did not have the energy to cope with her given his tenuous criminal justice status.

> I'm just putting my life back together. I'm still on work release. You know until next month . . . then I'll be free. And, honestly, I'm to the point in my life where I'm giving all I can. You know, what can I do? And that's what I always ask her [his teenage daughter] now. Well, what am I supposed to do? What do you want me to do?
>
> (Terrance, 33)

The stress of parole/probation and reentry, especially in contrast to the period of incarceration when they had few, if any, responsibilities, does not create an ideal environment for rebuilding the father-child bond. Fathers described being depressed, crying, and feeling despondent during this time. Here a father describes his frustration with his unsuccessful attempts to reconnect with older children with whom he did not bond in the past and who are now uninterested in establishing a relationship with him: "I cry, I cry, yeah...it should be like a video game where I can just hit the reset button...it is what it is" (Chris, 43).

The quasi-incarcerated state of P/P may also inhibit men's willingness to exert their parental authority or press custodial issues. For example, Terrance refused to intervene in the volatile situations that arose between his daughter and her mother because he worried that the police might be called to the house and he would be at risk for reincarceration. One of the primary stipulations of parole and probation is that individuals avoid all contact with law enforcement. Men were cautious about negotiating visitation and custody with their children's mothers, out of concern that the mothers might become upset and call the police. The fathers' perception of their compromised legal status may also hamper their interaction with the State's child protection agency, the Department of Children and Families. Several men with children under DCF supervision expressed a feeling that their ability to negotiate custody issues was compromised by a DCF bias based on their P/P status, and this sense contributed to their choice not to assert their parental rights.

Parole and Probation's Support of Fatherhood

While there are clearly ways that P/P conflicts with fatherhood, there are also several ways in which P/P supports men's attempts to reestablish themselves as fathers. For one, some services become available to probationers and parolees that they might otherwise have difficulty accessing, such as mental-health and drug treatment, counseling, and classes. These services may help position men to be fathers by stabilizing mental-health issues and reducing or eliminating their substance abuse. When these services keep men from reoffending and going back to jail, they are increasing their availability to their children. Many described fatherhood as a motivating force behind their efforts to desist from criminal activity and drug use.

Second, some men reported learning specific skills, especially relating to anger management and communication, that they used in their relationships with their children. Joe describes using nonjudgmental communication skills that he learned from a substance-abuse counselor to talk with his social daughter, who told him she was cutting herself:

> So I was shocked but I didn't show it in my face and my response was, you know, "I don't think they [people who cut themselves] are crazy, they might not have people to talk to and they just express themselves that way." . . . I wasn't really familiar [with cutting]. . . . But since I had been in the program, like my counselor's real cool and . . . he's been explaining certain things to me and luckily we just had this conversation like two days before . . . he was the one who told me when people are sharing certain things with you, you shouldn't openly express shock or awe . . . so I did that.

Third, for some men, the PO is a source of encouragement and support who helps them through this difficult period of transition.

[My parole officer] is one of the nicest guys around me. . . . All of the time when I had my dirty urines and stuff like that, he could have been put me back in jail . . . instead of putting me in jail, he put me in a halfway house through the program. At first I was mad as hell at him for doing that. But then I realized why he done that, you know. He said, "I don't want to put you in jail, man, because you . . ." Because he said that I'm an all right person. So after that, you know, I said, "Thank you very much." So you know what? He's my parole officer and plus, he's a friend of mines. . . . I got magic stuff for that man.

(Marcus, 42)

However, more often men did not share more than the basic information that was explicitly required and did not consider P/P to be helpful. When asked if his probation officer ever offered him assistance, Derrick replied:

Of course not. And this is what probation and parole officers do not do generally. They do not do this. [They ask]: "Is your piss clean, buddy? Have there been any incidents, any run-ins with the authorities?" These are the types of questions that they're concerned about. "Your next meeting with me will be on this date." It's not like, "Here, let me help you out." It's not that.

Interventions and Future Research

These qualitative data suggest that probation and parole affect African American men's ability to meet personal and community expectations of fatherhood. Further research to test the effect of "father-friendly" modifications to the P/P systems could lead to interventions that moderate this effect. Possible interventions include financial flexibility to recognize parental expenses, transportation or visitation services to facilitate father-child interaction, family and individual mental-health counseling, recognition of full-time childcare responsibilities as employment, family-friendly policies at halfway houses (e.g., increased visitation opportunities, house-sponsored activities that include children), and legal counseling about custody rights.

Impact of Fatherhood on P/P Goals

Discussion about intervention possibilities, however, must be predicated on frank deliberations about the value of fatherhood to criminal-justice goals, the offenders' children, and the offenders' children's mothers. If P/P is going to dedicate resources to father-child relationships, then the benefit of this investment to community supervision's dual mission to reduce recidivism and promote public safety must be demonstrated. The majority of people (51.8 percent) released from prison are back in prison within three years (Langan and Levin 2002). Blacks were more likely than whites to be rearrested, reconvicted, and returned to prison (Langan and Levin 2002). Could fatherhood programming help to reduce these rates of recidivism? Given the larger socioeconomic factors that shape recidivism, it may not be fair to expect that fatherhood initiatives alone can make a significant impact on reincarceration rates. However, creative ways to measure the effects of these interventions on criminal-justice outcomes will need to be developed.

Indeed, it is not yet obvious that increasing interaction between male former prisoners and their children would increase the reentry success of these fathers. There is an "underlying assumption that prisoners' families and friends . . . will be the major sources of concrete aid and social and emotional support" for people coming out of prison (Hairston, Rollin, and Jo 2004:1), but the literature is inconclusive about the effects of this family support on the former prisoner, especially as it relates to fatherhood (Stouthamer-Loeber and Wei 1998; Edin, Nelson, and Paranal 2001; Nelson 2004; Bahr et al. 2005). In this study, it was clear that children can be a source of inspiration for recovery; nevertheless, fatherhood was also a source of stress that led to relapse and criminal activity. In his third interview, Derrick talked about the issues that led up to his relapse and three-month incarceration shortly after his second interview.

> Eventually a lot of the pressures, the financial pressures, the social pressures—by social I don't mean like peer pressure but social as far as like my station in life. But a lot of different things do affect my decision making. And I ended up reverting right back to old behaviors as far as drug use, drinking like a fish. My wife was pregnant at the time. I was going to be a first-time father and I started to go downhill really fast.

The question of whether interaction with children reduces fathers' likelihood of going back to prison (and what kinds of interaction, specifically) requires further study.

Effect of Fathers on Children and Children's Mothers

In addition to understanding the positive and negative effects of fatherhood on prisoner reentry outcomes, the effect of the criminally involved fathers on children and children's mothers must also be considered in the development of future interventions. The participants in this study clearly demonstrated the capacity to assist their children's mothers and love and support their children. However, given high rates of recidivism, is it responsible social policy to encourage repeat offenders, many with untreated mental-health and substance-abuse issues, to reconnect with their children? Here, again, the issues are complex and the literature about the effect of fathers on children, especially low-income nonresidential fathers involved in the criminal justice system, is inconclusive (Roy 1999; Bennett and Fraser 2000; Hamer 2001; Harper and Fine 2006; Leite and McKenry 2006; Wiemann et al. 2006; Coley and Medeiros 2007; Gee et al. 2007). Joe talked about coming to his own realization about the effects of the criminal-justice system on fatherhood during a prison visit with his five-year-old son:

> Me and his [son's] mom was talking and he [my son] had the key in his hand and he started digging around the edge of the window. So I'm like . . . "Boo Boo, what you doing?" He's like, "I'm trying to break all the daddies out." . . . So I looked around and I saw all the kids like in the little visiting area and . . . all the daddies, and I started crying. . . . I know it's a lot of people who are incarcerated who have kids, a lot of kids who don't grow up with fathers.

The effects of fathers on their children's mothers, and the mothers' relationships with their children, must also be considered.

> [My return from prison,] it's like kind of tough for my kid's mom because, she's like real like, like, you know, aggressive, outgoing, like type of personality. And, you know, it's like me and her bumping heads now because she was used to being the boss for all these years

and having the final say in everything. But she can't do that when I'm
in the house.

(Joe, 29)

The study participants' narratives about their children's mothers
illuminate the stressors these women experience during the fathers' incarceration and reentry period, especially in terms of raising children.
These experiences, which have been extensively documented in the
literature, demonstrate the ways in which men's experiences, including parole and probation, are inextricably linked to the lives of their
children and their children's mothers (Jarrett 1994; Petersilia 2000;
Shapiro and Schwartz 2001; Coley and Morris 2002; Adimora et al.
2003; Arditti, Lambert-Shute, and Joest 2003; Clayton and Moore 2003;
Seaton and Taylor 2003; Travis and Waul 2003; Roy 2004; Freudenberg
et al. 2005; Roy and Dyson 2005; Pattillo, Weinman, and Western 2006;
Wiemann et al. 2006; Gee et al. 2007; Roy and Burton 2007).

Clearly, there is no "quick fix" to this situation. Men's desire to be
fathers must be balanced against the desire of children and their mothers to have the fathers actively involved in their lives and the need to
promote stability and healthy relationships within these families.

Middle-aged Fathers with Adult Children

The data also draw attention to the struggles that middle-aged men
face in parenting adult children. Research and social policy about fathers generally focuses on the transition to fatherhood (Nelson 2004;
Wiemann et al. 2006; Gee et al. 2007) and experiences of fathers
with young children, exploring how these men do or do not contribute, emotionally and financially, to the upbringing of their children
(Stouthamer-Loeber and Wei 1998; Roy 1999; Hamer 2001; Jayakody
and Kalil 2002; Nurse 2002; Haney and March 2003; Harper and Fine
2006; Letiecq 2007). The relationships between middle-aged fathers
and their *adult* children is less examined (Cochran 1997; Coley 2001).
Older men in this study were no less interested in their adult children
than younger men with babies and school-aged children. They discussed their appreciation of the care and work their children's mothers gave to raising their children, remorse about opportunities to be a
father that they had missed, and a desire to reconnect with their chil-

dren. Mending these relationships—whether the result is reunification or closure—could have a powerful impact on the future trajectory of both the fathers and their adult children. A greater understanding is needed of the effects of fatherhood across the lifespan, including how it relates to men's efforts to desist from criminal activity.

Conclusion

This research demonstrates the specific ways that the context of parole and probation shapes the capacity of African American men to fulfill biological-, social-, and location-fathering roles. Parole and probation affect the offender's finances, housing, time management, mobility, and spirit. P/P programs may also offer participants the opportunity to access substance-abuse and mental-health services that boost their parenting skills. Efforts to mitigate the negative consequences of P/P on the offenders' relationships with their children must be balanced against the criminal-justice system's mission to promote community safety and reduce recidivism and the needs of the children and the children's mothers. Further research is required to determine if parole and probation policies that improve African American men's relationships with their children can also improve the fathers' criminal-justice outcomes or reduce family and community level stress.

To the extent that African Americans are disproportionately represented among those on probation and parole, they are more likely than other racial or ethnic group to experience the consequences of these systems. Of course, this analysis says nothing about why it is that African Americans are overrepresented among those on probation and parole. Furthermore, we have focused here only on African Americans, so we do not know, from this analysis, whether their experiences with these systems are distinct from those of their white or Hispanic counterparts, although it is likely that they are, given the many forms of racism. Further research comparing the experiences of different racial and ethnic groups on probation and parole and the effects of these systems on their fathering relationships is therefore warranted.

Note

1. One fifty-five-year-old father had recently been disabled by adult diabetes and other health complications, but he was not born disabled and had been consistently employed for most of his life.

References

Adimora, A. A., V. J. Schoenbach, F. E. A. Martinson, K. H. Donaldson, T. R. Stancil, and R. E. Fullilove. 2003. "Concurrent Partnerships Among Rural African Americans with Recently Reported Heterosexually Transmitted HIV Infection." *JAIDS: Journal of Acquired Immune Deficiency Syndromes* 34 (4): 423–29.

Arditti, J. A., J. Lambert-Shute, and K. Joest. 2003. "Saturday Morning at the Jail: Implications of Incarceration for Families and Children." *Family Relations* 52 (3): 195–204.

Bahr, S. J., A. H. Armstrong, B. G. Gibbs, P. E. Harris, and J. K. Fisher. 2005. "The Reentry Process: How Parolees Adjust to Release from Prison." *Fathering: A Journal of Theory, Research, and Practice About Men as Fathers* 3 (3): 243–65.

Bennett, M. D., Jr., and M. W. Fraser. 2000. "Urban Violence Among African American Males: Integrating Family, Neighborhood, and Peer Perspectives." *Journal of Sociology and Social Welfare* 27 (3): 93–117.

Blankenship, K. M., A. B. Smoyer, S. J. Bray, and K. Mattocks. 2005. "Black-White Disparities in HIV/AIDS: The Role of Drug Policy and the Corrections System." *Journal of Health Care for the Poor and Underserved* 16 (4 Suppl B): 140–56.

Bonczar, T. P. 2003. *Prevalence of Imprisonment in the U.S. Population, 1974–2001*. No. NCJ 197976. Washington, D.C.: U.S. Department of Justice.

Carey, C. 2004. *No Second Chance: People with Criminal Records Denied Public Housing*. New York: Human Rights Watch.

Clayton, O., and R. B. Moore. 2003. "The Effects of Crime and Imprisonment on Family Formation." In *Black Fathers in Contemporary American Society*, ed. O. Clayton, R.B. Mincy, and D. Blankenhorn, 84–104. New York: Russell Sage Foundation.

Cochran, D. L. 1997. "African American Fathers: A Decade Review of the Literature." *Families in Society* 78 (4): 340–351.

Coley, R. L. 2001. "(In)visible men." *American Psychologist* 56 (9): 743–53.

Coley, R. L., and B. L. Medeiros. 2007. "Reciprocal Longitudinal Relations Between Nonresident Father Involvement and Adolescent Delinquency." *Child Development* 78 (1): 132–47.

Coley, R. L., and J. E. Morris. 2002. "Comparing Father and Mother Reports of Father Involvement Among Low-Income Minority Families." *Journal of Marriage and Family* 64:982–97.

Edin, K., T. J. Nelson, and R. Paranal. 2001. *Fatherhood and Incarceration as Potential Turning Points in the Criminal Careers of Unskilled Men*. Evanston, Ill.: Institute for Policy Research, Northwestern University.

Flavin, J. 2007. "Not Every Woman Is a Mother: Addressing the Invisibility of Criminal Justice Involved Women Who Do Not Have Children." Paper presented at the meeting of the Society for the Study of Social Problems, August 10–12, 2007, New York.

Freudenberg, N., J. Daniels, M. Crum, T. Perkins, and B. E. Richie. 2005. "Coming Home from Jail: The Social and Health Consequences of Community Reentry for Women, Male Adolescents, and Their Families and Communities." *American Journal of Public Health* 95 (10): 1725–36.

Gee, C., C. McNerney, M. Reiter, and S. Leaman. 2007. "Adolescent and Young Adult Mothers' Relationship Quality During the Transition to Parenthood: Associations with Father Involvement in Fragile Families." *Journal of Youth and Adolescence* 36 (2): 213–24.

Glaze, L. E., and T. P. Bonczar. 2006. *Probation and Parole in the United States, 2005*. No. NCJ 215091. Washington, D.C.: U.S. Department of Justice.

Hairston, C., J. Rollin, and H. Jo. 2004. *Family Connections During Imprisonment and Prisoners' Community Reentry*. Chicago: University of Illinois at Chicago, Jane Addams College of Social Work.

Hamer, J. F. 1998. "What African-American Non-Custodial Fathers Say Inhibits and Enhances Their Involvement with Children." *Western Journal of Black Studies* 22 (2): 117–27.

Hamer, J. F. 2001. *What It Means to Be Daddy: Fatherhood for Black Men Living Away from Their Children*. New York: Columbia University Press.

Haney, L., and M. March. 2003. "Married Fathers and Caring Daddies: Welfare Reform and The Discursive Politics of Paternity." *Social Problems* 50 (4): 461–81.

Harper, S. E., and M. A. Fine. 2006. "The Effects of Involved Nonresidential Fathers' Distress, Parenting Behaviors, Inter-Parental Conflict, and the Quality of Father-Child Relationships on Children's Well-Being." *Fathering: A Journal of Theory, Research, and Practice about Men as Fathers* 4 (3): 286–311.

Jarrett, R. L. 1994. "Living Poor: Family Life Among Single Parent, African-American Women." *Social Problems* 41 (1): 30–49.

Jayakody, R., and A. Kalil. 2002. "Social Fathering in Low-Income, African American Families with Preschool Children." *Journal of Marriage and Family* 64 (2): 504–16.

Langan, P. A., and D. J. Levin. 2002. *Recidivism of Prisoners Released in 1994*. No. NCJ 193427. Washington, D.C: U.S. Department of Justice.

Leite, R., and P. McKenry. 2006. "A Role Theory Perspective on Patterns of Separated and Divorced African-American Nonresidential Father Involvement with Children." *Fathering: A Journal of Theory, Research, and Practice About Men as Fathers* 4 (1): 1–21.

Letiecq, B. L. 2007. "African American Fathering in Violent Neighborhoods: What Role Does Spirituality Play?" *Fathering: A Journal of Theory, Research, and Practice About Men as Fathers* 5 (2): 111–28.

Nelson, T. J. 2004. "Low-Income Fathers." *Annual Review of Sociology* 30 (1): 427–51.

Nurse, A. 2002. *Fatherhood Arrested*. Nashville, Tenn.: Vanderbilt University Press.

Ogbu, J. U. 1981. "Origins of Human Competence: A Cultural Ecological Perspective." *Child Development* 52 (2): 413–29.

Pattillo, M., D. Weinman, and B. Western, eds. 2006. *Imprisoning America: The Social Effects of Mass Incarceration.* New York: Russell Sage Foundation.

Petersilia, J. 2000. *When Prisoners Return to the Community: Political, Economic, and Social Consequences.* Washington, D.C.: National Criminal Justice Reference Service. Available from http://www.ncjrs.gov/pdffiles1/nij/184253.pdf.

Petersilia, J. 2003. *When Prisoners Come Home: Parole and Prisoner Reentry.* New York: Oxford University Press.

Roy, K. 1999. "Low-Income Single Fathers in an African American Community and the Requirements of Welfare Reform." *Journal of Family Issues* 20 (4): 432–57.

Roy, K. 2004. "Three-Block Fathers: Spatial Perceptions and Kin-Work in Low-Income African American Neighborhoods." *Social Problems* 51 (4): 528–48.

Roy, K. 2006. "Father Stories: A Life Course Examination of Paternal Identity Among Low-Income African American Men." *Journal of Family Issues* 27 (1): 31–54.

Roy, K., and L. Burton. 2007. "Mothering Through Recruitment: Kinscription of Nonresidential Fathers and Father Figures in Low-Income Families." *Family Relations* 56 (1): 24–39.

Roy, K., and O. Dyson. 2005. "Gatekeeping in Context: Babymama Drama and the Involvement of Incarcerated Fathers." *Fathering: A Journal of Theory, Research, and Practice About Men as Fathers* 3 (3): 289–310.

Sabol, W. J., T. D. Minton, and P. M. Harrison. 2007. *Prison and Jail Inmates at Midyear 2006.* No. NCJ 217675. Washington, D.C.: U.S. Department of Justice.

Seaton, E. K., and R. D. Taylor. 2003. "Exploring Familial Processes in Urban, Low-Income African American Families." *Journal of Family Issues* 24 (5): 627–44.

Shapiro, C., and M. Schwartz. 2001. "Coming Home: Building on Family Connections." *Corrections Management Quarterly* 5 (3): 52–60.

Stouthamer-Loeber, M., and E. H. Wei. 1998. "The Precursors of Young Fatherhood and Its Effect on Delinquency of Teenage Males." *Journal of Adolescent Health* 22 (1): 56–65.

Travis, J., A. L. Solomon, and M. Waul. 2001. *From Prison to Home: The Dimensions and Consequences of Prisoner Reentry.* Washington, D.C.: Urban Institute.

Travis, J., and M. Waul, eds. 2003. *Prisoners Once Removed: The Children and Families of Prisoners.* Washington, D.C.: The Urban Institute.

Tripp, B. 2001. "Incarcerated African American Fathers: Exploring Changes in Family Relationships and the Father Identity." *Journal of African American Men* 6 (1): 13–30.

Wiemann, C., C. Agurcia, V. Rickert, A. Berenson, and R. Volk. 2006. "Absent Fathers as Providers: Race/Ethnic Differences in Support for Adolescent Mothers." *Child and Adolescent Social Work Journal* 23 (5/6): 617–34.

CHAPTER FIFTEEN

Fostering Fatherhood

Understanding the Effects of Child-Support Policy on Low-Income,
Noncustodial African American Fathers

CHERYL E. MILLS

In 1996, the passage of the Personal Responsibility and Work Opportunity Reconciliation Act (PL 104-193) placed noncustodial fathers at the center of a growing fiscal movement to transfer responsibility for social-welfare programs from the federal government to states. During this period of transition, policymakers focused on the elimination of entitlement programs for the poor in favor of welfare-to-work programs and strict enforcement of child-support responsibility. In accordance with conventional social norms, the father's role as the family's economic provider contributed to a policy environment wherein child support evolved as a political linchpin of the modern welfare state. Hence, focus on the financial role of noncustodial fathers increased despite decreases in the numbers of mothers and children involved in cash-assistance programs, known commonly as welfare.

This chapter examines the impact of child-support legislation on low-income, African American noncustodial fathers. The effects of social policy on this population compels attention because of well documented findings that reveal high rates of poverty, single-parent households, and corresponding welfare dependency within the African American population. I identify the extent to which policy guidelines endorse men's behavior and shape their attitudes toward payment of child support and engagement in social and emotional support of their children. The policy analysis focuses on the Temporary Assistance for Needy Families Act contained in the February 2006 reauthorization of the Personal Responsibility and Work Opportunity Reconciliation Act of 2005.

The chapter begins with an overview of child-support legislation, outlining contextual issues that oblige the goal and purposes of the policy, which is followed by a discussion of emergent issues that arise in the implementation of the social policy, including unanticipated and inadvertent effects on beneficiaries. The chapter concludes with policy recommendations for addressing the needs of low income, noncustodial African American fathers in service of the best interest of their children.

Policy Background

Over the past several decades a confluence of historic, demographic, and societal shifts affected the structure of American families, contributing to the social-policy environment within which welfare-reform legislation was crafted during the mid-1990s. Of most concern among these trends was the growing number of female-headed household and nonmarital births. The current social-policy strategy of requiring financial support from noncustodial fathers is a direct outgrowth of the increase in never-married mothers, as opposed to those who were widowed, separated, or divorced (McLanahan and Carlson 2002). For example, according to a U.S. House of Representatives Report (2004), between 1970 and 2002, the percentage of children living in single-mother families doubled, growing from 11 to 23 percent of the total children in the United States, and by 2002, nonmarital births accounted for about a third of all births.

At the same time, growing public and political belief supported the view that increased financial support from the noncustodial parent— usually the father—should replace welfare dependency on the government. In the 1980s, conservative scholars such as Charles Murray (1984), along with a conservative Congress, characterized the expanded welfare state of the 1960s as a failed system that induced dependency and created a cycle of poverty among participants. By the turn of the twentieth century, neoconservative and conservative politicians spanning the presidential administrations of George H. W. Bush and William J. Clinton conspired to reform Aid for Families with Dependent Children, a major component of the American welfare state. The Temporary Assistance for Needy Families program became the centerpiece of welfare reform, replacing the beleaguered AFDC program.

The Temporary Assistance to Need Families Act

In 1996, a redesign of the public-welfare system under the landmark Personal Responsibility and Work Opportunity Reconciliation Act changed public assistance from an entitlement program (AFDC) to the TANF program, based on work requirements. Over the ten-year period from 1986 to 1996, federal financing of social safety-net programs contracted, and the primary funding for these programs devolved to states through a block-grant formula. Social-policy formulations focused on reforming welfare to achieve four goals: to promote children's economic security through mandating income support from the noncustodial parent; to enlist the involvement of noncustodial fathers in contributing to the emotional and social development of children; to strengthen the institution of marriage as a means of reducing the frequency of nonmarital births; and to shorten periods of dependency and increase self-sufficiency among welfare users. These emergent goals of social-welfare reform highlighted the concerns of policymakers surrounding the precipitous shift in family structure over the past three decades.

Federal legislators sought to meet some of these goals by introducing laws to strengthen child-support collections and enforcement by linking eligibility and receipt of TANF benefits to cooperation on establishment of paternity. Additional reforms to welfare included aggressive child-support enforcement, work requirements, time limits, and family caps for AFDC/TANF participants. However, from the mid-1900s onward, when the federal government shifted responsibility for social-welfare programs to the states, the interaction of economic recessions collided with punitive welfare reforms, negatively altering economic opportunity for low-income families (Turner and McDaniel 2007).

Child-Support Enforcement

Earlier policymaking efforts to encourage and enforce parental responsibility, particularly among unmarried couples, began with the addition of Part D to Title IV of the Social Security Act. Enacted in 1975, this legislation directed states to establish a child-support-enforcement system for AFDC cases as a requirement for receiving federal funds. Strengthened enforcement followed in the Child Support Amendments (PL 98-378) of 1984 and the Family Support Act (PL 100-485) of 1988. Each of these pieces of legislation imposed additional conditions on states to set guidelines, establish paternity, use tracking and monitoring systems, and implement penalties for noncustodial parents failing to comply with child-support orders.

As a result of child-support legislation contained in the Personal Responsibility and Work Reconciliation Act of 1996 (P.L., 104-193 Sec. 103 [a] 401 [2]) and its subsequent reauthorization in 2006, collections from the noncustodial parent have been effectively established through provisions contained in the TANF block-grant program. Presently, to qualify for cash assistance from federal TANF funds, the custodial parent must agree to cooperate with child-support-enforcement agents and to assign the right to collected child-support payments over to the resident state. In partnership with the Federal Office of Child Support Enforcement program, state and local governments operate to locate the noncustodial parent for the purpose of establishing obligation and enforcing collection of child-support payments (U.S. Department of Health and Human Services 2006a).

Along with state assignment of rights to child-support collections, policies pertaining to state pass-through and disregard requirements are a critical yet often understated element of the child-support-enforcement system. Under changes in the 1996 PRWORA legislation the federal government eliminated pass-through and disregard requirements. Earlier legislation under AFDC required states to distribute (pass through) the first fifty dollars of child support collected each month to the custodial parent. This amount was disregarded in calculation of the family's AFDC benefits. Subsequent PRWORA legislation directs states to withhold the federal share of child support collected but allows discretion in establishing pass-through and disregard policies. Accordingly, states may retain 100 percent of monthly child-support collections as reimbursement for benefits a family receives. State-designed distribution plans include procedures that permit them to forward a portion of collections to OCSE, recoup monies owed to the state as a result of TANF payments to the noncustodial parent for the dependent child, and determine if any portion of the payment is passed onto the custodial family. Regarding the amount of pass-through funds a family receives, provisions included in the 2006 reauthorization of TANF recommend that states not exceed an amount of $200 for two or more children.

Presently, a majority of states neither pass through nor disregard any child support for families receiving TANF benefits (Koball and Douglass-Hall 2005). However, a small group of states have either continued their pass-through policies or altered the amount of child support collection that is disregarded. For example, in Alaska, California, Illinois, and New York, fifty dollars are passed through to the family, and that amount is disregarded in relation to TANF eligibility and benefits (Roberts and Vinson 2004). Ideally, to ensure a child receives maximum financial benefit from both TANF and child-support programs, state policy should pass through a higher percentage of the child-support contribution or increase the amount of funds that are disregarded in calculating welfare benefits. Otherwise, the pass-through amount lowers the amount of TANF funds the mother receives so that her eligibility for welfare receipt is compromised.

Since states have discretion in establishing policy regarding pass-through and disregard amounts, variability among states can produce income disparity within welfare-dependent families. Critics assert that when disregarded, pass-through dollars contribute to a dual class of TANF recipients (Meyer 2008). Most advantaged by multiple distribution arrangements is a family that receives full pass through, full disregard of the monthly child-support payment, and full welfare benefits, compared to a family that receives a TANF check only. Still, critics and supporters agree that as a result of a formula-driven, means-tested procedure applied to TANF eligibility, disparities between groups are minimal and short term. A predetermined benefit structure also minimizes any potential long-term disparities because a family becomes ineligible for TANF once its income reaches the established ceiling.

Greatly relevant to the discussion of pass-through and disregard strategies is the effect of policies on a parent's decision to participate in the enforcement program. A few studies indicate that the lack of pass-throughs and disregards promote reluctance on the part of fathers (Furstenberg 1992) and mothers (Edin and Lein 1997) to become involved in the formal child-support system. Conversely, Miller et al. (2004) found that compliance of noncustodial fathers with child-support orders increased with their knowledge that the full child-support collection was paid to the family. For such an obviously important reason, all states should incorporate reasonable pass-though and disregard policies, which are likely to have the effect of increasing collections and contributing to the greater goal of improving the financial well-being of welfare-dependent and low-income children.

Since the late 1990s, interest in developing disregard and pass-through policies has grown as policymakers continue to seek to move more TANF families from the welfare rolls. Despite impressive national statistics regarding exits from welfare in the mid- and late 1990s, ongoing welfare dependency persists among a cohort of slower leavers, prompting legislators and social policymakers to reconsider implementing pass-through and disregard policies (Meyer 2008). Flexibility in allowing states to develop such policies offers TANF families a means of receiving additional cash income and support to become self-reliant.

Accordingly, between 1997 and 2001 under demonstration waivers from the federal government, several states, including Connecticut, Wisconsin, and Vermont, each engaged in a pilot program involving pass-through and disregard policies. Implemented in 1997, the Wisconsin program was the only one in the country to provide a 100 percent pass-through and full disregard of child support collections to a TANF family until 2002 (Meyer 2008). General findings from the Wisconsin Child Support demonstration program reveal modest financial results for families involved in pass-through and disregard programs, with the greatest net benefit accruing to families who exit welfare (Cancian and Meyer 2007). Wisconsin families that exit TANF are eligible to receive the entire amount of monthly child support collected from the noncustodial father. Cancian and Meyer (2007) also found larger pass-through and disregard payment amounts to be associated with a statistically significant increase in the rate of paternity establishment and a smaller but statistically significant increase in the proportion of cases with child-support collections.

Outcomes for Vermont were similar to those in the Wisconsin project regarding increased collections from noncustodial fathers. Findings from participants in the Vermont study showed increases in child-support payments from the noncustodial parent and an increase in the average amount paid (Miller et al. 2004). As a result of demonstration projects, Vermont and Connecticut put into practice policies that allowed for full pass-through of collected child support and disregarded the first fifty and one hundred dollars, respectively. In each of these states, federal waivers have expired, but pass-through and disregard remain central to their child-support policy. Nevertheless, Vermont and

Connecticut remain among a minority of states that use pass-throughs and disregards.

As the preceding discussion indicates, major changes in enforcement policies since 1996 have garnered the attention of social-science researchers and social policymakers. At the nexus of ongoing discourse and debate among diverse stakeholders is the question of whether strict enforcement policies contribute not only to a reduction in the number of welfare-dependent families but also to an improvement in the relationship between welfare-dependent children and their fathers? Throughout the remainder of this chapter, welfare-reform strategies that involve withholding portions of child-support payments and the use of punitive and coercive sanctions against low-income non-custodial African American fathers are discussed. Critical consideration is given to the issue of how such policy strategies promote or reduce compliance through a set of inadvertent disincentives linked to child-support-policy development and implementation.

The Effect of Child-Support Receipt on Poverty and Welfare Use

Vigorous and strict child-support enforcement aims to reduce poverty among poor women and children and leads to lower welfare caseloads. Collections are purported to have the dual benefit of promoting self-sufficiency by reducing the mother's eligibility and reliance on public assistance and limiting the public tax burden associated with government support of TANF families (Wheaton 2004). Such reduced dependency on the federal government through use of public transfers and increased personal responsibility are hallmarks of contemporary welfare-reform policy designed to counter criticism that liberalized eligibility requirements for public-assistance receipt in the 1960s had undermined marriage and work and contributed to long-term dependency on government relief (Murray 1984).

However, the outcome of child-support collections as a result of strict enforcement policy and procedures diverges among children and families, depending on their level of poverty. A 1998 report from the U.S. House of Representatives indicated that improvement in child support collections from the noncustodial parent would not have lifted the majority of the 1.26 million families living in poverty in 1991 above the poverty level (U.S. House of Representatives 1998). Even if child-support-enforcement policy did not require that government payments be recouped and allowed full payment to be made to these 1.26 million families, only 140,000 of them would have received enough in payment to move out of poverty. However, Sorensen and Zibman (2000) estimate that child support reduces poverty for about half a million low-income children by a margin of 5 percent and reduces their poverty gap by 8 percent. The amount these families receive also constitutes a higher proportionate share of their income compared to nonpoor families. In addition, among poor children not on welfare, child support constitutes a significant portion of income and can have some effect on poverty reduction. In addition, outcomes for *working-poor* single mothers are more promising. Data show that for this latter group of mothers, aggressive child-support enforcement serves to prevent and also reduce child poverty (Sorensen and Zibman 2000).

However, riding on the presumed benefit of child support to improve the financial, social, and emotional well-being of poor children, PRWROA policymakers strengthened child-support-enforcement efforts. A conservative political climate and an improved economic environment allowed policymakers to reduce government involvement in public social welfare with the manifest goal of increasing self-sufficiency and personal responsibility among poor families. This political ideology resonated with a social environment dominated by the value of personal responsibility. Together, efforts to limit the American welfare state and a strong belief in individualism were reinforced in social policy though punitive sanctions against noncustodial parents who did not fulfill their child-support responsibilities.

Low-Income Noncustodial Fathers and Child Support

According to census estimates, approximately 80 percent of poor children live with a custodial mother. Recent statistics also indicate that nearly half of single mothers have never married and are less likely than previously married mothers to receive child support (Sorensen and Halpern 1999). Evidence also indicates that child-support payments play a significant role in rates of exits and reentry to welfare (Huang, Kunz, and Garfinkel 2002). Nonetheless, as a group of custodial mothers, those that never marry and receive TANF benefits are also least likely to have legally established child-support awards (Grall 2006).

Most studies confirm that because low-income and poor fathers have high rates of unemployment and low earnings, they have few financial resources to comply with child-support orders. Consequently, very poor children receive minimal benefits associated with child-support programs (McLanahan and Carlson 2004). Among families receiving TANF benefits, only 20 to 30 percent of poor fathers provide cash support to their children, and a slightly higher percentage contribute in-kind resources (Miller et al. 2004; Rangarajan and Gleason 1998).

Until recently, limitations in both census and administrative data restricted our understanding of factors associated with the payment of child support among low-income, noncustodial fathers. Information concerning behavior of noncustodial fathers was primarily linked to statistics obtained from small administrative databases used by public child-support-enforcement agencies. In addition, policymakers had little social science data on which to formulate theories about noncustodial fathers whose children receive TANF benefits. As a result, during the early welfare-reform era of the 1990s, policymakers based their approach to child-support enforcement and father involvement on studies involving custodial mothers and divorced fathers. Custodial mothers tended to offer a conservative assessment of the noncustodial father's behavior (Seltzer and Brandreth 1995; Sonenstein and Calhoun 1990). Moreover, child-support social-policy initiatives contained in the 2006 reauthorization of TANF reflected conclusions drawn from studies of divorced men, usually white, who earned higher incomes than never-married noncustodial fathers (Garfinkel and Oellerich 1989). Unfortunately, these were not the men whose behavior social policy was intended to address.

As a result of improper data, a distorted assessment of the noncustodial father's motivation, willingness, and ability to pay child support emerged. A major policy assumption growing from these data was that noncustodial fathers were "deadbeat dads": disinterested in the financial, social and emotional well being of their children who must be forced by the government to "man-up" to their responsibility.

Yet in contrast to labels that portray them as "deadbeat dads," many low-income fathers fulfill their child-support responsibility, despite the heavy burden payment places on their relatively low incomes (Holzer 2007). For example, Miller, Garfinkel, and McLanahan (1997) show that in 2000, one-third of low-income noncustodial fathers paid child support despite their median annual earnings of only $5,000, and, in fact, they paid proportionately higher payments than divorcees or middle-income fathers, at a cost estimated at 20 to 35 percent of their income. Nevertheless, other fathers are effected negatively by labor-market conditions and low wages. Related studies indicate that inner-city noncustodial fathers often cannot meet their child-support obligations (Stier and Tienda 1993; Furstenberg 1995) largely because of insufficient income (Sorensen 1997).

In the case of young fathers, most suffer from the same poverty that affects their families and communities. Studies of teenage and young-adult noncustodial fathers indicate that low income levels and a high incidence of poverty negatively effect their ability to comply with child-support payments (Pirog-Good and Good 1995; Lerman and Ooms 1997). Clearly, the issue of child-support collection is complex, and the response to enforcement by noncustodial fathers is as varied as the men themselves.

Child Support and Father Involvement

Focus on the nonmonetary role of fathers is a relatively recent outcome of welfare policy. Before TANF, child support was viewed by policymakers and some social scientists as a primary form of father involvement. Consequently, policy centered primarily on increasing collection of child support from absent fathers. Since then, policymakers have come to recognize the importance of noncustodial fathers in contributing to the emotional and social well-being of their children. Father-involvement programs that emerged under TANF espoused a philosophy that positive engagement strengthened the relationship between noncustodial parents and their children and served to mitigate negative effects of single parenting on child development.

Ideally, involvement denotes personal contact that increases social interaction and psychological attachment between father and child. Earlier studies of father involvement claim an association between the frequency of contact between the noncustodial father and payment of child support. Arditti and Keith (1993) are among several researchers to suggest positive interactive effects between visitation and payment of child support. This finding is supported by other researchers who note that increased contact with the child increases the likelihood that child support will be paid (Furstenberg et al. 1983; Seltzer, Schaeffer, and Charng 1989; Furstenberg and Cherlin 1991).

Subsequent studies show a correlation as well between the parental relationship and child-support payment. The often tenuous relationship between an unmarried noncustodial parent and a child's custodial parent is similar to that of divorced, nonresidential parents. The mother's control over the child-support money, spending behavior, access to visitation, and childrearing practices are factors that can adversely affect payment of child support (Demo and Ganong 1994; Fox and Blanton 1995; Aldous 1996). In addition, new and evolving research on fragile families implicates child factors such as age, gender, and birth order as bearing on the noncustodial father's payment of child support (Huang and Garfinkel 2003; Huang 2006).

As part of a TANF policy mandate, father-involvement programs also extend to relationships with mothers and are designed to reduce the number of children with absent fathers by affecting women's fertility. Pregnancy-prevention programs aimed at addressing unwanted births among unmarried women are part of this strategy. Family-planning programs encourage use of contraceptives and discourage teenage childbearing by promoting abstinence and "safe sex." Policy requiring "family caps" limit monthly benefits to children born to the mother at time eligibility for TANF is established and excludes future births from being added to the amount the family receives (McLanahan and Carlson 2002).

Over the past decade attention has also turned to multiple-partner families, that is, those families in which one partner has other children from previous relationships (Mincy 2006). Multiple-partner families have gained the interest of policy researchers since evidence from several states indicates that a substantial portion of these families receive welfare (Meyer, Cancian, and Cook 2005). According to Meyer, Cancian, and Cook, having multiple partners is an emergent family configuration prevalent among young, low-income African American and Hispanic American males that can influence patterns and frequency of involvement with their children and payment of child support. Multiple romantic relationships, including remarriage, further complicate the situation and can dissolve the noncustodial father's incentive to fulfill child-support obligations (Huang 2006).

Policy Impediments to Child Support and Father Involvement

In this section, three major policy impediments are identified and discussed in relation to their dire and inadvertent effect on noncustodial African American fathers: the formula and definition by which child support payments are determined; the "criminalization" of noncustodial fathers in the child-support-enforcement system; and penalties involving revocation of occupational and driver's licenses.

Payment Determination, Definition and Arrearages

States decide on the amount of child-support payment through calculations based on one of three models: percentage of income, income shares, and Delaware-Melson. By comparison to the percentage of income formula, the income-share and Delaware-Melson models appear more equitable, and the majority of states use the income-shares approach, which takes into consideration the self-sustaining need of each parent. In the income-shares model, the exact amount of payment is calculated according to a formula that takes into consideration the relative and combined income of both parents, child-spending patterns and self-sufficiency needs of the noncustodial parent, the number of children for whom support is to be determined, and the time a parent spends with a child after state-specific deductions are considered. The final determined amount also reflects adjustment for special conditions, such as joint custody and visitation from the noncustodial parent. In following mandatory guidelines set in 1988, a majority of states base determination of the noncustodial parent's contribution using the income-shares model. The fluctuating financial circumstances of low-income noncustodial African American fathers are seldom considered by courts and public-agency administrators in determining the amount of a child-support order. Furthermore, the use of a regressive formula penalizes many noncustodial fathers who pay a comparatively higher share of their income toward child support.

By and large, state policies and practices base payment requirements on the legal presumption that noncustodial parents have earnings from a full-time, full-paying job even when child support data do not provide evidence of employment or income (Turetsky 2001). According to an analysis of data from the 1990 Survey of Income and Program Participation, a majority of low-income noncustodial fathers worked or looked for work, but only one-fourth worked full-time, year-round, earning an average income of $6,989 when the poverty threshold for a single person was $6,800. Consequently, many noncustodial fathers report having to deprive themselves of basic necessities, including housing and transportation that gets them to work, in order to comply with a monthly $600 child-support determination on a low income, for example (Sullivan 1989). Payment determination that results in an amount the noncustodial father considers unrealistic in relation to his income is also a major disincentive associated with child-enforcement policy. In addition, procedures for establishing the amount of payment and enforcing the obligation often introduce more tension and conflict into frequently strained relationships with the child's mother. Most likely, interparental conflict will also have a negative effect on a child's behavior (Amato and Gilbreth 1999).

Regardless of the father's circumstances, the court is prohibited from forgiving or arbitrarily reducing the child-support payment. Every state, however, must have a process for adjusting child-support orders to reflect changes in a parent's circumstances (Turetsky 2001). The formal modification must be granted at the time a change in circumstances occurs. Otherwise, the original amount must be paid in full. Some states allow child-support awards to be set retroactively to the birth of the child whether or not paternity was established at the time and without consideration of a change in the noncustodial father's income (Sorenson 1997). When payments fall into arrears during incarceration, the father can be considered as being "voluntarily unemployed" and payment determination can be based on his earnings capacity. These and perhaps other reasons cause some noncustodial fathers to resent court involvement in determining child-support amounts (Sullivan 1989), preferring to make informal arrangements with the child's mother. Payment determinations are, however, left to family courts and agency administrators who often are insensitive to the negative effect of high rates of unemployment and incarceration among low-income noncustodial African American men. As a result, even well-intentioned fathers find themselves in a precarious state as they attempt to navigate within the child-support system.

Finally, a major oversight in the determination of child-support payment is consideration of variability in the cost or standard of living from one community to the other, even within a state. For example, if the cost and standard of living in a community are greater than what the formula awards but the father is able to pay more, the child does not receive the full benefit of his earnings. However, a more likely scenario is one in which the mother prefers to live in a community where the award amount is in excess of the standard and cost of living. The income formula can result in a payment determination in excess of the cost of living and financial support needed to ensure the child a commensurate lifestyle. Under such conditions, the percentage of income formula may yield an amount that may inadvertently disadvantages a noncustodial father whose income is taxed by wage withholding or garnishment. Some African American noncustodial fathers have further concerns that mothers who continued to live in poor and substandard conditions are spending money on themselves or redirecting child-support payments to support a new relationship. When there is no formal arrangement that taxes wages of the noncustodial father, his belief that child support is not fully benefiting the child can have a negative psychological effect on his social involvement. In the absence of a formal agreement, partial payment or total noncompliance with a child-support agreement is likely to result.

Past-due child-support orders or arrears are accompanied by varied and myriad penalties, including automatic reporting to credit bureaus. Similarly, financial institutions may freeze accounts and assets. Low-income noncustodial parents who are struggling with child-support debt are caught in a downward spiral that affects them and their children. Such noncustodial fathers who might be struggling to keep a job, continue their education, or provide for a current family have meager resources stretched to the point where there often is not enough money to go around.

It is common knowledge in most African American communities that before PWROA, under AFDC, many low-income fathers succeeded in circumventing the child-support-enforcement system, frequently with the cooperation of the custodial mother. This behavior followed a long tradition among unmarried couples in African American communities by which noncustodial fathers established paternity informally and made direct contributions of financial and in-kind resources to the child, who received full benefit of the father's contribution while the payment did not affect the mother's AFDC grant.

When viewed from a strengths-based perspective, noncustodial African American fathers have been known to provide their family with a mixture of support that is both instrumental and expressive. Both qualitative and quantitative studies indicate that noncustodial fathers are most likely to provide informal, in-kind support (noncash contributions) involving purchases of school clothing and toys, or visits in lieu of these payments (Edin and Lein 1997; Plotnick and Waller1999; Greene and Moore 2000). According to a recent U.S. Census Bureau report (Grall 2006), custodial parents receive more in-kind support (60 percent) than cash child-support payments (40 percent). In many instances, the unemployed, noncustodial father's behavior can range from assisting the mother with discipline, picking up children from school, or buying toys and school supplies, to preparing meals. Among some low-income working fathers, a regular cash contribution is often supplemented with a portion of income earned for an extra day of work or overtime work. Formal requirements to establish paternity as a means towards enforcement of child support have possibly curtailed these well-intended, informal practices among low-income parents, which produced direct and immediate benefits to children. Aggressive enforcement efforts that focus on establishing paternity, calculating payment, and enforcing collections threaten in-kind contributions and "off the books" payments and disrupt social interaction between non-custodial fathers and their children within economically fragile communities. Moreover, a punitive and formal system, in which only cash contributions in a fixed amount are acknowledged as support, can undermine many of the "fringe benefits" that noncustodial African American fathers are more likely to provide. In this regard, disruption of the informal child-support system that was an integral part of the African American community undermines policy goals of lifting children out of poverty. Ultimately, children bear the loss of valuable social interaction and emotional and psychological support when the father's contributions are reduced to a "cash-only" system.

The Criminalization of Child-Support Nonpayment

From her analysis of 1997 data on noncustodial fathers, Elaine Sorenson (1997) found that nearly 30 percent of low-income noncustodial fathers were incarcerated. Moreover, recent data from the U.S. Department of Health and Human Services (2006b) indicate that half of all incarcerated parents have open child-support cases. For African American men, the situation is dire. Mincy (2006) notes that by age thirty-four, up to one-half of African American men are fathers without custody of their children, and an estimated 30 percent have been to prison.

In 1998 the federal Deadbeat Parents Punishment Act (PL 105-187) established criminal penalties for failure to pay past-due child support in arrears of two years. Among states, penalties range from a misdemeanor in Alabama for "intentional failure to provide support" to a felony in Massachusetts for "willfully failing to comply with an order of support when the noncustodial parent is financially able or has the earning capacity" (Sussman and Mather 2003). Louisiana's statute (Act

801), signed into law in 2004, increased criminal penalties for nonpayment of child support. In cases of a second offense, willful nonpayment extending over a year or $5,000 in arrearages would constitute a crime resulting in a maximum fine of $2,500 or imprisonment with or without hard labor for a maximum of two years.

Moreover, a 2004 report by the American Bar Association notes that there are eighteen states where incarcerated men continue to accrue child-support debt, despite the fact that their earnings cease. In one-third to one-half of states, incarceration is considered "voluntary unemployment," and child support payments continue to accumulate, regardless of imprisonment (Turetsky 2001). The eighteen states that require noncustodial fathers to pay child support during incarceration are essentially creating a situation that makes it impossible for low-income men ever to dig their way out of child-support debts (Mincy 2006). Even in states where a support order can be adjusted, the process to petition the court is complicated and sufficiently drawn-out to discourage incarcerated parents who might be inclined to assert their right to seek modification of the court order.

Since arrearages continue to mount and in some instances the father's incarceration could extend beyond his minor child's eligibility for child support, long-term imprisonment cases deserve the most attention from policymakers. In thirteen states, arrearages constitute an element leading to more severe punishment for the initial crime of nonpayment. For example, in Illinois, willful refusal to provide support over a six-month period or in arrears of more than $5,000 constitutes a Class 4 Felony with a maximum penalty of three years in prison or a $25,000 fine. The noncustodial parents' penalty can be increased if arrears amount to $10,000 and an attempt is made to leave the state or if arrears are in excess of $20,000 (Sussman and Mather 2003).

Criminalizing the nonpayment of child support increases existing high rates of incarceration among African American men and further marginalizes their participation in the labor market. Additional criminal statutes related to nonpayment of child support or chronically delinquent payments enlarge the potential of incarceration for nonviolent offenses among African American men who are already in a high-risk category. A noncustodial parent that did not make child support payments before being incarcerated is unlikely to make them while incarcerated, after being released on parole, or upon completion of a jail term. Arrears, nonetheless, continue to compound a vicious cycle that most low-income and poor noncustodial fathers cannot easily escape.

Following unemployment, incarceration is the most likely cause of fathers' failure to pay child support. The interrelationship between unemployment and incarceration creates a situation of double jeopardy in which the nonpayment of child support and subsequent incarceration leads to further nonpayment and incarceration. As it relates to child-support enforcement, incarceration is not an effective solution to low income and poverty; instead, it tends to create and further extend these disadvantages among oppressed populations. Accordingly, poor children are as disadvantaged by punitive social policy that invokes incarceration as punishment for nonpayment as they are by the noncustodial fathers' original lack of payment. In both instances, the child does not receive needed child-support dollars.

Frequent incarceration ensures that noncustodial fathers will accumulate a bad work history and a criminal record, which further prevents employment. Some noncustodial fathers resort to "hustling" as an alternative to blocked opportunities in the legitimate labor market (Sullivan 1989). Among African American men, who are predisposed to fluctuations in the labor market (Mincy 2006), the extent to which incarceration further entraps them financially, contributes to noncompliance with support orders, and pushes them into poverty is not difficult to imagine. Contrary to conventional thinking, noncustodial fathers indicate that fear of incarceration can have negative effects that reduce compliance with child-support orders and contact with the child. The historic experiences of African American men with the court system contribute to a fear of unfair treatment and injustice that is triggered by even the smallest infraction. Consequently intimidated by the court system, many of these men will seek ways to avoid involvement and participation in child-support hearings.

The indirect effects of criminalization of child support can be as devastating as the direct impact. Having a felony record removes possibilities for obtaining a student loan, housing, credit, and even employment. In some states, the removal of voting rights further disenfranchises many African American men, reinforcing their position at the margins of civic society. According to Holzer (2001), second to incarceration, strict enforcement of child-support policies is a major factor oppressing young African American men, as it forces them into a downward spiral of debt, incarceration, and unemployment.

Withdrawal of Occupational and Drivers Licenses

Policy requiring withdrawal of occupational and driver licenses can impede the ability of a father to comply with child-support-payment arrangements. The suspension of driver licenses would clearly impede the efforts of many low-income fathers in obtaining or maintaining legitimate work in some unskilled and semiskilled occupations that often require operating a vehicle, such as a bus or taxi. Most jobs involving technical skills, including working in a barber shop, plumbing, or electrical or construction work require some form of license. Losing a license as penalty for nonpayment of child support places the noncustodial father in the untenable predicament of not being able to work so that he can pay child support, which perpetuates the cycle of further nonpayment, unemployment, and arrears.

Personal hardships do not occur only among low-income and unemployed African American noncustodial fathers. Many noncustodial fathers attend college and graduate school. These students frequently finance their education through loans, grants, and part-time work. Nonetheless, they must comply with child-support payments, frequently based on income levels before they enrolled in school or based on their capacity to earn. In the long term, dropping out of college to work may be less beneficial to the goal of increasing the father's earning power, which is related to enhancing his child's financial condition. When education is considered an important factor in low wages and unemployment among African American fathers, a man who is unable to complete higher levels of education may be contributing to the cycle of poverty from which he and his family are attempting to escape.

Discussion

The mismatch between the policy framework and the target population of low-income fathers has led to inappropriate assumptions and punitive policies being applied to low-income noncustodial fathers. The resulting system of child support explicitly aims to change the behavior of fathers to align with a child's need for financial, social, and emotional support while implicitly seeking to reduce and eliminate the financial dependency of poor families on the state and federal governments. This dual nature of the child-support system, however, serves to both facilitate and undermine social-policy objectives. For example, high rates of under- and unemployment and incarceration among low-income young African American fathers influence the efficacy of social policy aimed at fostering children's economic security. The disproportionately high numbers of African American fathers who fall into poverty, unemployment, and incarceration increase the likelihood of these men and their children being negatively affected by misguided social-policy formulations. Social policy based on negative bias and inaccurate or incomplete assumptions about the behavior of African American men ignores the influence of institutionalized factors, including poverty, persistent racial inequality and discrimination, and changing global labor markets. An emphasis on individual-level explanations alleges irresponsibility and lack of commitment to family values and enlists stereotypes that portray poor, noncustodial, unmarried fathers as lazy, amoral, and often uncaring. We see an example of the inadvertent outcomes of misguided social policy when men go underground or disappear from their children's lives because they feel hounded by oppressive and unreasonable collection enforcement.

As a result of their financial circumstances, many low-income noncustodial fathers might abandon all efforts at support and involvement as defined and measured through court-ordered formal behavior and monetary calculations. However, poor and low-income, noncustodial African American fathers have a history of in-kind contributions that should be valued and counted to offset a portion of cash payments, particularly if the child's social and emotional development benefits from his involvement.

Over the past ten years, changes in child-support policy have been recommended by African American noncustodial fathers participating in focus groups and by scholars studying the effects of multiple factors on compliance with child-support orders and involvement with children. Consistent with these recommendations, the following conclusions emerge from this chapter in support of modifications in child support policy:

- Develop a coordinated and concurrent procedure among child-support-enforcement officials and civil and criminal courts to initiate modification of child-support orders at the time of sentencing and before incarceration.
- Calculate realistic payment orders that balance a child's needs and the noncustodial father's ability to pay. Eliminate the regressive structure of assigning child-support payments.

- Increase "pass through" and reduce welfare-cost recovery to a minimum. Disregard a higher percentage of total child-support payment to allow for establishing self-sufficiency among TANF families.
- Reduce administrative "red tape" to allow for routine modifications in child-support orders based on negative changes in the noncustodial parent's ability to pay.
- Assign a value to "in-kind/noncash" support and consider this contribution as payment toward child-support orders.
- Establish a system for monitoring mother's use of payments that ensures the supported child's needs are being met based on the noncustodial father's contribution.
- Permit the amount of child-support payment to be counted as a tax deduction.
- Eliminate child support as a "penalty" factor in obtaining credit or other services.
- Establish and require job training and employment programs for unemployed and incarcerated fathers.

Conclusion

Similar to conventional views of poor, unmarried mothers receiving TANF benefits, noncustodial unmarried fathers are assumed to have a flawed moral character. These intermingling assumptions result in formulation of a penalty-driven child-support policy.

When social policy is formulated to reflect the reality of all stakeholders, benefits are likely to increase for the intended beneficiaries, and unanticipated should risks decrease. For poor African American children and fathers, current child-support policy has yet to fulfill the goal of alleviating poverty and improving psychosocial development. The relatively weak effect of current policy on the frequency of support payments and parent-child engagement among poor TANF families derives from a set of ill-conceived guidelines that are inconsistent with the circumstances of many poor and low-income African American fathers. As a result, many of the men who maneuver on the fringe of the labor market in low-wage and temporary employment or exit to the underground do not meet their obligations or enable their poor children to leave welfare and become self-sufficient.

Guidelines that divert collected payments away from poor children to federal and state governments satisfy goals of repaying a debt but can also perpetuate the poverty that social policy is designed to reduce. Similarly, punitive policy prescriptions further dissuade African American fathers from doing what little they can in support of a positive family life for their children. To be effective, social policy must balance the important goal of making parents responsible for their children with the reality of the social and economic conditions that challenge poor noncustodial African American fathers.

References

Aldous, J. 1996. *Family Careers: Rethinking the Developmental Perspective.* Thousand Oaks, Calif.: Sage.
Amato, P. R., and J. G. Gilbreth. 1999. "Nonresident Fathers and Children's Well-Being: A Meta-analysis." *Journal of Marriage and the Family* 61:557–73.
Arditti, J. A., and T. Keith. 1993. "Visitation Frequency, Child Support Payment, and the Father-Child Relationship Post-divorce." *Journal of Marriage and the Family* 55:699–712.
Cancian, M., and D. Meyer, eds. 2007. *The Child Support Demonstration Evaluation Research Summary.* Madison: Institute for Research on Poverty, University of Wisconsin.
Demo, D., and L. Ganong. 1994. "Families and Change: Coping with Stressful Events." In *Divorce,* ed. P. C. McKenry and S. J. Price, 197–218. Thousand Oaks, Calif.: Sage.
Edin, K., and L. Lein. 1997. *Making Ends Meet: How Single Mothers Survive Welfare and Low-Wage Work.* New York: Russell Sage Foundation.
Fox G., and Blanton, P. 1995. "Noncustodial Fathers Following Divorce." *Marriage and Family Review* 20 (1/2): 257–82.
Furstenberg, F .F., Jr. 1992. "Daddies and Fathers: Men Who Do for Their Children and Men Who Don't." In *Caring and Paying: What Fathers and Mothers Say About Child Support,* ed. F. F. Furstenberg Jr., K. Sherwood, and M. Sullivan. A report prepared for the Parents' Fair Share Demonstration. New York: Manpower Demonstration Research Center. Avaialable at http://fatherhood.hhs.gov/pfs92/ch3.htm.
Furstenberg, F. F., Jr. 1995. "Fathering in the Inner-City: Parental Participation and Public Policy." In *Fatherhood: Contemporary Theory, Research, and Social Policy,* ed. W. Margsiglio, 119–47. Newbury Park, Calif.: Sage.
Furstenberg, F. F., Jr. and A. J. Cherlin. 1991. *Divided Families: What Happens to Children When Parents Part.* Cambridge, Mass.: Harvard University Press

Furstenberg, F. F., Jr., J. L. Peterson, C. W. Nord, and N. Zill. 1983. "The Life Course of Children of Divorce—Marital Disruption and Parental Contact." *American Sociological Review* 48 (5): 656–68.

Garfinkel, I., and D. Oellerich. 1989. "Noncustodial Fathers' Ability to Pay Child Support." *Demography* 26:219–33.

Grall, T.S. 2006. "Custodial Mothers and Fathers and Their Child Support: 2003." Current Population Reports. Washington, D.C.: U.S. Census Bureau. Available at http://www.census.gov/prod/2006pubs/p60–230.pdf.

Greene, A. D., and K. A. Moore. 2000. "Nonresident Father Involvement and Child Well-Being Among Young Children in Families on Welfare." *Marriage and Family Review* 29 (2–3): 159–80.

Holzer, H. J. 2001. "Racial Differences in Labor Market Outcomes Among Men." In *America Becoming: Racial Trends and Their Consequences*, ed. Neil J. Smelser, William Julius Wilson, and Faith Mitchell, 98–123. Washington, D.C.: The National Academic Press.

Holzer, H. 2007. "Collateral Costs: The Effects of Incarceration on Employment and Earnings Among Young Men." Institute for Research on Poverty Discussion Paper no. 1331-07. The Urban Institute.

Huang, C. 2006. "Child Support Enforcement and Father Involvement for Children in Never-Married Mother Families." *Fathering* 4 (1): 97–111.

Huang, C., and I. Garfinkel, 2003. "Child Support Enforcement, Joint Legal Custody, and Parental Involvement." *Social Service Review* 77 (2): 255–78.

Huang C., J. Kunz, and I. Garfinkel. 2002. "The Effect of Child Support on Welfare Exits and Re-Entries." *Journal of Policy Analysis and Management* 21 (4): 557–76.

Koball, H., and A. Douglas-Hall. 2005. "Marriage Not Enough to Guarantee Economic Security." New York: National Center for Children in Poverty, Columbia University, Mailman School of Public Health. Available at http://www.nccp.org/publications/pub_632.html.

Lerman, R. I., and T. J. Ooms. 1997. *Young Unwed Fathers: Changing Roles and Emerging Policies*. Philadelphia: Temple University Press.

McLanahan, S., and M. Carlson. 2002. "Welfare Reform, Fertility, and Father Involvement." *Children and Welfare Reform* 12 (1): 147–65. Available at http://www.futureofchildren.org/usr_doc/6-mclanahan.pdf.

McLanahan, S. and M. Carlson. 2004. "Fathers in Fragile Families." In *The Role of the Father in Child Development*, 4th ed., ed. Michael E. Lamb, 368–96. New York: Wiley.

Meyer, D. 2008. "Child Support and Welfare Dynamics: Evidence from Wisconsin." *Demography* 30 (1): 45–62.

Meyer, D. R., M. Cancian, and S. T. Cook 2005. "Multiple-Partner Fertility: Incidence and Implications for Child Support Policy." *The Social Service Review* 79 (4): 577–601.

Miller, C., M. Farrell, M. Cancian, and D. Meyer. 2004. "The Intersection of Child Support and TANF: Evidence from Samples of Current and Former Welfare Recipients." New York: MDRC.

Miller, C., I. Garfinkel, and S. McLanahan. 1997. "Child Support in the U.S.: Can Fathers Afford to Pay More?" *Review of Income and Wealth* 43 (3): 261–81.

Mincy, R. B., ed. 2006. *Black Males Left Behind*. Washington, D.C.: Urban Institute Press.

Murray, C. 1984. *Losing Ground: American Social Policy, 1950–1980*. New York: Basic Books.

Pirog-Good, M., and D. Good. 1995. "Child Support Enforcement for Teenage Fathers: Problems and Prospects." *Journal of Policy Analysis and Management* 14:25–42.

Plotnick, R., and M. Waller. 1999. *Child Support and Low-Income Families: Perceptions, Practices, and Policy*. San Francisco: Public Policy Institute of California, 1999.

Rangarajan, A., and P. Gleason. 1998. "Young Unwed Fathers of AFDC Children: Do They Provide Support?" *Demography* 35:175–86.

Roberts, P., and M. Vinson. 2004. "State Policy Regarding Pass-Through and Disregard of Current Month's Child Support Collected for Families Receiving TANF-Funded Cash Assistance." Center for Law and Social Policy. Available at http://www.clasp.org/publications/pass_thru3.pdf.

Seltzer, J. A., and Brandreth, Y. 1995. "What Fathers Say About Involvement with Children After Separation." In *Fatherhood: Contemporary Theory, Research, and Social Policy*, ed. W. Marsiglio, 166–92. Thousand Oaks, Calif.: Sage.

Seltzer, J., N. Schaeffer, and H. Charng, 1989. "Family Ties After Divorce: The Relationship Between Visiting and Paying Child Support." *Journal of Marriage and the Family* 51:1013–32.

Sonenstein, F., and C. Calhoun. 1990. "Determinants of Child Support: A Pilot Survey of Absent Parents." *Contemporary Economic Policy* 8:75–94.

Sorensen, E. 1997. "A National Profile of Nonresident Fathers and Their Ability to Pay Child Support." *Journal of Marriage and the Family* 59:785–97.

Sorensen E., and A. Halpern. 1999. "Child Support Enforcement Is Working Better Than We Think." New Federalism: Issues and Options for the State. Series A, No. A-31, March. The Urban Institute. http://www.urban.org/UploadedPDF/Anf31.pdf.

Sorensen, E., and C. Zibman. 2000. "Child Support Offers Some Protection Against Poverty." Series B, No. B-10 Assessing the New Federalism. Washington, D.C.: Urban Institute. http://www.urban.org/publications/309440.html

Stier, H., and M. Tienda. 1993. "Are Men Marginal to the Family? Insights from Chicago's Inner City." In *Men, Work, and Family*, ed. J. C. Hood, 23–44. Newbury Park, Calif.: Sage.

Sullivan, M. L. 1989. *Getting Paid*. Ithaca, N.Y.: Cornell University Press.

Sussman, S., and C. Mather. 2003. "Criminal Statutes for Non-Payment of Child Support by State." Madison, Wis.: The Center on Fathers, Families, and Public Policy. Available at .http://www.cffpp.org/publications/pdfs/crimstat.pdf

Turetsky, V. 2001. "Realistic Child Support Policies for Low-Income Fathers." Kellogg Devolution Initiative Paper. Washington, D.C.: Center for Law and Social Policy, March 2000. Available at http://www.clasp.org/publications/realistic_child_support_policies.pdf.

Turner M., and M. McDaniel. 2007. *Racial Disparities and the New Federalism*. Washington, D.C.: The Urban Institute.

U.S. Department of Health and Human Services. 2006a. "The National Child Support Enforcement Strategic Plan for FY 2005–2009." Available at http://www.acf.hhs.gov/programs/cse/pubs/2004/Strategic_Plan_FY2005-2009.pdf.

U.S. Department of Health and Human Services. 2006b. Administration for Children and Families, Office of Child Support Enforcement Reentry and Child Support Issues. "National and State Research Overview Report." Available at http://www.acf.hhs.gov/programs/cse/.

U.S. House of Representatives. 1998. Report: House Ways and Means Committee Prints: 105-7, 1998 Green Book. Washington, D.C.: U.S. Government Printing Office. Available at http://www.gpoaccess.gov/wmprints/green/1998.html.

U.S. House of Representatives. 2004. Report: House Ways and Means Committee Prints: 108-6, 2004 Green Book. http://www.gpoaccess.gov/wmprints/green/2004.html.

Wheaton, L. 2004. "Cost Avoidance and Cost Recovery in California's Child Support Program." Urban Institute. http://www.urban.org/publications/410957.html.

CHAPTER SIXTEEN

Fatherhood Responsibility and the Marriage-Promotion Policy

Going to the Chapel and We're Going to Get Married?

DAVID J. PATE JR.

In the United States, the federal government first made economic provision for children without fathers through the Social Security Act
of 1935. The act included a variety of income-transfer programs for
low-income families. Of particular significance here is the public-
assistance program ("welfare"), which provided a variety of services to
poor families in which the father was absent. This program reflected
the Roosevelt administration's belief that the federal government had
a responsibility to provide for poor families that lacked access to a father's income. Eventually, the government made a distinction between
families whose fathers had died and those whose fathers were absent
because of divorce or nonmarital births. The former retained access
to funds through Supplemental Social Security; the latter were transferred to Aid to Families with Dependent Children, a means-tested
program.

In 1996, Congress passed the Personal Responsibility and Work
Opportunity Reconciliation Act, radically changing how the nation
provided income support to poor families. Aid to Families with Dependent Children became Temporary Assistance to Needy Families, a program that promoted job preparation, work, and marriage. In fact, one of
the four major goals of the TANF policy was the encouragement of the
formation and maintenance of two-parent families. From 1999 to 2006,
several bills, including the Fathers Count Bill of 1998; the Responsible Fatherhood Acts of 1999, 2000, 2001, and 2003; the Child Support

Distribution Act of 2001; and the Strengthening Families Act of 2003, were introduced with an emphasis on fatherhood but increasingly, after the 2000 election of George W. Bush as president, these bills included some aspect of a healthy-marriage program. Finally, the Healthy Marriages and Responsible Fathers Act of 2004 was included in the Deficit Reduction Act of 2005 as a part of the agreement that marriage was the priority. Responsible fatherhood would be included as long as the policy contained healthy-marriage activities. Thus, the reauthorized TANF program provided funding in the amount of $150 million per year for fiscal years 2006 through 2010 for healthy-marriage-promotion activities (at least $100 million) and the promotion of responsible fatherhood (not more than $50 million). Healthy-marriage-promotion activities included marriage education, marriage-skills training, public advertising campaigns, high-school education on the value of marriage, and marriage-mentoring programs. According to an online report of the Administration for Children and Families in the Department of Health and Human Services, at least 250 organizations have received grants to promote marriage (Administration for Children and Families n.d.). While the grantee organizations are quite diverse across religions, races, and citizenship, little is yet known about how the effectiveness of these activities might vary by race and income.

This chapter will discuss the healthy-marriage-promotion activities and examine the policy in the context of African American fathers with welfare-reliant children. This paper arises from a larger study undertaken to explore respondents' knowledge of and experiences with various policies stemming from the major shifts manifested in PRWORA. Specifically, I was interested in ascertaining single mothers' and fathers' knowledge of public-assistance, paternity-establishment, child-support, and marriage policy. For this particular chapter, I have included only the qualitative data from the nine African American single fathers included in the larger study. Their experiences suggest why a marriage policy is likely to be ineffective among low-income African American fathers.

Noncustodial Parents and the Healthy-Marriage-Promotion Policy

The marriage-promotion campaign arose in the midst of a debate over the causes of decreasing marriage rates and increasing nonmarital birth rates among African Americans. Wilson (1987) and Wilson and Neckerman (1986) introduced the term "marriageable men" and examined the relationship between marriage and employment in the 1980s. They found that a rise in male joblessness was linked to a rise in never-married births. Testa et al. (1989) concluded that a man with a job was more likely to marry the mother of his child born out of wedlock. Yet results of the effect of employment on marriageability have been mixed (Nock 2003; Wilson 2003; Lichter and Roempke Graefe 2007; Mincy and Pouncy 2007).

Some research (Lichter 2001; Lichter and Roempke Graefe 2007) discussed the intersection of earlier children and marriage; once women have nonmarital children, their likelihood of marriage decreases. And other research (Lichter, Batson, and Brown 2004; Edin and Kefalas 2005) has addressed attitudes toward marriage. While most find that black women continue to desire marriage, some have found lower rates of marriage desire among black men (South 1993).

Despite the lack of resolve over the causes of marriage decline, marriage-promotion policy entered the picture as the solution the U.S. government would endorse and fund. Since the policy has only been in effect since October of 2007, there is a dearth of information on the effectiveness of the healthy-marriage-promotion policy generally and its effects on low-income, noncustodial male parents particularly.

Before the passage of the Healthy Marriages and Responsible Fathers Act of 2004, most policy research focused on the purpose of marriage promotion. Some scholars saw the policy as an antipoverty program based on family structure (Rector et al. 2003; Berlin 2004); a program to promote the well-being of children (Grassley 2004; Ooms 2004; Horn 2005; Mincieli et al. 2007); a program to reduce the incidence of domestic violence (Rector, Johnson, and Fagan 2004); or a program to improve a couple's attitudes and relationship skills (Rector and Johnson 2004). Others thought marriage promotion would provide all-around social and economic benefits for African American men (Sitgraves 2008). The Heritage Foundation has been one of the program's most avid advocates.

However, some scholars criticized the program (Ainslie 2002), arguing that marriage for marriage's sake might lead to a higher divorce rate and more domestic abuse. Others (Lane et al. 2004) argued that marriage promotion is a heterosexist policy that blames black single mothers for demographic realities over which they have no control (black women outnumber black men starting around eighteen years old, which means many black women cannot marry within their race). Looking from the mothers' perspective, Mink (2002) argued that marriage promotion was yet one more way that government was attempting to control women's reproductive choices while avoiding addressing their poverty. Still others have argued that the policy might be useful to couples who are economically stable, but for low-income or poor parents, more appropriate policies would target increased access to education, skills, and employment (Coontz and Folbre 2002; DeAngelis 2004; Lichter and Roempke Graefe 2003).

Methodology and Sample

As mentioned earlier, for this paper I'm using the experiences of nine African American fathers who were part of a qualitative study

Table 16.1
Means of Key Variables for the Population in the Sampling Frame and the Qualitative Sample of Noncustodial Black Fathers

Variable	Dane County Population (N = 303)	Qualitative Sample of Dane County African American Men (N = 9)
Unemployment Insurance Earnings		
Year		
2002	$11,385	$5,999
2003	$11,992	$5,695
2004	$12,336	$4,698
Child Support Paid to W-2 Mothers		
Year		
2002	$1,979	$797
2003	$2,448	$2,078
2004	$2,487	$1,691
Arrearages Owed by Fathers on 12/31/2004		
Child support arrearages owed to the W-2 mothers (with interest)	$5,313	$5,695
Child support arrearages owed to the state for W-2 mothers (with interest)	$942	$3,472
Lying-in arrearages owed to the state for W-2 mothers	$1,256	$1,953

Table 16.2

Characteristics of Nine Noncustodial Black Fathers in Qualitative Sample

Noncustodial Parent Age	Number of Children Who Received W-2 at Time of Interview	Ever Live with Biological Children?	Type of Job at Initial Interview (2005)	Currently Lives with Mother and Subject Child	Highest Level of Education	Accused of Intimate-Partner Violence
30	1	Yes	Self-employed	Yes	GED	No
32	1	Yes	Unemployed	No	H.S. diploma	Yes
22	2	Yes	Unemployed	N/A	HSED	Yes
34	2	Yes	Unemployed	No	HSED	Yes
27	3	Yes	Manager	No	H.S. diploma	No
25	1	No	Unemployed	No	H.S. diploma	NA
26	1	Yes	Unemployed	Yes	H.S. diploma	NA
36	1	Yes	Unemployed	Yes	GED	No
27	2	Yes	Unemployed	Yes	H.S. diploma	Yes

Notes: The full qualitative sample consisted of twenty noncustodial white and black fathers and fourteen matched custodial mothers were interviewed. All partner-violence accusations were made by the partner or police.

of noncustodial (white and African American) fathers' and mothers' knowledge of and experience with various policies related to PRWORA (see Pate 2002). To explore and define the knowledge of current policies among noncustodial and custodial parents from April 2005 through September 2005, I conducted semistructured interviews with parents of children receiving public assistance. Respondents were drawn from African American fathers listed in Wisconsin administrative records, otherwise known as KIDS Information Data System. Key interview questions included: How did you get involved with the child support enforcement system? In what ways are you involved with your children? Why are you not married to the mother of your child?

Tables 16.1 and 16.2 compare information on all the fathers in this study with those in the initial sampling frame. Table 16.2 shows the characteristics of the nine men in this study. The nine fathers participating in this study were generally representative of the initial population. Fathers interviewed had low levels of formal earnings as reported in the state unemployment-insurance records. The overall population of fathers, which included white and African American fathers, paid an average of $2,487 in child support to W-2 mothers in 2004. The African American fathers' payments were somewhat under the average at $1,691. Arrearages to the mothers were about the same, but these nine fathers owed more to the state than the population of fathers as a whole.

The fathers ranged in age from twenty-five to thirty-six. Five fathers had only one child on welfare, three had two, and one had three. All but one father had at some point lived with his biological children, and four were currently living with the mother and children. None of the fathers had an education beyond high school, and seven of the nine fathers were currently unemployed.

Barriers to Marriage Promotion

The experiences and narratives of the African American men in this study highlight several potential barriers to effective marriage promotion, including their perspectives on marriage, their involvement with both biological and nonbiological children, and ongoing child-support payments and arrears.

Perspectives on Marriage

Although a few of the men in this study had been in long-term relationships with the mothers of their children, the majority of the men currently did not have a good working relationship with the mothers (note on table 16.2 that four of the men had been accused of domestic violence), though four currently lived with their children's mothers. Several fathers had seen marriages of family and friends terminate, and these experiences soured them on marriage. Eddie, a twenty-seven-year-old father of five children, is unemployed and lives with his girlfriend, De-De, who is the mother of two of his children. We discussed his rationale for not being married. Echoing some of the findings of previous studies (Edin and England 2007; Mincy and Pouncy 2007), Eddie's experience with his brother's and parents' "marriages" dissuaded him from taking that step himself.

> I assess everybody else's relationship. You know what I'm saying? My brother was with his girl for damn near ten years. The marriage didn't even last a year. You know what I'm saying. . . . My mother was married to my father. You know what I'm saying? He was in and out of prison. Every time he came out of prison, she was pregnant . . . that's how I came. He got a furlough, came home, and here I am. . . . And then [he] went back to prison. So my parents, you know, . . . my parents been together since eighty-seven, and they still ain't married. . . . Yeah. . . . So it's just like, man, marriage pretty much, it kind of scares me, man. You know what I'm saying? It is almost like, you know, I want to go and get counseling, you know, really go to marriage counseling, see if this is really what it is.

While several men indicated they would eventually like to marry, most wanted to do so under more desirable circumstances. Like most people, they had a concept of what constituted a good marriage and wanted to have that type of marriage. Consequently, they wanted to marry when the time was "right" to the "right" person. For instance, Kevin and Bilaal were fathers at a young age. Kevin and the mother were high school sweethearts and had their child when they were both seventeen. Kevin says, "We didn't get married because I felt that I was young and she was young. I felt that I didn't need to, I felt that I didn't even want nothing. . . . It's as simple as that." Kevin's reasoning is not illogical, as young marriages have a significantly higher risk for divorce.

Kevin is now twenty-five and father of an eight-year-old daughter who was visiting with him and his parents at the time of the interview. Although he is older and youth would no longer pose a barrier to marriage, he is now the survivor of a point-blank gunshot to the head. He lives with his parents and is on disability.

Bilaal is a twenty-two-year-old single man with two children. Currently he is unemployed but has been selling drugs to "make ends meet." He feels that this is his only option for survival. The mother of his children has a drug problem. Recently she was cited for neglect, and both of their children were placed in kinship care with his maternal aunt. I asked him if he foresaw his children living with him at some point in the future. He responded,

> Um, the only way I could see it is if I get married to a good woman. . . . Because I'm going to need that balance for them . . . I can't just be there with my kids like that, man. You know what I'm saying? I need my woman to help me. . . . If I have to, I will [help] though, you know what I'm saying . . . because I'm a man before anything. . . . I eventually [would like to] get married and have my kids come live with [me].

Bilaal's answer indicates a desire to get married; he sees that marriage would help him rear his children, as he doesn't view himself as being able to do it on his own. Yet to marry, he would want a "good woman." Most parents would not advise their children to marry partners who are too young or on drugs (or selling them) or unemployed. Although most of the men had contemplated and even expressed a desire for marriage, for men like Kevin and Bilaal, these serious issues pose barriers to an ideal marriage. Marrying under these circumstances or to the particular mothers of their children looks to them as a marriage doomed from the start.

Complex Fatherhood

Another issue is the role of the men as caretakers for nonbiological children or for several biological children from different mothers. At the time of the interview, 55 percent of the men in the sample were maintaining an emotional and financial relationship with their current and former spouses' children. This contributed to the stress on their limited resources. DJ, a self-employed man in his thirties, discussed his current living situation with the mother of their biological and other nonbiological children. His story was typical of a number of men in the population sample.

DJ: I got two kids. I'm taking care of three though.

Interviewer: Oh, you're taking care of three children. Who is the other one?

DJ: My girlfriend's brother's daughter [because he is incarcerated and the mother is unavailable] . . . and my daughter up here is seven. . . . But I [have] also been taking care of [another daughter] since she was three [from a previous relationship]. Okay. And that child, I've had that child since [she was] three and now she's twelve.

This scenario highlights several issues. First, when there are multiple children and mothers, fathers are often paying child support for several children, which puts them under financial stress and detracts from their marriageability in the eyes of potential spouses. Second, they could marry one of the mothers, but that obviously doesn't solve the problem for the other mothers. Marriage-promotion policy has been naïve about or negligent in addressing this issue, which is disproportionately common among low-income men of color.

The Child Support Enforcement System

As indicated in Cheryl Mill's chapter in this volume, in many ways the child-support system ironically may hinder father involvement and responsibility among low-income men. It can be a confusing and bureaucratic system, slow or unable to respond appropriately to changes in the fathers' economic situations, and the men frequently have difficulty navigating it. For instance, a few fathers discussed their initial relationship with the child-support-enforcement system. Kevin said that his initial contact with the system came when he had his first child at the age of sixteen.

I don't know exactly how it went, but that's how the courts do it. The letter said . . . I didn't have to pay till I was eighteen. I [had to pay] the birthing expenses, and then they put me on like regular child support [payments]. It was $1,500 a child. Yeah. . . . By the time I was eighteen, I had two kids [and $3,000 to pay for birthing expenses].

If Kevin had known to and been able to obtain legal counsel to dispute the birthing expense, there is a possibility that he would not have been responsible for it based on his income level at the time of the birth of this child.

Nor does the child support system consider disability a legitimate ground for not paying child support. As mentioned earlier, Kevin is a recipient of SSDI benefits, and he complains that the majority of his benefits check is garnished by the child-support office. He feels his ability to "make ends meet" is almost nonexistent. He lives with his parents, and because of the gunshot wound to his head, he has inconsistent memory. His mother agreed to sit in on the interview. I asked Kevin how much of his disability check is garnished for child support. He answered and his mother clarified,

Kevin: I pay monthly now. I pay $300 and some.
Kevin's mother: You know, they get, they get like 50 percent of his income. . . . And I think it's because he's living at home with his parents and he's not paying no bills, so they take 50 percent out. My niece said, they're supposed to take 17 percent out. They were taking 50 percent out [of his SSDI benefit check]. They get half. When he was getting the unemployment after his brother passed away, they [were] getting half of that. [Now] they're getting half of his SSDI.

One of the issues is that Kevin's percentage of garnishment is based on his previous job. Several of the men in the study did not understand the child-support policies and did not seek a modification of their child-support order. Therefore, they were ordered to pay an amount that is not based on the reality of their current income.

The child-support system is also a punitive system that may be effective for fathers who have money and are intentionally withholding it but punishes men who lack resources. In the scenario that follows, DJ discusses his current financial child-support issues. DJ's children live with him and their mother. On a daily basis, he provides financial and emotional child support to his biological children and a nonbiological child as well. I asked him if the child-support-enforcement office knows that his children live with him: "No. They don't know. What happened was . . . , I was in prison when [my daughter] was born. My girl[friend] . . . I guess [she] put the child support people on me.

Individual males [that I know] . . . nine times out of ten, they going to take care of their daughters."

DJ thinks that his girlfriend, the mother of one of his children, was probably "mad at him" and ordered child support enforcement to go after him. DJ does not understand that once the mother requests public assistance from the state, she is required to provide his name in order to receive the requested public assistance. He answered in the following manner:

> I really don't mind [paying] now, but by me being in prison, I had a whole lot of stuff on my hands. And I'm thinking like, how the hell are you going to put the people [child-support-enforcement staff] on me or whatever? And so it's like $1,500, or $40 a week, if I have a job. See, I'm self-employed, so they can't say nothing about my salary. . . . I'm scared to put my money in the bank because they fuck around with that, and then I'm going to be penniless.

Current child-support policy requires noncustodial fathers to pay or accrue child support while incarcerated. And, although he currently is residing with his children, DJ is still paying child-support arrears, which he would still have to pay if he got married. In addition, once in arrears, fathers can be jailed for failure to make their payments. DJ had already been incarcerated for nonpayment of child support. He was released once he was able to give them the requested amount of purge payment. If he had not provided the necessary funds to be released, then he would have had to serve an additional mandatory forty-one days in jail. So DJ expresses the sentiments I heard from many of the fathers who were previously incarcerated; they feel like they are still paying for a crime for which they served time.

In conclusion, these men provided evidence of the variety of challenges that confront their ability to be emotionally and financially responsible to their children. Several of these men are parenting both biological and nonbiological children and living with the mother of one their children. Also, several of the men have considered marriage as an option but later rejected the idea for a variety of reasons. However, many of them expressed frustration with their involvement in the child-support-enforcement system. Several of them did not understand the workings of the program and the rationale for their participation when they were financially and emotionally taking of their child or children.

Policy Implications and Conclusion

The intent of this study was to ascertain how the fathers understand the child-support-enforcement system and the proposed new policy on marriage. Frequently, the fathers directly answered that the marriage policy does not make sense to them and talked about the ways they currently simulate a marital relationship, such as providing financial and emotional support to their children and sometimes living with the mother of one of their children. Four of these men are living with the mother of one of their children and view themselves as having "set up" house with a selected mother of their choice. Despite a lack of economic resources, these men participated in their families' lives as caregivers and active participants in social networks. Several of the men cared for their own (and other) children on a daily basis. In fact, 90 percent of the men in the sample had ongoing contact with their children.

This research also highlights the importance of efforts to develop employment programs for men. Recent scholarly writing by Martinson et al. (2007), Mincy and Pouncy (2007), and Edin and England (2007) confirm the challenges confronted by low-income fathers in the present study. The Healthy Marriage Initiative alone can address only relationship and parenting skills. While such skills are laudable and necessary, these cannot compensate for the economic instability displayed by the men in this sample. Of the nine men in the study, only two were employed. Such dire straits do not make a good foundation for marriage. To begin to address those issues, a House bill (H.R. 3395) called the Responsible Fatherhood and Healthy Families Act of 2007 was introduced by Congressman Davis (Ill.) and by Senators Obama (Ill.) and Bayh (Ind.) in the Senate. If it had been passed, this would have provided $150 million in state grants for fiscal years 2008 through 2010 to conduct demonstration projects to promote economic opportunity for low-income parents (Govtrack.us n.d.).

Nor can the Marriage Initiative address shortcomings of the current child-support-enforcement system. One of the presumed goals of that system is to benefit the families of poor fathers. This research has shown that the effects of the child-support-enforcement mechanisms used, including imprisonment and tax interceptions, generally did not benefit the children of noncustodial fathers who lacked the ability to pay. More effort needs to be done to assure that the child-support order is realistic and frequently readjusted to the person's ability to pay.

In conclusion, the current healthy-marriage-promotion policy goals are unclear. Is it an antipoverty program? Is it solely intended to promote and sustain healthy relationships? The answers will not be available for a few more years as the funded sites have just begun to gather and analyze data from the participants in the various programs. However, data from this small study suggest that marriage promotion cannot be a successful antipoverty program if the partners involved are un- or underemployed or if fathers must continue to pay the state child-support arrears despite marriage to the mother or coresidence with the child. Moreover, the stability of marriages undertaken by partners with psychological, economic, or substance problems is questionable, and for men who have multiple children by multiple women, marriage will at best solve the problems for only one family. The men in this sample have lives filled with perceived and real obstacles, perceived and en-countered risks, and human and financial costs. Many of these fathers, and their potential spouses, are not ideal marriage partners because of their present challenges. Instead, policies aimed at reducing births among individuals unprepared to be parents and policies targeting im-provement of socioeconomic conditions of low-income fathers would have more long-term success. Until we address the needs of low-income mothers and fathers, pro-marriage rhetoric will fall on deaf ears.

References

Ainslie, K. F. 2002. "Is the President's Marriage Proposal DOA?" Washington, D.C.: Cato Institute. Available at http://www.cato.org/pub_display.php?pub_id=3435.

Administration for Children and Families. Undated. "Comprehensive List of Healthy Marriage Education Programs." Available at http://www.acf.hhs.gov/healthymarriage/pdf/june18_list_marriageedprograms.pdf. Accessed May 29, 2008.

Berlin, G. 2004. "The Effects of Marriage and Divorce on Families and Children." Testimony from the Hearings Before the Science, Technology, and Space Sub-committee of the Committee on Commerce, Science, and Transportation. 108th Congress.

Coontz, S., and N. Folbre. 2002. "Marriage, Poverty, and Public Policy: A Discus-sion Paper from the Council on Contemporary Families." Presented at the Fifth Annual Council on Contemporary Families Conference, April 26–28, 2002. Available at http://www.comtemporaryfamilies.org/briefing.

DeAngelis, T. 2004. "Marriage Promotion: A Simplistic 'Fix'?" Monitor on Psychology 35 (8). Available at http://www.apa.org/monitor/sep04/marriage.html. Accessed May 29, 2008.

Edin, K., and England P. 2007. *Unmarried Couples with Children*. New York: Russell Sage Foundation.

Edin, K., and M. Kefalas. 2005. *Promises I Can Keep: Why Poor Women Put Motherhood Before Marriage*. Berkeley: University of California Press.

Govtrack.us. N.d. http://www.govtrack.us/congress/bill.xpd?bill=h110-3395.

Grassley, C. 2004. "The Benefits of a Healthy Marriage." Testimony from the Hearings before the Subcommittee on Social Security and Family Policy, of the Senate Committee on Finance. 108th Cong.

Horn, W. 2005. Testimony from TANF Hearings Before the Subcommittee on Income Security and Family Support of the House Committee on Ways and Means. 109th Congress.

Lane, S. D., R. Keefe, R. Rubinstein, B. Levandowski, M. Freedman, A. Rosenthal, D. Cibula, and M. Czerwinski. 2004. "Marriage Promotion and Missing Men: African American Women in a Demographic Double Bind." *Medical Anthropology Quarterly* 18 (4): 405–28.

Lichter, D. T. 2001. "Marriage as Public Policy." Policy Report of the Progressive Policy Institute. http://www.ppionline.org/ppi_ci.cfm?knlgAreaID=114andsubsecID=144andcontentID=3781.

Lichter, D. T., and D. Roempke Graefe. 2003. "Is Marriage a Panacea? Union Formation Among Economically Disadvantaged Unwed Mothers." *Social Problems* 50 (1): 60–86.

Lichter, D. T., and D. Roempke Graefe. 2007. "Men and Marriage Promotion: Who Marries Unwed Mothers." *Social Service Review* 81 (3): 397–421.

Lichter, R. T., C. D. Batson, and J. B. Brown. 2004. "Welfare Reform and Marriage Promotion: The Marital Expectations and Desires of Single and Cohabiting Mothers." *Social Service Review* 78 (1): 2–25.

Martinson, K., J. Trutko, D. S. Nightingale, P. A. Holcomb, and B. S. Barnow. 2007. *The Implementation of the Partners for Fragile Families Demonstration Projects*. Washington, D.C.: Urban Institute. Available at http://aspe.hhs.gov/hsp/07/PFF/imp/index.htm. Accessed December 20, 2007.

Mincieli, L., J. Manlove, M. McGarrett, K. Moore, and S. Ryan. 2007. *The Relationship Context of Births Outside of Marriage: The Rise of Cohabitation*. Research Brief No. 2007-13. Washington, D.C.: Child Trends.

Mincy, R. and Pouncy, H. 2007. *Baby Fathers and American Family Formation: Low-Income, Never-Married Parents in Louisiana before Katrina*. Future of the Black Family Series. New York: Institute for American Values.

Mink, G. 2002. "From Welfare to Wedlock: Marriage Promotion and Poor Mothers' Inequality." *The Good Society* 11 (3): 68–73.

Nock, S. 2003. "Marriage and Fatherhood in the Lives of African American Men." In *Black Fathers in Contemporary American Society*, ed. O. Clayton, R. B. Mincy, and D. Blankenhorn, 30–42. New York: Russell Sage Foundation.

Ooms, T. 2004. "The Benefits of a Healthy Marriage." Testimony in the Hearings Before the Subcommittee on Social Security and Family Policy, of the Senate Committee on Finance. 108th Cong.

Pate, D. 2002. "An Ethnographic Inquiry Into the Life Experiences of African American Fathers with Children on W-2." In *W-2 Child Support Demonstration*

Evaluation, Report on Nonexperimental Analyses, Fathers of Children in W-2 Families, vol. 2, ed. D. R. Meyer and M. Cancian, 29–118. Report to the Department of Workforce Development. Madison: Institute for Research on Poverty, University of Wisconsin.

Rector, R. E., and K. A. Johnson. 2004. *Role of Couple's Relationship Skills and Father's Employment in Encouraging Marriage.* DAA04-14. Washington, D.C.: The Heritage Foundation.

Rector, R. E., K. A. Johnson, and P. F. Fagan. 2004. *Marriage Still the Safest Place for Women and Children.* No. 1732. Washington, D.C.: The Heritage Foundation.

Rector, R. E., K. A. Johnson, P. F. Fagan, and L. R. Noyes. 2003. *Increasing Marriage Will Dramatically Reduce Child Poverty.* CDA03-06. Washington, D.C.: The Heritage Foundation.

Sitgraves, C. 2008. *The Benefits of Marriage for African American Men.* Research Brief, No. 10. New York: Institute for American Values.

South, S. J. 1993. "Racial and Ethnic Differences in the Desire to Marry." *Journal of Marriage and Family* 55 (2): 357–70.

Testa, M., N. M. Astone, M. Krough, and K. Neckerman. 1989. "Employment and Marriage Among Inner-City Fathers." *Annals of the American Academy of Political and Social Science* 501:79–91.

Wilson, W. J. 1987. *The Truly Disadvantaged: The Inner City, the Underclass, and Public Policy.* Chicago: University of Chicago Press.

Wilson, W. J. 2003. "The Woes of the Inner-City African American Father." In *Black Fathers in Contemporary American Society*, ed. O. Clayton, R. B. Mincy, and D. Blankenhorn, 9–29. New York: Russell Sage Foundation.

Wilson, W. J., and K. Neckerman. 1986. "Poverty and Family Structure: The Widening Gap Between Evidence and Public Policy Issues." In *Fighting Poverty: What Works and What Doesn't*, ed. S. H. Danziger and D. H. Weinberg, 232–59. Cambridge, Mass.: Harvard University Press.v

The Myth of the Missing Black Father set out to challenge some of the negative stereotypes that have been foisted upon black men in general, but black fathers in particular. We were not attempting to assess the quality of parenting among the fathers, nor to place men in a good-dad, bad-dad paradigm, but rather to provide a panoramic view of fathering among black men. Without romanticizing these African American dads, this volume sought to challenge the dominant presumption of absence by showcasing the varying forms of involvement of African American men in the lives of their children across several typologies and contexts of fatherhood. They included married residential fathers, nonresidential fathers, fathers of multiracial children, social fathers, single custodial fathers, young inner-city fathers, college-athlete fathers, and fathers on parole and probation. While some fathers were more involved than others, clearly the portraits here indicate that even absent fathers—that is, fathers not resident with the child—frequently desire and attempt to parent.

Although black men have often had to enact their parental roles under the taxing circumstances of persistent institutional racism and social and economic marginalization, the unveiling of "black men parenting" is considered "breaking news" to the society at large. Through a combination of quantitative and qualitative research, we have tried to simultaneously highlight both the motivations of fathers to do well by their children and certain institutional structures and practices—

for example, parole and probation regulations and child-support collection and enforcement, as well as gender discrimination—that militate against the sincere efforts by many black fathers to live up to their responsibility as fathers.

What emerges from this volume as perhaps the most important finding is the consistent desire and intention on the part of these black men to be positive fathers to their biological children, grandchildren, step-children, and social children. Many of these fathers demonstrated competent nurturing of their children and a strong motivation to adopt and adapt to a role that has historically been the domain of mothers. Clearly, many felt impeded from doing so.

Accepting these findings and at the same time recognizing the existence of certain aggravating forces are major though insufficient steps toward dismissing the myth. Because studies on fatherhood, particularly among men of color, are relatively recent, there remain limitless research opportunities. We only skimmed the surface in an attempt to jumpstart future exploration. Foremost, we need to refocus research on men who are parenting, under myriad circumstances. Some avenues for research that would prove fruitful include comparative fatherhood studies by race and class, looking not only for differences among fathers of different races but areas of commonality that can be addressed through policy. The area of social fathers is just starting to be investigated and still is in need of differentiation among types of social fathers and the outcomes for them and for the children they parent. With most states now allowing single or gay men to adopt, there has been an increase in adoptive and gay fathering, and these are often interracial adoptions as well. Preliminary research questions would include, To what extent have these been black fathers? Under what circumstances and with what outcomes do such adoptions occur? Finally, scholars need to identify new strategies for disseminating these data to practitioners and the public and for assessing and advocating policies that facilitate good parenting among more fathers.

Contributors

KIM M. BLANKENSHIP is an associate research scientist at the Yale University School of Public Health, Yale School of Medicine, and associate director of Yale's Center for Interdisciplinary Research on AIDS. Her sociological work focuses on race, class, and gender analyses of law, policy, and health. Current research projects include analysis of the implementation and effects of community-led structural interventions to address HIV risk in sex workers in India; a study of the effects of the criminal justice system on HIV risk among drug users in Connecticut; and an analysis of the relationships among incarceration, policing, and race disparities in HIV/AIDS.

RONALD E. BULANDA earned his Ph.D. in sociology from Bowling Green State University in 2004. He is currently an assistant professor in the Department of Sociology and Gerontology at Miami University in Oxford, Ohio. His research interests primarily pertain to issues related to family structure, child well-being, and the predictors and consequences of parenting. Ronald's research has appeared in *Journal of Marriage and Family, Population Research and Policy Review, Marriage and Family Review,* and *Journal of Child and Family Studies.*

CASSANDRA CHANEY is assistant professor in the School of Human Ecology at Louisiana State University. Her general area of study is the sociology of African American families. Within this broad field, her primary research interests are African American romantic relationships and the effects of religiosity and spirituality on African American family life.

ERICA CHITO CHILDS is associate professor of sociology at Hunter College of the City University of New York. Her research interests focus on issues of race, gender, and sexuality in relationships, families, communities, and media/popular culture. Her book *Navigating Interracial Borders: Black-White Couples and Their Social Worlds* (2005) documented the attitudes and responses of black and white families and communities to interracial relationships. Her second book, *Fade to Black and White* (forthcoming) explores the images and meanings attached to interracial sexuality in media and popular culture.

ROBERTA L. COLES is associate professor of sociology in and chair of the Department of Social and Cultural Sciences at Marquette University in Milwaukee, Wisconsin, where she teaches courses on family, race and ethnicity, and social inequality. She is author of *Race and Family* and *Best Kept Secret: Black Single Custodial Fathers*. Other publications have appeared in the *Sociological Quarterly*, *The Sociological Review*, *Journal of Contemporary Ethnography*, *Journal of Aging Studies*, *Sociology of Religion*, and *The Western Journal of Black Studies*.

HEATHER M. DALMAGE is associate professor of sociology and director of the Mansfield Institute for Social Justice at Roosevelt University. She is author of *Tripping on the Color Line: Black-White Multiracial Families in a Racially Divided World* and editor of the volume *The Politics of Multiracialism: Challenging Racial Thinking*.

CHARLES GREEN Is professor of sociology at Hunter College of the City University of New York. He also teaches in the Ph.D. program in sociology at the CUNY Graduate School and University Center. In 1989 he was awarded a Fulbright Scholar in Sociology at the University of Dar es Salaam, Tanzania. His published works have been in the areas of race and ethnic relations, urban politics, Caribbean migration, and comparative-development issues. He is the coauthor of *The Struggle for Black Empowerment in New York City: Beyond the Politics of Pigmentation*; author of *Manufacturing Powerlessness in the Black Diaspora*; and editor of *Globalization and Survival in the Black Diaspora: The New Urban Challenge*.

KATRINA HOPKINS-WILLIAMS recently received her Ph.D. from the School of Human Ecology at Louisiana State University. Her dissertation was titled "'Yes, They're Out There': A Qualitative Study of Strong, Happy, Enduring Black Marriages."

MANSA BILAL MARK A. KING is currently assistant professor of sociology at Morehouse College in Atlanta. His research has focused on family studies and racial/ethnic inequality. King earned his doctoral and master's degrees in sociology at the Johns Hopkins University. His B.S. in psychology is from Howard University.

SUZANNE LAMOREY is associate professor in the Child and Family Development Program in the College of Education at the University of North Carolina at Charlotte. Her current research focuses upon the measurement and enhancement of the self-efficacy of parents and teachers as they participate in early-intervention efforts for infants and toddlers at risk for developmental delay. She is also involved in the development of preschool-personnel-preparation programs for nontraditional college students.

BETHANY L. LETIECQ is assistant professor of health and human development at Montana State University. She conducts research in partnership with marginalized or underserved groups, such as African American fathers, Native Americans, and informal kin caregivers to understand the ways in which social policies and systems facilitate or hinder family health and well-being. Letiecq teaches courses on family law and family diversity. She has published in such journals as *Fathering*, *Journal of Family Issues*, and *Family Relations* and is a member of the National Council on Family Relations.

TRACY MACINTOSH, M.S., M.P.H., is a research assistant at the Yale University Center for Interdisciplinary Research on AIDS. She is currently pursuing a medical degree at the Yale School of Medicine.

LOREN MARKS is associate professor in the School of Human Ecology at Louisiana State University. His qualitative research focuses on African American families and the influence of faith in family life. He and his wife, Sandra, are the parents of four children.

EUNICE MATTHEWS-ARMSTEAD is associate professor of social work and sociology at Eastern Connecticut State University and a licensed clinical social worker with a private practice. Before entering the academy she worked as a social worker both in direct service and administration primarily in the area of family and children services.

CHERYL E. MILLS is currently associate professor of social work at the Southern University School of Social Work, New Orleans, Louisiana. Her primary areas of research, publication, and teaching concern social-policy issues pertaining to families, poverty, social inequality, and education. Dr. Mills has developed, analyzed, and implemented local school-district education policy in her role as an elected official and engaged in policy training and administration in child welfare.

OLENA NESTERUK is assistant professor in the Department of Family and Child Studies at Montclair State University. The primary focus of her research is immigrant families and their adaptation to a new sociocultural environment in the United States. She is also interested in culturally diverse families, parenting, and family stress and coping.

AUREA K. OSGOOD is assistant professor at Winona State University. She teaches family sociology and social research. Her research interests include single parenthood, custodial single fathers, poverty, and welfare reform. She is currently researching welfare-reform work policies and child well-being.

DAVID J. PATE JR. is assistant professor of social work, University of Wisconsin–Milwaukee, Helen Bader School of Social Welfare; and faculty affiliate, Center for the Study of Cultural Diversity in Healthcare, School of Medicine and Public Health, and the Institute for Research on Poverty, both at University of Wisconsin–Madison.

KEVIN M. ROY is associate professor in the Department of Family Science at the University of Maryland at College Park School of Public Health. His research focuses on the life course of men on the margins of families and the workforce. Dr. Roy has published in *Social Problems, American Journal of Community Psychology, Journal of Family Issues,* and *Family Relations,* and has coedited a recent volume, entitled *Situated Fathering: A Focus on Physical and Social Spaces.* He received a Ph.D. from the Human Development and Social Policy program at Northwestern University in 1999.

DIANE SASSER is professor in the Louisiana State University Ag Center and Cooperative Extension Service. Her interests include parenting and marriage, and she is the project director for the Parents Partnering for Success Program.

RYAN D. SCHROEDER is assistant professor of sociology at the University of Louisville. He teaches criminology and deviance courses. His research interests include desistance processes, with a particular focus on the role of alcohol and drug use, emotional development, family processes, and religious transformations.

AARON A. SMITH is professor emeritus in the School of Social Work, University of South Florida–Tampa. Dr. Smith worked as a clinical research social worker for twenty years at Stanford University Medical School in a variety of clinical and teaching programs including neonatology, cardiovascular surgery, and heart and kidney transplantation. He is also the founder of the Florida Kinship Center, specializing in working with kinship care-giving relatives and their children. He is currently preparing articles on his pioneering work of fifteen years with parents of terminally ill children. Dr. Smith is the father of two daughters and six grandchildren.

JACQUELINE D. SMITH is a doctoral candidate in sociology at the Maxwell School for Citizenship and Public Affairs at Syracuse University. Her research interests include identity formation and representation among diasporic cultures both historically and in popular culture, with a focus on the African diaspora. She is especially interested in the ability of music to connect the many cultures of the African diaspora. This is her first publication.

AMY B. SMOYER is a research associate at the Yale Center for Interdisciplinary Research on AIDS and a doctoral student in the Social Welfare program at the City University of New York (CUNY) Graduate Center. Her social-work-practice background includes community organizing and housing administration in the field of

HIV/AIDS. Amy's current research interests include the impact of incarceration on community health, including HIV/AIDS and nutritional issues.

COLLEEN VESELY is a doctoral student in the Department of Family Science at the University of Maryland–College Park School of Public Health. Her research focuses on how contextual factors, including public and social policy, kin networks, employment, and immigration history shape low-income, racial-ethnic fathers' and mothers' experiences of parenthood throughout the life course. Colleen received an M.A. in human development and family studies from the University of Connecticut in 2006.